This book analyzes the complex, often violent connections between body and voice in narrative, lyric and dramatic works by Ovid, Petrarch, Marston and Shakespeare. Lynn Enterline describes the foundational yet often disruptive force that Ovidian rhetoric exerts on early modern poetry, particularly on representations of the self, the body, and erotic life. Paying close attention to the trope of the female voice in the *Metamorphoses*, as well as early modern attempts to ventriloquize women's voices that are indebted to Ovid's work, she argues that Ovid's rhetoric of the body profoundly challenges Renaissance representations of authorship as well as conceptions about the difference between male and female experience. This vividly original book makes a vital contribution to the study of Ovid's presence in Renaissance literature.

Cambridge Studies in Renaissance Literature and Culture 35

The Rhetoric of the Body from Ovid to Shakespeare

Cambridge Studies in Renaissance Literature and Culture

General editor
STEPHEN ORGEL
Jackson Eli Reynolds Professor of Humanities, Stanford University

Editorial board
Anne Barton, *University of Cambridge*
Jonathan Dollimore, *University of York*
Marjorie Garber, *Harvard University*
Jonathan Goldberg, *Johns Hopkins University*
Nancy Vickers, *Bryn Mawr College*

Since the 1970s there has been a broad and vital reinterpretation of the nature of literary texts, a move away from formalism to a sense of literature as an aspect of social, economic, political and cultural history. While the earliest New Historicist work was criticized for a narrow and anecdotal view of history, it also served as an important stimulus for post-structuralist, feminist, Marxist and psychoanalytical work, which in turn has increasingly informed and redirected it. Recent writing on the nature of representation, the historical construction of gender and of the concept of identity itself, on theatre as a political and economic phenomenon and on the ideologies of art generally, reveals the breadth of the field. Cambridge Studies in Renaissance Literature and Culture is designed to offer historically oriented studies of Renaissance literature and theatre which make use of the insights afforded by theoretical perspectives. The view of history envisioned is above all a view of our own history, a reading of the Renaissance for and from our own time.

Recent titles include

A complete list of books in the series is given at the end of the volume.

The Rhetoric of the Body from Ovid to Shakespeare

Lynn Enterline
Vanderbilt University

CAMBRIDGE
UNIVERSITY PRESS

PUBLISHED BY THE PRESS SYNDICATE OF THE UNIVERSITY OF CAMBRIDGE
The Pitt Building, Trumpington Street, Cambridge, United Kingdom

CAMBRIDGE UNIVERSITY PRESS
The Edinburgh Building, Cambridge CB2 2RU, UK   http://www.cup.cam.ac.uk
40 West 20th Street, New York NY 10011–4211, USA   http://www.cup.org
10 Stamford Road, Oakleigh, Melbourne 3166, Australia

First published 2000

Printed in the United Kingdom at the University Press, Cambridge

Typeset in 10/12pt Times   [CE]

A catalogue record for this book is available from the British Library

ISBN 0 521 62450 9 hardback

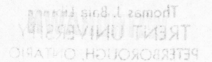

I dedicate this book to my parents,
Joyce and Robert Enterline

Contents

Acknowledgements

Were it not for many of the colleagues and friends named here, this book might never have found its way into print. Always a fabulous and absorbing interlocutor, Wayne Koestenbaum liberally gave both his time and attention when I first began to explore the idea for this book; I feel his inspiring presence everywhere in its pages. For his unwavering support, sensitive suggestions, gentle editorial presence, and impeccable timing, I owe Stephen Orgel an enormous debt. Leonard Barkan's close reading, at once magnanimous and authoritative, kept my spirits high even in moments of adversity; the book is much better for his suggestions. And Richard Halpern, who has generously read so much of my work over the years, helped me strengthen the argument in significant ways.

I am grateful to Patricia Rosenmeyer for informative conversations as well as for apt bibliographical suggestions; her work on the *Heroides* allowed me to refine my ideas about Ovidian narrative considerably. A number of colleagues at Yale – Peter Brooks, Ian Duncan, Kevin Dunn, Elizabeth Fowler, Ann Gaylin, Lynne Huffer, Heather James, David Marshall, Giuseppe Mazzotta, Tyrus Miller, Kathryn Rowe, Deanna Shemek, Sara Suleri Goodyear – carefully read much of this book while it was still in progress. I appreciate their numerous insights, queries, and suggestions. Jay Clayton's enthusiasm for this project came as a delightful surprise. Lena Cowen Orlin offered support and advice at a time when it was least expected – and thus all the more gratefully received. I would like to thank the Vanderbilt English Department, as well, for their collective enthusiasm for this project.

An earlier version of chapter 6 appeared in *Shakespeare Quarterly* 48.1 (Spring, 1977): 17–44 and a part of chapter 3 appeared as "Embodied Voices: Petrarch Reading (Himself Reading) Ovid" in *Desire in the Renaissance*, ed. Valeria Finucci and Regina Schwartz (Princeton: Princeton University Press, 1994). I thank both *Shakespeare Quarterly* and Princeton University Press for allowing me to reprint them here.

And finally, for long standing personal, moral, and intellectual support, I am deeply indebted to Carla Kaplan, Jonathan Lamb, Jeff Nunokawa, Bridget Orr, Adela Pinch, and Sharon Willis. I count myself fortunate indeed to call each a dear friend. Mark Mushkat has always believed in me and for that I remain grateful.

1   Pursuing Daphne

Purple notes

At the center of Ovid's *Metamorphoses* lie violated bodies. Sometimes male, at other times female, a few of these ruined forms elude the grasp of gender and its reductive nominations. Fractured and fragmented bodies from Ovid's poem cast long, broken shadows over European literary history. Sometimes, these shadows fall back on the poem that gave them shape. As Quintilian put it when deliberating the frequently heard charge that Ovid's manner is too ingenious, there is "some excuse" for his invention, since so much of it is required if this poem's author is to "assemble" such extremely diverse things into "the appearance of a unified body" ("res diversissimas in speciem unius corporis colligentem").[1] That a poem fascinated with the fracturing of bodies should have been passed down through the middle ages and into the Renaissance, thanks to Lactantius, predominantly in fragments, a reordered collection of pieces torn away from their original arrangement, is one of the ironies of literary history that continues to echo and ramify.[2] For it is not merely that the body's violation is one of the poem's prominent thematic concerns. As Philomela's severed "lingua" mutely testifies – her "murmuring tongue" designating both the bodily organ and "language" as such – dismemberment informs Ovid's reflections not only on corporeal form, but linguistic and poetic as well.[3] An elaborately self-reflexive poem, the *Metamorphoses* traces, in minute and sometimes implacable detail, the violent clashes between the poem's language and the many bodies of which it speaks. In this book, I contend that the violated and fractured body is the place where, for Ovid, aesthetics and violence converge, where the usually separated realms of the rhetorical and the sexual most insistently meet.

I take my cue in the following chapters from Philomela's severed *lingua*, "murmuring on the dark earth." In them, I analyze the complex, often violent, connections between body and voice in Ovid's *Metamorphoses* and several Renaissance texts indebted to it. In addition to

1

Ovid's *Metamorphoses*, I read lyric, narrative, and dramatic works: Petrarch's *Rime Sparse* (1359–74), John Marston's *The Metamorphosis of Pigmalions Image* (1598), Shakespeare's *The Rape of Lucrece* (1594) and *The Winter's Tale* (1610–11). My general purpose is twofold: to interrogate the deeply influential connections between rhetoric and sexuality in Ovid's text; and to demonstrate the foundational, yet often disruptive, force that his tropes for the voice exert on early modern poetry, particularly on early modern representations of the self, the body, and erotic life. After demonstrating the complex connections between Ovid's rhetorical strategies in the *Metamorphoses* and his distinctive way of portraying the human voice, I turn to works by Petrarch, Marston, and Shakespeare in which tropes for the voice allow each author to restage, in his own way, many of the dilemmas central to Ovid's representation of subjectivity, sexuality, and gender. I do not try to offer an exhaustive account of Ovid's presence in early modern poetry. Others have already attempted that greater task.[4] Rather, I have selected a few prominent texts to consider in detail, texts in which Renaissance writers are as captivated in their turn, as was Ovid, by the idea of the voice. At the same time, I have chosen texts in which desecrated and dismembered bodies are imagined to find a way to signify, to call us to account for the labile, often violent, relationship between rhetoric and sexuality as it was codified, transmitted, and rewritten in an Ovidian mode. In the chapters on Petrarch, Marston, and Shakespeare, I argue that Ovid's rhetoric of the body – in particular his fascination with scenes of alienation from one's own tongue – profoundly troubles Renaissance representations of authorship as well as otherwise functional conceptions about what counts as the difference between male and female experience.

To recall something of the extraordinary cultural reach of Ovidian narrative, and therefore something of my reasons for returning to analyze this legacy, I should observe here that Ovid's stories fascinate contemporary feminists writing about female subversion and resistance much as they once did medieval and early modern writers preoccupied with stories about love and male poetic achievement.[5] As the story of Philomela's tongue should make clear, an important hallmark of Ovidian narrative – by which I mean not only Ovid's poem but also the many European texts that borrow from it – is its unerring ability to bring to light the often occluded relationships between sexuality, language, and violence. The poems arising from that reflection have been at once deeply influential (in poetic practice) and sorely neglected (in critical practice). Such neglect of the foundational yet unsettling consequences of Ovidian rhetoric has come about, in part, because when viewed from the

perspective of the history of classical scholarship, it is only in recent years
that literary critics have reinvigorated a serious study of rhetoric by
analyzing the ways that various practices and forms of writing raise
difficult epistemological, ethical, and political questions. Much of this
theoretical work has just begun to reach criticism of the *Metamorphoses*.[6]
The habit of treating Ovid's stories piecemeal, rather than in light of the
poem's larger narrative strategies and self-reflexive fantasies, may have
furthered such neglect. Selective reading informs not only literary appropriations of Ovidian material but critical reception of it, too. As one
critic observes, because we inherit the *Metamorphoses* as a kind of
collection or anthology, "the temptation to read Ovid's tales and not
Ovid's epic is very strong."[7]

The opening chapter therefore situates several stories central to
feminist criticism – among them, Philomela, Medusa, Echo, Arachne, the
Bacchae – in the context of Ovid's larger narrative and rhetorical
strategies. It argues that Ovid's penchant for ventriloquizing female
voices occupies a crucial, if mysterious, place in the *Metamorphoses* as a
whole. But I open this study with the example of Philomela's amputated,
"murmuring" tongue because it so succinctly captures the characteristic
way that Ovid uses stories about bodily violation to dramatize language's
vicissitudes. Other bodies will be put to similar use as the Renaissance
authors examined here revisit Ovid's poem. Fantasies of fragmentation
permeate Ovidian narrative, and they do more than convey a message
about the body's vulnerability or, more importantly, the violence that
subtends the discursive production of what counts as the difference in
sexual difference. Scenes of dismemberment and rape, of course, do
convey both of these culturally laden meanings and I endeavor to keep
them in mind. But as Philomela's tongue suggests, violated bodies also
provide Ovid with the occasion to reflect on the power and limitations of
language as such. Before being cut out, for instance, Philomela's tongue
speaks about rape as a mark of the difference between what can and
cannot be spoken: she says "I will move even rocks to share knowledge"
of an act that is, literally, *ne-fas*, or "unspeakable" ("et conscia saxa
mouebo" 6.547; and "nefandos" line 540, derived from the verb *fari*, "to
speak or talk"). Of Ovid's representation of the rape itself – "and
speaking the unspeakable, he overwhelmed her by force, a virgin and all
alone" ("fassusque nefas et uirginem et unam / ui superat" lines 524–25)
– Elissa Marder points out that Ovid's text tellingly "insists on the
convergence between speaking the crime and doing the deed. One cannot
speak 'rape,' or speak about rape, merely in terms of a physical body.
The sexual violation of the woman's body is itself embedded in discursive
and symbolic structures."[8] When Tereus "speaks the unspeakable,"

language becomes a productive, violent act that is compared to rape even as the act of rape resists representation.

This book attends to the many places in Ovidian narrative where the idea of a speaking body – often literalized as the figure of a moving tongue – becomes a single, memorable image that brings together the usually separate realms of aesthetics and violence, representation and the body, language and matter. Further brief elaboration of the way Ovid tells the story of Philomela's tongue will therefore be a useful way to introduce the problems guiding the analyses that follow. In the middle of his story, the narrator begins to stutter over the word "unspeakable." Ovid's iterated *nefas* signals a kind of narrative impasse, a fixation on the poem's troubled failure to speak about an event that defies speech. *Nefas* stresses that all we get, from Philomela or the narrator, are mere words and signs about an event that escapes words and signs. Resistance to narration, however, only induces further narrative. Thus when Tereus literalizes his "unspeakable" act by cutting out her tongue, giving her an "os mutum" line 574 – literally, "speechless mouth" – Philomela finds recourse in art, weaving a tapestry to represent the crime. "Great pain" begets in her the very "talent" to which Ovid elsewhere often lays claim as a poet ("ingenium," line 575). She sits at a "barbaric loom" ("barbarica tela" line 576) that is, etymologically speaking, a loom of incomprehensible utterance (derived from the onomatopoeic Greek word, βάρβαρος, for the meaningless sounds on other people's tongues). On such an instrument, Philomela manages to weave threads that are "skillful," "expert," or "practiced" ("stamina ... callida," line 576), turning her body's bloody mutilation into "purple marks" on a white background ("purpureasque notas," line 577). Like her narrator, Philomela struggles at the limits of representation: where the narrator stutters at the effort to turn an unspeakable act into verse, Philomela is imagined to coax an expert weaving out of an unintelligible, hence "barbarous," instrument.

The work that Philomela produces, moreover, amplifies the problems raised by her "moving" tongue: her tapestry takes up where her tongue left off, telling us that in this story, presumed distinctions between language and action, the speakable and the unspeakable, aesthetics and violence verge on collapse. On her tapestry, Philomela weaves a set of purple "notae," a noun that, as Marder observes, suggests several divergent yet crucial meanings. *Nota* may signify a written character – a mark of writing used to represent "a sound, letter, or word." It may signify the "vestige" or "trace" of something, like a footprint. It may also designate a mark of stigma or disgrace, particularly an identifying brand on the body. And in the plural form used in Ovid's narrative, "notae," can, by extension, also suggest "a person's features."[9] Artist of her own trauma, Philomela sits down to translate something – an event, a body – that cannot be translated: rape is an "unspeakable" sound; the medium of its communication, a "barbaric" loom; the "notes" that represent it, neither letter, mark, nor physical imprint. Philomela's "purple notes" on a white background hover somewhere between being a self-portrait, a physical remnant of the crime (like a bruise), and a stigmatizing "brand or tattoo" that re-marks the violated body it was supposed merely to represent.[10] This weaving, in its turn, proves every bit as persuasive as the tongue Philomela once hoped would "move the very rocks to consciousness" (6.547). It moves her sister, Procne, to terrifying action. The tapestry then extends the confusion between the "speakable and the unspeakable" to another person (again, "fasque nefasque," 6.585) because the crime conveyed in these marks resists the "indignant words" Procne seeks with her "questing tongue" ("uerbaque quaerenti satis indignantia linguae / defuerunt," 6.584–5).

All the aspects of language enacted in this story of Philomela's rape and mutilation are not necessarily compatible, though each fleetingly shades into the other. Through her murmuring tongue and bruised marks Ovid invites us to reflect on the power and limitations of language in its several overlapping functions: instrumental, poetic, and rhetorical. As an instrument of communication or expression, language is necessary but inadequate to its task. As a sign hovering between literal and figural meanings, Philomela's "lingua" or "tongue" functions as a productive yet potentially violent distortion of the world (and body) it claims to represent. On Philomela's loom, signs become objects of aesthetic appreciation. And as a rhetorical tool, language wields enormous power, although its force may, without warning, exceed the control of the one who uses it. The figure of Philomela's severed "lingua" and her bruised "purple notes," moreover, refuse any final distinction between language and the body, or between ideas and matter. Ovid's narrator knowingly poises his text on a divide between what can and cannot be represented, aesthetic form and violence, poetic "ingenium" and barbarism, language and the body. And he mercilessly draws our attention, all the while, to the fading of that divide. Disquieting erasures such as these characterize the *Metamorphoses*: in Ovid's rhetoric of the body, poetic and rhetorical self-reflexivity can become "grotesquely violent and yet intensely moving."[11]

When I refer to Ovid's "rhetoric of the body," I mean not merely to designate a language that describes the body, but to draw attention to several other, more elusive issues. First, I mean to suggest that in the *Metamorphoses* Ovid refuses commonplace distinctions between the body's ability to speak and its ability to act: the narrator continually draws attention to such mysterious and complex images as that of Philomela's "moving" tongue. Capturing in one figure a Roman commonplace for the aims of rhetorical speech (*mouere*, to "move" one's audience), Ovid tells us that her tongue has motion and that it "moves" those who listen. Rhetoric, in the story of Philomela's tongue and tapestry, means taking the idea of symbolic action very seriously. It means acknowledging that the body is both a bearer of meaning as well as a linguistic agent, a place where representation, materiality, and action collide.

Second, by Ovid's "rhetoric of the body," I am referring to the sense conveyed throughout the *Metamorphoses* that our understanding and experience of the body itself is shaped by discursive and rhetorical structures. Ever alert to language's shaping force on what we know about our own body and the bodies of others, Ovid's poem frequently dramatizes in minute detail the action and effects of this productive, at times even performative, process. In it, the mark of an image, sign or figure repeatedly falls between the body and a character's perception of it. Between Narcissus and self-understanding falls an *imago*; between Pygmalion and womankind, a *simulacrum*; between Perseus and the body of the Gorgon, a protective, mirroring shield; between Actaeon's experience and understanding of his swiftly changing shape, a strange sound that "neither human nor any deer could make." Representation, in fact, becomes foundational to how we perceive the human race: the narrator imagines new beings arising from the stones of Deucalion and Pyrrha, but between our eyes and the bodies of these new humans arise forms "such as statues just begun out of marble, not sharply defined and very like roughly blocked out images" ("uti de marmore coepta / non exacta satis rudibusque simillima signis" 1.405–06). I call this introduction "Pursuing Daphne" in order to suggest the way that the form of the body – Daphne's sense for *figura* – both inspires and eludes the capture of language – Apollo's sense for *figura*. Like Daphne, the bodies in Ovidian narrative take shape under the formative pressure of figural language. And yet something about those bodies remains, like Daphne, forever fugitive.

To understand why Ovidian poetry insists on drawing such close connections between language, sexuality, and violence, this book directs attention back to the often overlooked scene of writing in the *Metamorphoses*. By "scene of writing" I am referring to two, related, matters: the poem's systematic self-reference, its complex engagement with its own figural language and with the fact of having been a written rather than a spoken epic; and its equally complex engagement with the materiality of reading and writing practices in the Roman world. Symbolically and historically resonant, this scene of writing, I contend, left indelible traces not only on Ovid's representation of the body but also on many of the later European works derived from his epic. The Ovidian narrator habitually emphasizes the poetic, rhetorical, and corporeal resonance to the various "forms" (*formae*) and "figures" (*figurae*) about which the poem speaks, deriving many of the *Metamorphoses*' erotic and violent scenes out of the entanglement of poetic and bodily "form." For example, Ovid's interest in the double nature of Daphne's beautiful "figure," for example, turns a story of rape into one of the first book's successive stories about the birth of certain poetic forms (in this case, epideictic). Similarly, the vacillation between the literal and figural meanings of "lingua" allows Philomela's mutilated tongue to tell another, related story about the uneasy relationship between a body and what is usually taken to be its "own" language. The specific metalinguistic resonance of one memorable scene in the *Metamorphoses* has grown somewhat dim, perhaps, because of material changes in practices of writing. But in Book 10, Pygmalion's statue undergoes a change from marble to flesh by passing through a stage like wax growing soft under pressure from the thumb:

> subsidit digitis ceditque, ut Hymettia sole
> cera remollescit tractataque pollice multas
> flectitur in facies ipsoque fit utilis usu. (10.284–86)

The ivory yields in his fingers, just as Hymettian wax grows soft in the sun and molded by the thumb is changed into many forms and becomes usable through use itself.

In a poem that habitually renders its interest in the "forms" and "figures" of its own language as erotic stories, it is no accident that this simile for the ivory maiden's animation refers to an actual tool for writing in the Roman world. As the narrator of the *Ars Amatoria* suggests in another erotic context when advising lovers to be cautious when counterfeiting, wax was the malleable surface used to coat writing tablets: "nor is it safe to write an answer unless the wax is quite smoothed over, lest one tablet hold two hands" (3.495–96). Ovid conveys Pygmalion's rapt attention to the body taking shape like wax under his fingers with a metaphor as weighted, in his day, as was the one Shakespeare uses for *Much Ado*'s Hero, stained with slander: "O, she is fall'n / Into a pit of ink" (4.1.139–40).

Renaissance authors, particularly those educated according to a humanist model of imitating classical precursors, were extremely sensitive to Ovid's rhetorically self-conscious verse. An important phase in the history of rhetoric is embedded in the subtle details of Renaissance returns to Ovidian narrative. Each chapter therefore focuses on the particular problems raised by a later writer's equally self-conscious revision of Ovidian rhetoric. Because of Ovid's frequent metapoetic, metalinguistic, and metarhetorical turns, however, he has often been condemned as an author marred by rhetorical excess, insincerity, and misplaced ingenuity.[12] It is therefore a revealing index of a shift in both taste and critical practice that *Titus Andronicus* – the Renaissance play that most consciously endeavors to bring the violated Ovidian body to the stage while rivalling his self-reflexive word play and rhetorical inventiveness – was once an embarrassment in the Shakespearean canon and yet has become, in recent years, the object of critical fascination.[13] One notable speech in that play, of course, prominently leans on a truly Ovidian juxtaposition of aesthetics and violence. When Marcus sees the tongueless and handless Lavinia before him, raped and mutilated because her attackers have read Ovid's story of Philomela, he speaks about her as if she were an aesthetic object, a marred beauty best understood in terms of the dismembering rhetoric of the *blason*. Pulled apart by the language of lips, tongues, hands, and fingers, hemmed in like Lucrece by Shakespeare's Petrarchan tropes of red and white, Lavinia endures yet one more male reading. She hears her "crimson ... blood" likened to "a bubbling fountain stirr'd with wind" that flows between "rosed lips;" she can signify very little as her cousin remembers the way her "lily hands" once trembled "like aspen leaves upon a lute" (2.4.22–47). Borrowing from Ovid's text as the two rapists did before him, Marcus reads Lavinia as more than Philomela: with her "body bare / Of her two branches," she exceeds Ovid's Daphne; the "heavenly harmony" of her former singing betters Ovid's Orpheus (2.4.17–18 and 44–51). Even Lavinia's reluctance to be interpreted yet again by the book written across her wounded body – her apparent attempt to flee when Marcus first sees her – is immediately, relentlessly pulled back to the story of Philomela. In a play dedicated to enacting the literal and figural pressure of the *Metamorphoses*, Marcus' demand, "Who is this? my niece, that flies away so fast?" (2.4.11) chillingly recalls Philomela's final flight, as a bird, to escape Tereus' angry beak ("petit ... siluas ... prominet inmodicum pro longa cuspide rostrum" *Metamorphoses* 6.667–73). Given the supremely literary origin for the horrible events written on Lavinia's body, Marcus' speech perpetuates the violence it haltingly tries to comprehend. But it does more than exemplify the play's larger fascination with language's devastations. A point of rupture in the history of literary taste, the speech has also become a kind of touchstone for each critic's sense of the relation between text and the social world, aesthetic form and cultural violence.

In a similarly well-known, if ostensibly more refined, poem that involves critical in ethical judgment, Ronsard captures in one word the collapse between language, a sense of aesthetics, and sexual violence that characterizes all the texts in this study. Wishing he were like Jove, transformed into the bull that raped Europa, the love poet aspires to write about a beauty that is "ravishing." In so doing, the poem imports Ovid's story of rape into its sense of its own attractions:

> Je vouldroy bien en toreau blandissant
> Me transformer pour finement la prendre,
> Quand elle va par l'herbe la plus tendre
> Seule à l'escart mille fleurs *ravissant*.[14]

I wish I were transformed into a whitening bull in order to take her subtly as she wanders across the softest grass, alone and isolated, ravishing thousands of flowers.

In the *Metamorphoses*, Europa is raped as the result of her aesthetic sense. The bull is so white, its bodily "form" so beautiful ("tam formosus"), its horns so "various" that "you would maintain that they were by someone's hand." Europa "admires" this bull ("miratur") and is, therefore, raped (2.855–58). Ronsard, too, imagines his beloved to be both subject and object of aesthetic appreciation; his brief phrase for her pastime, "ravishing flowers," joins her capacity for aesthetic pleasure to violence in true Ovidian fashion.[15] A chiasmatic exchange takes place between speaker and his second Europa – a suspicious slippage of agency that, as we shall see again in the chapter on Shakespeare's *Lucrece*, characterizes Ovidian narratives of rape. Here, the poet derives his aesthetic sensibility from "elle" while his own desire to "ravish" – expressed in his opening wish to be like the golden shower that fell into the lap of Danaë – suddenly becomes hers.[16] Through Ronsard's pun on *ravir*, moreover, Ovid's already metapoetic story becomes yet another meditation on the conjunction between rape and the "flowers" of rhetoric – in this instance, as in much Renaissance Ovidian poetry, Petrarchan rhetoric. Similarly, Perdita's desire, in *The Winter's Tale*, for the flowers that Europa, "frighted," let fall "From Dis's waggon" (4.4.116–18), borrows Ovid's favorite technique of turning metaphors – particularly metaphors about poetic language – into literal objects in the landscape. Invoked in the context of a debate about the relationship between nature and art, Ovid's text surfaces in the form of Proserpina's lost "flowers" and forces us to reflect yet again on the disquieting conjunction between poetic form and sexual violence.

This book is devoted to reading figures such as Philomela' "purple notes," Marcus' "lily hands," Ronsard's "ravissant," or Perdita's flowers. In such figures, poetic language and the ruined body insist on being read together. By taking us on sometimes intricate pathways through the erotic landscape of Ovidian and Petrarchan rhetoric, these figures keep asking us to ask: what, precisely, is the relationship between literary form, cultural fantasy, and sexual violence? And what, moreover, do these jarring conjunctions mean for the subjects of Ovidian narrative? It perhaps does not go without saying that I find the conjunction between aesthetic form and culturally inflected sexual violence disquieting, and hence illuminating, because I do not believe they are the same thing.[17] Ovid's deliberately troubling juxtapositions compel me to extend an already well-developed feminist critical tradition in which the question of how to read rape has become central to the question of how to read the *Metamorphoses*. But in order to expand the feminist critique of the thematics of sexual violence in Ovid's text, this book considers how representations of the body, subjectivity, and sexual difference are bound up with, and troubled by, the poem's intense rhetorical and aesthetic self-reflection.[18] If I direct attention to Ovid's characteristically ironic move from admiring the beauty of a *figura*, *imago*, or *simulacrum* to a distinctly rapacious "love of having" ("amor ... habendi" 1.131), it is because I believe the narrative's incessant turn of attention to the beauty of a mediating screen of poetic form allows one a certain (though certainly not inviolable) space for reflection, distance, and critique. To address the frequent juxtaposition of poetic language and violence in Ovid's *Meta-morphoses* and to understand the place of the embodied subject in it, therefore, I have taken a lesson from Philomela's purple notes and moving tongue, analyzing the scene of writing out of which such urgent figures emerge. I do so because I believe it important to understand the *conjunction* of aesthetics and violence, rhetoric and sexuality, in this influential tradition. I understand this to be a critical and productive interference between two different orders, not an utterly saturated translation of one into the other.

These readings suggest, moreover, that the problems raised by Ovidian rhetorical practice alter the sense of certain terms crucial to discussions of the relationship between representation, sexuality, and violence. That is, his rhetorical practice continually calls into question what we mean when we make such distinctions as those between male and female, subject and object, author and reader, agent and victim. At the same time, it also tells us that the relationship between a speaker's discourse and his or her mind, feelings, or experience is far from transparent. Ovidian narrative therefore troubles the link that, as John Guillory argues, is often made in debates over the canon between "representation" understood as a literary term and representation understood as a political term.[19] In this regard, the story of Philomela's severed tongue may once again be instructive. Marder observes that Philomela's murmuring *lingua* directs attention to a rupture between "access to language" and her "experience of violation." Ovid's emphasis on Philomela's "os mutum" and writhing tongue tells us that such an experience exceeds any words its victim can utter – that the very sense of violation is measured by the extent to which that experience is "unspeakable." Both Philomela and Procne are bound together by Philomela's bruised, purple notes and their brutally symbolic act of stopping the rapist's mouth with the body of his own child. The enraged sisters may speak a kind of body language, but it remains "a language without a tongue." In other words: "to speak in rage is to be 'beside oneself.' It is to abandon the possibility that one's speech coincides with the place of one's experience."[20] But such a rupture between one's discourse and "the place of one's experience" in the story of Philomela's rape characterizes many other Ovidian stories as well. One thinks of Echo in the *Metamorphoses* but also of Io, Semele, Byblis, and Actaeon; in the *Heroides*, of Cydippe; in the *Fasti*, of Lucretia.[21] This characteristic rupture between experience and discourse in Ovid's texts tells us that they cannot be understood merely to reflect this or that person's or social group's experience (the slide from textual to political "representation"). In fact, one could argue that the moment of speaking "beside oneself" that Marder locates in the story of Philomela and Procne typifies Ovidian narrative: the poet who developed the art of female complaint in the *Heroides* into its own influential genre also gives us a narrator in the *Metamorphoses* who constantly engages in acts of ventriloquism. Over and over, Ovid tries to speak as if he were a woman, to find a convincing "voice" for female suffering. He continually speaks "beside" himself in his poetry, a trademark displacement of voice with which Shakespeare in particular was fascinated. As soon as Ovid's poems provoke the Barthesian question – "whose voice is this?" – one can no longer say, with any certainty, whose "experience" of violence or desire the text is representing, or for whom its stories may be said to "speak."

Medusa's mouth

To analyze the relationship between rhetoric and sexuality in this tradition, then, I concentrate not on violated bodies alone but also on the voices imagined to issue from them. What Shoshana Felman calls "the scandal of the speaking body" has particular resonance for this tradition, concerned as these Ovidian texts are with bodies whose stories testify to the power, failure, and disturbing unpredictability of the human voice.[22] In all the texts examined here, the moment when the voice either fades or spirals out of the speaker's control is also the moment that speech is revealed at its most material. Recall, for example, the important yet evasive signifiers that neither Io nor Actaeon can utter because of the other, frightening noises that issue from their lips; or the unexpectedly deadly power of one word – *aura* – that the unfortunate Cephalus speaks in the forest. At such moments, we are also asked to consider language not merely as a mode of representation but as a (deeply unreliable) mode of action. As many characters discover to their peril, the performative dimension of Ovidian rhetoric is in excess of, or to the side of, thought. A material effectivity of rhetoric in the poem exceeds any functionalist account of language defined by the concepts of matter or intention. Though volatile, language's action in the *Metamorphoses* can be extremely effective – its forms of action at once profound and unpredictable for the speaking subject and the world to which that subject addresses herself.

Renaissance authors revisit these Ovidian rhetorical problems, moreover, because they were acutely sensitive to the way that Ovid tends to invoke a *uox* at the moment it is lost. Fascination with lost voices is crucial to this tradition's literary representations of a self. Thanks in large part to Petrarch's rendition of Ovidian figures, Philomela's lost tongue, Orpheus' failed voice, Actaeon's vanished speech, and Echo's subtly subversive repetitions became commonplace in the mythographic vocabulary of Renaissance self-representation. And yet in Ovid's and Petrarch's texts, each of these stories undermines generally functional assumptions about subjectivity, authorship, and language *from within* the voice itself. Merely mentioning Echo, Actaeon, or Orpheus here reminds us how important the fading of the human voice is for the *Metamorphoses*. Ovid's signature habit of intertwining figures for the voice with reflections on the poem's own scene of writing – captured most memorably in the story of Echo but prominent throughout the epic – gave rise to what I call a kind of phonographic imaginary in Ovidian poetry. Losing one's voice becomes a precise index of a variety of linguistic dilemmas that hollow out the poem's "speaking subjects" from within. Paying attention to the dilemmas specific to each text's mode of representation, I argue that in the Ovidian tradition these dilemmas are sometimes a matter of language as a differential system; sometimes a matter of a text's own rhetorical fabric; sometimes of its scene of address or enunciative structure; and sometimes of the specific literary history informing a particular narrative or trope. I call Ovid's trope of the voice "phonographic" because the kinds of self-endorsing fantasies that Derrida describes as "phonocentric" are no sooner entertained in the *Metamorphoses* than they are eroded.[23] Like much theoretical work undertaken in light of Derrida or Lacan, Ovid's text effectively dismantles empiricist conceptions of the voice. These chapters therefore consider tropes for the voice in Ovid's poem and its Renaissance heirs from a number of directions, demonstrating how these texts paradoxically endorse and unsettle the fantasies of phonocentrism. In them, I consider such problems as the bodily figure of the speaking tongue and the listening ear; how the voice itself may become an object of desire, even a fetish; the unexpected erotic consequences of apostrophe; voice and the language of music; the unconscious dynamics set in motion by ventriloquism; and the often unpredictable connections between speaking and carrying out an action.

The second chapter sets the stage for those that follow by examining the phonocentric illusion that sustains many of the stories in the *Metamorphoses* and yet is also eroded by them. I pay particular attention to the Ovidian narrator's place in the poem's recurrent fantasies and anxieties about the body's vocal power. Chapter 3 argues that Ovid's rhetoric of the body has a significant impact on the relationship between voice and idolatry in Petrarch's *Rime Sparse*. I place Petrarch's self-portrait as one obsessed by his own words in its Ovidian frame, analyzing the part that such figures as Ovid's Pygmalion, Narcissus, Actaeon, Echo, and Medusa play in constituting the fetishizing unconscious of Petrarchan autobiography. Chapters 2 and 3 provide a foundation for the rest of the book, since those that follow presume knowledge of the increasingly codified Ovidian-Petrarchan lexicon from which both John Marston and Shakespeare derive their figures. Chapter 4, on Marston's *Metamorphosis of Pigmalions Image*, considers the role that apostrophe, a privileged trope for poetic voice, plays in that poem's barely suppressed homoerotic scene and its attendant attempt to distinguish between pornography and what the narrator calls his own merely "wanton" verse. I place my analysis of Marston's epyllion between chapters on Petrarch and Shakespeare because his satire pushes Petrarchan discourse to its extreme, excising female voices altogether. Indeed, Marston's *Pigmalion* forges a path that Shakespeare quite pointedly does not take. Chapters 5 and 6 turn to *The Rape of Lucrece* and *The Winter's Tale*. Chapter 5 connects the problems haunting Lucrece's voice with the poem's representation of authorship and argues that in order to examine the consequences of Petrarchan rhetoric, Shakespeare stages a return to Ovid's text that differs profoundly from Marston's. And I analyze the unravelling of voice, authorial agency, and gender "identity" in *Lucrece*'s various Ovidian figures by looking at Shakespeare's language of musical "instruments" and of the borrowed tongue. Finally, chapter 6 examines what female voices in *The Winter's Tale* have to say about the play's

Orphic desire for a truly performative utterance. In the voices of Paulina and Hermione, Shakespeare stages an ethical critique of Petrarchan autobiographical discourse – a critique that hinges on a return to Ovid's text to listen once more to a number of its forgotten but still troublesome female voices.

In thinking through the many complex problems raised by figures for lost voices in the Ovidian tradition, I discovered a peculiar but telltale sign of Ovid's presence in Renaissance poetry: the scene of an impossible demand. This is usually, but not always, the demand for love or for pity from someone who will give neither. In the *Metamorphoses*, very few characters ever persuade their listeners to respond. Narcissus pleads in vain with his image, Echo with Narcissus, Apollo with Phaethon, Pentheus with his aunt and mother, Actaeon with his hounds, Orpheus with the horde of Bacchic women, Apollo and Pan with Daphne and Syrinx. It is as if the hopelessness of the scene – which Petrarchanism will codify as the lady's stony resistance to persuasion – augments the beauty, pathos, or rhetorical ingenuity of words spoken to no avail. This refusal does not become a question of deep psychological significance for the addressee, since nothing will change his or her mind. But it does instigate considerable aesthetic and rhetorical significance: resistance to another's address underlines language's formal beauty, its unexpected and uncontrolled duplicity, or, more generally, its moving force (for readers and audiences if not for the implacable addressee).

Let me illustrate this general observation with a few brief examples. When Lucrece speaks to persuade Tarquin to refrain, the delay caused by her words merely fuels his desire; his violent purpose, born from her resistance, "swells the higher by this let."[24] At the moment Lucrece utters the plea we know will have no effect, Shakespeare turns her into a second Orpheus. In *Titus Andronicus*, similarly, Lavinia becomes another Philomela when she fails to persuade the inexorable Tamora to relent: "'Tis present death I beg, and one thing more / That womanhood denies my tongue to tell. / O, keep me from their worse than killing lust / And tumble me into some loathsome pit ..." (2.3.173–75). Lavinia's way of wording the request for what we know she will not get – pity – suggests the very Ovidian rape it hopes to fend off. Much like Lucrece's painfully naive *double entendres* in her bedchamber, Lavinia's "tumble me" encourages what it tries to evade. Tamora responds only, "let them satisfice their lust on thee" (2.3.180). In Shakespeare's narrative poem and tragedy, the failure to persuade throws thought back upon how readily words escape control of the one who utters them. This insight about the conditions of becoming a speaking subject, as I hope to show, is deeply Ovidian. It is all the more so because this crisis is embodied in a story of rape. In Petrarch's hands, the beloved's refusal of the speaker's demand for love provides the very condition for writing poetry. It is therefore as a second Apollo, unable to persuade his Daphne to stay, that Petrarch inaugurates his autobiographical version of Ovidian narrative.[25] The *Rime Sparse*, and much love poetry derived from it, elevate this Ovidian scene of the failure to persuade into a virtual poetic ontology. Both the beauty of words themselves – Petrarch's famous form of "idolatry" – and the subjective condition of "exile" emerge as a kind of after-effect of language's failure to bring about the changes of which it speaks. My third chapter traces how deeply this Petrarchan "subjectivity effect" is indebted to Ovidian rhetorical self-consciousness, particularly as embodied in failed aspirations for the human voice. Actaeon's dismemberment, rather than Philomela's rape, becomes an emblematic analogue in the *Rime Sparse* for the voice's failure.

Understood most generally, this book analyzes the many ways that Ovid's fantasies and anxieties about the performative power of his own rhetoric inform each text's libidinal economy. It shows that the failure of the voice and attendant fascination with the scene of an impossible demand – the demand for love or pity, the demand that death return to life, the demand that words change the world rather than merely represent it – shape the Ovidian narrator's self-representation in the *Metamorphoses* and give distinctive shape to his representation of art, passion, and the body. Based on such an understanding of Ovidian rhetoric, the rest of the book shows that Ovid's many tropes for lost voices, at once foundational and disturbing, continue to unsettle Renaissance representations of authorial and sexual identity, whether male or female. In other words, I ask why Ovid's stories about lost voices or voices that fail to effect the change they seek draw to a close only when the body containing that voice is destroyed, dismembered, or raped. Such dire endings tell us that a struggle over the meaning of the human body – as molded by and yet resistant to culture's differential law – casts a shadow over what might otherwise seem to be the most abstract formal, symbolic, and tropological concerns of each text.

By exploring the paradoxical conditions of subjectivity that Ovid's influential tropes for lost voices reveal, I demonstrate something further still. In this tradition, it is the *female* voice – even when it falls resoundingly silent – that puts greatest strain on each poem's thinking about itself and its effects, about the connection between rhetoric and aesthetics, rhetoric and violence. The example of the way Marcus reads Lavinia's bleeding mouth in Ovidian-Petrarchan terms may have suggested as much. Female voices are not always heard (or rather, quoted) in these texts. Sometimes their glaring excision from representation is as

important to my argument as any speech could be. For example, one of
Ovid's most mysterious yet influential figures, that of Medusa, never
utters a word in the *Metamorphoses*. Thanks to Freud's 1940 essay
"Medusa's Head,"[26] we usually refer to the Gorgon's "head" and think
of her effect predominantly in terms of a visual trauma. But in Ovid's
text it is not Medusa's "head," or even her gaze, that petrifies. Rather, it
is primarily her silenced "face" or "mouth" (*os, oris*) that does its
enigmatic work. As I explore further in chapter 2, Ovid singles out
Medusa's *os* as the instrument of petrification. When laying what we
might loosely translate as her "head" on the sand, Perseus puts down
Medusa's "os" rather than, say, her "caput"; when the narrative of her
ghastly effect draws to a close in Book 5, it is again the "mouth" or
"face" of her final victim that, gaping across a line break, reflects the
speechless mouth of Medusa ("*oraque regis / ore* Medusaeo" [5.248–9]).
The Latin noun, *os, oris*, is at the root of the English "oracular." But
"os" is difficult to translate into one word, particularly as Ovid uses it.
For the narrator constantly reminds us of its etymological resonances,
tracing a tropological sequence with rich cultural significance for his
thinking about poetic voice and for some of our most deeply ingrained
ideas about language and persons. First designating a literal place on the
body, "the mouth as the organ of speech" or "the lips," *os* soon comes to
mean "the voice." In Augustan usage, it may designate specifically "the
mouth of a poet."[27] The phrase, *in ore habere*, means "to have on one's
lips;" *in ora uenire* means "to come into other's mouths," or (significantly
for writers like Ovid, Petrarch, and Shakespeare) "to become famous."
This noun for the mouth or lips then travels, as it were, *per ora* ("from
mouth to mouth") to develop related meanings: in general, a "mode of
utterance, pronunciation, eloquence"; then "the front part of the head,
the face," "the features"; then, a person's "expression." And finally, the
os signifies the face insofar as the face is interpreted to imply someone's
"gaze," "mood," or "character."

In Ovid's poem, an "os" or face deprived of the capacity to speak
acquires tremendous affective power. Over and over, the narrator stresses
the etymological link between a character's countenance and his or her
mouth, evoking the idea of a speechless face in order to signify the
moment when a self is most alienated from itself. Narcissus first perceives
that the beautiful "face" he loves (3.423) is merely a reflection when he
notices that the "lips" before him are moving without making a sound
("quantum motu formosi suspicor *oris* / uerba refers aures non peruenientia nostras" 3.461–2). And when no voice issues from Actaeon's
mouth, tears pour down the face that can no longer be said to be his
("uox nulla secuta est. / ingemuit: uox illa fuit, lacrimaeque *per ora / non*

sua fluxerunt," 3.201–03). In referring to the decapitated Medusa by her "os," then, Ovid is drawing on the rich phonographic imaginary of his "perpetual song," in which a speechless face reveals a terrifying otherness within the self. A long Greek tradition associating the Gorgon with disturbing oral fantasies, moreover, suggests that Ovid has a strongly vocal conception of Medusa's "os": "the name 'Gorgon' itself is from the Indo-European root *garj*, denoting a fearful shriek, roar, or shout." Similarly, "the visual arts of the seventh and sixth centuries BC show the Gorgon with a huge frontal face, a distended and grimacing mouth, a protruding tongue, and often sharp and prominent teeth."[28]

Medusa's implacable, silent mouth ("ore Medusaeo"), like Philomela's "speechless lips" ("os mutum"), will serve as an icon for the way that the *idea*, if not the actual sound, of the female voice is crucial to Ovidian reflection on the conditions, effects, and limitations of poetry and rhetoric. In this tradition, I found that whether the female voice is imagined to speak or to fall silent, it wields a telling (if unpredictable) power.[29] Therefore it is not the difference between speech and silence – nor the differences between male and female, power and impotence so often allied with it – that draws my attention. Even in silence, Medusa and Philomela achieve stunning effects. The perceived opposition between speech and silence, this book suggests, does not allow us to grasp anything new about the complex entanglement of rhetorical figures in the politics of sexual difference. Rather, such received antinomies as that between female silence and male speech (an antinomy that appeals to intuitive rather than critical notions of personal agency), betray what is most telling about each of these texts, deflecting attention from the way Ovidian rhetoric undoes carefully guarded presumptions about persons, subjectivity, agency, and gender.

Implicit in the way these readings are structured is my own deepening conviction that we cannot listen to female voices alone, or for that matter know what we (or these texts) mean by "female," without attending to the vicissitudes that are imagined to haunt male voices. Chapter 2 demonstrates that Ovid's representation and enactment of a "voice" – his own and those of his many characters – are crucial to the epic's larger narrative project and deeply affect its stories of violence and desire. As my brief comparison of Medusa's silent "os" to those of Narcissus and Actaeon should suggest, it is only in the context of, and in relation to, Ovid's many "male" voices that what counts as a "female" voice takes shape in the *Metamorphoses* and, in turn, in that poem's Renaissance heirs. It is only by analyzing the symbolic and libidinal economy of voices like those of Apollo, Orpheus, and Pygmalion that we can grasp the significance and force of what is said, or remains unsaid, by female characters such as Ovid's Echo, Philomela, and Medusa; Petrarch's Laura; and Shakespeare's Lucrece, Paulina, and Hermione. Reading each of these characters in light of the persuasive stories about male poetic activity that give both form and texture to their forms of resistance, I demonstrate that like Echo and Narcissus – or perhaps like Salmacis and Hermaphroditus – male and female voices in the Ovidian tradition are locked in a mutually defining, differential embrace.

When I use the term, "the female voice," therefore, I aim to designate a pervasive and seductive *trope*. I do not presume there to be a given – or more importantly, intelligible – phenomenon anterior to the language that gives it shape (for instance, "woman" or "the female subject"). In my last book, *The Tears of Narcissus: Melancholia and Masculinity in Early Modern Writing*, I analyzed the maternal body as a crucial figure in the discourse of early modern, "male" melancholia: this trope provided a number of authors with an effective chronological and material alibi for masking what is in fact a recurrent dislocation in poetic language.[30] The trope of a maternal body allowed each author to deflect and disguise the melancholic, "male" subject's ongoing displacement in language – a displacement that can be grounded neither in time nor in the material world, much less in the original loss of an empirical body. This seeming thing, the maternal body, turned out to be an *effect* rather than a cause of the symbolic order it is said to disrupt. In this book, I similarly understand the apparently intuitive concept of a "female voice" as a discursive effect rather than a prediscursive fact. At the same time, I also understand "subjectivity" to be a contradictory and fragile linguistic effect. Here, as in *The Tears of Narcissus*, I take the speaking subject to be always "in process," as much at risk in language as produced by it. Indeed, this fundamentally psychoanalytic insight – that the speaking "subject in process" is ceaselessly subject to failure – motivated my choice of topic. For there are few poems as relentless as the *Metamorphoses* in representing the speaking subject as an evanescent, fragile thing best grasped at the moment of its fading. As we shall see, the trope of the voice is crucial to this Ovidian insight about the self's fragility, for the poem captures such fading by attending to the sound a voice makes when it fails to work.

I believe that the misfiring implicit in any speaking subjectivity in the Ovidian tradition, moreover, is matched by a similar recalcitrance at the level of "gender identity." First, however, it must be said that the trope of a "female voice" easily invites and reinforces long-standing assumptions about what constitutes womanhood. One could certainly argue that the Ovidian-Petrarchan tradition both reflects and helps to reproduce culturally and historically restrictive definitions of what counts as natural and proper for "women." At first glance, we might decide that because the poems studied here generally associate proper feminine behavior with silence and improper, unchaste, or dangerous femininity with a too voluble tongue, they reinforce historically coded gender positions.[31] Such an idea does find solid endorsement in some aspects of Ovid's poem: oppositional female noise wends its dangerous way through the *Metamorphoses* in the form of the Bacchic horde. Because Ovid's poetry was an important part of the humanist curriculum taught young boys in Elizabethan grammar schools, we do well to be suspicious of its possible effects on the way women are represented in the literary texts of the period. Not only was the *Metamorphoses* extensively excerpted in the lower schools, but in the upper schools it was read in its entirety, set to be memorized as a model for rhetorical imitation.[32] As the flowering of Ovidian poetry in the 1590s by many such former school students indicates, Ovid's narrative and rhetorical manner were highly influential. The marginal notes to John Brinsley's school text translation of *Metamorphoses* Book 1, a work he undertook "chiefly for the good of Schooles," interpret Ovid's text for young students in order to promote prevailing ideologies of proper womanhood. Dedicated to the humanist pedagogical claim that imitating classical authors helps "reduce" the "barbarous" "unto civility ... whereby their sauage and wilde conditions may be changed into more humanity," Brinsley recommends Ovid's "singular wit and eloquence" for grammar school training because "neuer heathen Poet wrote more sweetly in such an easie and flowing veine." His schoolroom version of Book 1 ends, however, not where Ovid ended, but with a story he wants to emphasize: Apollo and Daphne. The laurel is useful "in physicke" and is, more importantly, "pleasant for students." The pedagogue's marginal comments tell pupils that Daphne's fate is generally about the voice – "of *lao phone*" – "because when a leaf or a branch" of the laurel "is burned, it seemeth to send forth a voyce by cracking." He further interprets this story of the voice as one that endorses marriage, chastity, and appropriate silence in a woman. "The Poet intending here to set downe the power of loue ... and withall the reward of chastitie, descendeth unto this next Fable, how Apollo ... was yet ouercom with the loue of Daphne, and how she for her chastity was turned into a Laurell." Before her metamorphosis, Brinsley describes Daphne as one who "cannot endure to heare of loue ... but contrarily solaceth herselfe to liue in the woods." She was therefore a "malcontent" because she lived "all alone without a husband, ranging of the unwayed woods." But after her metamorphosis into the laurel tree, Brinsley adds a note of approval: "*oscula ab os*, seemeth here to be taken for her little mouth" – a trait which, of course, "especially commends a virgin."[33]

Despite Brinsley's confidence about the text's collusion with the banal dictates of gender, however, the trope of the female voice – in the *Metamorphoses* and in many of the works to which it gave rise – unsettles the very ideas about gender hierarchy and identity on which it also relies. To take one of the tradition's more intractable problems: the claim that beauty causes rape permeates the *Metamorphoses* and finds its way into later representations of the crime. But as Katherine Gravdal points out, the Ovidian narrator "systematically" turns attention to the reactions of the victim: female characters in the *Metamorphoses* speak at length of their "pain, horror, humiliation, and grief." In numerous interior mono-logues or, as I hope to show, by such signs as Arachne's tapestry, Medusa's snaky locks, and Philomela's bruised message to her sister, "Ovid highlights the cruelty of sexual violation, showing the part of violence and degradation as clearly as the erotic element. Rape is not mystified or romanticized, but presented as a malevolent and criminal action."[34] Through numerous female voices in Ovid's poem and others, we see that "beauty" is more than merely the object of desire. Someone must become subject of and to beauty; and the *Metamorphoses* does not shy away from showing *at what cost*. As the following chapter will demonstrate, moreover, the narrator's poem-long meditation on the connections between rhetoric and violence gradually produces a series of voices and figures that contest the alliance between rape and poetry first proposed in the story of Apollo and Daphne – voices and figures that establish a position of considerable distance from the narrator's opening dramatization of poetic inspiration.

But this book contends, as well, that female voices do more work in this tradition than that of merely carrying the burden of protest against definitions violently imposed upon them. For example, Leontes' suspi-cion of his wife's too "potent" tongue, the subject of chapter 6, draws on deeply ingrained misogynist alignments of too much talk with lascivious feminine behavior. But *The Winter's Tale*, of course, is highly critical of Leontes and his jealous fantasies. I demonstrate that Shake-speare, in fact, leans on several of Ovid's stories about the power of female tongues to produce a kind of homeopathic cure for the king's delusion. Through the sound of the very "female" voice that triggers Leontes' jealousy, the play distances itself from the king's essentialist reduction of Hermione's tongue to her body and at the same time criticizes the psychologically and politically damaging effects implicit in such culturally pervasive ideas as those pertaining to "male" speech and "female" silence.

More important still, by focusing on Ovidian narrative, I am looking at texts characterized by ventriloquism, a mode Elizabeth Harvey aptly describes as a kind of vocal cross-dressing.[35] In addition to the frequent female monologues of the *Metamorphoses* – Byblis, Myrrha, Scylla, Medea, Hecuba – Ovid honed his art of transgendered *prosopopoeia* in his *Heroides*, an influential series of letters that explore the passions of legendary women as diverse as Penelope, Dido, and Phaedra. His distinctive talent for cross-voicing spawned a tradition in which subsequent male authors took Ovid's poetry as the *locus classicus* for their attempts to speak in or through the voices of women. It is a tradition renewed with remarkable vigor in late sixteenth-century England by such poems as Shakespeare's *The Rape of Lucrece* or Drayton's revision of the *Heroides* in *England's Heroical Epistles*. Taken together, these chapters suggest that a penchant for examining passionate female emotion through the device of interior monologue, the displacements inaugurated by the Ovidian practice of ventriloquism, the mutual implication of male and female voices, and the habit of disrupting the subject from *within* the voice itself – all of which characterize this tradition – trouble our assumptions about identity, personal or sexual. The problems raised when male writers try to "speak as a woman" inform my readings of the rhetoric of animation in the *Metamorphoses*, the connection between exile and autobiography in the *Rime Sparse*, and the displacements of personal and poetic agency in *Lucrece*. The chapter on *Lucrece* especially concentrates on the surprising effects of ventriloquism, for Shakespeare, while engaged in the highly self-conscious act of "lending a tongue" to the virtually silent heroine of Ovid's *Fasti*, undermines the certainty of difference that his trope of a "female voice" and the story of rape presume. And my final chapter follows ventriloquism into another genre, for one of the stranger effects of Leontes' vexed relation to the female "tongue" in *The Winter's Tale* is that the play should emphasize such a tongue in the context of transvestite theatrical practice.

Rhetoric is, above all, an art based on contingency. The intersection between Ovid's rhetorical practice and that of the poets borrowing from him, therefore, takes on the particular color of historical circumstance. I understand early modern impersonations of Ovid's "female" voices in light of the historically specific discursive or institutional practices that inform them. In the case of Petrarch's humanist return to the texts of ancient Rome, Ovidian metamorphosis comes to define a complex relation to figurative language that allows Petrarch to distinguish between his notion of the self and what *The Secretum* represents as Augustine's. In such Ovidian figures as Petrarch's Pygmalion, Augustine's theological and semiotic definition of idolatry runs aground on the shoals of Ovidian eroticism. In Marston's *Metamorphosis of Pigmalions Image*, I read the dynamics of apostrophe, a favorite Ovidian trope, and the narrator's lascivious invocations of female silence in relation to the homosocial institutional arrangements of the Inns of Court, for which the poem was written. In the chapter on *The Rape of Lucrece*, I situate Lucrece's attempt to gain a voice by imitating the *exempla* of Philomela and Hecuba in relation to contemporary pedagogical theory and practice, in which imitation of texts like Ovid's was integral to a humanist theory of rhetorical education. In the final chapter on *The Winter's Tale*, I argue that although Leontes hastily turns his rhetorical anxiety over Hermione's "potent" tongue into fantasies about her body, the play's own highly metatheatrical rhetoric reminds us that the material practice of cross-dressing on the English stage resists the very essentializing turn the king's jealousy takes.

It will be clear by now that throughout this book I view the voice as embodied. My readings suggest that linguistically, culturally, and historically determined ideas about what bodily differences signify give grain and texture to that seemingly most abstract entity, the voice.[36] What "embodiment" might mean is in flux, subject to the vagaries and contingencies of material practice and culturally sedimented fantasy.[37] If the writing ego is, throughout this book, a "bodily ego," that does not mean that I take either the ego or the meaning of the body as a given. The Ovidian tradition, in my view, tells us that the speaking subject's sense of the body's significance is always in process, at once corresponding to and at odds with its own and other bodies as given significance by a differential field of culturally invested meanings. I take it as axiomatic that these differential meanings are always shifting – that they do not actually work, in the end, to impose the law of difference and identity on which these violent stories about bodies and voices paradoxically depend.

I am transformed

My approach to the Ovidian tradition implies that by focusing on the trope of the voice, particularly at the moment of its fading, we come to a fuller understanding of what rhetorical and poetic dilemmas Ovid's erotic narratives bequeath to his heirs. And because I understand the embodied ego in Ovidian poetry to be an unstable, composite linguistic effect subject to recurrent failure, these chapters trace how this subject emerges in the wake of linguistic crisis. My approach therefore also implies that the various dilemmas inherent in Ovid's numerous metapoetic stories about embodied voices have profound consequences for the kind of speaking subjectivity they generate, both in the *Metamorphoses* and later works indebted to it. In Elizabethan England, the habit of allegorizing Ovid's poem gave way to another, transpersonal mode of reading: Ovidian metamorphosis was understood to be, as Jonathan Bate puts it, "psychological and metaphorical instead of physical and literal." New ways of reading Ovid – developing alongside but beginning to outweigh the practice of allegorical interpretation – led to an "implicit internalizing" of Ovidian narrative. Bate finds such internalizing "key to Shakespeare's use of Ovid" and I concur.[38] But a further question arises from this literary-historical observation. Exactly what kind of subjects emerge as a result of this collective "internalizing" of Ovidian narrative? We may come to a sufficiently detailed understanding of the impact that Ovid's rhetoric had on early modern English representations of the self, I believe, by thinking through at least three related issues: the specific rhetorical problems intrinsic to Ovid's representation of the voice in the *Metamorphoses*; the distinctive inflections that Petrarch, in turn, gave Ovid's stories and passed on to sixteenth-century readers; and the way Ovid's poetry was read and interpreted in Elizabethan grammar schools.

As to the first two aspects of Ovid's impact on literary subjectivity, my third chapter analyzes the way his rhetorical practice in the *Metamorphoses* influenced the poetic subject of the *Rime Sparse*. It is not Shakespeare alone who read Ovid's poetry as having internal and psychological significance. Petrarch, that eternally divided Actaeon, forges a new and highly influential representation of the self, I argue, by using Ovidian narrative against Augustinian autobiographical writing.[39] Petrarch does more than merely internalize Ovid: his autobiographical revision of Ovidian figures produces a radically fragmented subject that is always partially blind to its own history, a subject that never coincides with itself and that emerges only as an after-effect of the failure of self-representation. Petrarch's exile from himself, that is, his "partial" forgetting of "the other man" he once was (1.4), is constituted in the very movement of writing. The present iterative of Petrarchan autobiography – *mi trasformo* ("I am transformed" 23.159) – transfers the ceaseless displacements of Ovidian metamorphosis to the very process of trying to write one's own history. In the *Rime Sparse*, such constitutive blindness-in-representation recapitulates, as a trope of writing, the distance from self that in Ovid's *Metamorphoses* inhabits the moment of speaking.

Because of Petrarch's persuasive rendering of metamorphosis as the melancholy condition of a writing and desiring self, Elizabethan poets – be they Petrarchan or anti-Petrarchan – habitually read Ovid and Petrarch together, playing one off the other for different effect (ranging from satiric to tragic). Shakespeare, too, mined the poetry of both Ovid and Petrarch, using their texts as a kind of combined lexicon for representing the condition of the signifying and desiring subject. As

Petrarch read Ovid, and Shakespeare read Ovid and Petrarch together, they produced versions of the "voice" that must change our understanding of that term. Far from being expressions of a self that is given beforehand and that remains somehow greater than whatever can be forced into words, these voices anticipate the theory of the subject's simultaneous production and dislocation in language advanced by Lacan's "return to Freud." Where Lacan reads Freud's observation that "the ego is not master in its own house" as an insight into the conditions of speaking subjectivity, Petrarch and Shakespeare borrow Ovidian rhetoric to *enact* such an understanding of the self. Petrarch sees self-dispossession as the condition for poetic utterance:

> le vive voci m'erano interditte,
> ond'io gridai con carta et con incostro:
> "Non son mio, no ..."   (23.98–100)[40]

Words spoken aloud were forbidden me; so I cried out with paper and ink: "I am not my own, no ..."

Shakespeare, when taking up the task of "lending" Lucrece a tongue, represents her central difficulty in similar – that is, Petrarchan and Ovidian – terms. From Petrarch's constitutive lament, "Non son mio, no," we turn to a Lucrece whose coming into words revolves around a foundational paradox: the subject called by "the name of chaste" and who struggles to speak and write her grief is never fully author to her own "will" because, as the poem tells us, "She is not her own" (line 241). Self-dispossession – which the poem's story of rape presents in gendered terms as a question of Lucrece as someone else's property – is also, thanks to the poem's inaugural act of ventriloquizing Ovid's character, foundational to Shakespeare's representation of what it means to be an author. Reading from this literary-historical angle, we cannot separate the paradoxical condition of Lucrece-as-subject from the fantasies about authorship that so absorb Shakespeare's nondramatic narrators.

Petrarch's contribution to a new way of reading Ovidian narrative marked a decisive turn in European literary representations of self. But there is a second sociological, and therefore more broadly formative, reason for this shift toward an internalized version of Ovidian narrative in Elizabethan poetry. I briefly hinted at this reason above. Early training in classical Latin – aptly described by Walter Ong as a "male puberty rite" and more recently by Richard Halpern as a "mode of indoctrination based on hegemony and consent rather than force and coercion" – was central to humanist pedagogical theory and practice. "Mimetic" rather than "juridical," the humanist curriculum centered on imitation, a practice that "animates not only humanist stylistics but also humanist pedagogy."[41] Halpern argues that Erasmus's program of imitation as the chief means for achieving rhetorical *copia* inaugurated an educational curriculum in which schoolboys were inducted into self-regulation by way of an imaginary *identification* with a dominant model or, to put it in sixteenth century terms, with an "example." His Althusserian view of the humanist curriculum traces the process of the subject's "interpellation" through the ideological apparatus of the grammar school. Guided by an Erasmian theory of imitation, the schools encouraged students to become socialized in high culture rather than popular culture; and they did so by designing exercises that would encourage students to copy the rhetorical practices of classical Latin in order to internalize these practices as if they were their own. And as Bate and others discuss, Ovid's texts were central to this program for acquiring socially sanctioned rhetorical facility; he was particularly noted among classical authors for "sweetness" of style. The Elizabethan reception of Ovid is, therefore, not merely a matter of the waning of allegory in favor of psychological readings, but touches on the *formative* power of rhetoric in the grammar school's material practice, its attempt to marshal imitation and identification as a means for producing rhetorical facility in its "gentlemen" in the making.

Citing the evidence of Brinsley, who was following Roger Ascham's *Scholemaster*, Bate describes the method whereby the master would give students prose excerpts of classical poets – usually from Mirandula's *Illustrium Flores Poetarum*, which frequently epitomized Ovid – and ask them to translate back not merely into Latin, but into the style of the author in question. For Brinsley, this is "the first entrance into versifying, to turne the prose of the Poets into the Poets owne verse, with delight, certainty and speed, without any bodging; and so by continuall practice to grow in this facilitie, for getting the phrase and vein of the Poet."[42] Bate describes the common exercise of writing letters in the style of Ovid's *Heroides* as "the beginning of dramatic art." But as training designed to inculcate rhetorical facility, it might also be considered an exercise in discovering oneself through identification – or, as Erasmus's theory might formulate this relationship, in adopting the voices of others in order to find out one's own. We may grasp something of the way identification subtends the humanist educational theory of imitation by remembering one of Shakespeare's favorite classical *exempla*: Hecuba. In the schools, Ovid was taught as one of the most "copious" of authors and his Hecuba (*Metamorphoses* 13) provided an exemplary model for how to use *copia* to create great emotion. In humanist educational training, the voice of Ovid's suffering Hecuba became a "mirror" or "example" for pupils to imitate – a lesson for young men learning to develop their own style. As Bate argues, it is therefore hardly surprising that Gorboduc takes Hecuba to be "the woeful'st wretch / That ever lived to make a *mirror* of" (3.1.14–15).[43] Because of the pedagogical methods of the grammar school, we might consider imitation of classical examples an important social, imaginary, and personal practice as much as a stylistic technique. As I explore in chapter 5, Lucrece finds voice for her own grief by way of imitating Hecuba's just as Hamlet, later, will discover his own "passion" after witnessing someone else imitating Hecuba's. They both use Ovid's suffering Trojan mother as a mirror, that is, in and through which to understand and to express what they claim to be their "own" emotions.

It is important to note, as well, that Ovid's texts were not merely memorized, but set as exercises for learning to write in his style. The cultivation of style served a social function beyond the direct one of producing rhetorically capable subjects. The apparently immoral content of the *Metamorphoses*, once read away by allegory, could now be evaded by a method of education based on the positive valuation of rhetorical style over content. In trying to understand the attitude of schoolmasters toward the wanton material in classical texts such as Ovid's, T. W. Baldwin cites Robert Cawdry:

As in slaughter, massacres, or murther, painted in a Table, the cunning of the Painter is praysed, but the fact it selfe, is vtterly abhorred: So in Poetrie wee follow elocution, and the proper forme of wordes and sentences, but the ill matter we doo worthily despise.[44]

Citing this text to support his argument for what he calls the humanist "destruction of content," Halpern then invokes the allegory of the *Ovide moralisé* as counterpoint to the humanist project of acquiring rhetorical *copia*: "the older method subsumed dangerous contents within a larger ideological unity; the newer method decomposed this same material into harmless, inert atoms."[45] As he also suggests, however, the aim to imitate "cunning" style alone without approving "abhorred" content did not convince everyone: Juan Luis Vives, for instance, advocated that "obscene passages should be wholly cut out from the text, as though they were dead, and would infect whatever they touched."[46] As subsequent chapters will show, the scandalous content of Ovidian eroticism was barely contained by the humanist cultivation of his rhetorical style. Though Francis Meres famously stressed affinity of style – "the sweete wittie soule of Ovid lives in mellifluous and hony-tongued Shakespeare" – and Thomas Nashe praised the "silver tong'd" and "well-tun'd" nature of Ovidian verbal facility, nonetheless the erotic shape Ovid habitually gave his myriad reflections on rhetoric in the *Metamorphoses* continues to surface in Elizabethan poetry (particularly in the epyllion) just as allegorical reading never utterly canceled the illicit pleasure some readers clearly gleaned from reading the most heavily annotated of Ovidian texts.[47] Allegorical interpretation imposed an entirely new order of meaning on Ovid's text, and thus subsisted in a different order of understanding (whether accepted by individual readers or not). But an educational practice so thoroughly alert to nuances of rhetorical technique remained very much in touch with the "phrase and vein of the Poet." It was therefore precisely the kind of practice that would alert its well-trained readers to the way that the narrator of the *Metamorphoses* habitually translates rhetorical problems into erotic ones (and vice versa).

Admirable figures

There is a third, formal issue to consider if we are to account for Ovid's impact on literary representations of subjectivity. Understanding what happens in the process of internalizing Ovidian narrative – or what effect the extensive and repeated imitation of Ovid's verse might have had on young students of Latin – means taking careful stock of his language. Certain hallmark rhetorical practices carry within them dilemmas important to later "Ovidian" representations of the self. Ovid's reflections on the power and limitations of language in the *Metamorphoses* are legion, and they are foundational for what passes as a subject in this tradition. I have already discussed the Ovidian phenomenon of the impossible demand, a dynamic that Petrarch would turn into the very condition of love and the self. The failed address or impossible demand – so influential for Renaissance texts – might be thought but an instance of a larger problem in the epic: for Ovid, the self comes most memorably into being when the instrumental function of language breaks down. Such failures are most often dramatized in a story about a mouth that betrays its owner: Io, mooing, "is terrified by the sound of her own voice" ("mugitus edidit ore / ... propriaque exterrita uoce est," 1.637–38) and Actaeon utters an "inhuman" groan that "no deer could make" (3.237–39). Such failures find one of their most resonant, and painful, synecdoches in the literalized figure of Philomela's tongue, murmuring on the dark earth. The voice's excess – the fact that it doesn't always work as an instrument of communication or that it can mysteriously become more than mere instrument – generates a great deal of action in the epic out of words that mean too little (the cryptic oracle given to Deucalion and Pyrrha) or that do too much (Apollo's oath to his son Phaethon to grant him whatever he wishes as proof of paternity). The narrative veers back and forth between words that do not work and words that work all too well. On the one hand, we read that Pentheus' words are quite audible. His pleas are quoted directly in the text, but they make no difference: neither mother nor aunt acknowledge those "milder words" and therefore tear Pentheus limb from limb ("uerba minus uiolenta" 3.717). On the other, we find that although Jove wishes he or Semele could take back the words they have spoken, they cannot: "already her voice had rushed out into the air" ("exierat iam uox properata sub auras" 3.296). The god is therefore bound to honor the spoken promise that will kill her.

Captivated by the perils of speaking subjectivity – a peril that includes even the gods – Ovid continually renders these dangers as erotic dramas. In his hands, the abstract problems of language – its (often tenuous) role as a form of mediation between mind and world and its power to produce something new in the world rather than merely represent or describe it – assume a distinctly sexual guise. In many of the poem's dramas about lost voices, characters are caught, in rapt attention, by the mediating screen of an image, figure, or form; such devotion to an image alters both the world and that character's place in it. The *Metamorphoses* most memorably characterizes its speaking subjects, that is, by putting them in passionate relation to an image or figure. For love of an image whose "lips" can move but make no "audible sound," Narcissus dies and produces a flower. For love of a speechless *simulacrum*, Pygmalion generates a new race. From the failure of Apollo's voice to hang onto the *figura* he so desires, a new sign for poetry emerges. Here we are not far from Petrarch's ceaselessly announced "martyrdom" to the laurel, his beloved "first figure."

But desire is not the only momentous emotion attached to images in the *Metamorphoses*. As I examine further in chapter 2, because they confront Medusa's terrifying mouth (*os*), numerous male victims stand forever petrified by the force of this *monstrum*. We are told that Athena made the snaky *monstrum* – meaning a "sign, omen, or prodigy" – so that Medusa's rape "not go unpunished" (4.800); the goddess rhetorically extends the crime's effect on the world by memorializing it in an ominously potent sign. (Although it may seem that Medusa is being punished for her own rape, the narrative remains deliberately vague about who is being punished; we should note, for instance, that Medusa's victims are all men.) Petrarch, of course, was quite aware that his love for his one "figure" might lapse into petrification. His desire to be a second Pygmalion by making a picture of Laura speak finds its inversion in his own imprisonment as a marble statue: "The heavenly breeze that breathes in that green laurel ... / has the power over me that Medusa had

over the old Moorish giant, when she turned him to flint ... Her very
shadow turns my heart to ice and tinges my face with white fear, but her
eyes have the power to turn it to marble" ("L'aura celeste che'n quel
verde lauro / spira ... / po quello in me che nel gran vecchio mauro/
Medusa quando in selce transformollo ... / L'ombra sua sola fa 'l mio
cor un ghiaccio/ et di bianca paura il viso tinge,/ ma gli occhi ànno vertù
di farne un marmo" 197.1–14). A reader as attuned as Petrarch to the
rhetoric of the *Metamorphoses* understands that in it, images wield a
duplicitous power. He is therefore martyr to a sign that both kindles
desire *and* "tinges his face with white fear."

Ovid's narrator, too, dwells in loving detail on his characters' fascination with significant form – be the feeling aroused one of admiration or,
in the case of Medusa, terror. One of the more frequent words in the
Metamorphoses for this moment is "mirari": Narcissus "admires" his
image (3.424), Pygmalion "admires" his *simulacrum* (10.252), Europa
"admires" the white bull. But so, too, are "haerere" ("to stick," "freeze,"
or "fasten on with the senses") and "stupere" ("to be struck dumb")
other favorite Ovidian words for the effect of an image on its viewer.
Thus Narcissus "freezes (haeret) ... like a statue carved from Parian
marble" (3.419) before his watery reflection; and Perseus, half convinced
that Andromeda is a "marble statue," is "struck dumb" ("stupet") by
"the image of her beautiful face" (4.675–77). In the story of Perseus and
Medusa, the hero's immobilized attention to an image turns into a
permanent state of affairs: caught by the omen of the Gorgon's "os," one
viewer "froze (haesit), a marble statue" (5.183). Like the story of
Narcissus's love for the sheer beauty of his own *imago*, Medusa's story
tells us that in an Ovidian universe, the capacity for aesthetic pleasure
may give way, with but the slightest of turns, to a total evacuation of the
self. Ovid's many variations on this delicate balance emerge in Petrarch's
hands as the woes of one who, devoted to his "figura," lives forever
suspended "mezzo ... tra vivo et morto" ("a mean between the living
and the dead," 23.89).

In the *Metamorphoses*, therefore, significant form does more than
mediate between inner and outer worlds. Source of love or of terror, a
figure may also *change* both, though not in any predictable fashion. To
remember the poem's earliest exploration of language's productive force:
telling the story of the world's creation soon becomes, in Book 1, a thinly
veiled excuse for telling numerous stories about the constitutive power of
poetic language. In the tale of Deucalion and Pyrrha, a second creation
of human beings from stones takes place on Mt. Parnassus, the mountain
of poetry. The notion that language wields a creative force was important
to this creation story before Ovid. As Frederick Ahl reminds us,

etymological play informed the Greek tradition: accounts by Apollo-dorus (1.7.2) and Pindar (*Olympian* 9.41ff) suggest that the actions of Deucalion and Pyrrha reflect "the derivation of the word 'people' from 'stones' " (people: "ho LAos"; stones: "ho LAas" but also "ho LAos"). In Ovid's handling of the scene, Ahl suggests, human beings ("HUMani ... generis," 1.246) are derived from a gesture of "humiliation," as the pair "prostrate themselves on the earth" ("procumbit uterque/ pronus HUMi," 1.375–76).[48] But this new world is also generated from a metaphorical understanding of language. When the oracle speaks, "throw the bones of your great mother behind you" ("ossaque post tergum magnae iactate parentis," 1.383), Pyrrha recoils from the implied sacrilege in the literal level of the command. But Deucalion steps in, a poetic reader armed with a metaphorical interpretation of oracular speech that creates another world altogether: "our great mother is the earth: and I think that the bones of which the goddess speaks are the stones in the earth's body" ("magna parens terra est: lapides in corpore terrae / ossa reor dici" 1.393–4). In this story, both the literal sounds of words and their capacity to signify in more than one way assume the power to *produce* a perceived world rather than merely reflect or replace it. The Ovidian narrator, characteristically, directs our attention to a prolonged visual spectacle of the verbal mediation Deucalion has just enacted: as I described earlier, we watch the "form" of this second race slowly take shape "*like* the beginnings of forms made out of marble, not sharply defined and very like rough statues" (1.405). Like Deucalion's move into metaphor, Ovid pauses over the transitional moment – the "sed uti" – to make us look, as it were, at the shaping force of his simile as it brings a new race into shape by way of a work of art. The narrator's simile, in effect, works to claim Deucalion's constitutive verbal power as its own.

We may speak of the productive power of Ovid's poetry, then, in social terms – the important imaginary force his poetry exercised on students looking to develop their own voices according to the prescrip-tions of humanist rhetorical training – but also in poetic and rhetorical terms. In the *Metamorphoses*, language's mediations often acquire a constitutive rather than merely representative power. But we must also remember, as I suggested above, that the effect of appreciation for significant or figural forms may not be so beneficent as it seems in Deucalion's story about creating a new race of beings. Admiration for the beauty of an interposed form can quickly lapse, like the story of Europa's interest in the white bull or Arachne's "polished" tapestry, into narratives of violence. Thus Philomela's "skilled" weaving becomes, in Procne's hands, a dangerous message that inaugurates an act even deadlier than the one it reports. And if Deucalion's story tells us that language has the power to produce a new world rather than merely describe it, any given speaker in the poem may do no more than momentarily harness this power – "if," to phrase this through Diana's taunt to Actaeon, "he or she can." Productive as this rhetoric may be, its effects are not predictable. Nor does its power rest with any one speaker. As even Apollo discovers in his rash oath to his son, words may not always have the effect one intends. In moments such as Apollo's impotent regret for the consequences of his own words, we are not far from Lavinia's "tumble me" or Shakespeare's opening move, in *The Rape of Lucrece*, to blame Collatine's (Petrarchan) words of praise as the verbal event that produces a little too much admiration. The narrator holds "the *name* of chaste" [my emphasis] responsible for engendering in Tarquin a distinctly voracious "appetite" for rape. Alienation from one's own tongue is both a physical predicament in Ovidian narrative and, at the same time, the condition of being able to speak at all.

Pursuing Daphne

We must now return to reconsider an important problem in further detail. When thinking through the relationship between aesthetic form, rhetoric, and violence in the *Metamorphoses* or, for that matter, the relationship between male and female voices, we confront what has proved for some critics one of the poem's most troubling features: the story of rape. What seems to me most striking, however, is not simply that the poem associates sexuality with power or violence. Rather, it repeatedly links sexual violence to a sense of beauty – verbal and visual, general and specifically formal or technical. Out of rape and mutilation, Ovid generates images that are to make us pause and, like so many of the poem's characters, "admire" (mirare). Out of her own rape, Philomela weaves "skilled" threads; out of the rapes of others, Arachne weaves a tapestry so accomplished that it enrages Athena. Daphne's flight from Apollo, similarly, turns into a thinly veiled commentary on many aspects of poetic verse: in the god of poetry's eyes, Daphne embodies a "form" and "figure" in need of arrangement; her flight produces the "breath" that will become the voice of song. And where Philomela's story represents rape through what can or cannot be spoken by the "tongue" ("lingua"), Daphne's also meditates on poetry's specifically oral power. For in it, Ovid uses "os," or mouth, as the one word in which to capture sexual violence and poetic speech at once. In the final simile for Apollo's chase, that of a dog pursuing the hare, the god of poetry's desire to possess Daphne turns into an image of a dog's outstretched mouth: "she escapes the teeth and leaves *the outstretched mouth* behind her: so the god and the maiden" ("et ipsis/ morsibus eripitur *tangentiaque ora* relinquit: / sic deus et uirgo" 1.537–38). In a poem in which "amor" is, throughout, "amor sceleratus habendi" ("the cursed love of having"), this simile for Apollo's "outstretched mouth" tells us that poetry, too, is implicated in the voracious force of eros, a force whose devastating effects it is the narrator's project to "sing."

As chapter 2 demonstrates, it is not in Daphne's story alone that Ovid associates the violence of rape with the technical beauties of poetry, be they "form," "figure," or rhythm. Critics no longer look beyond rape in Ovid's poem; several have called our attention to the necessity of asking why it happens with such predictable regularity.[49] But it is by no means clear how to read these rapes or, indeed, what questions might expand our treatment of them. My own attempts to address this issue are many. They are scattered throughout these readings, as is my sense of how to ask questions that do not reduce the complexity of either the fact of social and sexual violence or the vicissitudes of poetic language. I can give here a brief sense of my own thinking on the matter by saying that from an Althusserian perspective, one might argue that in the *Metamorphoses*, the call from the law that hails or "interpellates" the female subject *is* rape.[50] One English term translates a variety of Latin ones covering a range of actions from sexual violation to abduction; but Ovid's poem also tends to identify the various acts along this continuum, from Tereus' brutally physical assault on Philomela's body to the abductions of Europa and Persephone.[51] And the poem is inclined, moreover, to identify acts we might prefer to separate because of its (metarhetorical) preoccupation with *forma*, or female "beauty": that is, Ovid's women define what counts as "beauty" by resistance or flight from threatened rape, whether in the form of abduction or violation. Indeed, as my students often tell me, being a woman in Ovid's poem means to embody the principle of resistance. Women discover, like Daphne, that "beauty" ("forma") is not really itself. Beauty is created in the eyes of desire, as one scene after another tells the story of rape as the accident, "one day x saw y." And it is *"augmented* by flight" ("auctaque forma fuga est," 1.530). Or in one of the poem's most influential stories of sexual assault, it is Philomela's verbal and visual resistance to Tereus' multiple violations that allows the narrator to emphasize both the complexities of rhetorical speech (her Orphic attempt to "move stones") and the formal qualities of visual and/or written art (her tapestry's moving "purple notes").

Where Althusser's subject recognizes his subjection in the call of a policeman on the street, Ovid's women recognize their subjection *as* women when suddenly hailed by a god bent on rape. They recognize themselves as subjects in the violent call of someone else's desire. And they become the female beauty they are called upon to embody by turning Althusser's moment of recognition into flight. But flight only embroils them further in the very *forma* from which they flee, since in the eyes of masculine law in this poem, resistance and flight enhance beauty and nearly come to define it. Thus Caenis, ravished by Neptune, might be a fitting spokeswoman for many of the poem's victims. Bid to choose what she wishes in payment for having been raped, Caenis responds by seeking the only way out: "Grant me that I not be a woman" ("mihi da, femina ne sim," 12.202). Caenis' request strikes my ear, at least, as an epitome of Althusser's notion of "internal distance." For him, internal distance "presupposes a retreat" or "internal distantiation" from the ideology to which a text "alludes and with which it is constantly fed." In its blunt confrontation with the conditions of being a woman in the poem, "Mihi da, femina ne sim" makes us understand "in some sense *from the inside* ... the very ideology" of sexual difference which the *Metamorphoses* also deploys.[52] Such a claim – that in the *Metamorphoses*, rape is represented as the call that interpellates the female subject *as* "femina" – suggests to me that Ovid's text, like many of Freud's, is more a critique of the systematic violence and subordination embedded in patriarchal culture than mere repetition or perpetuation of it.[53]

I believe, therefore, that deciding the "male" narrator's place in Ovid's aesthetically self-reflexive representations of rape is not as straightforward a matter as some would have it. Nancy Miller, for instance, believes she can separate Arachne's art from Ovid's. Reading the story apart from the rest of the *Metamorphoses*, she celebrates Arachne's "feminocentric protest" and censures the narrator's control, personifying Ovid's character to the detriment of her author. When Athena rends Arachne's tapestry and destroys her human shape, Miller blames the narrator for "deauthorizing" Arachne's voice. But before we follow Miller, remember that the status of the voice is not so simple in the *Metamorphoses*. The condition for having a voice at all in the poem, in fact, is that *it will be lost* – or, as Miller puts it, "deauthorized."[54] Even Orpheus loses his body (and therefore song) to the Bacchic horde. And the poem's narrator, the "voice" that stands to benefit most from the voices that others lose, concludes his most blatant bid for immortality – his song will bring him an "indelible name" that lasts as long as the Roman empire lasts – with an irony born of metamorphosis: "*if* the prophecies of bards have any truth to them, I shall live" ("siquid habent ueri uatum praesagia, uiuam" 15.879). In a book where prophecy of Rome's continued status as "eternal city" culminates a narrative of "endless, cyclical change" that destroys all other cities, Ovid pointedly lets us wonder about the efficacy of linking his own "perennial" fame to Rome's future.[55] Arachne joins the ranks of every other artist in the poem, including, by implication, the narrator. That Arachne's body and art are destroyed only to issue into another story incorporates that story into the narrative movement of metamorphosis; but it is a movement from which the Ovidian narrator is too canny to claim that he alone is exempt, even though he may try. No narrator who tells a story like that of Echo's tricky repetitions can claim, without irony, that though his body may be destroyed, he will live because his words are uttered by other mouths, transferred "on the lips" of other people ("ore legar populi" 15.878).

More important still, Ovid's description of Arachne's skill fashions her in the mold of contemporary aesthetic judgment. Arachne represents many of the poem's previous rapes with a skill that Ovid describes in some detail. Indeed, Ovid brings the contemporary lexicon for poetic excellence to bear on Arachne's indignant representation of rape. Like other neoteric Roman poets she is "docta" (somewhere between learned and cultured).[56] Like the poet's wearing of ivy in Horace or Propertius, her tapestry's border represents "clinging ivy" ("nexilibus ... hederis" 6.128). Of this line, W. S. Anderson comments on the association between ivy and poetry, suggesting that Ovid may be "seeking a floral symbol with connotations to rival those of Minerva's olive."[57] Like the fame Ovid wishes for at the end of the *Metamorphoses*, Arachne has achieved a "memorable name" ("nomen memorabile," 6.12 for Ovid's "nomenque erit indelebile nostrum" 15.876). And like the unnamed Olympian god whose artistic sensibility shapes the world in the first lines of the poem, Arachne generates the material for her work by arranging and organizing a rude, chaotic mass of material. For the "rudis ... moles" of chaos in Book 1, line 7 we find Arachne's "rudem ... lanam," a mass that she weaves on a "polished spindle with smooth thumb" ("leui teretem uersabat pollice fusum," 6.22). The weaving that represents so many violated women is as refined and "polished" as the verses to which contemporary Roman poets lay claim. Arachne's tapestry, moreover, recapitulates the rapes narrated earlier in the poem itself and she finishes her work with a characteristically Ovidian signature: the border of the tapestry is "filled with flowers and clinging ivy intertwined" ("nexilibus flores hederis habet intertextos" 5.128). This line leaves one uncertain whether the flowers are figures *in* the tapestry or actual, "real" flowers incorporated into its weaving. Like the fading of so many of Ovid's figures into objects in the landscape, Arachne's "polished" representation lapses back, at the edges, into the natural world.[58] One might claim that Arachne, far from being "deauthorized," becomes a *surrogate* for Ovid's narrator.[59] Through her tapestry, he may speak about rape through the "as if" of metaphor: Arachne's art allows the narrator to speak, momentarily, "as if" a woman.

In the figures on Arachne's tapestry, then, Ovid recapitulates his own poem by signalling that its seemingly endless series of rapes may look very different if seen through the victim's eyes.[60] Arachne's work gives readers a chance to ponder the details of a female character's version of the subject of rape, a weaving comparable to the one that later in the same book is destined for the eyes of Philomela's sister alone. That Arachne's "perspective" disappears is not unusual. No single perspective survives the bewildering shifts of Ovid's metamorphic narrative, a narrative whose "favorite topic" is, precisely, the dissolution of such identity.[61] Similarly, as I suggest in chapter 2, Perseus borrows Medusa's "mouth" (again, "os, oris") to conquer where his own words could not: when Ovid "speaks" through Arachne's tapestry or Perseus persuades through Medusa's mouth, exact determinations of agency and attendant judgments of culpability become thankless and reductive tasks. Indeed, the stories of Echo, Medusa, and Philomela make clear that one of the central problems in Ovid's poem is that ownership of one's "own" words and control over their effect are endlessly uncertain.

My joint focus on the general influence of Ovidian rhetoric and on the particular pressure exerted by the trope of the female voice on each text offers a view of early modern "masculine" subjectivity coincident with what I take to be the most promising axiom of psychoanalytic work for feminist criticism: that no subject is ever as coherent, as much an "identity," as it imagines itself to be. The "male" subject in these texts is, rather, internally fractured and fragmented, a composite formation fissured by multiple and contradictory demands. And when a woman is imagined to speak in these texts, we see most clearly that the "male" subject is the *effect*, rather than the cause of signification – that he can never master the field of difference over which he may nonetheless claim dominion. Poetic ventriloquism in the Ovidian tradition, like the theatrical practice of cross-dressing, places enormous pressure on the discourse of masculine "identity." The fractured condition of the subject in Ovidian narrative by no means implies a reduction in male power, however. On the contrary, the very fragility to which the female voice draws attention in these texts leads to violent fantasies (like rape) that work to reclaim the very hierarchy that seems momentarily at risk.

Stressing the continued pertinence of the hypothesis of the unconscious to early modern literary discourses of the self, my third chapter on "verbal fetishism" in the *Rime Sparse* demonstrates the sometimes unexpected consequences of Petrarch's autobiographical use of Ovidian figures. Drawing on the distinction between Pygmalion's vocal address and the statue's silence to explore the vicissitudes of his own fragmented voice, Petrarch shapes an influential structure of difference for representing the male self. But as I suggest, Ovid's female voices – Echo, Medusa, Diana – do occasionally break through the reflexive surface of Petrarchan self-absorption, signalling that self's fragility and undoing the explicit representation of sexual difference that founds the discourse of love. Recent feminist criticism, alert to the complex relation between experience and discourse, has turned attention to the rhetoric of the Petrarchan *blason*, a mode of describing female beauty that dismembers the very thing it praises. Stemming from one of two models – Gayle Rubin's "traffic in women" or the analysis of homosociality that runs from Freud to Eve Sedgwick[62] – feminist critics sometimes portray the *Rime Sparse* and the genre the cycle inaugurated as a well-oiled poetic and rhetorical machine, one that produces a discourse of "masculine" desire and self-reflection based on the objectification, exchange, fragmentation, and finally silencing of women. In a highly influential article, Nancy Vickers ends with a persuasive version of this view: in the *Rime Sparse*, "silencing Diana is an emblematic gesture; it suppresses a voice, and it casts a generation of would-be Lauras in a role predicated upon the *muteness* of its player" (emphasis mine). Here Vickers echoes early work by Laura Mulvey, whose "Visual Pleasure" she cites, particularly the claim that "man can live out his phantasies and obsessions through linguistic command by imposing them on the silent image of woman still tied to her place as bearer of meaning, not maker of meaning."[63]

This groundbreaking feminist work clearly enabled my own slightly different version of "verbal fetishism" in the *Rime Sparse*. But it remains only part of the story, occluding the foundational, if disruptive, effect that Ovid's rhetoric had on Petrarchan autobiography – and by that route, on early modern discourses of the desiring self. I emphasize the Ovidian background to Petrarchan autobiography and focus on the differential work of male *and* female voices in the *Metamorphoses* and beyond because I believe that a narrow focus on the Petrarchan *blason*, without an extended consideration of Ovid's influence on the discourse of autobiography in the *Rime Sparse*, can produce a too monolithic view of subjectivity and masculinity (or of gender more generally) and a too pessimistic view of the regulatory force of his rhetorical practice. My third chapter stresses that Diana is not in fact "silenced": instead, her few but crucial words *prohibiting* the poet's speech are foundational to the discursive and erotic paradoxes of Petrarch's self-representation. By focusing on the effects of Diana's quoted taboo, rather than on her being silenced, I hope to reconsider the unconscious currents that trouble the apparently smooth waters of masculine poetic agency. Taken together, these chapters suggest that if we read Shakespeare's *The Rape of Lucrece* and *The Winter's Tale*, and Petrarch's *Rime Sparse* in light of their complex debt to Ovidian voices, we will enrich current feminist analyses of the reifying *blason* and thereby understand more fully the impact of Petrarchan rhetoric on Shakespeare's representations of gender and subjectivity.

As my last book made clear, moreover, my own understanding of psychoanalytic theory differs from the one articulated here by Vickers or Mulvey. Pursuing lines laid out by critics like Janet Bergstrom on "multiple identificatory positions, whether successively or simultaneously" and Jacqueline Rose on the "failure" of any identity, male or female, I take the import of Freud's analysis of fetishism, for instance, to be that the "male" subject is fractured, always in the process of being forged out of immanent contradictions.[64] I join my focus on the Ovidian intertext with a psychoanalytic analysis of Petrarch's verbal fetishism because such an approach, while reading the speaking subject's symbolic and libidinal economy in a particular way, also maintains that the fetish is an important sign of the subject's splitting. As I discuss in Chapter 3, the fetish signifies both the price of achieving a "masculine" identity and the impossibility of ever entirely doing so. I believe, in short, that the contradictions inherent in the discourse of masculinity – many of which I examine in this book – may begin to explain the extraordinary, and unsettling, proximity of aesthetics and violence in the Ovidian tradition.

And finally, it is to counter what I believe to be an overly pessimistic view of the effects of Petrarch's "scattering" rhetorical practice that I concentrate on the crucial role of Ovidian rhetorical self-reflection in the *Rime Sparse* and beyond. As my discussion of the *Metamorphoses* should make clear, in Ovid's poem rhetoric can indeed be a dangerously potent tool. But it is never merely instrumental – and certainly never merely the instrument of "men." Contrary to Mulvey's description of masculine "linguistic command," the *Metamorphoses* teach one male character after another – Apollo, Orpheus, Pan, even Jupiter himself – that such command is never more than an enticing fantasy. Even the briefest encounters with Echo, Philomela, Medusa, and Arachne, moreover, instruct readers that female characters, even when "silenced," may still be "makers" rather than mere "bearers" of meaning. In Ovid's text, rhetorical speech is never entirely in control of any one subject: no speaker in the *Metamorphoses* is the final owner, author, or controlling agent of the words he or she speaks. In Ovidian narrative, language, like the body, exceeds the speaking subject. What I hope to demonstrate is that it is most often the voices of female characters – or the idea, if not the sound, of such a voice – that instruct male characters that this is so.

For Ovid the effect of rhetorical speech, while exceedingly potent, remains fundamentally unpredictable. Its power never rests unequivocally with any one party. The *blason* may be determining, therefore, but it is not mechanically deterministic: "a limit on the field of the possible rather than an irresistible compulsion."[65] And it had to share terrain with other aspects of Petrarch's rhetorical practice, among them the ones I stress here: inaugural tropes for the voice that over the course of centuries amounted to a venerable tradition of cross-voicing. "Female" voices in this tradition – Medusa, Daphne, Syrinx, Echo, Arachne, Philomela, Diana, Ceres, the Bacchae, and their early modern daughters, Laura, Lucrece, Hermione, and Paulina – are tropes that carry us beyond identity and the voice as such into a kind of phonographic imaginary. In this imaginary place, unsettling stories of difference echo, pointing beyond what can, in fact, actually be said by or heard in any voice. And though we encounter many terrible moments when silence is violently forced on a woman, this book suggests that if read carefully, phonographic traces of these lost, silenced voices persist long enough to disturb the symbolic and libidinal economy in which they play such a necessary part.

2 Medusa's mouth: body and voice in the *Metamorphoses*

This chapter analyzes the connections among rhetoric, sexuality, and subjectivity in Ovid's *Metamorphoses* to enable us to see why disquieting convergences like the one between Daphne's use of *figura* – the form of her body – and the narrator's – Apollo's poetic tropes – continue to inform Renaissance appropriations of Ovidian narrative, particularly later imitations of Ovid that claim to speak to a difference between male and female experience. By examining what the often violent intersection between rhetoric and sexuality means for the speaking subjects of Ovid's poem, moreover, I hope to give a sense of how important it is for a feminist critique of the *Metamorphoses* and its afterlife that in it we encounter what Simone Viarre, following Roland Barthes, calls a "fusion between poetry and rhetoric" – a thoroughgoing conversion of rhetoric into a "poetic technique."[1] In other words, the punning movement of *figura*, the resonant word that signifies both Daphne's body and the god of poetry's speech, suggests a crucial place where a feminist analysis of the *Metamorphoses* might intersect widely acknowledged aspects of Ovidian poetic practice.

I have already emphasized Ovid's habit of turning poetic and rhetorical self-reflection into stories of desire and sexual violence: Apollo's rapacious desire for Daphne is also a poet's love for a figure; Pygmalion's desire to "move" his statue is also a sexual version of a rhetorician's aim to "move" his audience; Perseus first uses Medusa's *os* (against Atlas) as a kind of rhetorical prosthesis, enforcing the compliance that his "soothing words" cannot; the aetiological story of the Gorgon's head, in its turn, converts a rape and a beheading into the origin of the fountain of poetry; and so forth.[2] My readings in this chapter move between Ovid's pervasive metapoetic and metarhetorical reflection in the *Metamorphoses* and his representations of gender and sexuality, paying close attention to his many figures for the human voice in order to ask what difference these figures make for the poem's distinctive way of defining embodied subjectivity.[3] I suggest that the idea of the voice gives a singularly Ovidian texture to the poem's announced topic – the "form" of the human body and the myriad possible changes to it. In my introduction I also put particular emphasis on Ovid's trademark habit of ventriloquizing female voices – a rhetorical technique Quintilian calls *prosopopoeia*[4] – because I understand this displacement to be part of the narrator's general strategy of attenuating in order to redirect attention to the connection we generally take for granted between a voice and the body that contains it. I return to consider what Ovid's penchant for ventriloquism implies for the poem's thinking about gender and sexuality at the end of the chapter. But before we can properly understand the effects of Ovid's transgendered *prosopopoeiae*, we must first examine how the narrator's strategy of distancing body from voice impinges on two things: the poem's representation of subjectivity; and those aspects of Ovid's narrative that seem to be matters of strictly formal, symbolic, or rhetorical concern. Both characteristics of the *Metamorphoses* – its particular way of representing subjectivity as alienation from one's own tongue and its corollary fascination with the power, and limitations, of rhetoric – would prove extremely influential in the European poetic tradition to which it gave rise.

In the pages that follow, I analyze a number of the *Metamorphoses'* most influential stories about bodies and voices in light of the narrator's prominent rhetorical strategies and fantasies. Put most generally, the chapter argues that although the metarhetorical economy of the poem may seem, in the beginning, to propose an unsurprising narrative of sexual difference to account for its various voices – unsurprising because consonant with normative ideas about gender and desire – nevertheless Ovid's rhetorical practice undermines that narrative over the course of the poem. But before we can understand how this continuing struggle over the meaning of bodily difference shapes Ovid's various voices (or, for that matter, the many Renaissance tropes for the voice that derive from his), we must first consider the provenance and trajectory of the voice in the *Metamorphoses* as a whole. Over the course of my analysis, this will mean looking closely at a constellation of related Ovidian figures: the lips or face (*os, oris*), the breath (*animus*), the tongue (*lingua*), and, more generally, the figure of apostrophe and gestures of address. The first three sections, "Phonographic histories," "Reading lips," and "The rhetoric of animation" delineate how the idea of the speaking voice – the seductive idea behind all these figures – arises from a particular concatenation of literary and material histories, governs the narrator's self-presentation in the epic, and shapes Ovid's investigation of supposed differences between male and female subjects and desires. The final three sections, "Beauty and the breeze," "Resisting voices," and "Other voices, other loves," demonstrate that although Ovid's narrator begins the *Metamorphoses* by turning his own metarhetorical reflection into a (highly influential) story of gender difference and hierarchy based on sexual violence, we soon discover that his ostensibly "female" voices sharply criticize this opening fantasy – and that they have something very different to say about the intersection between the poem's rhetorical and libidinal economies. Overall, my account of the poem makes two related suggestions. First, Ovid's emotionally charged yet self-reflexive stories about *Amor* epitomize Althusser's notion of "internal distance" – a text's "internal distantiation" from the ideology to which it "alludes and with which it is constantly fed."[5] And second, by so consistently forcing the usually separated realms of sexuality and rhetoric to meet, the narrator draws attention to the fact that while his characters act as if the body's meaning and value are given, that ostensible meaning is nonetheless unstable, the product of a fiercely unresolved cultural and psychic battle.

Phonographic histories

The idea of a lost voice or speechless face occurs over and over in Ovid's poem, suggesting that the link between mind and voice in the *Metamorphoses* is at best a fragile one, easily broken. Ovid's narrator repeatedly attaches stories of bodily transformation and/or violation to moments when characters try, in vain, to change events or reveal their true intentions by speaking about them: the deaths of Actaeon, Pentheus, and Orpheus; the vain protests of Daphne, Io, Syrinx, and Philomela; the impasse between Narcissus and Echo; the tardy regret of either Apollo or Jove for oaths they have already given. Stories like these establish a considerable distance between a speaker's purpose and the effect of the sounds that actually fall from his or her mouth. They tell us that for Ovid, the fiction of the speaking voice is as mysterious as it is foundational. Keeping this mysterious fiction in mind, notice that Ovid's stories about the voice follow a conventional opening claim that this written poem is, instead, a "song" the narrator is singing (1.4). The narrator who claims himself to be "singing" a *perpetuum carmen* habitually frames long sections of the poem as singing contests; dwells on images of the human face insofar as it is an instrument of speech; makes frequent use of apostrophe as the trope best suited for introducing or bidding farewell to various characters; and keeps pointing to speakers' mouths as organs from which fall words of unpredictable force, revelation, or beauty. The narrator's endeavor to sing a song coextensive with the history of the world is thus refracted in the many scenes that concentrate on the potential power of this or that character's tongue, lips, breath, or voice.

This isn't a surprising observation to make about a poem in which an entire book is given over to the singing "voice" of the poet Orpheus. But as the lethal attack on Orpheus' mouth by the Bacchae might suggest (10.7–19), this same narrator with a "singing" voice also keeps inventing nightmare inversions of any implicit claim for the voice's revelatory or instrumental power, inversions that question any necessary, transparent, or even minimally effective connection between the mind and the sound one makes with one's lips. We need to remember, then, that when Ovid's narrator defines extreme alienation of the self from itself as the moment when a character is startled by the effect of her words or the sound issuing from her mouth, these failed voices tell us as much about the narrator and his rhetorical aspirations as do the more confident "programmatic" scenes of the singing contest.[6]

Ovid pairs this larger programmatic interest in singing or speaking voices with a favorite body part: the mouth. References to the *os* – the lips and mouth – traverse the *Metamorphoses*, appearing approximately 250 times. And the *os* provides Ovid, as well, with a resonant figure to frame the epic: in the opening and closing books, the narrator refers to two different speaking faces – those of Lycaon and Pythagoras. That both these prominently placed stories highlight the *os* in particular should tell us that this word occupies a crucial place in Ovid's thinking about his own narrative act. Analyzing these *ora* will also allow us to grasp something of what Ovid's fascination with the idea of the lost voice implies for the poem's thinking about what it means to be subject to language. First, Pythagoras. When the philosopher explains the theory of metempsychosis that brings the last book of the *Metamorphoses* to a close, a conventional trope for ending his own discourse marks Pythagoras as yet another of the narrator's surrogates: "not to wander too far out of my course, my steeds forgetting meanwhile to speed towards the goal …" (15.453–55). Pythagoras helps the narrator bring his own "steeds" toward the "goal" of the poem in which he plays a part. But the narrator introduces this surrogate by a significant synecdoche: he draws attention not to Pythagoras's person but simply to his "learned mouth." A thinker Ovid calls upon to rival Lucretius' Empedocles, Pythagoras ponders "*primordia mundi / et rerum causas*" (67–68) and was "the first," we are told "to open his lips with these words – learned yet not believed" ("*primus quoque talibus ora / docta quidem soluit, sed non et credita, uerbis*" 73–74). Vatic and impotent, the philosopher's mouth may be "learned" ("*ora docta*") but that learning changes nothing.

Pythagoras' concluding discourse on the nature of things is supposed to remind us of Ovid's opening account of creation – the narrator's own, similar meditation on *primordia mundi et rerum causas*.[7] The figure of

Pythagoras' inspired *os*, moreover, reminds us that the *only* part of the body to which the narrator refers when the previously "unknown figures" of humankind first appear on earth after creation is the *os*: "os homini sublime dedit" ("he gave to man an uplifted face" 1.85). But like Pythagoras' unheeded lips, this first story about *os hominis* takes an infelicitous turn. With "indignant lips" (*ora indignantia* 1.181), Jove tells the story of Lycaon, the first character to lose his human shape. And it is Lycaon's inability to speak because of the change in the shape of *his* lips that marks this loss of humanity:

> territus ipse fugit nactusque silentia ruris
> exululat frustraque loqui conatur: ab ipso
> colligit os rabiem ...   (1.232–34)

terrified, he himself flees and having arrived at the silence of the countryside, howled and in vain attempted to speak: of itself his mouth collects foam ...

In the section of Book 15 devoted to Pythagoras, Ovid uses the *os* – the lips, mouth or face – as a metonymic figure for person in order to evoke a sense of what counts as "learned" discourse. In Book 1, this same metonymy indicates what in this poem counts as the difference between "human" and animal. But by contrast to Lucretius, who uses *rabies* to indicate the prophetic frenzy on a speaker's lips – "spumea rabies uaesana per ora effluit" (5.190) – and to Vergil, who uses the same noun as an index of prophecy on the Sybil's lips (*Aeneid*, 6.49), Ovid depicts Lycaon's metamorphosis by using *rabies* to capture an attempted utterance of considerable savagery. The foaming mouth of Lycaon, the poem's first human character, evokes the disturbing idea of a mouth not gifted with poetic prophecy but afflicted by the morbid disease of animals.

Framing the *Metamorphoses*, the mouths of Pythagoras and Lycaon seem to be inverse figures: one suggests learning, the cultivation of human potential, the other the complete loss of such cultivation.[8] But before we draw the conclusion that this difference marks some kind of linear, progressive movement across time and the epic – a dubious proposition in a poem dedicated to constant change and tending toward moments of startling irony – we should note that these two characters have rather more in common than might at first seem to be the case. That is, both Pythagoras and Lycaon strike us as human because of their desire to communicate and, more importantly for Ovid, because of their *failure* to do so.[9] Such failure, I submit, defines the human in the register of Ovidian desire – understood not only as "the cursed love of having" ("amor sceleratus habendi" 1.131) but also as the gap between the noise one makes with one's lips and what one actually thinks one wants to say or do by means of those sounds.[10] Where Lycaon encounters a physical impediment – the actual shape of his lips – Pythagoras encounters a different, but no less intractable, problem: learned though his "mouth" may be, the words he speaks, no matter how true, are "not believed." These two predicaments – a physical change to one's mouth and a misfiring of the words one does, in fact, utter – will continue to characterize Renaissance depictions of subjectivity that arise from figures drawn out of Ovid's poem. Like Lycaon, Pythagoras (and by implication, the narrator) finds a voice that can do little more than cry out in the wilderness.

Both of these stories repeat the significant cultural and etymological trajectory I traced earlier in my introductory remarks on Philomela's mutilated, "speechless face" (*os mutum*). Although it quickly evolved to designate a person's face or features and eventually her "mood" or "character," the noun, *os, oris* was first used to denote the "lips" or mouth. The stories of Lycaon and Pythagoras, alongside Philomela's, tell us that a person's identity or character is crucially tied, for Ovid, to its etymological origin in the idea of the capacity for speech. The narrator's pronounced attention to mouths, lips, tongues, and speaking faces as defining features of humanity and personal identity is part of what I have called the "phonographic imaginary" that shapes both the larger narrative strategies of the *Metamorphoses* and the many erotic stories told in it. I call Ovid's representation of the human voice phonographic because, as we have just seen when the subject "Lycaon" flickers briefly into view precisely when estranged from the sounds issuing from his own *os*, the kinds of self-endorsing fantasies that Derrida describes as "phonocentric" are no sooner entertained in the *Metamorphoses* than they are undermined.[11]

Several post-structuralist readings of the story of Echo and Narcissus (by John Brenkman, Clair Nouvet, and Gayatri Spivak) have already attended to one influential place in the poem where the relationship between language, subjectivity, and voice becomes deeply problematic.[12] Commenting on Echo's iterative "replies" to Narcissus, for instance, Nouvet writes that "we must reevaluate our entire understanding" of the dialogue between them "as the story of a distortion introduced into a stable, original statement." Rather, we should see that when Echo "seems to send back Narcissus' utterance with a different meaning than the one he intended (a meaning which would be 'hers' and not 'his')," we are forced to acknowledge the possibility "that this 'other' meaning might already have been 'meant' by the original statement." In other words, "we can no longer decide on its 'true' intended meaning. The echo is not a distortion which affects the intended meaning of a statement. It marks the impossibility ... of connecting a statement to the intention of a speaking consciousness."[13] Brenkman similarly points out that the Echo scene reveals only to occlude the aberrant grounds out of which we produce "character" as "voice-consciousness" from the impersonal, differential structures of language: "the dissemination of signifiers in the play of repetition and difference between utterance and echo is turned into a character's speech by linking a proper name, 'Echo,' to a set of signifieds. The result is the crystallization of a character and the representation of a voice-consciousness."[14] What is most striking about the *Metamorphoses*, from the perspective of this study, is that the erosion of a speaking subject from within her own voice – or rather, from within the convincing literary *effect* of "voice-consciousness" – is not the import of Echo's story alone. Rather, it is one of the narrator's central obsessions. In other words, Narcissus' question to Echo and, by implication, to himself – *ecquis adest?* ("is anyone there?" 3.380) – is a question we might justifiably ask of many of Ovid's characters, startled as they are by the unexpected sounds that fall from their lips.

Notice, too, that the body part chiefly at issue for Narcissus is once again the speechless *os*. He gazes in rapt attention at the beautiful lips in the pool that make no sound even though they seem to be moving ("quantum motu formosi suspicor *oris* / uerba refers aures non peruenientia nostras" [3.461–2]). From that observation of an *os* that makes no sound, Narcissus deduces the other within: the line that follows next is his famous lament, "iste ego sum." The dissemination of "differential signifiers" in his story means, as well, that we distinguish Narcissus' *os* (with a long o) from another, slightly different, *os* (with a short o) – Echo's *ossa* or the "bones" into which she dissolves: "ossa ferunt lapidis traxisse figuram" (3.399). First, Ovid estranges the idea of the speaking face when Narcissus complains that he cannot hear the words from his own reflected lips. And second, by pairing Narcissus' *os* with Echo's *os*, he opens up a differential movement within one of the poem's central words for speaking subjectivity.

This is not the only time Ovid does this to the *os*. Recall another resonant example of the speechless face, again from Book 1. The story of Io's metamorphosis captures what it means to be a subject by estranging the speaker from the noise that falls from her lips: "and with the effort to protest, a lowing sound issued from her mouth / and frightened by the sounds, she is terrified by her own voice" ("conatoque queri mugitus edidit *ore* / pertimuitque sonos propriaque exterrita uoce est" [1.637–38]). In Io's story, Frederick Ahl detects a complex interlacing of puns and anagrams. But the one that most concerns us here is that on the changed *ōs* of the "cow" or *bōs* she becomes ("bos quoque formosa est,"

3.612).[15] Through such figures as Narcissus' and Io's alienated *ora* and the literal play of signifiers associated with such alienation, the poem reminds us that as speaking subjects, we produce our fictions of person, and of self, from an impersonal network of differential relations (whether oral or graphic). Chief among these fictions of self is the phonocentric illusion of a voice – a voice that the narrator no sooner emphasizes than he dislocates, capturing that dislocation in his frightening motif of lips that may move but whose sounds do not correspond to what either we, or their owners, expect. We may now add to Philomela's story those of Lycaon, Pythagoras, Narcissus, and Io, characters whose sounds cannot achieve the effect their owners intend, whose moving lips are less than, or perhaps more than, mere instruments of the mind. It will not be necessary to rehearse Actaeon's story here to put him on this list as well. Io's terrified moo, Philomela's murmuring tongue, Lycaon's rabid foam, Actaeon's groans, Narcissus' confusion at the sight of his own soundless lips: each of these stories proposes an unnerving distance from the self-endorsing fantasy that Derrida calls "s'entendre parler."[16] Any being-in-language, these alien and alienating faces suggest, is but a fugitive illusion.

Ovid's poem-long preoccupation with the failed voices of both narrators and characters – and with their visual equivalent, the image of an *os mutum* – derives, in part, from his reflection on the history of epic as an oral genre, a song sung by a poet to his listening audience.[17] Mikhail Bakhtin would no doubt remind us that the *Metamorphoses'* many tropes for the voice, the mouth, and the speaking or speechless face are signs of epic's lengthy literary history – that authors like Ovid are "pouring" contemporary "artistic experience" into "pre-existing forms."[18] And indeed, Ovid establishes epic ambitions in the very first lines through the trope of the poet's singing voice and the invocation to the gods to help him sing his *carmen*.[19] But the fact that this momentarily epic "voice" in the poem's opening continues to tell stories about what it means to speak or to be unable to speak, to sing or to be silenced, is not merely evidence of the epic form in general. It also testifies to the particular tradition of Hellenistic poetry from which Ovid's poem springs and within which it defines itself: "the intervention of the figure of the narrator – focussing the reader's attention on the act of narration itself – is a well-known feature of the self-conscious literary stance of the Hellenistic poets."[20]

But Ovid's self-conscious, Hellenistic narrative stance relies on still further fantasies about the poet's voice – fantasies that are graphic as well as oral. I've called the poem's imaginary phonographic not only because Ovid so consistently disrupts the fantasy of phonocentrism but because his metarhetorical figures continually grapple with the tension between the fiction of a speaking voice and the poem's own self-conscious (Hellenistic) scene of writing. Composed very late in the literary history of ancient epic but still opening with conventional epic diction and figures, Ovid's *Metamorphoses* opens with the fiction of an inspired poetic voice, the voice of a *uates*. But this fiction derived from a proximity between singer and listening audience that Roman readers knew very well had been lost long ago.[21] Ovid's figure of his own singing voice, in other words, could not help but remind contemporary readers of the opposite – that his poem is a *written* poetic performance. The poem's knowingly conventional trope of an inspired singer would remind his readers that they were just that: *readers* rather than a listening audience. By contrast to the conditions presumed to have given rise to the tropes of primary epic, Ovid's "voice" speaks to the reader's distance from the poet's voice and the poem's scene of writing – reminding us of his (and our) own belatedness in his unsettling habit of emptying out the poem's subjects by means of their own tongues. Out of the programmatic conventions of Hellenistic poetry, the narrator of the *Metamorphoses* forges his own, idiosyncratic version of what it means to compose a self-consciously written epic in which the narrator, alongside the various poets in the poem, still lays claim to a singing "voice" despite the fact that the conditions of primary epic have long since vanished.

In addition, we should note that many of the *Metamorphoses*' hallmark figures for the poet's narrative act also speak to the pressure of specific material writing practices far removed from epic origins. As we must examine more closely in a moment, the concluding lines of the *Metamorphoses* propose a complex mingling of the oral and the written. It is a closing consonant with Ovidian practice: he is a poet fond of alluding, both overtly and obliquely, to the medium of the written word. The *Ars Amatoria*, for example, gives explicit writing lessons to lovers; the narrator warns them to obliterate all traces of previous characters left in wax tablets when counterfeiting another's handwriting (3.495–96). The story of Byblis' desire for her brother stages a lengthy writing scene: picking up tablets, Byblis "writes and erases" what she cuts into the wax until the surface is completely filled with her words ("tenet ... ceram. / incipit et dubitat, scribit damnatque tabellas,/ et notat et delet ... plena reliquit / cera manum," "she holds the wax, begins writing and pauses, writes on the tablets and hates what she writes, both noting and erasing ... the wax, now full, releases her hand" 9.522–65). Because of such erotically charged dramatizations, I pointed to the image of wax melting in Pygmalion's fingers as a telling figure, suggesting that the statue melts the way it does because wax tablets were an important medium for

Roman writing.[22] I would also argue that it is no accident that Pythagoras' chief metaphor for his theory of metempsychosis – a theory often noted for its proximity to Ovidian metamorphosis[23] – is that of the changes taking place to a piece of wax. Similarly, the metapoetic figures surrounding Daphne's flight may mean that readers wonder if the bark that surrounds her body suggests, as well, that she has become Apollo's book – since the same noun *liber, -bri*, means both the bark of a tree and a book written for publication ("mollia cinguntur tenui praecordia libro" 1.549). Thus by the time we arrive at Byblis' story, whose name in Greek means "book," we can hardly avoid considering the phonographic, as well as erotic, complications of her internal debate about whether a written or a spoken proposition to her brother would have been more convincing.

But alongside Ovid's erotically charged allusions to the material conditions of ancient methods of writing, we would do well to remember, when thinking about the historical conditions that inform this phonographic imaginary, that the *Metamorphoses* was written during the retreat of Roman rhetoric from public debate. It was the product of a poet schooled in the art of declamation who knew, as everyone else knew, that oratory no longer carried the same political weight it was once thought to bear. "School-orations" (*scholastica*), ingenious exercises replacing "genuine public speech," became a highly mediated form of rhetorical display in which the presumed power of a speaker's voice to move or to change anything of which it speaks – rhetoric's aim – was badly compromised from the outset.[24] Ovid's recurrent fantasy about a voice that fails in its purpose may well mark something of such diminished expectations for rhetorical performance. In such political circumstances as those surrounding the shift toward declamation as a form of display under the principate, Ovid's exaggerated tropes of orality – that is, the power of Orpheus's voice to move even stones – as well as his attendant fascination with the many unexpected ways a voice can fail could not help but underline oratory's decline in public life.

But it is not merely because training in Roman declamation was predominantly oral that one might want to look closely at the precise contours of the voice in Ovidian poetics. It is also the case that the voice became the focus of explicit training and comment as the declaimer's chief instrument. Quintilian, for example,

recommends the learning by heart of passages which will require loud, or argumentative, or colloquial, or modulated intonation ("clamorem et disputationem et sermonem et flexus" 11.3.25), and it seems probable, therefore, that the rehearsal, either by the master for imitation or by the pupil for criticism, of sections of speeches for this strictly limited purpose of *pronuntiatio* was what *declamatio* originally meant. The great exponents of *pronuntiatio*, of course, were the best actors of the stage; and the Roman student of rhetoric, who frequently had ... to impersonate historical or mythological personages in his exercises, and to simulate their emotions, needed to be something of an actor.[25]

That an intensely rhetorical poem written by a former student of declamation should focus on the voice so frequently cannot surprise when we remember such training. Nor is his penchant for dramatizing the voices of mythological *personae* given the frequency of similar *prosopopoeiae* among declaimers. Read in the context of such an educational program, moreover, a debate like the one Byblis stages with herself – whether the modulations of her voice would have been more persuasive than her written words – might be thought to be a poet's displaced meditation on the difference between writing poetry and training for declamatory display. As we continue to think about the way the narrator represents himself and his own narrative act in the opening and closing lines of the epic, we should remember the historical contingencies – literary, material, political – that influenced Ovid's scene of writing and thus, in turn, helped give such a distinctive shape to his fictions about the power and limitations of the voice.

Reading lips

Once we see that the *Metamorphoses'* many stories about the fate of its characters' voices – male and female – refract the poet's representation of his own, we would do well to take a closer look at the complex figures that represent the narrator's relation to his "song" in the poem's opening and closing lines. In particular, the poem's final verses will enable us better to grasp the specifically "graphic" half of Ovid's phonographic imaginary because, as we will see more closely below, they ask us to imagine that both the poem and the poet's name are a kind of permanent writing never to be erased. But first, remember that Ovid begins the poem by calling on the gods to "breathe on these my undertakings." The poem's opening lines make the narrator a vessel for divine breath or, quite literally, "inspiration":

> In noua fert animus mutatas dicere formas
> corpora; di, coeptis (nam uos mutastis et illas)
> *adspirate* meis primaque ab origine mundi
> ad mea perpetuum deducite tempora carmen.   (1.1–4)

My mind is moved to tell of bodies changed into new forms. Gods, *breathe on* these my undertakings, for you yourselves have wrought these changes, and bring down the perpetual song from the origin of the world to my present time.

To begin singing his song, the poet's "mind" "moves" to speak by drawing breath from somewhere else. The very first word that names an authorial presence in the poem is "mind" or *animus*. Strictly speaking, this "mind" is etymologically consonant with the invocation, "coeptis ... adspirate meis," ("breathe on my beginnings") because *animus*, the narrator's word for himself, is derived from ἄνεμος, a noun designating the wind both external and internal to the body.[26] Cicero, for example, refers to the Greek root for both *animus* ("mind") and *anima* ("soul") when he derives the former from the latter, observing that he does so because the first meaning of *anima* is "air, breeze, wind" and that it therefore eventually signifies "the vital principle or breath of life."[27] Mind and voice, on such an etymological understanding, are indissolubly linked: the movement of air that enables speech – the ἄνεμος inside the body – defines one's mind or *animus*. Nor is Ovid's opening reference to a speaking *animus* unique in the poem. This constellation of ideas – inner self (both mind and soul), voice, and the breeze – becomes one of the poem's prominent concerns.[28] Both *animus* and *anima* surface hundreds of times in the narrative. We learn, for instance, that the derivation of Pythagoras' *anima* and the narrator's *animus* from "the breath of life" is pertinent to Ovid's representation of life and death: birth is the entry of an *infans* (literally, "without speech") into the "common air" ("infans ... communes exit in auras," 7.126–27); and death comes when a speaker exhales his or her *anima* onto the wind (either *aura* or *uentus*).[29]

As a metaphor for one's mind or thoughts, the wind suggests that like ἄνεμος, *animus* exerts a force that can, without warning, exceed the body that contains it. Thoughts come and go in the mind like the breeze; sometimes they work for the thinker, sometimes against. Ovid's metaphor means that one's thoughts, fickle as the wind, cannot always be said to express what one intends or even what one thinks one desires. Such an analogy between *animus* and ἄνεμος, in other words, entertains an idea of interior life consonant with Freud's theory of the unconscious: the wind is a force that exceeds the subject's declared intentions and desires. And insofar as Ovid associates ἄνεμος with the idea of a speaking consciousness, the poet's opening trope for himself touches on the problem of being subject to language as an impersonal force that a speaker may harness but that always originates elsewhere. Ovid's pervasive idea of *anim*ation, in other words, traces a kind of pneumatic movement through the poem that both fills up speaking subjects and empties them out. For the wind that can give you a voice – the ἄνεμος in *animus* and *anima* – can also take it away. The death of Orpheus, which the final section examines in more detail, succinctly captures the close, etymologically resonant connection that the narrator draws between the

mind, the mouth, the voice, and the passage of air inside and outside of
the body:

> ... ad uatis fata recurrunt
> tendentemque manus et in illo tempore primum
> inrita dicentem nec quicquam uoce mouentem
> sacrilegae perimunt, perque os, pro Iuppiter, illud
> auditum saxis intellectumque ferarum
> sensibus in uentos anima exhalata recessit.   (11.38–43)

... they ran back to kill the bard who, holding out suppliant hands, for the first
time spoke in vain, nor did he move any of them with his voice; the impious
women slew him and – Oh Jupiter! – through lips that had been heard by stones
and understood by wild beasts, his soul fled, exhaled on the winds.

Where the voice or *animus* of the poem's narrator takes inspiration from
the movement of external air – the breath of the gods – Orpheus' voice
and inner self (his *anima*) mingle, in death, with the breeze circulating
around his body. We should not be surprised, therefore, when a series of
apostrophes allow the narrator to take his poem back from the dying
Orpheus, apostrophes that work hard to suggest that this narrative
animus or speaking voice is picking up where Orpheus' leaves off ("Te
maestae uolucres, Orpheu, te turba ferarum, / te rigidi silices ..."
11.44–45).

The story of Daphne's flight, "swifter than the breeze," to escape the
menacing "breath" from Apollo down her neck similarly derives from
this network of associations between wind and voice as the vital principle
of life. So, too, does the story of Cephalus and Procris. In this story, in
fact, the breeze quite literally inverts the rhetoric of animation. Not only
is the wind an agent that bears voice and *anima* away, but the word for
breeze – *aura* – causes yet another death through the mouth. One day
Cephalus indulged in an elaborate apostrophe to the wind or *aura* ("*aura*
petebatur ... *auram* exspectabam ... / '*aura* ... uenias' cantare solebam")
and was overheard by someone. His signifier is then transformed on
other lips into the personal name, "Aura" (7.811–23). No longer master
of his own spoken word, Cephalus does not know that the eavesdropper
has personified his signifier, telling Procris her husband is in love with
"Aura." His spontaneous poem, addressed to the breeze, soon turns
deadly: Procris spies on her husband out of jealousy, is herself overheard,
mistaken for an animal, and killed by his javelin. Cephalus no sooner
identifies his wife's "voice" ("uox ... fidae / coniugis, ad uocem praeceps
amensque cucurri," 843–44) than she dies, like Orpheus, orally: "she
looked at me and *exhaled her spirit on my mouth*" ("me spectat et in me /
infelicem *animam nostroque exhalat in ore*" 7.860–61). Keeping such
stories as those of Orpheus and Procris in mind, it is not difficult to see

why Petrarch's seminal pun – *L'aura/Laura* – emerged as a reading of
Ovid's poem. The Petrarchan breeze does more than commemorate the
story of Apollo and Daphne, fleeing "faster than the breeze." *L'aura* is a
figure that captures Ovid's preoccupation with the intimate relation
between the poetic subject as "voice-consciousness" and the impersonal
(or transpersonal) movement of the wind.

Where Ovid opens his *carmen* with the figure of its author's singing
animus helped along by the breath of the gods, he imagines an equally
compelling fantasy of vocal animation in the final lines of the *Metamorphoses*. In these famous verses, Ovid tells the story of his own metamorphosis, as a poet, into a kind of eternal presence beyond the life of his
body.

> Iamque opus exegi, quid nec Iouis ira nec ignis
> nec poterit ferrum nec edax abolere uetustas.
> cum uolet, illa dies, quae nil nisi corporis huius
> ius habet, incerti spatium mihi finiat aeui:
> parte tamen meliore mei super alta perennis
> astra ferar, nomenque erit indelebile nostrum,
> quaque patet domitis Romana potentia terris,
> *ore legar populi*, perque omnia saecula fama,
> siquid habent ueri uatum praesagia, uiuam.   (15.871–79)

And now I have finished a work which neither Jove's anger nor fire nor iron nor
gnawing age shall have power to destroy. That day which has authority only over
my body may when it pleases put an end to the uncertain span of my life; with the
better part of me I shall soar immortal high above the stars and my name shall
not be extinguished. Wherever the sway of Rome shall extend over the conquered
lands, *I shall be read by the tongues of men* and for all time to come, if the
prophecies of bards have any truth in them, by and in my fame shall I live.[30]

In a moment we will take a closer look at what the figure of the reader's
os (1.878) means for the author's self-definition as *animus*. But first, it is
important to observe that at the end of his poem, the narrator has added
a distinctly graphic resonance to the figures with which he represents
himself. In place of his corporeal form, the form of his poem and his
name will give the narrator a life beyond that of the body. He tells us,
more precisely, that he possesses an "indelible" name that cannot be
erased ("nomenque erit indelebile nostrum" 876). The adjective, *indelebile*, is Ovid's invention.[31] It derives from *deleo, -ere*, a verb whose first
meaning is graphic: "to remove [written characters or other marks] by
wiping or scratching out; to efface, to wipe clean (a tablet)."[32]

To see the importance that Ovid attaches to the trope of a name one
cannot erase – *nomenque erit indelebile nostrum* – we should remember
that he was fond of including his own name as a way of drawing

attention to himself as the author of his poems. In the *Tristia*, he compares himself to Actaeon as someone who saw something he shouldn't, only to distinguish himself as one who managed to achieve a "name" recognized by a "crowd of learned men": "I bear a great name throughout the world; and a throng of learned men are acquainted with Naso" ("grande tamen toto nomen ab orbe fero, / turbaque doctorum Nasonem nouit").[33] In the last line of *Ars Amatoria*, the narrator writes his own name into the poem by imagining the hands of readers as they inscribe "Naso" on the bodies of their erotic victims: "Ut quondam iuuenes, ita nunc, mea turba, puellae / inscribant spoliis 'Naso magister erat'" ("As once the youths, so now let young women, my entourage, write upon their spoils, "Naso was Master").[34] Closing the *Metamorphoses* with a similar signature, Ovid declares his poem will confer on him an "indelible name" that may last as long as Roman *imperium*.

To lay claim to his place as author, Ovid likes to represent himself as a signifier – a *nomen* that will be spoken *or* written and hence recognized by "crowds" of readers. Representing himself as a subject within a social discourse, Ovid lays claim to a place as author or *magister*. But the *Metamorphoses'* newly coined *indelebile* also suggests – as does the imagined scene of readers writing Ovid's name on the bodies of their lovers in *Ars Amatoria* – that we think a little further about the heavily graphic emphasis in Ovid's fantasies about his own social, authorial identity. The written signifier of the author's name inscribes him as the poem's ghostly presence, still there somehow in or around his poem even if his body has disappeared. Ovid's idea of an unerasable name appears, moreover, when the narrator turns to address himself to another. The author's *nomen* can have force only if carried on by the hands or mouths of readers; Ovid's continued presence depends on the fantasy of a reading counterpart who recognizes and is dedicated to speaking or writing his words and his name. The moment of the authorial subject's ostensible immediacy in and transcendence of language is qualified because his identity as author depends on the signifying work of others. I would therefore call Ovid's final scene of address a phonographic *imaginary* in order to evoke the strong, Lacanian sense of "imaginary" as Laplanche defines it: a "dual relationship based on ... the image of a counterpart," of "another who is me" and that "can exist only by virtue of the fact that the ego is originally another."[35]

The form that this constitutive "other" may take is quite specific: the poem's author will transcend writing because his name and his *opus* will be "read aloud" on the *os* or "lips of the people" ("ore legar populi" 15.878). In such an address, the idea of Ovid's written *opus* and *nomen* return to the vocal resonances that have characterized the poem's depiction of character since the moment the narrator announced he would sing a *perpetuum carmen*. Once again, Ovid asks us to consider the *os* – this time, *os populi*. Because his written words will be spoken on the lips of the people, the poet will "achieve fame for all time." Ovid then ends the poem with the declarative prediction, *uiuam*, "I shall live." Ovid's phonographic imaginary (the dynamic relation between himself and his readers) turns the idea of his poetic voice into a fantasy about the transforming effect of a reader's voice on a poet's "indelible," written letters. The *Metamorphoses* receives its author's signature at the moment that it predicts its own future scenes of spoken reading, readers' lips becoming the corporeal means by which the fictional time of the *perpetuum carmen* extends indefinitely. In a poem devoted to the anti-thetical processes of *anim*ation and petrification, we must not forget the fiction proposed by the poem's frame: the poetic *animus* that inaugurates the poem first claims to be part of a divine wind and then imagines its own perpetual "animation" by means of an oral reading of his written words. Animation is not merely (or not only) a vivifying principle for Ovid. It is, quite strictly speaking, a *poetic* principle: "breath" and with it the sound of the voice are crucial to the narrator's self-representation in the poem. His poetic *animus* "moves" like the wind ("animus fert … dicere") through the "changing forms" of bodies and of written letters to produce a song that is "perpetual" not merely because of its temporal scope, but because it is imagined to be a writing continually revivified by the "lips" and breath of others. Both this signature effect and the oral fantasy of letters spoken aloud are marshalled to animate the poet, to revivify "part of me" by carrying that "me" beyond the body and beyond time ("parte tamen meliore mei super alta perennis / astra ferar").

One further aspect of material history helps to situate this distinctively Ovidian figure of the reader's devoted *os*. Bakhtin observes that because of their formation before the advent of signifying practices bound to writing (or printing), genres like ancient epic and lyric offer so many tropes for the voice because they are not "organically receptive" to the "mute perception" of silent reading.[36] Ovid's closing figure of readers' lips speaking the written words of the *Metamorphoses* out loud, in other words, also asks to be read in terms of ancient practices of writing and reading. And as Bernard Knox has shown, reading in antiquity was almost always a reading out loud.[37] The readerly habit of vocalizing written words provided Ovid with a convincing material substitute for the epic fantasy of singing one's verses to a live audience. The final figure of his reader's speaking *os* does more than call upon a contemporary practice to stand in for the absent audience of primary epic, however. It also allows Ovid to transform the ancient habit of vocalizing written texts into a kind of authorial ontology: "I shall be read aloud on the lips of the people . . . I shall live" ("ore legar populi . . . uiuam").

As we'll see in subsequent chapters, such a phonographic definition of authorial subjectivity was lost on neither Petrarch nor Shakespeare. If Ovid's mode of self-representation – the figure of the *os* and its attendant rhetoric of animation – derived from a complex network of literary, material, and political histories, we may grasp something of the profound effect that Ovid's particular way of inflecting these histories had on Renaissance authors by remembering Shakespeare's phonographic figures for his poems to the young man:

> Your monument shall be my gentle verse,
> Which eyes not yet created shall ore-read,
> And toungs to be, your beeing shall rehearse,
> When all the breathers of this world are dead,
>   You still shall liue (such vertue hath my Pen)
>   Where breath most breaths, euen in the mouths of men.[38]

Similarly, Petrarch's recurrent dream about the breezes touching Laura's hair where he cannot (*Rime Sparse*, no. 52) and Shakespeare's Pygmalion fantasy about a "chisel that can cut breath" (*The Winter's Tale*, 5.3.77–79) indicate that Ovid's rhetoric of the speaking subject's *animation* carried considerable persuasive force.

There is yet another text worth remembering briefly alongside the written *imperium* imagined to hold sway over the tongues of the *Metamorphoses*' readers. Two epistles from the *Heroides* – by Acontius and Cydippe – draw on ancient reading practices quite directly to entertain the fantasy of an author whose words are potent enough to conquer a reader's tongue and body. These letters tell us that Cydippe's sexual subjection to Acontius is the literal subjection of a text's reader to its author. Because she is a creature of habit and therefore read aloud the words of a marriage vow that Acontius had inscribed on an apple and rolled in front of her, Cydippe is pledged by her tongue against her will to marry the writer of those words. She begins her complaint, therefore, by noting that she has had to remember, contrary to custom, to read Acontius' second missive in silence: "Pertimui, scriptumque tuum sine murmure legi / iuraret ne quos inscia lingua deos" ("All fearful, I read what you wrote without so much as a murmur, lest my tongue might swear, without knowing it, by some divinity").[39] Reading another's words aloud in this story subdues the unlucky owner of that tongue to the hand of the one who wrote them. Cydippe surrenders, and the *Heroides* ends by acknowledging the inescapable power of one more author: "doque libens uictas in tua uota manus" ("and I freely yield my vanquished hands in fulfillment of your prayers" 21.240). In this story, the *Metamorphoses'* subjection of reader's lips to writer's words for the sake of authorial self-representation becomes a relationship of sexual domination.[40]

Despite the similarity between Acontius' triumph over Cydippe's tongue and Ovid's claim that his words will survive on the lips of readers, however, important differences separate Ovid's narrator from Acontius. The ostensibly animating, vocal figures representing the narrator in the *Metamorphoses'* frame suggest something unexpected: the voice "singing" this *perpetuum carmen* can never entirely be said to belong to its author. The breath that inspires his song comes from somewhere else (from the gods) and will be passed, at the poem's closing, onto the lips of future generations (his readers). The voice that enables the narrator to "sing" about "bodies changed to new forms" precedes the poem's author and carries on beyond the life of his body. More striking still, the phrase that appears in the final lines of the poem so unequivocally to declare the narrator's eternal presence turns out, as well, to originate with someone else. Thus when Ovid claims "ore legar populi ... uiuam," he is echoing Ennius' famous epitaph, "uolito uiuus per ora uirum" ("Living, I fly through the mouths of men").[41] Like his predecessor, this author claims to "live" *per ora*. Similarly, commentators often note that beginning with *iamque opus exegi*, the narrator revisits a series of highly conventional topoi in his closing passage. Most obviously, he echoes Vergil and Horace (particularly *Odes* 3.30, "exegi monumentum"). But he also draws on a host of other texts known to us now only in fragments.[42] In other words, Ovid's final lines may claim to represent something essential to the author – *parte ... meliore mei* – and thus to constitute a culminating moment of authorial self-presentation.[43] But the self depicted in these lines turns out to be a palimpsest of other voices, a complex fabric of quotations.

Such a narrator, phrasing the fantasy of his own survival by way of commonplaces and quotations, resembles no character in his poem so closely as his own Echo. Like the narrator she, too, reveals herself by piecing together the sounds made by others. She, too, is preserved beyond the death of her body merely as "voice" and "sound":

> ... uox tantum atque ossa supersunt:
> uox manet, ossa ferunt lapidis traxisse figuram.
> inde latet siluis nulloque in monte uidetur,
> omnibus auditur: sonus est, qui uiuit in illa.   (3.398–401)

... only voice and bones remain; then voice remains, as they say her bones were transformed into a figure of stone. Then she hides in the woods and is seen nowhere on the mountain, but is heard by everyone; it is sound that lives in her.

With this sound heard by "omnes," we are very close to the narrator's self-portrait as sound – a sound heard by everyone because carried along on reader's lips for as long as Rome's *imperium* lasts.

There is, of course, an even more general sense in which Echo is a compelling figure for Ovid's narrator. Few writers have so fundamentally based their poetic project on recycling the stories, and sometimes the words, of other previous discourses and texts. Recalling the revisionary declaration, *in noua fert animus* (1.1), E. J. Kenney observes that "the whole scope of his poem demanded that he reshape and reinterpret the myths."[44] Like Echo's literal repetition of Narcissus' words, Ovid's metamorphic project reshapes both the stories of myths and, quite often, the particular form given them by previous poetic texts. That Echo should dissolve to "uox" alone, then, I take as another sign of our phonographic narrator – or at least, of his imaginary. In her capacity as *uox* preserved beyond the body, Echo doubles her narrator, struggling to find precisely such vocal preservation himself: "it is sound that lives in her" ("sonus est, qui uiuit in illa"); and "I shall live, read aloud on the tongues of people" ("ore legar populi ... uiuam"). We therefore find an unexpected turn in the poem's final line because Ovid makes repetition a condition not merely of his character's fate but of his own. Derrida has variously demonstrated that sheer iterability is the condition of language. Ovid appears to make it the condition of being an authorial subject. By so doing, the poet confronts the fact that despite his own desire for survival in and through his verse, his written text is also, precisely *because* it is written, "made to do without him."[45]

The relationship Ovid sets up in the last line is not entirely analogous to Echo's, however. As an author who hopes to be given life on the "lips of the people," the narrator is, rather, proposing to play Narcissus to the *reader*'s Echo. I have suggested that by signing the last lines of his poem with his *nomen*, Ovid tries to lay claim to ownership of the poem and hence (according to this fiction) of himself. And though something of Ovid may indeed be preserved in his poem – or the many poems generated out of his – the form of such preservation continues to call into question the status of the subject behind the utterance. Although the poet pictures his own survival on his readers' lips, his own earlier story of the same circumstance stresses two problems the final lines occlude: even the most faithful, literal revoicing alters the original; and every "original" utterance is, as Nouvet suggests, inhabited by an echo within. Taking Narcissus' position in the fictional game of voicing and revoicing does little to secure authorial presence in the poem's words and generates, instead, an unending future of echoing readers. Because Echo's repetitions tell us that meaning is no one's to own – a problem of *différance* not obliterated by mere temporal priority – and because Ovid recalls this scene in the final lines of self-representation, the projection involved in "connecting a statement to the intention of a speaking consciousness" is also part of the predicament in which the poem's author finds himself (either with respect to his poem as linguistic artifact or as part of literary history).

Ovid's final lines, then, erode their own declaration of transcendence in a variety of ways. Both the figure of readers's lips, repeating the text out loud, and the borrowed phrases that Ovid pieces together to imagine his transformation-by-reading tell us that Ovid's place as author of this text – what he calls "the better part of me" – is, like Echo's, neither that of origin nor final destination. Despite the dream that somehow the poem's words will preserve their author somewhere "beyond the stars," the author's "voice" is in a strange way displaced and temporary. The only voice the narrator finds, we might say, is a collective, transpersonal fiction: as a speaking subject he is inhabited by the Other; his voice exists only in relation to the voices of others, at the level of the imaginary. The poem's closing figure of the reader's *os*, in sum, tells us that the author's voice in the *Metamorphoses*, like the many failed voices that make up the body of the poem, exceeds the command of its imagined "speaking" subject.

Will the poem's future readers, repeating Ovid's words out loud, be any more faithful than Echo? Certainly the literary history of the *Metamorphoses* would suggest otherwise. These readings, even the most faithful "translations," return to the initial text only to change it. The course of European literary history will therefore tease out an effect similar to the echo-effect that Nouvet locates within the poem. That is, ensuing revisionary returns to Ovid's poem ask us to consider whether the "other," new meanings revealed in later poetry "might already have been 'meant' by the original" narrative.[46] We might well believe that something of the author, like something of Narcissus, persists even in the alteration. But despite the last lines, that "something" is not "voice-consciousness." Self-dislocation rather than self-presence defines the narrative "voice" of the *Metamorphoses*. We see evidence of such negative knowledge about the author's disarticulation in the impersonal, differencing networks of language, I submit, in the many scenes in Ovid's poem in which speakers are startled by the sound of their own tongue.

Ovid's tone in these final lines about his survival as vocalized text is therefore quite complex. At once assertive and ironic, he prefaces his final declaration of eternal life, *uiuam*, with a qualification: "*if* the prophecies of bards have any truth in them," ("siquid habent ueri uatum praesagia," 15.879). Such a mixed tone is entirely consonant with the last book's equivocal subject matter: the fate of Rome and the status of the other poets who had praised it. As Leonard Barkan comments, Ovid's final book points straight toward the contradiction between his declaration of eternal Roman *imperium* and Pythagoras' view of "history as an arena of unending change." Because Pythagoras' "example is of the passing from Troy to Rome," Barkan writes, "we can hardly avoid the implication that the present form will also dissolve ... Whether we see the subject of the speech as mutability, dissolution, metempsychosis, or endless cyclical change, we must recognize that Pythagoras is no celebrant of the eternal *pax Romana*." And because Pythagoras' speech is "tightly bound up with the spirit of Ovid's whole poem and rather strikingly at odds with the Augustan empire,"[47] Ovid's last line – "if the prophecies of bards (*uatum praesagia*) have any truth in them" – also implicitly criticizes Vergil, conveniently caricatured as celebrant of that empire.[48] For Ovid, the honorific Roman word for the poet as a bard or "seer" – *uates* – is often less than honorific. Satirizing Vergil's status as *uates* in the opening of the *Amores*,[49] Ovid uses the word again in the closing moments of the *Metamorphoses* to let us know that his predecessor is one of his targets. Although Ovid claims that his fame will last as long as Rome's *imperium*, he also connects Rome's fate to Troy's. The context of Book 15 therefore signals that this *imperium* is rather less secure than the narrator's seeming boast – or his account of Vergil's claims – might lead one to think.

Ovid's last lines strike a precarious balance between irony and confidence in the matter of Rome's future. My analysis of Ovid's phonographic figures suggests that such precariousness applies, as well, to the author's figures for himself as vocalized text. Indeed, Ovid links the idea of his own permanence as a writing and speaking subject to the idea of Rome's *imperium* by way of a strangely mixed series of figures. At once boasting and funereal, his concluding verses turn the poem into a kind of epitaph that perpetually announces its author's continued absent presence. Like the final lines of the *Ars Amatoria*, the last verses of the *Metamorphoses* imagine the appearance of the author's name, written or spoken, as a kind of military victory; for the author's triumph over the bodies of lovers in the first ("inscribant spoliis") we find another over the poet's own body and the tongues of the rest of the Roman world in the second. Such conclusions, clearly the product of a poet skilled in the discourse of *militia amoris*, are more than merely assertive. They bring together two literary and cultural practices that are worth briefly remembering here: the epic boast (or εὖχος) and funerary epitaphs.[50] With respect to the εὖχος, Sheila Murnaghan describes the function of the hero's boast in the *Iliad* as part of the "constant impulse to replace bodily engagement with speech." She observes that "by boasting, a hero is able to go on using his voice rather than his body as a way to impress himself upon the world." Such an impression takes two characteristic verbal forms: "a name and a narrative, perhaps a genealogy."[51] In place of a hero's particular genealogy, Ovid has written the genealogy of the world, appending his name to that rather grander story. In Ovid's rendition of the epic εὖχος – at once aestheticizing and ironic – it is precisely the poet's narrative ("iamque *opus* exegi") and the poet's name ("*nomen*que erit indelebile nostrum") that are to replace his body in its battle against time. He claims that his words subdue not a particular antagonist on a particular battlefield, but time and the tongues of everyone else who speaks in the Roman world.

And with respect to the funeral monument, Jean-Pierre Vernant describes the Greek epic hero's relationship to language and body in death, a description that may help us see a little more clearly why the closing lines of Ovid's poem sound like an epitaph for its author:

When his body disappears, vanishes, what remains below of the hero? Two things. First of all the σῆμα, or μνῆμα, the stele, the funeral memorial erected on his tomb, which will remind the generations of men to come of his name, his renown, his exploits ... Second, parallel to the funeral monument, there is the song of praise that faithfully remembers high deeds of the past ... the poetic word ... snatches them from the anonymity of death.[52]

Two artifacts, stele and song, replace the hero's body upon its death; signs remain the only means for the hero to "impress himself upon the world." Ovid's final lines turn the poem itself into a kind of stele, turning his written text into a kind of monumental verbal artifact that will impress its author upon the world after his death. And indeed, several phrases in Ovid's closing lines for *his* song – *iamque opus exegi* and *nomen indelebile* – have long reminded commentators of the highly conventional trope of building a poem as building a monument.[53] As Jesper Svenbro points out of epitaphs on Greek funerary monuments, moreover, these texts frequently called upon passers-by, as does Ovid in these final lines, to lend their voices to the letters inscribed on the stone by reading the words out loud.[54] When Ovid echoes the suggestive line attributed by Cicero to Ennius' epitaph ("Living, I fly through the mouths of men"),[55] he is engaging in a literary version of a complex phonographic, social ritual. The ritual can extend life from Ennius to Ovid, we are asked to imagine, by way of a multitude of animating tongues.

If we keep both the heroic boast and the epitaph in mind when reading Ovid's final lines, we come to see that in addition to political irony there is also something we might call an irony of the subject. On the one hand, if we attend to ancient reading practices – for poems as well as epitaphs –

we hear a seductive fantasy behind the figure of the reader's speaking lips: Ovid marshals the ancient habit of vocalizing written texts into a kind of vivifying, epic battle against the mortal body and time. Because the very idea of metamorphosis, as Charles Segal comments, "militates against [the] preservation of the unique personality and his unforgettable deeds," we are not surprised to find Ovid close with the figures of a *nomen indelebile* and a poetic text as a kind of stele as a way of overcoming that contradiction.[56] As passers-by are summoned to read words carved in tombstones out loud, to lend their breath and life to letters carved on a monument, readers' speaking lips are to give voice to the poem's written words and thereby assure the author's continued presence "above the stars." And as my comparison of this boast with Acontius' trick for conquering the reluctant Cydippe should suggest, the poet's continued presence beyond death requires subjection – the subjection of all other living tongues in Roman territory. But on the other hand, if we attend to what these lines *do* – to how they come to signify these ideas – we feel a significant skeptical undercurrent pulling against this boastful proposition for authorial presence and mastery. The self-conscious interlacing of conventional topoi, the citations of Ennius and of Horace, the graphic figure of an unerasable name, the (funerary) idea of a reader's speaking lips lending life to written letters, the allusion to Echo's iterations in the mouth of the reader as Other: all these poetic and rhetorical concerns mean that deeply Ovidian questions remain. Whose "voice" are we supposed to be hearing? Whose conquering "poetic word" is this? Ovid's closing figures may well propose a phonographic rhetoric of animation predicated on a fantasy of subjecting others to the overwhelming power of one's words. But at the same time they also convey a certain skepticism about whether anyone really owns these words. Impersonal and disconcertingly hollow, the poem's concluding verses ask us to inquire along with Narcissus – or is it with Echo? – "is anyone here?"[57]

The rhetoric of animation

We've seen that the narrator of the *Metamorphoses* oscillates between a dream of linguistic animation – the tenacious fiction of voice-consciousness – and an uneasy sense that language, especially (and disturbingly) *spoken* language, exceeds the subjects who try to use it. Once we perceive that the numerous stories the narrator tells about alienated and alienating voices have as much to do with the predicaments of the poem's author as they do with the those of his characters, we are in a better position to ask how the poem's many dislocating voices bear upon Ovid's representation of the body in general and of gendered bodies in particular. I have implicitly been suggesting that figures such as Echo's *uox*, Io's terrified moo, and Philomela's murmuring *lingua* unhinge the fantasy about the self as speaking consciousness that Ovid's opening rhetoric of animation initially proposes. Such figures remind us of the various ways that we are subject to the impersonal, mechanical functioning of language, by which I mean that it is, by definition, made to do without us. They therefore darken the narrator's closing vision of personal transcendence by way of the voice. Similar effects often follow from the sound of women's voices in Ovid's poem, as we'll see in further detail. But before we look at the way the idea of a female voice qualifies the more optimistic overtones to Ovid's rhetoric of vocal animation, I must first be a little more precise about what kind of relationship pertains between the poem's various voices and the bodies that contain them. I will then be able to clarify exactly what sort of story the narrator proposes in order to give that relationship an erotic, and distinctly gendered, shape.

When Ovid imagines his own preservation as author in the poem's final lines, he proposes a dialectic between two apparently different entities: the mind (represented as voice-consciousness) and the body. The poet's body will die but the "better part of him" will survive because other lips read his poem out loud.[58] The first thing to notice is that Ovid's closing fantasy of surviving beyond his body's death – and the materiality of the written word – repeats the images that Pythagoras used to describe the process of metempsychosis earlier in Book 15. Specifically, Ovid tells us that as a voiced name and text, the author will survive whatever "fire ... or the gnawing tooth of time" can do to his body (15.871–12, "nec ignis / ... nec edax abolere uetustas"). These tropes explicitly recall those that Pythagoras used: *anima*, the philosopher declares, persists despite "the burning pyre or the wasting power of time" ("siue rogus flamma seu tabe uetustas" [15.156]). Concerning Ovid's self-representation in the last lines, therefore, Simone Viarre remarked that the evident parallels with Pythagoras transform the narrator into "un héros ... pythagoricien."[59]

Pythagoras' narrative about transcending the body depends on a distinction between *anima* and the *formae* and *figurae* it temporarily occupies:

> omnia mutantur, nihil interit: errat et illinc
> huc uenit, hinc illuc, et quoslibet occupat artus
> spiritus ecque feris humana in corpora transit
> inque feras noster, nec tempore deperit ullo,
> utque nouis facilis signatur cera *figuris*
> nec manet ut fuerat nec *formas* seruat easdem,

sed tamen ipsa eadem est, animam sic semper eandem
esse, sed in uarias doceo migrare *figuras*. (15.167–72)

All things change, nothing dies: the spirit wanders and comes now here, now there, and occupies various bodies, moving from animals into human bodies and from human to animal form, but never dies – just as pliant wax, stamped with new *figures*, does not remain the same as it was nor preserve the same *forms* yet still is the selfsame wax, so the soul is always the same, but I teach that it passes into a variety of *figures*.

At the end of his long speech, Pythagoras again describes the process of moving through bodies as one of changing *formae* (455).

With this simile, Pythagoras tells another of the poem's many narratives about the body that carry metapoetic weight. The two nouns Pythagoras opposes to *anima* – *figura* and *forma* – convey both corporeal and linguistic meanings.[60] As with Ovid's pun on Philomela's *lingua*, these nouns, too, vacillate between designating the form of the body and forms of language. I have already outlined the various meanings of *figura*. *Forma* bifurcates in the same two directions. *Forma* can refer to corporeal form, material appearance, contour, figure, shape; it can also refer to physical beauty: the narrator tells us that Daphne's *forma* is "augmented" by flight and that the *forma* of Pygmalion's statue captivates its maker. But as the rhetorical undercurrent in both stories about beautiful female "forms" should also alert us, *forma* also refers to style of composition and generally to poetic or rhetorical forms of speech.[61] The word certainly occurs in numerous ekphrastic scenes in Ovid's poem that ask readers to compare the poem's "form" to other forms of art – which, given the narrator's interest in the connections between visual and verbal registers, is often sculpture (i.e. 1.405–6; 4.675–77). And finally, *forma* also came to designate the grammatical quality, condition, or "form" of a word. Varro uses the word *forma* to designate the literal means by which one discerns the inflected *differences* between words in Latin.[62] In his description of writing love letters in *Ars Amatoria*, Ovid directly plays on these corporeal and linguistic senses: "barbarous language" in a woman's letter, the narrator warns, may do harm to her compositional style or "pretty form" ("et nocuit formae barbara lingua bonae," 3.482). It should therefore come as no surprise that the god of poetry wants to lay hands not only on Daphne's *figura* (1.547) but also on her *forma* (489, 530): when figure and style are missing, a poet's words are indeed "inperfecta" (526).

We might therefore understand the distinction Pythagoras proposes between *anima* and its changing bodily "forms" as the culminating thematic expression of the poetic, rhetorical, and grammatical aspects of *forma* and *figura* that occasionally surface in the *Metamorphoses*. That

Pythagoras should choose wax as the vehicle for his simile indicates, as would a similar comparison to "ink" today, that something other than corporeal form is also at issue. When Ovid alludes to this speech in the context of his closing meditation on the power of his poem to defy the ravages of time, he reminds us to think again about the metapoetic undercurrent of Pythagoras' speech. The narrator's allusion draws on that undercurrent in order to propose a significant analogy for his rhetoric of animation: like the *anima* that Pythagoras claims moves through the material forms of bodies, the narrator's *animus* moves through the material forms of the poem's letters (an idea derived, in part, from the culturally persuasive practices of vocalizing written letters in texts and epitaphs). When the last lines move from Ovid's written text to the reader's speaking *os*, we are reading a poet's specifically verbal rendition of the theory that material form is a vehicle for the soul or mind that lives beyond it.

If we read the figure of the poet's speaking *animus* in the *Metamorphoses'* first line alongside Pythagoras' theory of the imperishable *anima*, we may also wonder if the *mutatas formas* of which the narrator's "mind turns to speak" in the poem's opening are indeed something more than "the changing forms of bodies." Suspended by the grammar of Ovid's opening construction, particularly by the delayed agreement between the general neuter plural, *noua*, and the noun it modifies, *corpora* – "*In noua fert animus mutatas dicere formas / corpora*" – we are briefly encouraged to think of *mutatas formas* very generally – perhaps even as the changing "forms" of language that provide this revisionary, Hellenistic narrator with the material for his poem. Over the course of Ovid's narrative, this double focus expands. In addition to *forma* and *figura*, Ovid uses a number of words to convey a corporeal, physical meaning on the one hand and a rhetorical, poetic, graphic, or generally linguistic one on the other. Recall some of the poem's more prominent words for designating corporeal and poetic form at once: *pes* (physical foot and metrical foot); *membrum* (part of the body and part of a speech or literary work); *imago* (visible form or shape and representation, simile); *lingua* (corporeal tongue and language); *signum* (an identifying mark and the impression or mark in a piece of wax); *simulacrum* (a body's outward appearance and statue or image); and *mouere* (to move physically and to move by means of words). As increased scholarly attention to Ovid's metapoetic moments attests, this double focus only grows as the narrative proceeds. By the time we arrive at the death of the poet Orpheus, his *anima* "exhaled on the winds," we should not be surprised to read that Orpheus's *membra* – fragments of the poet's body and of his sentences[63] – lie scattered on the shores of a river. Such a double focus is, of course, consonant with the feature so often noted about the *Metamorphoses*: the continual movement between literal and figural meanings.

I am comparing Ovid's closing figures to Pythagoras' in order to suggest that Ovid's narrator develops a kind of metempsychotic poetics: the changing "forms" and "figures" of the poet's words are the material means by which his *animus*, his internal wind or voice, shapes the poem and at the same time allows him to develop the compelling fantasy that its author may achieve continued presence in the world by means of that poem. "Mutatas formas" provide an exceedingly convenient topic, one that enables the narrator to speak about bodies and the forms of poetry at the same time (hence the overall impression that the poem keeps shifting through the various poetic forms or genres as it proceeds). Ovid therefore makes sure to remind us that this is the case in the story of Apollo's love for Daphne's *figura* and *forma* and again in the tale of Pygmalion, where an artist falls in love with a "form" of his own making. By calling attention to the poem's double focus, of course, I am proposing nothing more than the kind of reading early modern writers proposed for Ovid's text. By confessing to an idolatrous, Apollonian passion for the name or *figura* of Laura, Petrarch made clear that he interpreted Ovid's changing "forms" and "figures" this way. Marston named his Ovidian narrative *The Metamorphosis of Pigmalions Image* in order to ring satiric changes on "image" as a word that can mean statue and reflection as well as poetic trope. But it is perhaps Andrew Marvell who most succinctly captured the sense of the other story that was always implicit in Ovid's treatment of corporeal "form":

> Apollo hunted Daphne so,
> Only that she might Laurel grow.
> And Pan did after Syrinx speed,
> Not as a Nymph, but for a Reed.[64]

If Ovid's narrator encourages us to draw an analogy between Pythagoras' theory of metempsychosis and his own poetic practice, however, this analogy is haunted by certain contradictions. Pythagoras posits an absolute distinction between mind and body, between *anima* and its material *formae* or *figurae*. Such a division between immaterial *anima* and material *forma* might reassure as a theory for the soul. But as a poetic practice it encounters some resistance. First, the voice so closely associated with the narrator's *animus* is, like the wind, itself a material substance. It seems to me that Ovid turns to sound and air because they are the least substantial substances he can find – and therefore less likely to direct attention to the contradiction. Second, a metempsychotic poetic, strictly adhered to, means that the forms and figures of language that so fascinate this poet's poet are merely contingent; what happens when the poet's *animus* moves between forms and figures is finally beside the point. The logical consequence of such a metempsychotic poetic creed is, in fact, profoundly antipoetic.

And third, we might well object that the one *forma* from which the poetic mind cannot distinguish itself is linguistic form. And we have already seen that when the poem draws attention to *that* form (its own form), it quickly becomes clear, as in the case of Echo, that the poetic *animus* depends upon previous forms and figures of language for continued existence. Such a "mind" or voice is *shaped* by the very forms it wants, according to the end of the poem, to transcend. In this regard, we cannot fail to notice that to clarify his theory, Pythagoras must lean heavily on a poetic figure:

> utque nouis facilis signatur cera figuris
> nec manet ut fuerat nec formas seruat easdem,
> sed tamen ipsa eadem est, animam sic semper eandem
> esse, sed in uarias doceo migrare figuras.   (15.169–72)

Just as pliant wax, stamped with new *figures*, does not remain the same as it was nor preserve the same *forms* yet still is the selfsame wax, so the soul is always the same, but I teach that it passes into a variety of *figures*.

Pythagoras' simile claims that there is a certain organic unity to *anima* that persists despite all changes of figure: "animam sic semper eandem." Understood this way, it could be read as the narrator's *apologia pro figuris suis*. Such an *apologia* implies that the poem's unity and coherence revolve around the poet's own *animus* – a "mind" that remains *sic semper idem* despite the poem's teeming array of changes. But the poem's evident preoccupation with the forms and figures of literary history, as we've already seen, encourages a certain skepticism about the scheme of temporal priority assumed by such a comparison. One is encouraged to ask several questions. If poetic *animus* or voice-consciousness anchors the poem's bewildering diversity of changing *formae* and *figurae*, whose *animus*, precisely, is it? How do we know when (or if) the many voices of literary history, on which the poem so deliberately relies, become one voice? And if we claim to hear a single voice (or controlling intention) in what is, rather, a subjectivity-effect achieved from a relationship *between* voices, do we not participate in the error of personification that the narrator so relentlessly exposes in stories like those of Echo and Procris?

The tenor of Pythagoras' simile for metempsychosis, moreover, is that *anima* subsists despite the changes in its material embodiments. But the vehicle represents this imperishable, immaterial *anima* as a piece of "pliant wax." Pythagoras claims, on the one hand, that *anima* differs from its material forms. But on the other hand, he uses a simile that equates *anima* with precisely that from which it is said to be distinct: a material form (wax). In this unexpected reversal where *anima resembles* matter, the philosopher's simile begins to unravel his careful distinction. This waxy figure, one might say, resists its speaker's mind; it leaves something of its own form behind, shaping the very mind that wants to argue the proposition that it is absolutely "the selfsame" apart from the forms it takes. One could say that Pythagoras' "mind" requires the mediation of poetic form in order to appear just as much as Ovid's revisionary narrator requires the many forms and figures of literary history to bring his *animus* to light. Pythagoras' unstable figure, in other words, inaugurates the kind of struggle between the speaking subject's expression in language and dislocation by it that we have seen hollow out the narrator's voice as well as the voices of his many characters.

Beauty and the breeze

In Pythagoras' speech, the distinction between *anima* and *forma* seems supremely indifferent to which of the two genders *anima* assumes as it migrates through various bodies. This is, of course, unusual in a poem so preoccupied with the vicissitudes of erotic life. But we need not look far to find such engendering. Elsewhere in the *Metamorphoses*, the corresponding difference that Ovid's narrator proposes – between the singing voice of poetic *animus* and the forms and figures of which it speaks – is not nearly so neutral. The important and highly influential metapoetic and metarhetorical reflections of Book 1, for example, transform the distinction between material form and poetic breath into a violent story about sexual difference. In the first book of the *Metamorphoses*, whose subject is not only the creation of the world but the creation of poetry, the stories of Apollo and Pan mirror each other. In each case, a poetic voice emerges at some considerable cost to the female body to which it tries to speak: both Daphne and Syrinx change beyond recognition. In each, the narrator proposes a brutal division of labor – male voice versus female *forma* – in the production of poetic song. Such a division defines what counts as "female" and what "male" by pitting one against the other. Most important to this analysis, however, is the fact that the narrator associates these singing male voices quite carefully and literally with the movement of ἄνεμος – internal breath and external breeze. The poem's first two attempts to dramatize the narrator's proposed rhetoric of animation, in other words, embody that rhetoric in rape, characterizing sexual violence as an aggressive collusion between the male voice and the wind.

In the first of Ovid's stories to embody the difference between *animus* and *forma* – Apollo's attempt to subdue Daphne – we find that the narrator dwells once again on one particular part of the speaker's body: the mouth. In an extended epic simile, the narrator compares the god of poetry's *os* – from which beautiful words should fall – to that of a dog's voracious muzzle, "outstretched" and snapping in pursuit of its prey:

> ut canis in uacuo leporem cum Gallicus aruo
> uidit ...
> alter inhaesuro similis iam iamque tenere
> sperat et extento stringit uestigia rostro,
> alter in ambiguo est, an sit conprensus, et ipsis
> morsibus eripitur tangentiaque ora relinquit:
> sic deus et uirgo ...   (1.533–39)

Like a Gallic hound that sees a rabbit on the open plain ... the one hopes now, even now, that he has her and grazes her footsteps with outstretched muzzle while the other does not know whether she is caught and flees those jaws, leaving behind the mouth closing on her: so the god and the virgin ...

Moving in concert with Apollo's impending jaws, Ovid's poetic principle of ἄνεμος turns as rapacious as the god of poetry. When Apollo "breathes down" Daphne's fleeing neck ("et crinem sparsum cervicibus adflat" 1.542), the breeze joins in. The breeze, in fact, accomplishes the very things Apollo cannot. Unlike the frustrated god, the wind lays Daphne's body bare of clothing. Where Apollo longs in vain to arrange her dishevelled hair ("inornatos capillos"), the wind is more successful:

> Plura locuturum timido Peneia cursu
> fugit cumque ipso uerba inperfecta reliquit,
> tum quoque uisa decens; nudabant corpora uenti
> obuiaque aduersas uibrabant flamina uestes
> et leuis inpulsos retro dabat aura capillos
> auctaque forma fuga est ...   (1.525–30)

While he was trying to say more, the daughter of Peneus ran away in timid flight although still pleasing in appearance, and left him with his words imperfect; the winds laid her body bare, vibrating her opposing garments with gusts of air that block her path, and a light breeze blew her dishevelled hair behind her; her form is augmented by flight ...

The *aurae* cooperate with Apollo's breath and increase his desire. And it is, of course, a golden arrow (*aura*tum) allied with the wind (*aura*) in both name and action that causes this strife since it kindles Apollo's unrequited love. But the wind also anticipates Daphne's transformation into a sign for Apollo's status as a poet. There are several synonyms for "wind" in this passage: *uentus, aura, flamen*. One of them, *flamen*, can mean either "gust of wind" or "breath." But it also can mean "a note

sounded on a wind instrument." Thus the line about the wind as *flamen* –
"obuiaque aduersas uibrabant flamina uestes" – begins the reluctant
Daphne's metamorphosis into a poet's instrument: the *flamen* strips her
bare by making her "opposing" clothing "vibrate" (*uibro, -are* being a
verb used to describe movements of both body and voice).[65] Daphne
therefore must flee the wind as swiftly as she flees the wind's ally, the god
of poetry. We come to understand that when Daphne flees "faster than
the breeze" ("fugit ocior aura" 1.502), she is more than merely agile. She
is also a very good reader of the poem in which she appears.

Hard on the heels of Daphne's story follows a condensed version of
the same circumstance: Pan pursues Syrinx in a manner as violent as
poetic. As if she has learned a lesson from her predecessor, Syrinx
doesn't stick around long enough to hear any of Pan's attempt to
persuade her ("talia uerba refert restabat uerba referre" 1.700). But the
form that Pan finally seizes nonetheless gives a poetic shape to the wind
that comes from inside his body. In place of the failed voice of rhetoric,
Pan acquires the "sweet" breath of pastoral poetry:

> corpore pro nymphae calamos tenuisse palustres,
> dumque ibi suspirat, motos in harundine uentos
> effecisse sonum tenuem similemque querenti.
> arte noua uocisque deum dulcedine captum
> "hoc mihi colloquium tecum" dixisse "manebit,"
> atque ita *disparibus calamis conpagine cerae*
> inter se iunctis nomen tenuisse puellae.   (1.706–12 [emphasis mine])

Instead of the nymph's body Pan held marsh reeds, and when he sighed, the
winds moving through the reed made a soft sound, like a complaint. The god,
captivated by the sweet new art for the voice, said, "this conversation with you is
left to me," and so the reeds of disparate length, *held together by wax*, kept the
name of the maiden.

In his first book, Ovid uses the fate of Daphne and Syrinx to unfold two
influential, etiological accounts for the poetics of animation. In each,
moreover, he makes a suggestion seminal for the literary history his
poem inaugurated: aesthetic form is born from a woman's resistance to
rhetorical persuasion.

When the two gods next appear together in concert – in Book 11 Pan
challenges Apollo to a contest by disparaging his skill – Pan is still
playing the reed pipes that once were Syrinx, and Apollo is still wreathed
in the laurel that once was Daphne ("ille caput flauum lauro Parnaside
uinctus" 165). And once again, the narrator represents poetry as a matter
of the *os* and of animating the natural world: Tmolus, god of the
mountain and judge of the contest, turns "his face to Phoebus's face"
("sacer *ora* retorsit / Tmolus *ad os* Phoebi" 163) and the entire forest

follows suit ("uultum sua silua secuta est" 164). But in this contest, female form has become an utterly silent partner in the collaboration between *animus* and *forma* necessary for a male voice to sing. Wreathed in Daphne's laurel, Apollo is no longer a lover encumbered by imperfect words. Rather, he is the very picture of an artist ("artificis status ipse fuit" 169) and so triumphs over Pan and his reed pipes. But Apollo's former ally, the wind, must assist the god's voice nonetheless. That is, everyone listening agrees that Apollo is a better singer than Pan, except for Midas. The god avenges himself by giving Midas ass's ears. But Midas, for his part, manages to keep his disgrace hidden – except from his barber. And the barber, unable to keep the news to himself – literally, "wanting to let it out to the wind" ("cupiens efferre sub auras" 184) – relieves his desire for speech by "burying his voice" in a hole in the ground. But a patch of reeds (what else?) springs up on the spot. When they are full grown, the wind moves through these reeds, releases the buried words, and so completes Apollo's revenge by exposing Midas' shame to the world in its own kind of disembodied voice ("leni nam motus ab austro / obruta uerba refert" 192–93).

In this battle between female form and male ἄνεμος – the partnership between breath and the wind – we encounter a fierce economy for poetry that is at once symbolic and sexual. Nor does this economy, with its terrible effect on female form, stop with the metapoetic reflections of Book 1. But it does take unexpected turns. We have already seen that Cephalus' brief poem to *Aura* – a series of apostrophes amounting to the tripartite anaphora dear to Roman poetry – comes out into the air only at the cost of his wife's death. Although *aurae* seem to move in concert with Apollo's voice when he wins the laurel and his singing contest with Pan, in Cephalus' case the allegiance between wind and voice can no longer be said to correspond in any way to the speaker's desire. Rather, the wind severs the link between what Cephalus loves (Procris) and what he says ("Aura," wind). And this divorce transforms the speaker's poetic figures into a verbal event with lethal consequences. As we have already seen in the narrator's self-portrait and in many of the poem's other stories about the *os*, however, a speaker's intention has little to do with Ovid's definition of the voice. Cephalus therefore finds, like his narrator, that both voice and wind may suddenly veer out of control.

By the time we reach the story of Orpheus' attempt to bring his wife back to life, the narrator has developed a full-blown, complex fantasy about the power and limits of vocal animation. Indeed, it is complex enough that it can be extended to the realm of the visual arts: Orpheus rewrites his own failure by telling the wish-fulfilling story of Pygmalion's life-giving art. When the narrator uses Orpheus' story to dramatize his own rhetoric of animation, he expands his dream about the voice to include the fantasy of a poet whose song conquers death – a dream that, as we've already seen, shapes the narrator's self-portrait in the poem's closing lines. But in Book 10 we read about this dream only in light of its failure; the league between poet and wind shifts once again. The book opens with Hymen traveling "through the upper air" ("aethera digreditur" 10.2) because he has been called upon by "the voice" of Apollo's son, Orpheus ("uoce uocatur" 3). But we learn immediately that his voice called Hymen "in vain." Clearly Orpheus' desire for his wife means that he *wants* to reverse his father's infelicitous poetic legacy. That is, Orpheus wants to use his voice to animate a beloved form ("auidusque uiuendi," 56). But he fails in his attempt. Taken together, the stories of Apollo, Pan, Cephalus, and Orpheus tell us at least two unsettling things about the relationship between *animus* and *forma*, mind and body: the voice and its effects are easily separable from intention and may all too easily betray the speaker's mind or desire; and one of several kinds of violation – rape, metamorphosis, death – are nonetheless required of beautiful female forms if male voices are to be raised in song. The first predicament, as we have seen, is applicable to *all* speaking subjects in the poem, regardless of gender. But the second appears to displace this problem within the voice, about which the poem is always aware, onto a story of sexual difference. Such displacement effectively occludes the contradictions inherent in the phonocentric fantasy of voice-consciousness, disguising a problem *within* any speaking subject as a sexually violent clash *between* gendered subjects. The narrator embodies the potential for any poetic speaker to be alienated from his/her own tongue in stories about the difference between "his" voice and "her" resistant form.

Pygmalion's animating art also conforms to this narrative, extending from Apollo to Orpheus, about a conflict between female form and male voice. As we come to expect, Ovid turns a story about desire into one that is also about art – since the lover in Ovid's source was a king, not a sculptor – and he is therefore able to use the story to comment on the power and limitations of the poem's own rhetoric of animation. In addition to the graphic trope of softening wax, the narrator satirizes the sculptor's delusion in terms that are as rhetorical as they are sexual. He tells us that Pygmalion believes his statue "wants to be moved" ("uelle moueri" 10.251); points out that it is Pygmalion's *words of prayer* to Venus, rather than his technical prowess, that really do the trick; and tells us, moreover, that the organ to begin the process of animation is not the sculptor's hand but his *os*. First, the prostitutes whose behavior disgusts Pygmalion change to stones, their "faces" or "mouths" hardening to flint – "sanguisque induruit *oris*" (241). Therefore, it is the sculptor's mouth rather than his hand that brings his new, improved female form to life: "he kissed her while she was lying on the couch; she seems to grow warm; he moves his mouth to her again" ("incumbensque toro dedit oscula: uisa tepere est; / admouet *os* iterum," 281–82). In place of women's hardened *ora*, Orpheus tells of Pygmalion's animating lips. In later chapters we will see that when Petrarch and Shakespeare read the story of Pygmalion in relation to that of his narrator, Orpheus, they were similarly struck by the poetic and rhetorical aspects of a tale that seems, on first reading, to be simply about the visual arts.

But if we do think of Pygmalion's story in rhetorical terms, we notice a certain sexual division of labor once again. Pygmalion's beloved *simulacrum* acquires neither name nor voice; like Orpheus' dead wife, the statue remains merely object, rather than subject, of the poem's representational economy. And like Eurydice, who says only "goodbye" to the husband who says so much, Pygmalion's statue says nothing about what she thinks of her lover's desire. In other words, both Eurydice's death and the unnamed statue's silence in the Orpheus–Pygmalion sequence of Book 10 conform to the larger fantasy first proposed in Book 1 with Apollo and Pan. In this fantasy about a masculinized *animus* as voice-consciousness, the power of the male *os* requires a silent (or silenced) female form if it is to be heard. And this form, moreover, must *resist* the speaker's demand.[66] In this network of related stories, the narrator gives a culturally familiar, gendered hierarchy to the difference between *animus* and *forma*. And in such a hierarchy, the options for female form are grim: silence, rape, metamorphosis, death.

But at this point a complicated question arises. How far does Ovid's narrator participate in the violent conflict inaugurated by Apollo to dramatize the rhetoric of animation? Such a question will take some time to answer. We can begin, however, by thinking about the narrator's role in Book 10, the book whose controlling narrative revolves around animation. It is only after Eurydice dies twice that Orpheus tells the stories that make up this section of the poem, so we might note that Ovid's narrator predicates an entire book of the *Metamorphoses* on Eurydice's absence. But in asking how far the narrator participates, or stands apart from, such fantasies, there is a further aspect to remember about this struggle between male voice and absent or violated female form: between Books 1 and 11, Apollo and Pan pass from heterosexual conflict to homosocial contest. Daphne and Syrinx become increasingly vestigial signs, their bodies first transformed and then understood to be symbolic conduits for a competition between male artists. Similarly, Ovid's narrator engages in a well-known bit of competition with Vergil at

the death of Orpheus, revising his famed predecessor's version at the end
of the *Georgics*. Ovid's apostrophes to the dying Orpheus evoke the
rhetorically compelling fiction that the narrator gains back his voice
when Orpheus "breathes out" his *anima* on the winds. At the same time,
however, Ovid's apostrophes to the head of Orpheus are clearly a way of
competing with his predecessor, Vergil. When Vergil represents Orpheus'
head floating downstream in the *Georgics*, someone also calls out a series
of apostrophes. But in this case, Vergil's narrator records, through the
voice of yet another storyteller, the apostrophes uttered by the mournful,
decapitated head of Orpheus as it devotes its dying breath to call out to
Eurydice.

> tum quoque marmorea caput a ceruice reuulsum
> gurgite cum medio portans Oeagrius Hebrus
> uolueret, Eurydicen uox ipsa et frigida lingua,
> a miseram Eurydicen! anima fugiente uocabat.
> Eurydicen toto referebant flumine ripae. (4.523–27)

Even then while Oeagrian Hebrus carried and rolled that head, severed from its
marble neck, in midstream, his voice and cold tongue called on Eurydice, oh
unhappy Eurydice!, with fleeting breath. The banks of the whole river echoed,
Eurydice!

Vergil's *tour de force* of sounding and resounding voices is not one that
Ovid, captivated with the idea of animated nature, voice, and "fugitive
breath" ("anima fugiente uocabat"), would be likely to forget. Notice
that Vergil's narrator is quoting the words of his temporary narrator,
Proteus, who is quoting, in turn, the words of Orpheus as they echo
down the banks of the river when the poet died. But when Ovid's
narrator tells the story of Orpheus' head floating downstream, he puts
his own apostrophes to Orpheus in place of those that Vergil's Orpheus
addressed to Eurydice. Refusing Vergilian indirection, he stakes a claim
for the right as heir to Orphic vocal power. But at the same time, these
emulous apostrophes to Orpheus push Eurydice still further into the
shadows of the forgotten. Instead of Orpheus' lament for Eurydice, we
hear Ovid's lament for Orpheus: "Te maestae uolucres, Orpheu, te turba
ferarum, / te rigidi silices, te carmina saepe secutae / fleuerunt siluae ..."
(11.44–46) ("The mournful birds wept for you, Orpheus, the crowd of
beasts, the flinty rocks, the trees that had so often followed your
songs ..."). In the programmatic narrative that brings Vergil's *Georgics*
to a close, the connections between Orpheus' voice and the poet's are
important but heavily mediated by the divagations of indirect discourse.
They are suggestive but understated. In Ovid's rendition, however, the
narrator boldly substitutes his tropes for those of Orpheus. Ovid

competes with Vergil, in other words, by assuming the extraordinary poetic voice that Vergil records only second-hand. He changes the focus from Orpheus' personal mourning for Eurydice to his own poetic desire for Orpheus. Or perhaps it would be more accurate to say that Ovid's desire here is for a voice such as Vergil's. In either case, Ovid derives considerable competitive profit from his predecessor's idea of a tongue devoted to Eurydice even to its last breath. But the glaring light of competition should not blind us to the fact that his self-inflating revision of Orpheus' mournful lament completes the process inaugurated by Apollo and Pan – that of excluding female voices and bodies from a scene that turns into yet another singing contest between male poets.

Resisting voices

When we first consider how far Ovid's narrator participates in the various masculinist fantasies with which he dramatizes his own rhetoric of animation – the stories of Apollo, Pan, Orpheus, and Pygmalion – we discover several disquieting emotions: a desire to rape, a desire to escape from female form altogether, or profound indifference to what the "beloved" woman might say or want. Various kinds of misogyny define the libidinal parameters of what counts as a "male" voice and "male" desire in these connected stories. But further reflection brings us to a contradictory undercurrent. That is, while at times the narrative suggests affinities between the narrator and his ostensibly "male" version of vocal animation, nonetheless Ovid's characteristic, pervasive irony also opens up a certain distance between them. Such distance is particularly obvious, for instance, by the time we reach the Pygmalion–Orpheus sequence. Central though the fantasy of animation may be to Ovid's narrative project, nonetheless the narrator is pointedly mocking the artist's fetishistic exuberance as he describes Pygmalion's activities: "he kisses and thinks his kisses are returned ... grasps it and thinks his fingers are pressing into her limbs, fears that he is leaving bruises ... he brings it gifts pleasing to girls," and so forth. And as classical scholars observe, Ovid's version of the myth of Orpheus is similarly defla-tionary.[67] Adept at putting an ironic distance between himself and his characters when needed, Ovid's narrator casts a particularly cool eye on the artistry of both Pygmalion and Orpheus. At the same time, it is this ironic narrator who never allows us to forget that the reason for Pygmalion's delusional version of rhetorical animation is misogyny. Imitating Orpheus' turn away from womankind, Pygmalion creates his *simulacrum* because of sexual disgust: he blames prostitution on one party only – calling it one of "the faults nature had so liberally given the female mind" (244–45) – and, the narrator reminds us, appears to believe that fondling an inanimate piece of ivory is a less repugnant sexual practice.

By the time we reach Book 10, moreover, we can scarcely avoid noticing a certain clash in narrative point of view over the question of "male" desire. Apollo and Pan call rape "love." So, too, does Orpheus: at the opening of Book 10, Orpheus buys into his father's catachresis, calling Pluto's rape of Proserpina *amor* ("famaque si ueteris non est mentita rapinae, / uos quoque iunxit Amor," "If the rumor of that old rape is true, you two were also joined by love" 10.28–29). But the last time we heard the story of Proserpina's rape – in the voice of Orpheus' mother, Calliope – we found a rather different account of the same event. That is, Calliope focuses her version of the rape around another mother's grief and a daughter's fear (5.341–550). Calliope also recalls the comments of a witness to the crime: Arethusa protests to Proserpina's mother that "a woman ought to be asked, not carried off" ("roganda, / non rapienda fuit" 5.415–16). Interested primarily in the victims' anguish and a female witness's complaint, Calliope reminds those who might be listening to the poem's dissenting voices that when her son, Orpheus, calls such sexual violence *Amor*, his is but one view of the matter.

If we are fully to assess how far Ovid's narrator is implicated in the erotic and at times violent fantasies that define the rhetoric of animation, we must ask still further questions. What would happen if we could listen, rather than merely speak, to Eurydice? Or if not to her, to any of her other fugitive sisters? And indeed, if we take time to listen to the female voices that accompany the stories we've been examining thus far, we detect a critique of the fantasies of rape, silence, and death that pervade the poem's metarhetorical reflection. Calliope's mournful version of what her son later calls "love," for example, puts us on notice to listen for other sounds of discord or dissent. These emerge most forcefully when the Bacchae encounter Orpheus. Along with Calliope's song, Bacchic voices register something of the Ovidian narrator's distance from the masculinist love story that shapes Book 10's reflection on rhetoric and animation. Heartily agreeing with the narrator's ironic attention to the permutations and effects of misogyny in Book 10, this roving band of women raise a violent outcry against its singer, Orpheus, as "nostri contemptor" (11.76). Their protest brings this section of the *Metamorphoses* to a close. It is not merely because the Bacchae have the last word that they are important to this analysis of Ovid's phonographic imaginary. It is also because their noise drowns out Orpheus' voice: he dies because neither the women nor the stones they throw can hear the sounds that fall from his mouth. The powerful vocal *clamor* of Ovid's Bacchic horde constitutes a significant protest against the symbolic and libidinal economy of animation, the predication of successful male poetic voices on repeated violations against the female body.

Indeed, once we've understood the violent and sexual shape that the narrator's rhetoric of animation can assume, we see that this Bacchic interruption carefully opposes the story about poetic voice and form associated with Apollo and his son. Not only does a horde of women conquer Orpheus' singing voice with their own shrill cries, but the narrator defines their appearance on the landscape in terms that should be, by now, extremely familiar.

> Carmine dum tali siluas *animos*que ferarum
> Threicius uates et saxa sequentia ducit,
> ecce nurus Ciconum tectae lymphata ferinis
> pectora uelleribus tumuli de uertice cernunt
> Orphea percussis sociantem carmina neruis.
> e quibus *una leues iactato crine per auras,*
> "en," ait "en, hic est nostri contemptor!" et hastam
> *uatis Apollinei uocalia misit in ora* ...
> clamor et infracto Berecyntia tibia cornu
> tympanaque et plausus et Bacchei ululatus
> obstrepuere sono citharae, tum denique saxa
> non exauditi rubuerunt sanguine uatis ...   (11.1–19)

While the Thracian bard led the trees and *minds* of animals and following rocks with such songs, behold, the Cicones, breasts covered with skins of wild animals, perceived Orpheus from a hilltop joining songs to the music of his lyre. And one of these, *her hair streaming in the gentle breeze*, said "see, see, here is the man who scorns us!" and *threw her spear at the tuneful mouth of Apollo's bard* ... the uproar and the Berecyntian flutes with discordant horns and drums and blows and shrill cries of the Bacchae drowned out the sound of the lyre, then at length stones grew red with the blood of the bard who went unheard ...

Various figures in this dense passage reverse the fictions of both Orpheus' voice and his father's. And by doing so, they implicitly criticize the controlling story about vocal animation fundamental to Ovid's *perpetuum carmen*. By the time we reach Book 10, we realize that it is no accident that one of the Bacchae aims her spear at Orpheus' mouth. But other programmatically significant figures gather around Orpheus' last breath. Instead of the mind or *animus* that Orpheus was once able to move even in animals, the Bacchae force the poet to exhale his own *anima* on the breeze. Rather than hair like Daphne's, tossed on the "light breeze" ("leuis ... aura"), Orpheus faces Bacchic hair, streaming on breezes that, although "light," are far less suited to his desire (again, "leues ... auras" 1.6). In place of either Syrinx-as-reed-pipe or the *flamen*

Daphne's hastily spoken *figura*: the mere idea of the female voice disturbs Ovid's initial programmatic story about Apollo's triumphant voice and its allegiance with the wind. These resisting voices tell us not only that this masculinist version of the poem's dream of rhetorical animation is extremely violent – predicated on repeated violations of other bodies – but that its tone is a little too naive, too quick to claim the laurel leaf of victory. Apollo may not learn this lesson from Daphne directly. But he will learn it soon enough: by the beginning of Book 2, the god of poetry comes bitterly to regret the sound of his own voice after swearing an oath to grant any request that his son, Phaethon, might make ("Paenituit iurasse patrem ... 'utinam promissa liceret / non dare'" 2.49–52). The reed pipe's "complaining sound" and the unexpected effects of Daphne's *figura* prepare the way for Echo's alienating repetitions. For these sounds, just as surely as Echo's *uox*, point to the potential distance between voice and consciousness. They reveal an otherness within the fiction of the poetic voice that profoundly qualifies the rhetoric of animation as we have delineated it thus far. They remind us, in fact, that the ἄνεμος that passes through the subject's body (whether *anima* or *animus*) cannot always be relied upon to work in the speaker's service, no matter how much that speaker tries to hoard its power.

There is yet another female voice in the *Metamorphoses* that performs this critical function, creating a distance internal to Ovid's opening fiction about the origins of poetry in rape and the power of the would-be rapist's voice. But this is a voice that we are never actually said to "hear." I refer to the story of Medusa's silent *os*, a *monstrum* that bridges Books 4 and 5. Like the metapoetic stories of Apollo and Pan, Medusa's story offers yet another account of the origin of poetry. As I have suggested, in fact, her story is also about the movement between rhetoric and poetry, since before giving rise to the fountain of poetry, Medusa's *os* appears first in the narrative as an aid to Perseus' failing words. As such, Medusa's terrifying, speechless mouth offers a rather different account of both poetry and rhetoric than the one Ovid associates with the songs of Apollo and Orpheus. In Medusa's story, Ovid imagines an avenging *os* comparable to the *clamor* of the Bacchae – a frightening pair of lips that constitute an internal form of protest against, and revenge for, the male rhetoric of vocal animation.[69]

In the figure of Medusa, we read at least two stories of origin: in the first, Athena turns Medusa into the Gorgon after Neptune raped her (4.793–803); in the second, the blood flowing from the Gorgon's decapitation gives rise to the Heliconian fountain of poetry. She is, Ovid tells us, the fountain's "mother" ("uidi ipsum materno sanguine nasci"

5.259). Like the stories of attempted rape in Book 1, the poem associates the origin of poetry with extraordinary violence against the female body: Medusa is raped, metamorphosed, beheaded. But in the case of this metapoetic figure, we encounter a strangely decapitated kind of verse that has little to do with *animus* or "mind." As Minerva discovers from the Muses on Helicon, Medusa's blood gives birth to poetry because a winged horse sprang from that blood and the blows from his beating feet – "factas pedis ictibus undas" (5.264) – carved out the fountain. As Stephen Hinds points out in some detail, the horse's beating hooves literally enact the meter of poetry: both *pes* (foot) and *ictus* (a blow or pulse) are the technical Roman terms for the rhythm or "blows" of metrical feet.[70] Such an etiology for poetry points not to the movement of a singer's "mind" or intention – "my mind is moved to tell," "animus fert dicere" (1.1) – but points, instead, to the movement of feet and of accident. These chance blows give rise to a rhythm that becomes the differential structure of poetic verse. Medusa's decapitation, a strange kind of "origin," is an appropriate literalization of this insight into the mechanical conditions of verse, a network of differences between sounds that determines the possible forms a poet's *animus* may take.

Medusa's effect on the voice turns out to be as unsettling as this etiological account of the Heliconian fountain might suggest. When Perseus "holds out the Gorgon's mouth" in battle – "Gorgonis extulit ora" (5.180) – death comes quickly, and significantly, through the voice, the tongue, and the *os*. Perseus subdues one of his foes mid-speech and the narrator records the exact moment of death by interrupting his own indirect discourse:

> "adspice" ait "Perseu, nostrae primordia gentis:
> magna feres *tacitas* solacia mortis *ad umbras*
> a tanto cecidisse uiro"; pars ultima uocis
> in medio suppressa sono est, adapertaque uelle
> ora loqui credas, nec sunt ea peruia uerbis.   (5.190–94)

"See, Perseus, the origin of my family: you will carry a great consolation for your death to the *silent shades* for having been killed by such a man" – but the last part of his voice was cut off in the middle of its sound; you would think his open lips wanted to speak but they were no longer a passageway for his words.

When another foe dies at the sight of Medusa's *os*, the narrator again points to the dying man's face and lips: "marmoreoque manet uultus mirantis in ore" ("the astonished face remains with marble lips," 206). The narrator then ends the battle with a fearful mirroring of this soundless *os*: "Perseus ait oraque regis / ore Medusaeo silicem sine sanguine fecit" ("Perseus spoke and with Medusa's mouth, made the king's mouth a stone without blood" 248–49). And finally, one of the first deaths at the banquet anticipates such work even before Perseus unveils Medusa's implacable mouth. One warrior's decapitated head literally "breathes out" its mind and, half-dead (or literally, "with half a mind") still continues to speak: "ibi *semianimi* uerba exsecrantia *lingua* / edidit et medios animam exspirauit in ignes" ("there the half-animate [or half-conscious] tongue poured out words of execration and in the middle of the altar fires breathed out its mind" 5.105–06). The imminent threat of Medusa's as yet unveiled *os* prompts the narrator to imagine a dead, but still moving, tongue. He associates her fearsome power with a tongue deprived of mind or intention (*semi-animus*) if not, however, of motion.

We have seen the *Metamorphoses* vacillate between a rhetoric of vocal animation and its own internal critique of that rhetoric as wishful fantasy. The narrator opens by dramatizing this rhetoric in an aggressively masculinist form. But he soon asks us to "hear" in many of the poem's female voices what we never can actually hear in any one voice – a phonographic critique of the voice that alienates the subject from within its own tongue. Both the poetics of beating feet and accident, associated with Medusa's decapitated head, and the idea of death through the mouth, associated with her *os*, are particularly memorable embodiments of Ovid's critique of his own fictions of voice-consciousness. Her mouth harbors an unexpected kind of oblivion in the notion of the "voice," the very faculty that Ovid strives to ally with *animus*, to make his own, while at the same time acknowledging his failure to do so. If Medusa's mouth traumatizes in both Ovid's poem, in other words, she does so because her *os* is a *monstrum* – meaning "prodigy, portent, sign" as much as "monstrous thing" – for speaking beings. Consonant with many of the poem's other female voices (Echo's mimicking *uox*, Philomela's tongue), Medusa's mouth draws attention to the narrator's unsettling habit of disentangling the generally functional relationship between language and the mind, between cherished notions of personal agency in language and what it actually means to be the "author" of a text or singer of a song. And if we read the figure of Medusa's decapitated *os* in light of Philomela's severed, yet still murmuring *lingua*, we see that in both, Ovid's critique of the voice operates according to a rhetoric of the dismembered body. Such a rhetoric asks us to think twice about the synecdoches that are the basis for our all too easy transitions from a part of the body – the mouth, tongue, lips, or face – to an idea of a whole body, person, or presence.

But Medusa's *os* does more than play a part in the poem's internal critique of its own rhetoric of animation. It also becomes a form of revenge for the story of rape allied with that rhetoric. When Athena changes Medusa into the Gorgon, the narrator tells us the following:

> hanc pelagi rector templo uitiasse Mineruae
> dicitur: auersa est et castos aegide uultus
> nata Iouis texit, neue hoc inpune fuisset,
> Gorgoneum crinem turpes mutauit in hydros.
> nunc quoque, ut attonitos formidine terreat hostes,
> pectore in aduerso, quos fecit, sustinet angues.   (4.798–803)

It is said the ruler of the sea raped her in Minerva's temple: Jove's daughter, having turned away, hid her chaste face behind her aegis, and in order that this might not go unpunished, she turned the Gorgon's hair into unsightly snakes. And now, in order to terrify her astonished enemies with this horrible thing, she wears the snakes which she made on her breast

Many readers protest, with good reason, that Medusa is being punished for her own rape. But notice that Medusa is not the only one punished by her metamorphosis – or rather, that if this metamorphosis is a form of punishment, it does not stop with Medusa. The poem's deliberately imprecise phrase, "neue *hoc* inpune fuisset," suggests two things with this "hoc": "in order that Neptune's crime not go unpunished" and "in order that this – that is, the crime of rape – not go unpunished." When Minerva transforms Medusa into a sign or portent (*monstrum*), she becomes a kind of talisman to one of the poem's most frequent forms of violence: rape. And the Gorgon-as-sign mysteriously obscures the question of agency, making one wonder who, precisely, is punishing and who being punished by this metamorphosis. That is, the fact that Medusa's metamorphosis originated in rape may explain why her ghastly *os* is wielded *only* against men. Only male lips and tongues freeze, mid-speech or semianimate, before Medusa's severed, snaky *os*. Such confusion about who punishes and who is being punished when Medusa becomes the Gorgon reiterates the rhetorical confusion of agency implicit in Perseus' battle with Atlas, where the hero, frustrated in his attempts to persuade, uses Medusa's mouth in place of his own. And it reminds us more generally of the poem's ongoing, unnerving critique of the speaking subject's belief in his or her own vocal agency. Medusa's mouth wields a negative kind of performative power: petrification by *os* sounds a note of caution within the poem's dream of words capable of conquering death, of bringing about the events of which they speak.

When we are told that Medusa is a *memorabile monstrum* (4.615; 5.216 and 241), she becomes a terrible kind of warning about the crime of which she is also the product. In a poem dedicated to etiology – to explaining the causes of various literalized figures in the landscape – Medusa's memorial function is common enough. But in a poem that captures its own rhetoric of animation in the visual sign of Daphne's beautiful *hair* tossed on the breeze, the transformation of Medusa's most beautiful feature, her hair, produces a powerfully self-critical image. Those snakes, born of Medusa's violated, "clarissima forma" (4.794), remind readers of the *price* women constantly pay in this poem for being seen to embody the idea of beautiful form on which so many male voices rely. In the terrifying effects of Medusa's raped body-turned-speechless *os*, then, we encounter yet another form of revenge for Apollo's poetic mouth, breathing down Daphne's neck as she turns in flight.

As dramatized by Apollo and Daphne, Pan and Syrinx, Cephalus and Procris, and Orpheus and Eurydice, Ovid's rhetoric of animation proposes a violent version of sexual difference. Embodied in a continuous narrative of crime and revenge – a struggle over poetic voice that leads to a series of ravaged female bodies – the poem's rhetorical reflection pits one sex against the other. At the origin of poetic acts over the course of the poem, Ovid tells us about female bodies that are raped (Daphne, Syrinx, Medusa), dead (Eurydice, Procris), and dismembered (Medusa). We should include in this list the violated body of Mother Earth, too, since not only a new race, but the idea of metaphor, springs from Deucalion's interpretation of the following sentence: "throw the bones of your mother over your shoulder" ("*ossa*que post tergum magnae iactate parentis" 1.383). From one *ōs* (face or lips) to another *ŏs* (bone): here, as with the story of Medusa giving birth to the Heliconian fountain, the generativity of poetry's differences (between sounds, between literal and figural meanings) derives from the idea of a mother's body in bits and pieces. But such violence does not "go unpunished." As if in payment for the violence that poetry's "voice" does to language's material forms, Orpheus encounters the devastating effects of Bacchic noise and the rest of the world of men the terrifying portent of Medusa's mouth.

Other voices, other loves

Bacchic *clamor*, Echo's repetitive *uox*, Syrinx's complaining sound, Daphne's unhappy *figura*, the Gorgon's implacable *os*: all these female "voices," whether low, shrill, or chillingly inaudible, are integral to the poem's critique of its own seductive, mutually reinforcing fantasies of animation and speaking consciousness. Over the course of the *Metamorphoses*, they trace the poem's internal distance from its own rhetorical practice, speaking – if they can be said to speak – for Ovid's critique of the fictions of voice-consciousness. Having seen this much, we are now in a position to notice something further. If the poem's opening symbolic economy, its rhetoric of animation, encounters fierce pockets of resistance over the course of the narrative, so, too, does its opening *libidinal* economy. To conclude my analysis of the trope of the "female" voice in the *Metamorphoses*, I want to suggest that just as these voices unhinge the persuasive fantasy of the single voice, they work just as surely to unravel the culturally pervasive fantasy of a single direction (or object) for desire, or, for that matter, of a single connection between erotic life and the gender of one's body.[71]

One of the poem's most frequently narrated events, rape, is crucial to any analysis of the poem's sexual politics. Since Leo Curran first tried to grapple with this issue in Ovid's poem, critics have often noted that rape is one of its most prominent and disturbing narratives.[72] By reading this narrative of sexual violence against the background of Ovid's larger rhetorical practice, we have perceived the internal distance that the trope of the female voice establishes from it. And I've suggested in this regard that the idea of absolute difference signified by rape serves to displace a problem within any speaking subject onto a story of conflict between gendered subjects – that as part of Ovid's phonographic imaginary, the metapoetic story of rape defines "male" bodies and desires in opposition to "female" ones in a way that leads, with a leaden sense of inevitability, to a vicious circle of crime and revenge. If we are to understand anything further about how rape functions in the *Metamorphoses*, or about the kind of role it plays in Ovid's representation of gender and sexuality, however, we must also read it in the context of the poem's larger libidinal economy. And central though it may be to the poem's metarhetorical reflections, rape is, nonetheless, one story among many others in a poem dedicated to the permutations and vicissitudes of *amor*. When we remember Ovid's increasingly polymorphous representation of sexuality, eroticism, and fantasy over the course of the *Metamorphoses*, we begin to see that he is as adept at unsettling the rigid binarisms of gender identity proposed by his opening stories of poetic origin as he is at undermining the fictions of personal identity conferred by the idea of the human voice.

Put schematically, the *Metamorphoses* questions the coherence and inevitability of sexual difference in a number of ways. First, when the poem ostentatiously engenders its own important distinction between *anima* and *forma* in the story of rape, it requires us to pay attention to the *process of conferring* gender – to the way that its various poetic tropes and genres impose meaning on bodily forms (and, by extension, on the desires portrayed as attached to those forms). And if we are asked to attend to the violence of this process, it is not hard to realize, in turn, that conferred meanings can also be contested. Certainly we have heard a number of voices in the poem raised in protest. Second, as the *Metamor-*

phoses progresses, the narrator famously tells multiple, contradictory, and polymorphously labile stories about the many forms of desire. Repeatedly imagining that his characters discover the cultural or natural "law" governing acceptable desires and objects only when they have already violated or decided to revise it,[73] the narrator continues to juxtapose these other "unlawful" loves to the heteronormative ones that rule the newly created world in the opening of the poem. Because the *Metamorphoses* represents so many erotic possibilities other than the ones with which it begins, the narrative eventually disentangles the gender of one's body from traditionally coded objects of desire. It does not take long to discover that in an Ovidian universe, just about *any* object can become erotic. Orpheus devotes himself to "tender boys" and one woman falls in love with another (Iphis and Ianthe). Narcissus falls for an *imago* and then himself, and Pygmalion falls for a statue of his own making. Byblis tries to seduce her brother and Myrrha succeeds with her father, who enjoys calling the disguised Myrrha "filia" in bed while she calls him "pater." Many characters simply prefer the hunt, or the company of other chaste hunters, to anything else, while still others devote themselves with such passion to memory of the dead that they, too, change their form. Even the exact shape of the beloved object's body means very little: we learn that Jupiter thinks Io just about as lovely in the form of a cow as a girl ("bos quoque formosa est" 1.612) and that Apollo is also pleased by Daphne's arboreal form. And through Europa's eyes, the narrator tells us just how very attractive that lovely white bull was, wandering through the fields ("formosus obambulat herbis / quippe color niuis est," etc. 2.851ff). In addition to *amor* written as rape, other desires and dispositions are entirely possible in Ovid's poem: among them, desire for a family member, for oneself, for someone of the opposite sex, for someone of the same sex, for boys who look like girls, for girls who dress as boys, for inanimate objects, animals, the chase, or simply no sexual relations at all.

Because of the exuberant exchange of objects in the *Metamorphoses*, as well as the permutations of passion that are *without* object, the poem begins to separate desire from its apparent rootedness in objects. Indeed, the narrator appears to be far more interested in the sheer force of *amor* (akin to Freud's notion of the *Trieb* or drive) than in the particularity of what this or that character desires. In some cases, passion exceeds not only the object but the subject, too. Thus figures like Midas, with his unlucky lust for gold, and Erysichthon, stricken with a hunger so overpowering that he eventually eats himself, are but further extensions of the poem's representation of *amor*, represented throughout as the "cursed love of having" (*amor habendi*).[74] Indeed, the combined effect of discovering what is "permitted" or "lawful" by way of transgressing the law – the definition of what counts as "normal" by way of what counts as "perverse" – and the overall impression that subjects and objects are far less important than the sheer force of desire and fantasy means that Ovid's poem bears a strong resemblance to Freud's antifoundationalist theory of polymorphous "perversity" in the *Three Essays on the Theory of Sexuality*. Indeed, one may wonder about the infinite variety of objects in Ovid's poem whether Laplanche's reformulation of Freud's hypothesis in *Three Essays* doesn't apply, as well, to the *Metamorphoses* – that is, whether sexuality in the poem isn't, "from the beginning, without an object."[75]

One therefore may wonder whether the myriad narratives of this love or that love aren't about objects at all but are, rather, fantasies invented to answer primary questions. That is, fantasies work to explain, and to cover over, a traumatic misfiring between experience and understanding (what Lacan calls "the Real" and what Petrarch, as we shall see in the next chapter, represents as love's constitutive blindness to its own history). As Laplanche comments with evident pertinence to a poem devoted to etiological myths, original fantasies, "like myths," claim "to provide a representation of, and a solution to, the major enigmas" that confront us as we enter into language and culture: "whatever appears to the subject as something needing an explanation or theory, is dramatized as a moment of emergence, the beginning of a history."[76] Taken as a whole, the dizzying erotic permutations of the *Metamorphoses* make the poem seem less a fixed representation of gender, difference, and desire than a series of originary histories that are offered, albeit provisionally, as ways of explaining the overwhelming, traumatic nature of *amor*. Certainly the poem's fascination with the phantasm of bodies "in bits and pieces" suggests that sexuality remains, for Ovid, fundamentally traumatic.

Of the *Metamorphoses*' many ruined bodies, however, Orpheus' is one that speaks eloquently to the poem's contradictory rhetorical and libidinal currents. Son of Apollo who equates rape and *amor*, Orpheus' "moving" voice carries on the poem's masculinist dream of animation; but he also pays dearly at the hands of the Bacchae for embodying this performative dream of a voice that can change the world. His *membra* lie scattered on the stream, his dying tongue still moving in his severed head as sign of the poem's mournful distance from its own fantasy about the voice's power: "flebile lingua / murmurat exanimis, respondent flebile ripae" ("mournfully the exanimated tongue murmured, and the banks mournfully responded" 11.52–53). At the same time, Orpheus' own erotic history – turning away from all women once one woman has died to give his "love to tender boys" – recalls the misogyny of his character, Pygmalion, and mirrors Ovid's homosocial gesture of replacing Orpheus' dying address to Eurydice in the *Georgics* with his own final apostrophe to Orpheus. And yet the momentary fit between Orpheus' homoeroticism and poetic homosociality is fleeting. Apollo's son goes on to sing a song teeming with discordant, unruly, and polymorphous desires that challenge the heteronormative rules governing the poem's metarhetorical story of rape and homosocial contest. "Author of giving love to tender boys,"[77] Orpheus begins with his father's own shifting erotic allegiance – his grief for the lovely Hyacinthus – and then convincingly impersonates, in turn, a man's passion for his statue; a daughter's unquenchable lust for her father (Myrrha); a goddess's fearful plea to her beloved boy (Venus); and the conflicting desires of a young man in love with a woman who might bring him death and the woman who is herself torn between her deadly contest for chastity and unexpected love for a *puer* (Hippomenes and Atalanta). Standing in the contradictory crosscurrents of the poem's libidinal as well as symbolic economy, Orpheus' scattered body and dying tongue attest to the Ovidian subject's internal contradictions – as subject of language and of desire.

But Ovid's narrator does more than conduct a thematic critique of gender, more than simply pry apart the seemingly inevitable or "lawful" relationship between genders, desires, and objects. He accompanies this critical dramatization of what desires count as lawful with the equally unsettling rhetorical practice of ventriloquism (or, as Quintilian and the declaimers might have it, *prosopopoeia*). Just as Orpheus gives a convincing voice to the passions of Myrrha, Venus, and Atalanta, the poet who would write the many "female" letters of the *Heroides* is also constantly engaged in a process of cross-voicing over the course of his epic. Perhaps the *Metamorphoses*' most resonant figure for its narrator's penchant for transgendered *prosopopoeiae* is Tiresias, the "seer" in the poem who inhabited both a male and a female body. We've seen that Ovid's zero-sum game of rape and revenge provides a powerful (and powerfully influential) definition of what it means to occupy a male or a female body. And yet, his narrator so often speaks "as a woman" during the course of narrating a rape – speaks, for instance, in the voices of Calliope, Philomela, Arethusa, Arachne, Caenis – that his means of telling the story unsettles the very differences that this deeply cultural form of sexual violence appears to confer. Indeed, the frequency with which Ovid tells the story of rape in a woman's voice reminds us how profoundly our sense of the meaning of what counts as male or female depends for its definition upon the other gender; such consistent cross-voicing enacts an elliptical critique of identity reminiscent of the one proposed by the psychoanalytic view of "sexual difference."

To take full stock of the poem's libidinal economy, in short, it is crucial to remember that its various dissonant female sounds, tongues, and lips – those of the Bacchae, Medusa, Syrinx, Echo, Daphne, Philomela, and others – are just as much surrogate figures for Ovid's narrator as those more tuneful voices attributed to Apollo, Pygmalion, Orpheus, or Pan. By remembering them, we come to see that Ovid's transgendered *prosopopoeiae* disturb the story of gender identity, difference, and desire that the poem's repeated narrative of rape produces. Taken overall, the many voices in Ovid's poem speak *against* each other. Rather than coalescing into one authorial voice, the poem's many voices speak against this compelling fantasy, alienating the fictions of identity (for both voice and sexuality) from within the very stories that also propose them. But that *clamor* need disturb us only if we subscribe to a view of fixed identity, gender, and desire that Ovidian rhetoric continually puts into question.

I may bring my reading of the *Metamorphoses* to a close by returning to the figure of Philomela's severed *lingua*. Like the figure of Medusa's mouth, I take Philomela's tongue to be emblematic of the work that Ovidian ventriloquism performs – as a kind of ongoing internal critique of the poem's own rhetorical and libidinal economies. For when Philomela protests Tereus' rape, her outcry does more than register yet another protest against sexual violation. It also allows the narrator to interrogate his own position as author by using Philomela's severed tongue to signify his own contingent relation to the text. That is, Ovid's narrator engages in a provocative act of cross-voicing that relies on a highly charged sense of sexual difference that it also confounds. The enraged "tongue" that speaks out against rape is, and is not, Philomela's; it is, and is not, Ovid's. "Her" moving but voiceless *lingua* becomes a terrible indexical sign of sexual difference, the violent residue of rape. But at the same time, it is also a sign for the narrator, striving through this speaker to find words that will capture an event that is *nefas*, "beyond speech." Signifying the narrator's predicament as well as Philomela's – how to speak about the unspeakable – the severed tongue marks an elliptical movement of "differential articulation" that makes each gender's story begin to revolve around the other's.[78] Justifiably famous for such acts of cross-voicing – the monologues of Byblis, Myrrha, Medea, Hecuba, Scylla, to name a few beyond the ones examined here – Ovid's narrator engages in a series of transgendered *prosopopoeiae* that counters the violent story of absolute sexual difference (difference, we might say, unto death) with a more elusive, elliptical narrative of mutual determination. Ovidian ventriloquism reminds us that even in such predicaments of difference as the one conferred by rape, the fate and definition of one sex relies on that of its "other."

Through the anxious figure for authorship that is Philomela's murmuring *lingua*, moreover, the narrator reminds us that while our understanding of what the gendered body means (both culturally and personally) derives from symbolic structures – a *lingua* is at once an organ, the "tongue," and "language" – our bodies are nonetheless just as resistant to the differencing semiotics of culture as they are molded by them. Indeed, we could say that the figure of Philomela's *lingua* testifies to the discursive shape of *all* bodies regardless of the gendered "form" they take. Understood etymologically, the pun on *lingua* tells us that like the "dying" organ that follows in "the footsteps of its mistress" ("et moriens dominae uestigia quaerit" 6.560), our "tongue" returns to us, insofar as it can return, only after having taken shape and meaning through the tongue we have learned to speak. But read in context – the context of distance and protest – Philomela's murmuring tongue also suggests that despite language's shaping force, despite the "tongue" we are given with which to speak, signs of resistance against that culturally determined form remain to be read. Both the poem's protesting female voices – their tones of anger, sorrow, and complaint – and the narrator's fondness for adopting those voices as figures for his own situation as author powerfully register that resistance.

The figure of Philomela's murmuring tongue, like the other female tongues we have heard, testifies to the recurrent dislocations of Ovidian rhetoric. Understood in light of the larger ventriloquizing narrative in which it appears, her *lingua* signifies that our tongues are both makers and bearers of meaning, at once agents in language and subject to the linguistic agency of others. Perseus and Medusa, Narcissus and Echo, Orpheus and the Bacchae, Apollo and Daphne, Pan and Syrinx, the narrator and the reader: we have seen that each one of these partners defines the other, that each voice comes to signify in a complex, differential relationship that challenges any recourse to phonocentric notions of singular agency in discourse. A story like that of Philomela's *lingua*, murmuring its discontent while separated from its owner, is but one telling moment in a narrative highly conscious of its own ventriloquizing and elliptical maneuvers. And highly conscious, as well, of the destabilizing effect that these rhetorical turns may have on generally functional conceptions about both identity and gender. Her ventriloquized story speaks, as do these other stories, to the subject's phonographic alienation from its own voice. But her story also speaks to the poem's fiercely unresolved conflict over what the differences between human bodies mean. Along with the many other female figures for Ovid's contingent position as author of this text, Philomela's ventriloquized tongue tells us that the voices in the *Metamorphoses* may come to signify only at some considerable distance from the body whose coherence, meaning, and value we mistakenly take as immanent.

3　Embodied voices: autobiography and fetishism in the *Rime Sparse*

Writing in the name of love

Petrarch's complex encounter with Ovid's *Metamorphoses*, as critics of Renaissance literature know well, left an indelible mark on the history of European representations of the poet – particularly as that poet represented himself, or herself, as the subject of language and of desire. In rereading and rewriting Ovidian stories, Petrarch necessarily worked through a relationship fundamental to the *Metamorphoses'* poetic project: the mutually constituting, and mutually interfering, relationship between rhetoric and sexuality. Any attempt to account for Ovid's place in the *Rime Sparse*, therefore, will implicitly be commenting on rhetorical and erotic problems that ramify, extending throughout the mythographic lexicon of Renaissance poetic self-representation.[1] In order to examine how the rhetoric of Ovidian eroticism affects Petrarch's portrait of himself in love, I consider several Ovidian characters crucial to Petrarch's representation of himself as a "martyr" to an idol "sculpted in living laurel" (12.10; 30.27): Apollo, Pygmalion, Narcissus, Actaeon, Diana and, finally, Medusa.[2] In this chapter, I ask several related questions: precisely how – and with what formal and libidinal effects – does Petrarch read Ovid? What does that reading suggest about the relationship between language and sexuality in the *Rime Sparse*? And what does Ovid's presence in the *Rime Sparse* mean for the Petrarchan subject, particularly when the poet who would rival Pygmalion is tormented by language as well as desire? For Petrarch, like Apollo, gets his laurel leaf – a signifier in return for his impossible demand – but as soon as he reaches the tree, he finds only "such bitter fruit" that his "wounds" are more aggravated than comforted (6.13–14).

The characteristic turn to Petrarch's Ovidianism that affected the way future writers appropriated the *Metamorphoses*, of course, was his project of adapting Ovidian figures to his own epideictic purpose by turning them into figures of his own story. The sheer metamorphic virtuosity of Petrarchan autobiography in the first canzone (23) suggests how profoundly autobiography would become, in the poetry of "Petrarchism," a gravitational center anchoring the difficult, often violent, certainly labile relationship between rhetoric and sexuality in the *Metamorphoses*. But Petrarch, by writing that the "first laurel" casts its shadow over all other "figures" (23.167–69), defines himself through a desire that Ovid saturates in the vagaries of language. The story of Apollo and Daphne – as the god of poetry violently, erotically, but nonetheless poetically "breathes" down her neck and yearns to "arrange" her tangled hair – concisely captures Ovid's penchant for turning stories about bodily "form" into commentary on poetic form. For Ovid characterizes the extremity of Daphne's reluctance linguistically – "immediately, the one loves but the other flees *the name* of love" – just as he turns her "beauty" to poetically useful purpose: Daphne's *forma* provokes the god of poetry and so it is her *figura* that she prays to lose (1.489, 530, 547). Indeed, the struggle between "the one and the other" (*alter* and *altera*) becomes as much one of the god of poetry's ability to *persuade* Daphne as to catch her. But his prayer breaks off with words "imperfect," for though he "would have said more," she runs away too quickly. In this metarhetorical scene of failed persuasion, Ovid systematically couples the erotic story with various aspects of rhetorical speech. He turns to trope by making Daphne's *figura* the body and the "figure" that the god of poetry wants – Apollo's similes being the verbal means deployed to lay his hands on that figure – and shifts from tropological to semiotic self-reflection when Apollo plucks the laurel, the sign for poetry.[3] His ensuing paean then plays on the much loved palindrome in Latin on the words for love and for Rome (AMOR-ROMA) after he plucks the laurel leaf from another anagram: the branches, or RAMOS, of her tree. That one needs to account for the collapse of the rhetorical and the sexual becomes somewhat brutally clear when one remembers that Latin writers use *ramus*, or branch, as a euphemism for the penis.[4] Following in Apollo's footsteps, Petrarch too would generate poetry from anagrammatic play on the actual letters of his laurel tree.[5] Ovid's text, in forging a connection between body, desire, and language – witness the frequent metalinguistic puns on *forma*, *figura* and *membra* – constantly confronts the violence latent in both rhetoric and sexuality. Yet the *Rime Sparse* poses a question underlying the *Metamorphoses* with new urgency: in Petrarch's internal landscape of Ovidian stories, the question becomes, what precisely is the poet's place, as a subject, in relation to the often violent interplay between language and *eros*? The much studied figure of Actaeon, suspended between his vision of beauty and the dismemberment attending his loss of voice, attests eloquently enough to the complexity of this intersection in both poems: "and still I flee the belling of my hounds" (23.160).

Although numerous artists in the *Metamorphoses* become surrogates for the narrator,[6] and such stories as Apollo's or Pygmalion's seem to comment on and to complicate that narrator's continuing and intense self-reflection, Ovid nonetheless distances himself from the erotic component of his own stories. No longer declaring himself, however ironically, "master" of erotic experience (*magister* in the *Ars Amatoria*) or victim of love (as in the *Amores*), the narrator of the *Metamorphoses* weaves no erotic fiction for himself. The narrator's distance – his habit of directing attention away from eros and violence as content to the violence and erotics of signification – is differently worked into the texture of Petrarch's exclusively, even obsessively, poetic relationship to Laura. Of course, his allusions to the *Metamorphoses* shape a persona very different from Ovid's narrator, for Petrarch weaves a new, suffering "voice" by directing Ovidian irony against himself. In the *Rime Sparse* a distance seems to surface *within* the poetic subject, pitting the self against itself, rather than, as in Ovid, *between* the narrating subject and his erotic stories.[7] In Petrarch's hands, Actaeon's dismemberment becomes an emblem of his internal condition. Such a distance within – named by turns error (*errore*) or exile (*'l duro esilio*) – might, in a Christian vocabulary, be called a sense of sin. In psychoanalytic terms, it might be called the effects of denial or the splitting of the subject.[8]

By shifting to a psychoanalytic account of the signifying subject, however, I aim to do more than experiment with another way of reading Petrarch's self-alienation. Looking behind the Augustinian frame for Petrarch's linguistic and erotic predicament to focus instead on the Ovidian figures with which Augustine may seem to be at odds, I am emphasizing the aspect of Petrarch's self-portrait that transgresses the theological discourse within which his semiotic and erotic project is often read. I stress the Ovidian texture of Petrarch's "martyrdom" to a figure and bring psychoanalytic theory to bear on that intertextual relationship in order to explore the complex connection between rhetoric and sexuality without subsuming one to the other. But I am also suggesting something specific about the Petrarchan subject: precisely by reaching back to Ovidian metamorphosis as a way to counter the discursive logic of conversion, memory, and right reading that governs "Augustinus'" understanding of the self,[9] Petrarch's specifically autobiographical revision of Ovidian stories paradoxically produces a discourse of the self in love that looks forward to the alienated linguistic subject, and the story of its desire, adumbrated by recent psychoanalytic theory. Where in the *Secretum* Augustinus says of his conversion "I was transformed into another Augustine" ("transformatus sum ... in alterum Augustinum"), one realizes when reading canzone 23 that in calling this a transformation,

Petrarch uses the very verb that evokes Ovid's metamorphoses: *trasfor-mare*.[10] In contrast to a past split that produced two Augustines – *transformatus sum* signalling the difference between a narrating and a narrated self – the poet-as-Actaeon writes, "I *am* transformed" (159). He thus modifies the temporality of Augustine's autobiographical division into two selves with an Ovidian representation of subjectivity *as* crisis: the poetic subject is caught in a continual process of metamorphosis, "a mean between living and dead" ("mezzo ... tra vivo et morto," 89). Neither this nor that, the poet rivals many an Ovidian subject's anguish when caught between forms. A *spirito doglioso*, he is trapped in a process of self-alienation that includes the very process of writing about that self: "I shall speak the truth; perhaps it will appear a lie, for I felt myself drawn from my own image and into a solitary wandering stag from wood to wood *quickly I am transformed* (*mi trasformo*) / and still I flee the belling of my hounds" (159–60). The difference between *transformatus sum* and *mi trasformo* marks a shift from autobiography divided between a narrated and a narrating self to autobiography as a continuing process of metamorphosis in which the self's alienation through trans-formation includes the very attempt to write a history of the self. This continuing disjunction emerges most forcefully in the *Rime Sparse* as forgetting and repetition. Both suggest that the self's inability to totalize or transcend – an inability modeled on time's differential movement in Augustine's *Confessions* – is the condition of memory and of writing.[11] The effect of this transforming process becomes most resonant for a psychoanalytic understanding of the signifying subject when Petrarch, complaining of martyrdom, claims he can neither relinquish the "one" figure that torments him nor remember, though he try, the whole of his own history: "And if here my memory does not aid me as it is wont to do, let my torments excuse it and the one thought which alone gives it such anguish that it makes me turn my back on every other and makes me forget myself beyond resistance" (15–20). With this painful fixation on an idolized sign that forces the self to "forget" itself we might compare Freud's theory of the unconscious – the blind spot that nonetheless shapes one's desire.

In the *Confessions*, the autobiographical text that profoundly influ-enced Petrarch's poetic practice, Augustine represents desire as cause and effect of language: for Petrarch, as for Augustine, "language engenders desire, and it originates in desire."[12] But the question still remains how one is to read this language. For the sense that language both constitutes and impoverishes the self – which Petrarch certainly shares with Augus-tine – fuels many of Petrarch's favorite stories from the *Metamorphoses*. Throughout Ovid's poem, some kind of figure, representation, or sign intervenes between a subject and his or her world, forever altering that relationship. In the stories of concern here, an *imago* "like a statue" (*signum*) falls between Narcissus and any other lover, a statue (*simulacrum*) falls between Pygmalion and womankind, and a laurel leaf as a sign for poetry bars Apollo from the beautiful figure of his desire. While such intervention directs attention to the beauty of the "form" in question, the subject's captivation with this form also gives rise to an absence – or better, an indefinite postponement – that nonetheless seems to constitute the subject. Thus Apollo becomes "himself" – produces an epideictic poem rather than *verba inperfecta* – when he receives a signifier in return for his demand for love. In the scene anticipating Petrarch's conversion of Laura as absent referent into linguistic absence, the only thing the god actually gets for the body he demands is the laurel leaf as "his" signifier. Daphne's resistance, we might say, is moved within, displaced in the scene's seeming resolution, for this signifying "closure" withholds as much as it gives. As the leaf replaces Daphne's body – the literal object Apollo said he wanted – a certain refusal of his demand is reified, turned into a signifier. The laurel leaf signifies poetry and, since it is part of an etiological story, its origin in Daphne's refusal. When the laurel replaces bodily form, the poem shifts attention from the absent referent to the absence that constitutes signification.[13] The Ovidian narrative crucial to Petrarch's self-portrait shadows the displacements founding desire in language when Apollo stops demanding an object (even as a tree she recoils from his kisses) and turns his demand for love into discourse, which takes the form of a poem in praise of something *other* than Daphne (Rome).

Addressing himself to this question of desire in language, John Freccero offered a powerful account of Petrarchan idolatry by reading the linguistic condition of the self in Augustinian terms, contrasting the *Rime Sparse* with Augustine's attempt to render the world intelligible by grounding language and desire in God as "the ultimate end of desire." To Augustine, Petrarch's pose would be "deliberately idolatrous," challenging the allegorical project of right reading: on Freccero's account, Petrarch undermines the "fig tree," the allegorical conversion story, by remaining with the laurel, the "autoreflexive" story of idolatry. Deploying the distinction between right and wrong reading in *De Doctrina Christiana*, he writes that Petrarch is self-consciously guilty of enjoying what he should use: "to deprive signs of their referentiality and to treat poetic statement as autonomous, an end in itself, is [Augustine's] definition of idolatry." Freccero thus reads Petrarch's idolatry – his dream of "an autonomous universe of autoreflexive signs" – according to a "theological problematic."[14] But the *Rime Sparse*, I have been

suggesting, offer another frame of reference for reading linguistic idolatry: the rhetorically self-conscious world of the *Metamorphoses*, whose
characters appear in the cycle as so many figures for the laurel, the "first
figure" of the poet's adoration (23.167). When Petrarch represents his
own condition through Pygmalion's formally mediated fascination with
himself – *operisque sui concepit amorem* ("with his own work he falls in
love" 10.249) – his allusion to the elaborately and explicitly sexual
rendition of "idolatry" in the Ovidian sense asks critics to think again
about the discourse of verbal fetishism. For Petrarch concludes the
paired sonnets on Simone Martini's painting of Laura by alluding to a
distinctly sexual subtext for his love:

> Quando giunse a Simon l'alto concetto
> ch'a mio nome gli pose in man lo stile,
> s'avesse dato a l'opera gentile
> colla figura voce ed intelletto,
>
> di sospir molti mi sgombrava il petto
> che ciò ch'altri à più caro a me fan vile.
> Però che 'n vista ella si monstra umile,
> promettendomi pace ne l'aspetto,
>
> ma poi ch' i' vengo a ragionar con lei,
> benignamente assai par che m'ascolte:
> se risponder savesse a' detti miei!
>
> Pigmaliòn, quanto lodar ti dei
> de l'imagine tua, se mille volte
> n'avesti quel ch'i' sol una vorrei!   (78)

When Simon received the high idea which, for my sake, put his hand to his stylus,
if he had given to his noble work voice and intellect along with form

he would have lightened my breast of many sighs that make what others prize
most vile to me. In appearance she seems humble, and her expression promises
peace;

then, when I come to speak to her, she seems to listen most kindly: if she could
only reply to my words!

Pygmalion, how much you must praise yourself for your image, if you received a
thousand times what I yearn to have just once! (translation modified)

Petrarch compares this visual *figura* to the poet's written *figura*, the "idol
sculpted in living laurel."[15] As is usual with Petrarch's veiled eroticism,
"that which" Pygmalion "received a thousand times" seems not to refer
to sexual favors (which crown Pygmalion's activities in the *Metamorphoses*), but merely to the lady's verbal response. When he turns away
from the blunt sexuality of Ovid's scene, that which the poet would have
"just once" – words – seem themselves to become erotic. As with Apollo,

Petrarch substitutes words for sexual relations. But in a further turn toward Pygmalion's love for his sculpted *simulacrum*, linguistic form usurps bodily form when this verbal artist makes words themselves the objects of his desire.

It is because of Pygmalion's rather startling literary career, the sheer persuasiveness of his poetic-erotic project, that I think a feminist and psychoanalytic reading is called upon to study the considerable literary appeal of fetishism. For feminist criticism, as many have argued, might have much to gain by reconsidering the poetic inscription of subject–object relations according to a linguistically attuned psychoanalytic theory. By means of this fetish, Laura is preserved, as Daphne for Apollo, or the statue for Pygmalion, for her lover's exclusive "use" – a use that conforms itself with stunning instrumental virtuosity (and considerable Ovidian irony) to exactly the shape imposed by the subject: like wax, the statue warms to Pygmalion's fingers, becoming "usable through use itself" ("ipsoque fit utilis usu," 10.286). In his apostrophe to Pygmalion, Petrarch figures an Augustinian understanding of idolatry through an intensely Ovidian meditation on the self's love for the figures of its own making. In Ovid's poem, Petrarch discovers not only idolized or reified signs (Augustine's sense of idolatry), but a peculiarly self-reflexive idolatry: in the stories of Narcissus and Pygmalion, the fixated subject is himself the author of the figure or sign he adores.[16] In the *Secretum*, Petrarch makes amply clear that for him Pygmalion's fixation on the ivory image of his own making recapitulates the predicament of Narcissus, frozen in front of the "image" of his own "form" (3.416). In Ovid's text, Narcissus' story does obliquely anticipate Pygmalion's sculpture: Narcissus freezes before his *imago* and is himself compared to a statue, "a figure (*signum*) formed from Parian marble" (419). The precise symmetry of these two stories, in which either the loving subject or the beloved object may be a statue, anticipates the mirroring reversals that characterize the relationship between Laura and her author.

From a subject like a sculpture to an object that is a sculpture, Ovid's stories of Narcissus and Pygmalion are implicated in each other: through the story of the statue, of becoming inanimate or animate, love for oneself as an "other" and obsessive love for oneself in another object are placed in complex chiasmatic relation to each other. Where looking at this sign or figure (*signum*) prompts Narcissus to declare *iste ego sum* only to dissolve in tears, Petrarch depicts himself as one similarly fascinated, to his harm, by an image. And so Augustinus refers to Simone's painting when he rebukes Franciscus not merely for loving an image for its own sake, but for loving himself, as poet, in that image:

"What could be more senseless (*insanius*) than that, not content with the presence of her living face, the cause of all your woes, you must needs obtain a painted picture by an artist of high repute, that you might carry it everywhere with you, to have an everlasting spring of tears, fearing, I suppose, lest otherwise their fountain might dry up?"[17] In this fetish, Narcissus and Pygmalion meet. Once again, Petrarch turns a dense Ovidian image to autobiographical account (weeping before a painting). In sonnet 78, moreover, the poet's imagined attempt to speak to the painting reminds us that these two stories were also about rhetoric, as both Ovidian lovers attempt to persuade, to invoke, or to move the image into a response by some kind of speech. Where Narcissus pleads his case with the *imago* itself, Pygmalion strikes upon a happier idea, turning away from the image to pray to Venus for a woman "like" his ivory maiden. In both cases, Ovid closely records the actual words the lover speaks to hold onto the image of which he is the author.

Such a fantasy as that of Pygmalion's animating success implicates the artists who use him in the very narcissistic relationship they outline. Ovid turned a story about a king in love with a statue into a story specifically about an artist's love for his own work; his version makes Pygmalion's a story about the artist's "escape into creative art from the defects of reality."[18] He then places Pygmalion's successful artistic endeavors in the frame of Orpheus' song: the sculptor's desire, and his success in giving life by giving form, thus become part of the wishful *fort-da* game of Orpheus' own desire.[19] And as we saw in the last chapter, Orpheus, for his part, is one of the *Metamorphoses*' most prominent figures for the rhetorical achievement to which the narrator aspires. In a similar, artistically self-reflexive move, Petrarch compares Pygmalion's desire to his own and in so doing, eroticizes his own words. But he does far more than this. In sonnet 78, Pygmalion himself turns into a very precise version of the poet. He becomes a love poet in the *epideictic* tradition. To Petrarch, Pygmalion's pleasure is more than pleasure: "Pigmaliòn, quanto lodar ti dei / de l'imagine tua" (literally, "Pygmalion, how much you must praise yourself for your image" [12]). This "lodar ti" casts Pygmalion in Petrarch's image, reminding the reader that Petrarch is indeed the poet of praise, the one who derives his poems and the name of his object from the same word: *lodare*, or the Latin *laudare*, is the etymological and literal basis for the changes on *laura* which generate the figures of the *Rime Sparse*. Petrarch thus becomes a consummate Pygmalion, as had Ovid before him, by reshaping a previous story into one made better because reconstituted in his image and thus made "useful through use itself."

Actaeon ego sum

Though the *Rime Sparse*'s structure of address gave a distinctive turn to the conventions of erotic description by which male poets in the Renaissance fetishized and dismembered the female body,[20] these conventions owe much to Ovid's rhetoric of the body. As soon as Apollo looks on Daphne, a *blason* seems to emerge: "He gazes at her hair ... he looks at her eyes gleaming like stars, he looks on her mouth ... he praises her fingers and her hands and her arms ... what is hidden, he believes even better" (1.497–502). This amorous look – and the enumeration of eyes, lips, fingers – would generate a long and varied literary history of erotic idealism. But it is important to remember that the *Metamorphoses* regularly fragments the human body and that dismemberment produces effects as horrifying as Apollo's gaze is idealizing. Thus Ovid frames Pygmalion's love for his *simulacrum* by recalling Actaeon's fate: when Pygmalion's narrator, Orpheus, dies, he is compared to "a doomed stag in the arena" falling "prey to dogs."[21] Whether violent (the death of Actaeon or Orpheus) or erotic (Apollo's lingering enumeration), dismemberment is one of the *Metamorphoses*' chief (dis)organizational principles as the narrator "turns his mind to tell of bodies changed into new forms" (1.1).

Petrarch reworks Ovid's rhetoric of body parts by incorporating it into the epideictic strategies of poetic autobiography. He captures the aesthetics and the violence of dismemberment in Ovid's poem: praising the body of Laura, as Apollo praises Daphne's, as so many beautiful parts, he also takes the story of Actaeon as his own. Where a fantasy of the *corps morcelé* – the "body in bits and pieces" – informs the *Rime Sparse*'s dismembered subject and fetishized object, so it frames the seemingly happy story of Pygmalion's *simulacrum*, for his narrator's *membra* are scattered, torn apart by instruments also "scattered" across the landscape (10.35, 50).[22] As Nancy Vickers suggestively argues in comparing Freud's theory of castration to Petrarch's "scattered rhymes," dismemberment and fetishism are part of the same amatory and defensive process.[23] According to Freud's simultaneously sexual and signifying etiology, Pygmalion's exclusive love for his statue, the object of his own making, would be a fetishistic love for a substitute – a transference of significant value from a prized body part to an external object that is henceforth required for gratification. Thus Pygmalion's *simulacrum* and Petrarch's *figura* eclipse the subject's interest in any other erotic investment: all pleasure (corporeal or aesthetic) is invested in this idol alone. Pygmalion's ivory maiden permanently replaces womankind in her maker's eyes; Petrarch is "governed" by Laura's veil only.[24] But as Freud makes clear, the fetish works precisely to defend against dismemberment – specifically, the dismemberment of castration. And it is this form of dismemberment, Vickers suggests, that the rhetoric of bodily fragmentation seems both to evade and to evoke.

What psychoanalytic theory shares with Ovid's and Petrarch's Pygmalion is a sense that while the fetish reveals much more about the loving subject than about the object with which he is captivated – remember that in Ovid the *simulacrum* is not named, while in Petrarch she takes her name from *his* rhetorical activity of praise – the fetish so absorbs the subject because it compensates for a profound disappointment with the "defects of reality." As we shall see, both Pygmalions suggest that the loving subject rejects the real world as deficient, incomplete. For Freud, of course, the fetish is both a memorial to, and an attempt to cover up, a particular lack that affronts the young boy's narcissistic investment in the form of his own body: the fetish replaces "a quite special penis that had been extremely important in early childhood but was afterwards lost. ... It is a substitute for the woman's (the mother's) phallus which the little boy once believed in and does not wish to forego." Symbol and symptom, the fetish signifies the price of masculine identity, for masculinity achieves its (always contradictory) coherence by acknowledging the law of exogamy. This taboo on incest, in turn, is personified in "the father." The fetishist, however, "attempts to substitute the rules of his own desire for the culturally predominant ones."[25] As his object-sign acquires "value" and "significance" by displacement, his devotion becomes an "artful" evasion of what the child "ascribes" to the father's "role."[26] A symbolic substitute – and symptom of a culturally demanded renunciation only nominally accepted – the fetish works by contradiction: it both affirms and denies the traumatic loss that it replaces (and preserves).

For Vickers, the "scattered rhymes" work according to this logic of fetishism, denying the very dismembering the poet practices and to which he alludes: "Woman's body, albeit divine, is displayed to Actaeon, and his body, as a consequence, is literally taken apart. Petrarch's Actaeon, having read his Ovid, realizes what will ensue: his response to the threat of imminent dismemberment is the neutralization, through descriptive dismemberment, of the threat. He transforms the visible totality into scattered words, the body into signs; his description, at one remove from experience, safely permits and perpetuates his fascination." The subject's memory (the play on *membra / ri-membra*) and the "body" of his poems are constituted by signs that "re-member the lost body" and thus, "like fetishes, affirm absence by their presence."[27] Here it is important to remember that the male child's "troubling encounter with intolerable female nudity" (103) is a cultural encounter with woman's body as it is read – and *given* significance – as "lacking parts." Woman's body is interpreted, that is, according to the taboo that legislates exogamy and that the sheer weight of cultural practice personifies in the father. If Freud's little boy sees a woman's body as dangerously mutilated, he does so because that body is offered to him to read as it has been rendered legible for him by a symbolic, not a natural, order. Legislated, that is, as that which comes to represent all those losses under the sign of what he may *yet* lose if he does not obey the law.[28] A symbolic cover for the lack the "male" subject wants to refuse but must "know" just the same to become socialized, the fetish allows him to love women by occluding their difference. The fetish is riddled with ambivalence, a historical relic of the narcissistic subject's attempt to retain his pleasure without submitting to the law of sexual difference through which "he" may come to be.

The Lacanian proposition – that sexual difference be read literally – is concisely distilled in the differential, enunciative structure through which the *Rime Sparse* so persuasively transmitted Ovidian stories: difference between *io* and *voi* depends on a difference between lau*ro* and lau*ra*. Pygmalion's fetish, however, would signal a certain resistance to the meaning attributed to this differential structure. And the *Rime Sparse*'s figures do indeed dismantle any simple gender identity. As both Giuseppe Mazzotta and Nancy Vickers rightly stress, the images for possible gender positions remain remarkably fluid. "If the analogy between Actaeon and the poet collapses," Mazzotta observes of madrigal 52, "he now insinuates he is like Diana. The shift of perspective is hardly surprising in Petrarch's poetry: he often casts himself, as is well known, in the role of Apollo and, in the same breath, casts Laura as the sun. The shift implies that the categories of subject and object are precarious and reversible."[29] In canzone 29, for instance, the poet becomes Dido: "My thoughts have become alien to me: one driven like me once turned the beloved sword upon herself" (29.36–9). Or in canzone 23, giddy transformations of gender are nonetheless articulated within a binary structure that shapes the fictions of a self represented as "male" or "female" by turns.[30] Defined by what Mazzotta aptly calls the "elliptical" structure of the *Rime Sparse*, the autobiographical subject's masculinity is always at risk, confronted with an other that is, by turns, his other *and* a mirror. Read psychoanalytically, dismemberment and idolatry suggest that the formal relationships of Petrarchan (and, by extension, Ovidian) poetics implicate the libidinal, and thus social, history of two different subjects resisting a tradition that is extremely consistent – rigid even – when it comes to representing the meaning and cultural value of sexual difference. But that entanglement of formal and historical concerns, however, will not be the history of conscious understanding (a history of ideas), but rather a study of its disruption – of the effect of a subject as it is produced in (an unpredictable) relation to a larger discursive field that is already laden with the weight of tradition.[31]

Like the story of Actaeon's dismemberment, Pygmalion's idol has struck many as having a phallic resonance.[32] In Ovid, Pygmalion's artistry is caused specifically by a flaw in womankind: after "seeing" female sexual crimes (the prostitution of the Propoetides), he carves his statue out of "disgust" for the "faults nature had so liberally given the female mind" (10.243–45). In the *Rime Sparse*, Petrarch renders his idolatry less specifically and rather more retroactively than Ovid's Pygmalion. But he nevertheless effectively conveys the sense that he finds the rest of the world impoverished by comparison: in his state of arrested infatuation, the poet "breathes many sighs," that, to him, "make what others most prize vile" (78.5–6). In the fiction of sonnets 77 and 78, of course, the poet is commenting on a painting of Laura by someone else's hand. Because he must distinguish Simone from other painters who have won fame "in the art of looking" in order to praise him as a painter of Laura (77.2, 5–14), the poet's explicit disdain is turned against a vague, general group of "others."

> s'avesse dato a l'opera gentile
> colla figura voce et intelletto,
>
> di sospir molti mi sgombrava il petto
> che ciò ch'altri à più caro a me fan vile.   (78.3–6)

... if he had given to his noble work voice and intellect along with form

he would have lightened my breast of many sighs that make what others prize vile to me.

This broad censure may include Simone's *figura*, the visual image being inferior to the poet's *figura*. Turned into a vague "something dear" or valuable "to others," that which is "vile" to the poet may also be understood specifically – that is, as other women, particularly in a poem that ends with an apostrophe to the artist who was "disgusted" with the female mind. But Pygmalion's particular distaste seems to have turned into a far more general disgust with worldly things. The poet's sweeping revulsion seems to have been produced by occluding its origin in the very specific distaste of Ovid's Pygmalion for what nature gave womankind; these lines seem to fashion the poet's disappointment by alluding only very evasively to Pygmalion's generative misogyny. True to the split in fetishistic pleasure, the poems to his painted idol affirm and deny their origin. Sonnet 78 relies on the Ovidian text, with its very specific reason for Pygmalion's creative act, and deflects attention from it by referring so very generally to "that which others most prize" as "vile to me." Similarly, Petrarch's self-designation as an Actaeon suspended *before* mutilation by his hounds hints at these contradictory, but nonetheless entangled, attitudes. Though invoked, Actaeon's dismemberment is never recounted in the *Rime Sparse*; this suspension renders his fate all the more indelibly as a dark subtext resonating beneath or beyond the cycle.

Taboo, and the punishment for violating it, informs the libidinal scene of both poems. As is frequently noted, Pygmalion's love for the image of his own making is not only fetishizing, it is incestuous. The artist himself does not "dare say" in his prayer what he really wants ("timide ... non ausus ... dicere" 274–6) and the desire of Myrrha for her father retrospectively casts some doubt over her grandfather's desire. When lying to her father to say she would like to marry someone "like" him, Myrrha quotes the words of her grandfather, Pygmalion, turning the narrative back on itself: Pygmalion's prayer, "'similis mea,' dixit 'eburnae'" reappears in her metrically identical answer, "'similem tibi' dixit at ille" (10.276, 364). Pygmalion and Myrrha employ the language of substitutes in order to avoid saying what is prohibited – that neither wishes, in fact, to enter into the play of substitutions at all.[33] This sense of violation, moreover, informs the visual and the vocal imagination of both poems. Petrarch's very rhymes, of course, violate Diana's injunction against speaking about what he has seen ("Make no word of this" [23.74]). Similarly, Ovid's story of Pygmalion exists precisely because of a violated prohibition on looking: Orpheus takes over the narrative of the poem, and tells the story of Pygmalion, only because he has lost Eurydice by disobeying Pluto's injunction not to "look back." We are thus able to read the narrative of Book 10 in the first place only because Orpheus disobeyed an injunction not to look. Recall, too, that the Actaeon story, central to the rhetorical and phantasmatic work of the *Rime Sparse* and echoed in the death of Orpheus, revolves around a taboo against looking. As Vickers suggests, criminal offense hangs heavy in the air when Diana forbids the intruder to speak about what he has, mistakenly, seen: "You would now tell the story of me seen before you, my robe put aside, if it were permitted that you be able to tell it" (3.192–93). The mountain on which unlucky Actaeon is torn to pieces is already "stained with the blood of many slaughtered beasts"; nymphs smite their breast and cry out when he enters the grove (143, 178). In the *Rime Sparse*, not only does the poet as Actaeon stumble on what he should not see, but he writes poems about what he should not tell.

As Freud conceived it, a fetish is a contingent, foundationally *acci-*

dental object attached to the traumatic scene of castration. Few texts, I might add, stress as repeatedly as the *Metamorphoses* that the occurrence and the object of desire are accidental: in the continuing narrative of that *amor sceleratus habendi* ("cursed love of having" 1.131), the emphasis falls heavily on the sheer transgressive force of *amor* rather than on the many objects desired. A statue or an image, that is, can become just as desirable as another human, and those human forms designated as forbidden by "law" easily become erotic.[34] In the story Petrarch chooses to represent his own desire, of course, the bad luck of stumbling across Diana naked proves fatal. *Fortuna* and *error*, the Ovidian narrator tells us, rather than *scelus*, are to blame. And so, in the *Rime Sparse* too, it is "the contingency of the encounter, the involuntary experience that Petrarch stresses."[35] Freud's account of fetishism is comparable to Ovid's and Petrarch's unlucky Actaeon because it is the accidental quality of the traumatic scene that founds the possibility of the "perception" of castration: "The setting up of the fetish seems to take its cue from a process which is reminiscent of the halt made by memory in traumatic amnesia. Here too interest stops on its way, perhaps at the last impression before the uncanny, traumatic one is seized as a fetish."[36] In Freud's exposition, a threat alone – and the eventual traumatic inscription in the subject of sexual difference as castration – produces in *some* males the socially sanctioned "normal" result of heterosexual desire. Thus I understand the ideological persuasiveness of the "experience" or "perception" of castration, or of the "truth" of sexual difference, according to a view of sexuality's traumatic and social character as set forth by Slavoj Žižek: "Ideology is not a dreamlike illusion that we build to escape insupportable reality ... it is a fantasy-construction which serves as a support for our 'reality' itself: *an illusion which structures our effective, real social relations and thereby masks some insupportable, real, impossible kernel.*" Not only will subjects never have a nonimaginary relation to their real conditions of existence (Althusser), but their representations (such tenacious "fantasy-constructions" as the Diana–Actaeon story) structure social relations so effectively precisely because they offer a means of evading or "masking" trauma – which, in Žižek's terms, amounts to the construction of the unconscious in the subject around the Law's "senseless" and "non-integrated" "injunction."[37]

Further reflection on the relationship between the poetic "I" and his linguistic practice suggests that Petrarch's verbal fetishism occludes another disappointment: although the beloved, like Daphne, disappears as the cycle's absent referent – her body ceding place to his letter – Petrarch's language is itself marked by the very absence it decries in the real world. Citing Freccero's assessment that Petrarch's language is "idolatrous in the Augustinian sense," Thomas Greene stresses that his remains a self-consciously failed attempt. Where Freccero allows that "pure auto-reflection of the sign" is impossible, Greene observes that "the question is whether this service" to the signifier *laura* "ever really works." Though Petrarch attempts to "create" himself in relation to the signifier, *laura*, "one might argue rather that he creates himself out of *failed* signifiers."[38] When it comes to Laura, his *ingegno* and *arte* are somehow "lacking" (308.12–14). Her absence as referent returns to haunt the language of the cycle as language's own lack: poetic-erotic melancholy repeats thematically as an erotic story what happens in actual semiotic practice.[39] Petrarch's differential signs – the difference between *lauro* and *laura*, or between *velo* and *vela* as self-reflexive signs for poetry – repeat the differential structure of the cycle itself. In an observation that describes Petrarch's lyrics in terms reminiscent of de Saussure's definition of the sign as a relational entity produced from a synchronic network of differences, Mazzotta writes: "each poem's autonomy is unreal ... the origin of each lyrical experience lies always outside itself ... and each reverses and implicates others in a steady movement of repetition." Rendering the logic of differentially produced signs explicit, the cycle evokes "plenitude and wholeness" only as they vanish; "emblems of origin" remain "unavoidably elusive."[40]

Such language about language as something that fails, or as a structure without an origin, suggests a further connection between the *Rime Sparse* and psychoanalytic theory. First, Lacanian theory and Petrarchan practice converge around the dismembered body "in bits and pieces," not simply as a theme or a symbol for erotic danger and desire – Actaeon as motif – but around the weaving of this story of sexual difference (as male visual trauma) into a specifically linguistic problem of meaning and structure.[41] In both, a synchronic network of differential, interdependent signifiers constitute a system in which any one element is meaningful only in relationship to what it is not. Absence haunts the erotic and the linguistic self-understanding of the cycle; the loss in one reflects loss in the other. The poetic form that most succinctly captures such a conception of semiotic functioning in the *Rime Sparse* is, of course, the sestina. The signifier, Lacan insists, is constituted in its absence from itself, an absence in which the subject, as a "speaking subject," is utterly implicated. It is in the translation of a linguistic into a sexual scene that Lacan locates the work of culture: "The phallus is our term for the signifier of his alienation in signification," by which he means to suggest that "it is in the *name of the father* that we must recognize the *support* of the symbolic function which, from the dawn of history, has identified his person with the figure of the law."[42] On this account of the signifying subject,

Petrarchan self-consciousness concerning his words' failure and his own linguistic "exile," receives the support of "the name of the Father" in the form of Actaeon and the prohibition on the female body in the form of a naked Diana.

Ovid and Petrarch place particular stress on the linguistic crisis from which dismemberment follows, or better yet, to which it is compared. As we saw earlier, Petrarch's allusion to Actaeon's vision replaces a past conversion into two selves (*transformatus sum*) with a continuing crisis of metamorphosis (*mi trasformo*). This Ovidian crisis includes the attempt to write an autobiographical account of the self's continuing alienation from itself. After he "stood to gaze on" the only sight that "appeases him," the poet undergoes a transforming process continuous with the moment of writing:

> ... l'acqua nel viso co le man mi sparse.
> Vero dirò; forse e' parrà menzogna:
> ch' i' senti' trarmi de la propria imago
> et in un cervo solitario et vago
> di selva in selva ratto mi trasformo,
> et ancor de' miei can fuggo lo stormo   (23.155–160)

... she sprinkled water in my face with her hand. I shall speak the truth, perhaps it will appear a lie, for I felt myself drawn from my own image and into a solitary wandering stag from wood to wood quickly I am transformed and still I flee the belling of my hounds

In a canzone whose every word transgresses Diana's foundational command – "make no word of this" – the poet's own shape is drawn, like his words, away from its "proper image" ("la propria imago"). No sooner is he returned to his earthly body ("terrene membra," 151) than he must flee his hounds; no sooner does he wish to coincide with his utterance than his words appear to lie. Where the speaker remarks that he was returned to his body only that he might suffer more (152), the dual figure of the *imago* also implies that the language in which he finds himself serves the same purpose – to increase his torment. Drawn from a *proprio imago*, an "image" in both a linguistic and a corporeal sense, the poet uses bodily disfigurement to figure the linguistic error of which the poem speaks and from which it cannot escape ("Vero dirò; forse e' parrà menzogna"). For as itself a poetic figure, the vanishing "proper image" reinscribes the very problem to which it refers.

In Ovid's text, dogs tear Actaeon's flesh because he cannot say his own name – because Diana's prohibition interferes between the subject and a language that, quite literally, is no longer merely his instrument, no longer the transparent medium of his intention: "He longs to cry out, 'I am Actaeon (*Actaeon ego sum*). Know your master.' But words fail his spirit (*uerba animo desunt*); the air resounds with barking" (III.229–30). This is the linguistic crisis that becomes the very condition of poem 23: "Make no word of this." The horror in Ovid's scene is attached, as much as anything else, to the way the sound of human words recedes before the sound of hounds barking. But, as Lacan would suggest of this not-speaking, "no one would think of that ... if there weren't beings endowed with an apparatus for giving utterance to the symbolic ... so as to make one notice it." One might ask, why are animals represented as beings that don't speak? Because of the human habit of projecting itself as a signifying subject: "You only know what can happen to a reality once you have definitively reduced it to being inscribed in a language."[43] Because his mouth changes to a stag's, Actaeon cannot pronounce his *nomen* and the subject is lost before the barbarity of the nonsignifying animal world. Further, it is on the change in the shape of Actaeon's lips that the representation of canine "reality" hangs: before Actaeon's metamorphosis, each dog achieved a quasi-human status because he, too, bore a name given by his master. Ovid draws out the pathos of the hunter hunted, increasing the barbarity by citing every name no longer available to Actaeon: "While he hesitates he sees his hounds ... Melampus and keen-scented Ichnobates are the first to give signals by barking ... then others run faster than the quick wind: Pamphagos and Dorceus and Oribasos ..." and so on (206–25). At the intersection between human and nonhuman, the signifying and the nonsignifying, the dogs appear all the more inhuman precisely because, once personified by names and trained by "signals," they now devour the speaker who defined each in a community founded on a rudimentary sort of language. When *Actaeon ego sum* literally fails to work, the dogs lapse back into a state understood only in relation to not-speaking, or "known," as Lacan puts it, once "reduced to being inscribed in a language." In this soon to become emblematic crisis of identity, we should recall Lacan's position that the subject represents itself as a subject for "the Other," which is not another subject, but another signifier. This is what Actaeon is trying to do – to use a signifier (Actaeon) to represent himself, as a subject, for another signifier (in this case, the other names for his hounds). But all he gets in return is barking because his lips cannot form that word and the dogs, once personified through signifiers of their own, literally cannot recognize the "sound" that "though not human, is still one no deer could utter" ("gemit ille sonumque,/ etsi non hominis, quem non tamen edere possit/ ceruus" 237–39). If one is defined retroactively as a subject by means of the differential movement of the signifier within a system of exchange with other speakers, it is because one's address to another requires the impersonal intervention of the Other. In this intervention, the fact of getting an answer or meeting with silence on the part of the actual interlocutor is beside the point: it is to the chain of signification in which both parties are assumed to be embedded, as subjects, that the signifier is addressed.[44]

The proper name – crucial to Actaeon's linguistic impasse – is also crucial to Ovid's representation of his place as a subject, as author, in his text. As we have seen, Ovid often inscribes his own name in his work. At the end of the *Metamorphoses*, he imagines his own permanence by way of signifiers: his name (*nomen*) and his work (*opus*) will survive because readers will read his text aloud. In the *Tristia*, he compares himself to Actaeon as someone who saw something he shouldn't only to distinguish himself as one who managed to achieve a name recognized by a "crowd of learned men": "grande tamen toto nomen ab orbe fero, / turbaque doctorum Nasonem nouit" ("I bear a great name throughout the world, and a throng of learned men recognize Naso," 2.119–20). In claiming a place as author, Ovid repeatedly represents himself as a signifier – a *nomen* heard throughout the world. In both the *Metamorphoses* and the *Tristia*, moreover, he offers this signifier to an audience who, in contrast to Actaeon's hounds, are fully signifying subjects (readers who are "learned"). Like Petrarch, who represents himself as a *lauro* in poems addressed to *Laura*, Ovid's favorite way to represent himself as author is as a signifier for the Other.

This shared habit of self-representation means that Actaeon becomes a very dark figure for authorship in both poems. Actaeon's failure to control language – his being controlled by the words usually taken to be instruments of the mind – is woven into a story of a prohibited looking that causes bodily dismemberment. As Jane Gallop observes, "castration for Lacan is not only sexual ... it is also linguistic: we are inevitably bereft of any masterful understanding of language, and can only signify ourselves in a symbolic system that we do not command, that, rather, commands us."[45] The Symbolic order is for Lacan a "phallic" order because linguistic absence is grafted onto a culturally organized sexual "absence." Such a theory could find few stories more apt than Actaeon's. The subject's sudden, unexpected imprisonment by the language he (mistakenly) assumed to be secondary or instrumental to thought is precisely what both the Petrarchan and the Ovidian Actaeon, in different ways, enact. But in taking up Actaeon's story as a figure for his own as a poet – which Ovid does in the *Tristia*, Petrarch in the *Rime Sparse* – each represents the condition of the poetic subject so that, as Žižek puts it, "the subject of the signifier is a retroactive effect of the failure of its own representation ... *the failure of representation is its positive condition*."[46]

It is not that there is more to "Actaeon" than he can say, that he exists somehow more completely outside the distortions of language. Rather, it is because he must represent himself as a signifier for another signifier – for the Other – that the lack that founds the possibility of this exchange becomes the "positive condition" for his existence as a subject.[47] The structure of address (Actaeon's to his hounds, Ovid's to his readers, Petrarch's to Laura) introduces the lack in the signifier by referring to the Symbolic network of language that is the condition of the possibility of both parties to the exchange. From a Lacanian perspective, it is no accident that the subject's precipitation in such a differential structure – his alienation from "him"self in signification – is rendered as a sexual story about seeing the female body as a trauma leading to a phantasm of the viewer's dismemberment. Nor is it an accident that so many future self-defining male writers used Actaeon's predicament as an emblem for their own condition. That story, however, would be precisely a "support" lent to the absence necessary to symbolic functioning, a support in which culture has, in practice, identified the "person" of the father "with the figure of the law" (though it need not). In Ovid's text, the scattered members of Pygmalion's narrator, Orpheus, recall those of Actaeon and qualify Pygmalion's happier fate. These *membra* remind one that culture's foundational story of sexual difference informs not only the erotic but also the linguistic project of both poems. That this horrible fate transcends personal pathology is suggested by the ever increasing popularity of Actaeon as a figure for expressing the inner condition of "man."[48]

The stories of Actaeon and Pygmalion suggest that the different forms of the human body – as given meaning by cultural laws – continue to cast a shadow over what might seem to be the most abstract formal, linguistic, and rhetorical concerns of both poems. Actaeon's story collapses bodily dismemberment into the disappearance of a name (in Ovid) or into the foundational distortions of poetic "images" (in Petrarch). Each poem reads the first in terms of the second, inscribing the accidental sight of a naked woman into "male" subjectivity realized *as* linguistic crisis. So, too, both Pygmalion stories weave desire into linguistic or rhetorical self-reflection, attesting to the body's continuing pressure on each poem's figurative strategies. In *The Ego and the Id*, Freud wrote that "the ego is first and foremost a body-ego." Of this evocative comment, Laplanche elaborates that the ego is an imaginary organ, a "projection or metaphor of the body's surface" that "is constituted outside of its vital functions, as a libidinal object." This body-ego would take its shape, moreover, "from the perception of a fellow creature," which "perception," I have argued, is inseparable from the social codes of sexual difference that give perception meaning.[49] A certain phantasm of the body's unity structures the subject's perception – but also its symbolic activity. In both poems, it is in the recurrent images of dismemberment, as well as in Pygmalion's fetishized statue, that one may recognize the ego of the writing subject.[50]

The art of looking

By focusing on Petrarch's Ovidian alienation from his own voice, we have understood that an unresolved struggle over the meaning of the human body in the *Rime Sparse* informs the cycle's figurative and rhetorical strategies. But we are also in a position to ask what Petrarch's representation of himself as alienated from his own tongue means for the nature of the poet's vision; his interrogation of the visual in relation to the verbal order repeats a similar investigation in Ovid's stories of Pygmalion, Narcissus, and Actaeon. Remember, then, that Petrarch's paired sonnets move between a poem in praise of a painting to one in search of that painting's missing words. The sequence opens with Simone's visual act:

> Per mirar Policleto a prova fiso
> con gli altri ch'ebber fama di quell'arte,
> mill'anni non vedrian la minor parte
> della beltà che m'àve il cor conquiso.
>
> Ma certo il mio Simon fu in Paradiso
> onde questa gentil donna si parte;
> ivi la vide, et la ritrasse in carte
> per far fede qua giù del suo bel viso.
>
> L'opra fu ben di quelle che nel cielo
> si ponno imaginar, non qui tra noi,
> ove le membra fanno a l'alma velo;
>
> cortesia fe', né la potea far poi
> che fu disceso a provar caldo et gielo
> et del mortal sentiron gli occhi suoi.   (Sonnet 77)

Even though Polyclitus should for a thousand years compete in looking with all the others who were famous in that art, they would never see the smallest part of the beauty that has conquered my heart.
But certainly Simon was in Paradise, whence comes this noble lady; there he saw her and portrayed her on paper, to attest down here to her lovely face.
The work is one of those which can be imagined only in Heaven, not here among us, where the body is a veil to the soul;
it was a gracious act, nor could he have done it after he came down to feel heat and cold and his eyes took on mortality.

From Simone's heavenly vision that transcends mortal eyes, the poet turns in the next sonnet to lament that Simone's painting neither hears nor responds to his address.

In pondering such interference between visual and verbal art,[51] Petrarch revisits a problem central to Ovid's narrative: the bereaved Orpheus sings a song that includes the story of Pygmalion's visual pleasure only after having himself disobeyed Pluto's command not to look back. Orpheus may either look on Eurydice or sing about her – but not both. From the disastrous, prohibited glimpse of Laura-as-Diana in canzone 23 to his praise for Simone's transcendent vision – "ivi la vide ... non qui tra noi" ("there he saw her ... not here among us") – Petrarch revisits the narrative trajectory of *Metamorphoses* 10 and 11. His engagement with Ovid's poem reminds us that both poets are writing, with infinite care, about the complex relationship between acts of writing and speaking and acts of looking. As we saw in canzone 23, Diana's injunction prohibits the Italian poet from gazing on the body he desires. But by rewriting Pygmalion's story in sonnets 77 and 78, Petrarch finds a mediated way to gaze at his idol. He can imagine getting a glimpse of Laura, that is, if he looks through one of two screens: Simone's painting or Ovid's poem. True to the double epistemology of fetishism, Laura's veil both has and has not been "stripped off." The poet may gaze on the painting as often as he likes, but veils of allusion and of paint still stand between his loving eyes and the figure that eludes him.

The "art of looking" in sonnets 77 and 78 recapitulates the difference between the position of Ovid's Orpheus (who sings only before and after his disastrous look) and that of Ovid's Pygmalion (whose art grants him the luxury of gazing upon his beloved). In other words, the narrative displacements of *Metamorphoses* 10 define Petrarch's visual desire in these sonnets: an unmediated glimpse of his beloved – the "Paradise" granted to Simon or to Pygmalion – will never be his own. Such a glimpse may be had only from an Orphic distance, in one artist's song about another artist's vision. Hovering between Orpheus and Pygmalion, Petrarch reads his own story out of the vacillation between one figure and another. Once again, the Ovidian narrator's ironic critique of a character in his poem (his knowledge that Pygmalion's story is but a phantasy) defines and divides the Petrarchan subject from within.

If we read sonnets 77 and 78 together, then, we understand that despite the idea of a heavenly vision, seeing is no more a transcendent experience than speaking for the autobiographical subject of the *Rime Sparse*.[52] In the first sonnet Petrarch writes about another man's visual paradise; and he certainly hopes to give himself a place among those other artists who compete in "the art" of looking. But by the end of the second sonnet, the desire to look on Laura ends by *depriving* the speaker of something important: "if only she could respond to my words" (78.11). The visual figure of Laura merely echoes Paradise. It cannot heal the "exile" or "death" that inhabits the poet's mind, art, and world. Indeed, the long shadows of several Ovidian prohibitions fall on Petrarch's version of the sculptor's infatuated gaze. Because he condenses so many Ovidian characters into a mythographic palimpsest of his own unhappy situation, Petrarch's unending desire to gaze on Laura is defined by Diana's taboo *and* Pluto's. The combined stories of Actaeon's and Orpheus' prohibited gazes tell us that this poet may see only the veil of Laura's painted or written *figurae*, never the woman herself. It is not merely that Petrarch and Ovid, as poets, prefer verbal to visual signs. These various love stories and the theory of fetishism both suggest, rather, that the preference for verbal over visual signs means that when it comes to being a speaking male subject, there is *something very wrong with looking*.

In the *Metamorphoses*, the fantasy of Pygmalion's gaze on his beloved is differently mediated, but even in his "success" story, mediation intervenes. Ovid's narrator, Orpheus, imagines a magical moment when the veil of sculpture slips away to reveal a woman's bodily form. He describes an idyllic moment when Pygmalion may touch, love, and look without the interference of a screen of any kind: "nec nuda minus formosa uidetur" ("no less beautiful is the statue naked" [10.266]). The line implies that Pygmalion can take off the statue's clothes as easily as he has put them on. But we cannot forget that this moment of her unveiling is narrated by the poet whose gaze on his beloved deprived him of the very presence he so anxiously desired. Because of the look forbidden by Dis ("ne flectat retro sua lumina .... flexit amans oculos" 51–57), Orpheus loses the Eurydice whom his voice had almost won. Because of the power of his voice, the infernal couple call Eurydice but after his look, "she instantly slipped into the depths" (10.57).

It may be tempting to suggest that Ovid resolves these displacements when Orpheus dies because at the end of his song (and his life), Orpheus is permitted precisely those things permitted his character, Pygmalion – to look and to touch. But at this point, a third voice intervenes: that of Ovid's narrator. In a scene that carries Orpheus' nostalgia for his mate into the poem's own discourse, the narrative turns round on itself, circling back around the pivotal figure of the rediscovered Eurydice. The narrator describes how Orpheus may now "look back" on Eurydice once more:

umbra subit terras, et quae loca uiderat ante,
cuncta recognoscit quaerensque per arua piorum
inuenit Eurydicen cupidisque amplectitur ulnis;
hic modo coniunctis spatiantur passibus ambo,
nunc praecedentem sequitur, nunc praeuius anteit
Eurydicenque suam, iam tuto, respicit Orpheus.   (11.61–66)

His shade fled under the earth and he recognized those places he had seen before, and searching through those fields of the blessed he found Eurydice and embraced her with loving arms. Here now both walk with conjoined steps, now he follows her as she proceeds, now he walks before her and now Orpheus may look back safely on his Eurydice.

Where his terrible mistake was to turn his eyes back, in death Orpheus repeats his act. But it is only after his soul has been exhaled through his mouth (Ovid's version of Petrarch's "non qui tra noi") that he may walk before her and look back ("re-spicere") without loss.

In this *re-* of *re-spicere*, Ovid involves Orpheus' visual act in his own narrative act as he "looks back" to the poem's earlier story. Indeed, the happy couple appear to embody the narrative's temporal disjunction: though "joined" in their steps, the two still walk apart. Ovid pictures them as she walks before him or as he before her ("uiderat *ante/* cuncta *re*cognoscit ... iam ... *re*spicit). The last line, too, captures the "look back" at the level of proper names. Ovid frames the line with Eurydice's name first and Orpheus's last ("Eurydicenque suam, iam tuto, respicit Orpheus"); the proper name Orpheus therefore "looks back" across the final line to the name of "his Eurydice." In other words, their union and Orpheus' visual pleasure must still be told sequentially, unfolded in sentences. Similarly, one name must always "follow the preceding" name ("praecedentem sequitur"). Although the scene conveys a desire for a here and a now ("nunc ... nunc ... iam"), such immediacy always evades Orpheus. In whatever situation he finds himself, the acts of speaking and of looking always interfere with each other. Orpheus' forbidden look was once the reason for his singing. And now, the moment of his safe looking must pass back to another voice – that of Ovid's narrator. As in the earlier scene, when Pygmalion's unimpeded view of his statue's "beautiful nakedness" was mediated through the voice of one who was forbidden such a view, this scene also carves out a certain deferral, a certain distance, in the now of Orpheus' imagined visual pleasure.

Wherever we enter Ovid's overlapping stories about artists who want to speak about the beauty they see, we find only displacement, deferral, and mediation. The story of Orpheus' transgressive gaze frames that of Pygmalion's gaze, one that risks transgression but is miraculously fulfilled because the artist does not "dare" utter the words that would actually say what he wants. It is the narrator, Orpheus, and not Pygmalion, who "utters" the exact words that Pygmalion fears to let pass his lips: "he did not dare say, 'my ivory maiden,' but said, 'one like my ivory maiden.' " When it comes to saying the actual words that reveal his desire, Pygmalion's voice slips away, ceding place to Orpheus'. Orpheus' voice occupies the ternary place from which a story like Pygmalion's can be told. Similarly, when Orpheus' own desire to look on Eurydice is fulfilled, the poem's narrative passes back to the narrator; his intervention allows the singer's transition from speaking back to looking. This is the Ovidian distance, this the narrative disjunction between the look and the voice, that Petrarch captures in the image of Laura's ever present veil. Laura's veil, the sign that he may not see everything, prompts poetry in praise of what it hides. An inescapable (linguistic) distance haunts the desire to look in both Ovid's and Petrarch's poems just as it haunts the desire for a speaking voice.[53] A consistent deferral of, and prohibition on, the now of visual pleasure persists in the way both poets represent Pygmalion's "success" story. In the visual register of both the *Rime Sparse* and the *Metamorphoses*, the misfiring that produces desire persists, in the Lacanian sense that desire is the remainder produced by demand because one must speak.

In Orpheus' song as much as Petrarch's *Rime*, of course, this misfiring is enabling: it generates considerable discourse about the failure of speech. If in canzone 23 the poet's voice falls away like Actaeon's, in sonnet 78 the lady's fetishized "form" seems to come to his aid in the form of Pygmalion's statue. Both the conceit of Laura's silent picture and the trope of apostrophe are the technical means by which the poet wrestles with the larger deferrals that language's written form insinuates into the imagined plenitude of "voice." As we have seen, the poem ends with a seductive figure, an apostrophe: "Pigmalión, quanto lodar ti dei / de l'imagine tua, se mille volte / n'avesti quel ch'i' sol una vorrei!" Silenced by Laura-as-Diana in 23, here the poet derives the fiction of his own speaking from *Laura*'s silence. Now it is the lady, not the poet, who is silenced by an image, a painted *figura*, whose very materiality seems to draw her from herself. In the painting, this would-be Pygmalion confronts a visual form that refuses vocal animation. It seems that the poet can throw his voice only so far:

> ma poi ch'i' vengo a ragionar con lei,
> benignamente assai par che m'ascolte:
> se risponder savesse a' detti mei!   (Sonnet 78)

... but then when I come speak to her, she seems to listen most kindly: if only she could reply to my words!

Here Petrarch stresses what critics often omit in discussing Ovid's version of Pygmalion. The statue-turned-maiden never speaks: the only "speaking" agency in Ovid's poem is the artist's – and the narrator's, as he articulates, through Orpheus' story and the story Orpheus tells, his own impossible demand for a poetics of animation.

Within the thematic frame of sonnet 78, Simone's painted "figure" seems to produce, by means of Laura's mute opposition, the fiction of the poet's voice. From a "figure" without "voice or intellect" Petrarch derives his own vocal performance, his apostrophe to Pygmalion. When Petrarch returns to Ovid's story of Pygmalion through the trope of apostrophe, such a figure for the poet's voice should make readers aware how deeply the fantasy of the living statue is a visual and tactile expression of the phonographic imaginary that shapes Ovid's rhetoric of animation. As Petrarch cannily reads Ovid in these lines, it is "intelletto" ("voce ed intelletto," 1.4) – the understanding mind or "animus" in Ovid – that his narrator's many projections of "voice" in the *Metamorphoses* are trying to bestow.

And so on first reading, we might think Petrarch achieves temporary relief (or closure to the poem's dilemma) by means of the fiction of vocal address to his more successful predecessor. Where in 23 Laura-as-Diana forbids his speech, in 78 it is she who remains as silent as a picture. Defined in eternal opposition, in a negative relationship to "Laura" in her many guises, here the poet produces an apostrophe in opposition to her silence. The reversal implies that the poet has the voice and "intelletto" that she lacks. On this reading, the final apostrophe would be quite enabling, a return from the melancholy writing about self-dispersal in writing, "non son mio, no." But this apostrophe, I submit, offers a solution that is, at best, provisional. Even as he invokes the fiction of his own speaking consciousness in contrast to her figural silence, the speaker's words recall the Ovidian narrator's irony about Pygmalion's delusion. And that undercurrent of irony turns the speaker, once again, against himself. For Petrarch uses a conditional clause to allude to Pygmalion's joy: "Pigmaliòn . . . *se* mille volte / n'avesti" ("Pygmalion . . . *if* you received a thousand times"). The "se" echoes the first "se" of the poet's own impasse, "se risponder s'avesse a' detti mei" ("if only she could reply to my words"). The position of the poet and of Pygmalion mirror each other syntactically; and Ovid's sculptor is recast in Petrarch's (unsuccessful) image. As we saw earlier, the Ovidian artist similarly enters Petrarch's poem in the shape of the epideictic poet, of one who uses the signifier "lodar" or "laudare" to "praise," as well as to enjoy, his statue ("quanto *lodar* ti dei"). We expect the "se" clause of the apostrophe to apply to Petrarch alone: if only I could have what Pygmalion had! But "*if* you received . . . what I yearn to have" applies here, instead, to Ovid's Pygmalion. In other words, the "fact" of his forbear's success becomes provisional, a matter of the loving artist's *desire* rather than his achievement.

The conditional wording of Petrarch's apostrophe therefore reminds us that Ovid tells the story of an inanimate "form" that responds to its maker's amatory address with considerable irony: "he gives kisses and *thinks* his kisses are returned" ("oscula dat reddique *putat*"). It is Pygmalion, not the narrator, who "*thinks*" the statue "wants to be moved."[54] What Petrarch recalls when he says "if" is the sculptor's deluded attribution of emotion to his statue. The apostrophe to Pygmalion relies, in part, on the idea of a moving voice, on the fiction of an Orphic voice that can animate the inanimate. But it simultaneously signals, because it says "if" – and because the entire scene is staged as the poet's frustrated wish – that this trope, along with Pygmalion's story, is a fantasy. Pygmalion's animating success with his "figure," evoked in the apostrophe, is the dream that everywhere else the poet tells us is impossible. One might say that the poem points to apostrophe as itself the illusion, acknowledged by the preceding stanza to be one: the poet knows very well that speaking cannot animate a figure. Like Pygmalion before him, the poet writes that "she *seems* to listen most kindly" ("benignamente assai *par* che m'ascolte"). But unlike his predecessor, the poet signals in his self-conscious allusion to Ovid's ironic narrator that such "seeming" response on the part of Laura's dumb and mute painting remains but his own deluded projection.

The concluding apostrophe, though offered as a kind of resolution, subtly points out its own lack of authenticity. This is the only kind of "voice" the poet finds. In sonnet 78, then, we find a fetishistic fluctuation over the poetic voice itself. "I know, but still . . ." captures both the wish and the irony subtending the rhetoric of animation. The only difference, though a crucial one, between the Latin and Italian poet is this: where Ovid usually embodies the epistemological split between two agencies (between the author and his characters),[55] Petrarch assumes both in one agency, carrying Ovidian irony within the voice of the writing "I." In her many guises, Laura – as the prohibiting Diana, as the mute statue – captures the poet's knowledge that his voice will fail, will never recuperate the deferrals of which and through which he "speaks." Within the apostrophe to Pygmalion – a trope that endeavors to project a voice that may then redound to the credit of the speaker – the allusion to Ovid's poem constitutes yet one more self-ironizing performance because the poet is doing what he knows very well to be an illusion.

If we attend to Petrarch's complex engagement with Ovidian rhetoric, then, we discover that it is not the thematics of speech and silence, nor the fact of one character's speech versus another's silence, that is most important for understanding the generative force of sexuality on the poetics of the *Rime Sparse*. Rather, the dilemmas confronting the poet when he "speaks" keep recalling the (Ovidian) pressure of prohibition and transgression – a pressure that shapes and interprets the male or female body for the gazing subject in a deeply cultural way. In the *canzone delle metamorfosi* and the apostrophe to Pygmalion, moreover, we have seen it is not the fact of Laura's speech or silence but rather the disruptive relationship *between* his voice and hers that matters most for understanding the implications of verbal fetishism. In sonnets 77 and 78, the poet's voice is both established and emptied out in its relation to Laura's mute picture. As Mazzotta observes of this deprivation, it is mutual: "Like Narcissus, who gazes at his reflected image – discovers that he, too, is a shadow – Petrarch looks at Simone's painting of Laura and 'sees' in it his own mute reflection."[56] Laura does not speak often in the *Rime Sparse*. But when she does, her voice commands unusual power. In canzone 23, when the poet translates Actaeon's linguistic crisis into the story of dismemberment, he does so because of a few simple words from her: "Di ciò non far parola." Out of Laura's words of taboo, Petrarch forges the portrait of himself as one condemned to try to look at and speak about what is forbidden. In other poems he calls the sound of Laura's voice "angelic" ("in voce ... soave, angelica, divina" 167.3–4) and claims that it draws him "like the sound of the sirens" ("di sirene al suono" 207.82). I therefore believe it is the *idea* of Laura's voice, if not the actual sound, that is foundational to the errancies of Petrarchan autobiography. Whether in speech or in silence, the trope of Laura's "voice" becomes a telling index of the poet's blindness to himself – to his own history and his own love – a blindness that goads him to still further attempts at self-representation.

Memorable monsters

One further Ovidian figure – Medusa – ominously captures Petrarch's sense that there would be something very wrong with looking at the beloved form that he claims he so much wants to see. This figure, of course, inverts the story of Pygmalion on which we've been concentrating. As Freccero aptly puts it,[57] Medusa's petrifying power attests to "Pygmalion's folly." In sonnet 197, for instance, the idea of turning to stone tells us that the speaker, rather than his beloved, resembles Pygmalion's statue: "ma gli occhi ànno vertù di farne un marmo," "but her eyes have the power to turn it [my heart] to marble" 197.14). Medusa is thus an extremely revealing figure for the discourse of verbal fetishism.

The first time Medusa appears in the *Metamorphoses*, Ovid calls her a "memorable monster" (4.615). We should understand *monster* in its primary sense here (from *moneo*, *-ere*, to point out, to warn) as a memorable "sign, portent or prodigy." In sonnets 51 and 197, Petrarch uses the figure of Medusa much as he does Actaeon or Pygmalion – to signal a complex autobiographical engagement with both the rhetorical and sexual registers of Ovid's *Metamorphoses*.

Although modern readings of Freud's "Medusa's Head" essay tend to associate Medusa with a strictly visual trauma, Petrarch's return to Ovid's Gorgon points, instead, toward a trauma that is both visual *and* oral. Before we can explore the dynamic interference between seeing and looking, however, we need to understand Medusa's effect on the thematics of sight in the *Rime Sparse*. In sonnet 51 – a poem that immediately precedes yet another famous allusion to Actaeon's vision of the naked Diana (52) – the poet avoids naming Medusa directly. But by alluding to a specific moment in Ovid's text (when Perseus uses the Gorgon's head against Atlas), he conjures her elusive presence and thereby is able to name himself. For Medusa's effect – petrification out of "fear" – allows him to inscribe the word "petra," or rock, that is his signature. Combining Ovid's story of Apollo and Daphne with that of Perseus and Medusa, the poem opens with a beautiful, dazzling sight only to close with a terrifying vision:

> Poco era ad appressarsi agli occhi miei
> la luce che da lunge gli abbarbaglia
> che, come vide lei cangiar Tesaglia,
> così cangiato ogni mia forma avrei.
>
> Et s'io non posso trasformarmi in lei
> più ch'i' mi sia (non ch'a mercé mi vaglia),
> di qual petra più rigida s'intaglia
> pensoso ne la vista oggi sarei,
>
> o di diamante, o d'un bel marmo bianco
> per la paura forse, o d'un diaspro
> pregiato poi dal vulgo avaro et sciocco;
>
> et sarei fuor del grave giogo et aspro
> per cui i' ò invidia di quel vecchio stanco
> che fa co le sue spalle ombre a Marrocco.

Had it come any closer to my eyes, the light that dazzles them from afar, then, just as Thessaly saw her change, I would have changed my every form,

And, since I cannot take on her form any more than I have already (not that it wins me any mercy), my face marked with care, I would be today whatever stone is hardest to cut,

either diamond, or fair marble white for fear perhaps, or a crystal later prized by
the greedy and ignorant mob;

and I would be free of my heavy, harsh yoke, because of which I envy that tired
old man who with his shoulders makes a shade for Morocco.

Nearly exhausted by desire, the poet claims to envy Medusa's first victim,
the "tired old man," Atlas (13), who was transformed into a mountain in
the fourth book of the *Metamorphoses*. Laura's dazzling visual form
reminds the poet of Daphne and Medusa at once. This troubling link
tells us that Laura's is a form he both wants and does not want to see.
Because the story allows Petrarch to name himself in his verse ("di qual
petra . . ."), it momentarily suggests a transparency of the self to itself.
But the letters of his name appear in the sonnet only in the context of
Ovidian metamorphoses that displace his sexual identity. Here, the
gender fluidity that is the effect of the cycle's larger elliptical rhetorical
strategy becomes overt. Dazzled by Apollo's light, the poet compares
himself to Daphne, changing his form as she changed hers ("come vide
lei cangiar Tesaglia / così cangiato ogni mia forma avrei" 1–4). He then
claims that though he has failed, he has nonetheless tried very hard to be
"transformed" or metamorphosed "into her" ("trasformarmi . . . in lei"
[5]).

Such indeterminacy about the gendered and sexual meaning of the
body, as we have seen, is a hallmark of a psychoanalytic definition of
fetishism – a sign of the failure immanent in even the most persuasive
cultural fictions of masculine identity. And such indeterminacy leads,
moreover, to the poem's final allusion to Ovid's Medusa (13–14).[58]
Much like Freud's (in)famous interpretation of Medusa as a sign of
castration anxiety, Petrarch's sonnet alludes to Medusa in the context of
an imaginary scene in which a male observer fantasizes being "transformed into her." But I read Freud's equation between Medusa and
castration in light of his larger theories of sexuality in which, as we have
seen in his speculation on the fetish, "castration" is a name for the way in
which for speaking beings, events are separated from understanding – a
disjunction that renders the regime of masculinity at once traumatic and
incomplete. Understood in light of such essays as "The Splitting of the
Ego in the Process of Defense" or "Fetishism," castration designates a
young boy's encounter not with the female body *per se*, but with the
cultural taboo that retrospectively interprets that body for him in a
culturally significant, and terrifying, way.[59]

In the figure of Medusa in sonnet 52, the blindness at the heart of
Petrarchan autobiography and of fetishism converge. Because here, as in
canzone 23, the speaker conveys the alienating effect of an Ovidian figure

on his sense of self in the present iterative verb for metamorphosis, *trasformare*. And true to the hesitations of fetishism we've traced throughout the *Rime Sparse*, Petrarch's representation of Medusa mixes ideas of sexual difference with those of sexual indeterminacy: the speaker perceives her as other, as alien, and yet *also* longs to be transformed into her. Thus the figure of Medusa evokes both the culturally pervasive regime of identity-through-difference and a sense of resistance to that regime. The emotions the speaker associates with seeing Medusa and becoming a rock – and thus, for Petrarch, with naming him (or is it her?) self – are both desire and "fear." Desire and terror converge when the self – "qual petra" – can be named only at the cost of a certain oblivion to itself.

But the Medusan effect – the self's internal distance from itself – is not confined to the poet's vision alone. In sonnet 197, we understand how profoundly it affects his voice, too. When Petrach actually names Medusa (197.6), he alludes to the same moment in Ovid's text as he did in sonnet 51, the conflict between Perseus and Atlas: "L'aura celeste ... po quello in me che nel gran vecchio mauro / Medusa quando in selce transformollo" ("The heavenly breeze ... has the power over me that Medusa had over the old Moorish giant [Atlas], when she turned him into flint" 197.1–6). As we've seen, the confrontation between Perseus and Atlas is the first time Medusa appears in the *Metamorphoses* and her ghastly *os* shores up Perseus' failing physical *and* rhetorical power. He asks for hospitality but Atlas refuses and, "adding force to his threats" ("uimque minis addit" 4.651), pushes Perseus away. The hero persists in trying to persuade Atlas "with soothing speech" ("placidis miscentem fortia dictis" 4.652), but when he realizes that neither his strength nor his words are strong enough, he reaches for Medusa: "he held out from his left hand the ghastly Medusa face/mouth" ("ipse retro uersus squalentia protulit *ora*," 656). And as Perseus' victory at the wedding banquet reminds us, Medusa's *os* derives its power from the idea of a trauma that is at once visual and oral, the "portent" of her face becoming one of the *Metamorphoses*' most frightening metarhetorical figures for the self's distance from the sound of its own voice.[60] In three of the stories crucial to Petrarch's representation of his own condition – that of Narcissus, Actaeon, and Medusa – we encounter the unsettling work of Ovid's critique of the fantasy of voice-consciousness. Just as Medusa's *os* is associated with the idea of a dead yet moving tongue, Narcissus first perceives that the beautiful *os* or "face" he loves (3.423) is merely a reflection when he notices that the *os* or "mouth" before him is moving without making a sound.[61] And when no voice issues from Actaeon's mouth, tears pour down the face that can no longer be said to be his.[62]

What I am suggesting is that Petrarch associates Medusa not only with the general idea of rhetorical power, but specifically with Ovid's phonographic imaginary – with the estranging distance of the self from its own speech that Petrarch will call his peculiar form of linguistic "exile." We can best see the consequences of this association in sonnet 197, "L'aura celeste." Remember that throughout the *Rime Sparse*, Petrarch uses the pun on "l'aura/Laura" to recall the breezes that blow through the *Metamorphoses* as the poem's chief fiction for poetic inspiration (poetic *animus*, derived from the Greek ἄνεμος for wind or breeze, and particularly prominent in the story of Apollo) and embody them in his beloved. *Laura* is more than a name for Daphne; it is also *l'aura*, Petrarch's rich word for Ovid's pneumatic, animating definition of poetic voice. And the slightest orthographical alteration – either "a" or "o" – allows him to name either his beloved or his voice. But by the fifth line of sonnet 197, however, we discover that this shared poetic principle, this Apollonian breeze, is itself the Medusa.

> L'aura celeste che'n quel verde lauro
> spira ov'Amor ferì nel fianco Apollo
> et a me pose un dolce giogo al collo,
> tal che mia libertà tardi restauro,
>
> po quello in me che nel gran vecchio mauro
> Medusa quando in selce transformollo;
> né posso dal bel nodo omai dar crollo
> là 've il sol perde, non pur l'ambra o l'auro.
>
> dico le chiome bionde e 'l crespo laccio
> che sì soavemente lega et stringe
> l'alma, che' d'umiltate et non d'altro armo.
>
> L'ombra sua sola fa 'l mio cor un ghiaccio
> et di bianca paura il viso tinge,
> ma gli occhi ànno vertù di farne un marmo.

The heavenly breeze that breathes in that green laurel, where Love smote Apollo in the side and on my neck placed a sweet yoke so that I restore my liberty only late,

has the power over me that Medusa had over the old Moorish giant, when she turned him to flint; nor can I shake loose that lovely knot by which the sun is surpassed, not to say amber or gold:

I mean the blond locks and the curling snare that so softly bind tight my soul, which I arm with humility and nothing else.

Her very shadow turns my heart to ice and tinges my face with white fear, but her eyes have the power to turn it to marble.

Consonant with the problem that Medusa's *os* raises for the relationship between mind and voice in the *Metamorphoses*, Petrarch's poetic breeze, "l'aura," turns against him, making the poet's face ("il viso") "white with fear."[63] The speechless face of Ovid's Medusa metamorphoses, in Petrarch's hands, into the poet's own terrified face. An Ovidian distance between the voice and the face, or of the poetic subject from his own inspiration, defines the action of the breeze in this Medusan sonnet. Petrarch's repeated allusion to the story of Perseus' rhetorical extension of Medusa's *os* tells us that his compelling, mythographic story about a dangerous vision of his beloved cannot be disentangled from the self-dispossession that haunts his voice. As in Petrarch's allusions to Actaeon and Pygmalion, these allusions to Medusa testify to an unsettling distance within the voice and the gaze, estranging the self from eyes and tongue at once.

In this anxious phonographic moment, moreover, it is impossible to disentangle the poet's voice from Laura's with any assurance. Sonnet 197 tells us that the speaker, as much as Laura, can be reduced to the silence of a statue. But as in the *Metamorphoses*, male and female voices are locked in a mutually defining embrace. And so in this sonnet, both the poem's speaker and his forbear, Apollo, are subjected *to* "L'aura celeste." Ovid's first book might encourage us to associate Petrarch's "l'aura" with Apollo's voice alone, the conventionally gendered version of this trope. But in this poem, Petrarch's pun on *L'aura/lauro* in line 1 draws renewed attention to the usually unmarked fact of each word's gender: the breeze seems, then, to pass *between* Daphne, "L'aura celeste," and the (masculine) "lauro." Over the course of the first line, a female breeze breathes through a male body: "L'aura celeste che'n quel verde lauro / spira" ("The heavenly breeze that breathes in that green laurel").[64] Formerly inanimate and mute before the solicitations of Petrarch's version of Pygmalion, Laura as Daphne and then Medusa inspires the speaker (read "inspire" in the strict etymological sense). *Her* breath, "l'aura celeste," opens the poem and eventually wields a rhetorical power over him as formidable as Medusa's over Atlas.

"L'aura celeste che 'n quel verde lauro" captures, in a single line, the unending vacillation of voice between bodies that occasionally surfaces in the present iterative metamorphoses of the *Rime Sparse*. If in sonnet 51 the poet sought to be "transformed into her," in this sonnet the breeze that breathes through both parties answers his wish by changing him into her at the level of the signifier: a *l'aura* moving in a *lauro*. Petrarch's Medusan sonnet therefore captures the strange displacements of rhetorical and sexual agency in Ovid's text when Perseus uses Medusa's "face" or "mouth" to effect the change his words could not. A surrogate mouth, a rhetorical tool of tremendous force, Medusa's *os* comes to Perseus' aid (and later Petrarch's), as a mysteriously dangerous image of vocal and sexual power. In Petrarch's fetishizing autobiographical version of Ovid's text, Medusa signifies the poet's voice *and* Laura's – a "heavenly" yet restless "breeze" that transforms one into the other, ties one to the fate of the other. Neither the actual sound of this voice, could we but hear it, nor a vision of the particular body that contains it would reassure us that the speaking voice of this poem (or the *Rime Sparse*) is the same thing of which it speaks.

Petrarch's autobiographical return to metamorphosis – to the voices of Pygmalion, Actaeon, and Medusa – evokes a danger that is at once sexual and rhetorical. We've seen that Petrarch's way of representing verbal fetishism through these Ovidian figures consistently signals "two epistemological scenes" when it comes to the linguistic form through which a poetic subject comes to be. But it seems to me crucial, nevertheless, to distinguish between an actual fetish and these poems about verbal fetishism. For according to psychoanalytic theory, the fetish would be the one substitute that freezes the signifying process, denying the "senseless" injunction of the letter that offers the female body to the male subject-in-the making as the visual explanation for his traumatic inscription in language. Founded on an initial substitution, a fetish allows the subject to fix on *one* image as that which cannot be substituted for others like it. This refusal of substitution is, of course, a refusal to enter into the network of language's structure of deferral and difference. But the fetish, initially a substitution, does not continue in a tropological sequence: thus, as Julia Kristeva argues, a fetish "is not a sign," nor can a sign be a fetish. In *The Revolution in Poetic Language*, she asks, "isn't art the fetish par excellence, one that badly camouflages its archaeology?" If entry into the Symbolic requires obedience to the Law-of-the-Father, she further asks, doesn't the subject continue to believe that "the mother is phallic, that the ego – never precisely identified – will never separate from her, and that no symbol is strong enough to sever this dependence?" For her, though "the subject of poetic language clings to the help fetishism offers," nonetheless it is a symbolic subject; though the "poetic function" may "converge" with fetishism, "it is not identical to it." In contrast to a fetish, the figures of poetry continue to signify.

In the *Rime Sparse*, of course, Laura's exceedingly textual veil is never stripped away. And though Medusa conjures a terrifying vision of petrification, that freezing produces further signifiers – "petra" or "l'aura" – for which others are substituted. In the *Metamorphoses*, it is only as a veiling *simulacrum* that the maiden may be, as it were, "seen" in the narrative *nuda*; once she becomes flesh, the narrative glances away. This *simulacrum* may be "seen" at all, it seems, because it signifies the desire of its narrator, Orpheus. "The text is completely different from the fetish because it signifies ... it is not a substitute but a sign (signifier/ signified) and its semantics unfurled in sentences."[65] Because it "signifies the unsignifying," a text is still a sign even as it gestures to the other side of signification. On such an understanding of linguistic subjectivity, and of the difference between fetishism and poetic language, I would suggest that these seemingly fetishized female figures be read as signs pointing to the cultural conditions legislated for becoming a "speaking-subject." They are assigned a peculiar place: these idols become signs of what the culturally fashioned male subject of poetic language must renounce if "he" is to accede to symbolic form. Diana, Eurydice, Pygmalion's maiden, Medusa, Laura: over and over in the *Metamorphoses* and the *Rime Sparse*, female forms become signifiers for what is in excess of the voice, in excess of signification, and in excess of the culturally imposed order of sexual difference. But the female "form" thus positioned only returns as a reminder that represents what is missing in language, and thus in the subject. Female form, that is, is not merely turned aside on the threshold of the linguistic. Her form returns from this initial turning aside to represent that (enabling) absence that is the "positive condition" of the poetic "speaking" subject. The absence of Laura – but also of Eurydice – always informs the fantasy of Pygmalion's love for a name- less, living idol. Both Ovid's and Petrarch's Pygmalion suggest that although the poet's voice may be empty, it is not, however, disembodied.

In tracing the nature and effects of Ovid's phonographic imaginary, we have seen that tropes for the voice – both male and female – shape the representation of subjectivity in both the *Metamorphoses* and Petrarch's autobiographical revision of that poem in the *Rime Sparse*. At the same time, these tropes play a crucial role in each poem's fiercely unresolved struggle over what human bodies mean and what their differences signify. We've also seen that various figures of vocal self-dispossession – Philomela's tongue, Echo's repetitive *uox*, Medusa's mouth, Actaeon's lips, Diana's prohibition, Bacchic noise – darken the dream that both poets entertain, in their different ways, of an Orphic voice powerful enough to bring about the changes of which it speaks. Such figures betray a profound anxiety about the voice's limitations as an index of authorial subjectivity as well as its unpredictable relationship to both mind and world. Most important of all, the violent narratives of desire and dismemberment within which these figures for lost voices emerge warn us that we cannot separate the contradictions haunting this phonographic imaginary from the way each poem grapples with the question of the sexualized body's significance and value.

Ovid's culturally laden fantasies and anxieties about embodied voices are no less foundational to John Marston's *The Metamorphosis of Pigmalions Image*, one of the most biting satires in the tradition that Ovid inspired. Dedicating himself to the task of exposing and satirizing the connections between rhetoric and sexuality in Petrarchanism, Marston selects Pygmalion, the figure who so memorably visualizes the Ovidian–Petrarchan dream of vocal animation, to conduct his critique. One of the clearest indications of what drew Marston's attention to the story of the inspired statue is his emphasis on Ovid's carefully chosen verb, "to move" (*mouere*). This verb for the ends of rhetorical speech appears frequently over the course of Marston's short poem. The narrator uses it to point out Pigmalion's predicament ("his dull Image, which no plaints could move" stanza 13); to capture the aim of Pigmalion's spoken prayer ("thus having said, he riseth from the floor . . .

Hoping his prayers to pitty moov'd some power" stanza 25); to describe the effect of the statue's animation on her maker ("he found that warmth, and wished heate / Which might a Saint and coldest spirit move" stanza 37); and to characterize the stated goals of Petrarchan poetry ("Tut, women will relent / When as they finde such moving blandishment" stanza 29 and "Ladies, thinke that they nere love you / Who doe not unto more than kissing move you" stanza 20).

Marston, like both Ovid and Petrarch before him, is drawn to the rhetorical dimension of the story and turns it into a provocatively eroticized commentary on his own scene of writing. Indeed, *Pigmalions Image* does more than simply draw our attention to the metarhetorical fantasy of a voice capable of moving even stones. Marston's narrator also tells an increasingly lewd series of poetic-erotic jokes that capitalizes on the fantasmatic work of apostrophe – the trope for the voice we've seen play such an important role in both Ovid's poetry and Petrarch's. To recall two prominent instances: in Petrarch's address to Pygmalion in sonnet 78 and in Ovid's address to the dying Orpheus, apostrophe emerges as the rhetorical equivalent of the story Orpheus tells of Pygmalion's successful animation. Apostrophe, as much as the story, relies on the fiction that a speaker's voice is capable of making an "absent, dead, or inanimate entity ... present, animate, and anthropomorphic."[1] Marston's narrator, who is as sensitive as Petrarch's to the way Ovid's story of Pygmalion embodies his rhetoric of animation, turns at least ten times to address imaginary audiences over the course of his satire. In the thirty-nine brief stanzas that make up Marston's epyllion, eight of these addresses take the form of formal apostrophe. One of these imaginary audiences is particularly noteworthy for our analysis. In a memorable scene to which we'll return in a moment, Pigmalion turns aside from his beautiful, ivory "imagerie" to address the poet to whom this metarhetorical fiction is most indebted:

> But when the faire proportion of her thigh
> Began appeare: O Ovid would he cry,
> Did ere Corinna show such Ivorie
> When she appear'd in Venus livorie?
>   And thus enamour'd, dotes on his owne Art
>   Which he did work, to work his pleasing smart.[2]

Pigmalion's cheeky apostrophe – his rhetorical turning away from the sexual attractions of "his owne Art" to speak to the author who inaugurated this phonographic fantasy of a relationship between creator and created – tells us that Marston, no less than Ovid, finds the story of animation particularly useful for posing questions about the erotic undercurrents of rhetorical and poetic relations.

But it is not only the rhetoric of address that is central to Marston's ironic vision of Ovid's story. So, too, is Ovid's etymologically precise rhetoric of vocal *anim*ation. In the midst of Pigmalion's "extasie," for instance, the narrator tells us that on the statue's "lips," the sculptor thinks he sees breath – "so sweet a breath," indeed, that it "doth perfume the ayre." He then asks us to picture Pigmalion, down "on his knees," praying for just such an animation:

> ... he all his sences charmes,
>   To invocate sweet Venus for to raise her
>   To wished life, and to infuse some breath,
>   To that which dead, yet gave a life to death.   (Stanza 22)

The pervasive Ovidian idea of the poet's animating breath – which Marston represents as Pigmalion's desire to "instill" a stone with "celestiall fire" (stanza 24) – profoundly determines the action of the satire. The poem's prose prologue, for instance, tells us that Pigmalion asks for Venus to "*enspire* life into his Love," to turn her into a "breathing creature." As we examined in some detail in chapter 2, Ovid represents his narrator's speaking presence in the *Metamorphoses* as an *animus* "breathed upon" by the gods ("in noua fert animus ... dicere ... di, coeptis ... adspirate meis, *Metamorphoses* 1.1–3). And he reinforces this etymologically resonant figure for his own inspired voice with a series of erotic and violent stories about the collusion between the poet's voice, breath, and the wind. Marston's numerous apostrophes, with their fiction of vocal animation, his fascination with the idea of "moving" a stone, and his repeated image of breath as a trope for life and poetry at once ("enspiring life"), reveal him to have been a good reader of Ovid's metarhetorical reflections. As such, he did not fail to hear, and push even further, the resonances between the story of Pygmalion's love and Ovid's opening, inspirationalist fantasy about poetic authorship.

A poem of questionable taste, *The Metamorphosis of Pigmalions Image* generally receives little more than passing commentary. My reason for pausing to examine it in some detail is Marston's evident interest in the rhetorical and libidinal economies of Ovid's phonographic imaginary. But there are several other compelling reasons for attending to Marston's rhetoric of the body at this point in my analysis. First, Marston's poem satirizes the discourse of Petrarchanism by way of that shared Ovidian character, Pygmalion, whose rather peculiar literary career we have been examining in some detail. As I hope to show, Pygmalion's verbal fetishism is just as important to this poem as to Petrarch's, but the consequences of that symbolic and libidinal economy for Marston's representation of the female voice and body are rather different than in

either the *Metamorphoses* or the *Rime Sparse*. Second, Marston's epyllion, like *The Rape of Lucrece*, the near-contemporary narrative poem I
discuss in the next chapter, presumes familiarity with both Ovidian and
Petrarchan figures, reading one in terms of the other. This habit of
critically juxtaposing Ovidian and Petrarchan rhetoric is one Shakespeare
not only shared with Marston but carried beyond the boundaries of
narrative verse. In my last chapter, a reading of yet another animated
statue in *The Winter's Tale*, we'll see the movement between Latin and
Italian poets emerge once again as theatrical metacommentary. A close
analysis of the way Marston reads one poet in light of the other will
therefore give us a useful coign of vantage from which to discern what
might be distinctive about Shakespeare's phonographic, Ovidian figures.
And finally, as we'll see when looking at Shakespeare's representations of
the voice in *Lucrece*, he also uses apostrophe as a key to open the door of
the Ovidian tradition – an important way to register his understanding of
its trademark representations of subjectivity, gender, and desire. If we are
to discriminate with any precision between the consequences of this
pervasive trope for representations of male and female experience, it will
help us to understand how apostrophe functions in another contemporary Ovidian narrative before turning to read Shakespeare's.

That fayre Image

Before we can explore the nuances of Marston's several apostrophes, or
examine the way his various representations of the voice intersect the
libidinal economy of *Pigmalions Image*, we must first note something of
the literary-critical context and insights that inform his satire on contemporary amatory verse. Marston wrote *The Metamorphosis of Pigmalions Image* in 1598 for his contemporaries at the Inns of Court. Like
Marston, his peers at the Inns had been trained in the rhetorical
curriculum of the humanist grammar school; and many, like him,
continued their studies at university.[3] Moreover, the men at the Inns
were all trained, just as Ovid had been, in the rhetorical techniques of
legal disputation. Indeed, the practice of holding public "moots" or
mock disputations to debate the finer points of complex cases sounds
remarkably similar to the Roman practice of declamation, that public
display of invention to which the orator's practice had been reduced
when Ovid began thinking about the connections and interference
between oratory and poetry.[4] Both their experience with the public
display of forensic rhetorical skill at the Inns of Court and their more
general education in the humanist curriculum meant that this group of
men constituted a particularly good audience for Ovid's metarhetorical

renditions of erotic experience. As Jonson's barbs in *Poetaster* attest, Marston's peers did not fail to notice the close fit between literary style and taste at the Inns and Ovid's. Written for such a coterie, Marston's epyllion is a rude and often savagely funny attack on the conventions of contemporary love poetry, particularly Petrarchan love poetry.[5] One might attribute the considerable aggression in Marston's tone, therefore, not only to his temperament but also to the literary-social milieu in which he found himself – to that intensely competitive crowd of young men at the Inns who were less devoted to studying the law than they were to the general imperative of "advancement and employment."[6] Given the audience for which it was written, it can be no surprise that while brief, Marston's attack on contemporary taste, performance, and form in *Pigmalions Image* is quite sharp.

The perception at the heart of this, Marston's first (and evidently very successful) publication was one that he evidently shared with Andrew Marvell. Marvell drily observed of contemporary amatory verse, "Apollo hunted Daphne so / Only that she might Laurel grow" and one could read *Pigmalions Image* as a dramatic enactment of this literary-critical insight into the unspoken aim of Petrarchan poetry. Where Marston's satire differs from Marvell's critique, however, is that he chooses Ovid's figure of Pygmalion over Apollo as the appropriate one with which to burlesque the ostensible claims of Petrarchan love poetry. Like Marvell, Marston swiftly dismisses the claim of love: his "Pigmalion" is moved not by the qualities particular to his beloved but by the "shadow" of his own poetic "imagerie" or "conceit" – by "the wondrous rarenesse / Of his owne workmanships perfection" (stanzas 11, 28, and 3). In other words, Marston is as clear as Marvell that it is not love of his mistress, but a fascination with the "Laurel" or poetic "image" replacing her that "moves" her inventor.

By dramatizing Pygmalion's story rather than Apollo's, moreover, Marston deftly criticizes another important facet of Petrarch's Ovidian version of Augustinian idolatry. What draws the satirist's fire is not merely that the Petrarchan poet loves his own images more than he loves his mistress, but that he loves what he sees of *himself* in those images. As we saw in the last chapter, Petrarch understood the profound similarity between Pygmalion's and Narcissus' love very well. In fact, he exploits this similarity to draw a deliberately self-ironizing portrait of himself as another Narcissus, forever weeping over an empty figure (Simone's painting of Laura). Marston is quick to attack the Petrarchan poet for just this failing. The poem's title, *The Metamorphosis of Pigmalions Image*, pointedly vacillates between subjective and objective genitive. Gesturing toward the Narcissus immanent in Pigmalion, Marston's title invites us to ask whether the poem concerns "the image that belongs to Pigmalion" or "the image that reflects Pigmalion." In case we don't pause long enough to notice the ambiguities in his title, Marston hammers the point home in the possessive pronoun of the third stanza:

> Hee was amazed at the wondrous rarenesse
> Of his owne workmanships perfection.
> He thought that Nature nere produc'd such fairenes
> In which all beauties have their mantion,
>   And thus admiring, was enamored
>   On that fayre Image himselfe portraied.   (Stanza 3)

Marston opens his poem by noting that very little, if any, of a woman's particularity, autonomy, or difference resists the self-interested pressure of the Petrarchan love story. Fading, like the referent, before the self-reflexiveness of Petrarchan poetic "images," the mistress who ostensibly began as the "Idol" of the poet's "soul" (stanza 26) pales before the splendor of that "fayre Image *himselfe* portraied."

Pigmalions Image, then, takes aim at precisely the symbolic and libidinal economy we examined in the last chapter: the poetic discourse of verbal fetishism. The narrator's joke on idolatry recalls Petrarch's self-portrait as a belated Pygmalion who loves the name or figure of Laura as much as the woman herself. The spectacle of Pigmalion's idolatrous "extasie" charges – as Petrarch would have been the first to recognize – that love poets formed in his image were at least as enamored of the name or "imagery" of their ladies as they were of their persons. We learn immediately that the poem's protagonist, Pigmalion, is a fetishist in a strictly linguistic sense: he "hates" the "substance" of woman and is obsessed only with the "shade" or "image" of one (stanza 1). Hence the Ovidian pun in the poem's title – on "image" as "statue" and poetic "trope" or "figure" at once – succinctly captures the way verbal fetishism puts poetic figures in place of female corporeal figures. Throughout Marston's brief satire, therefore, the narrator insists on Pigmalion's preference for a turn of phrase – for an "image" (stanza 2 and *passim*), a "conceit" (7), a "shadow" (28), an "imagery" (4), an "idol" (14), and a "shade" (1) – over the mere fleshy "substance" of womankind (1).

The narrator also unfolds his satire on Petrarch's idolatrous division of word and body – handed down, we remember, from Apollo and Daphne's dispute over *figura* – in a particularly Ovidian way. That is, he imitates Ovid's (often similarly comic) habit of moving between literal and figural levels of meaning. Such movement generates increasingly lewd jokes whose leering sexual overtones are designed to mock Petrarch's rather more refined discourse of unrequited devotion to his idol. For example, Pigmalion spends a lot of time ogling his "image" –

And naked as it stood before his eyes
Imperious Love declares his Deitie.
O what alluring beauties he descries
In each part of his faire Imagery!   (stanza 4)

– and then begins to "dally" with its "Ivory breasts" (stanza 13). In this, one of the poem's more pointed jokes on verbal fetishism, the narrator reduces a poet's love for his own *figurae* to the scene of an adolescent Pigmalion pawing his image. Mindlessly slipping back and forth from figure to referent – "Her breasts, like polisht Ivory appear" (stanza 8) – Pigmalion forgets that her breasts appear "like" ivory because they *are* ivory. The absurd portrait of the artist's literalist illusion broadly lampoons the serious semiotic and epistemological issues Petrarch was exploring through the discourse of idolatry (i.e., whether there is a connection, as Dante proposed, between desire, language, and knowledge; and whether or not, as Augustine proposed, a speaking subject can know the self of which it speaks). When Marston's Pigmalion forgets his own "as if" of poetry's tropological intervention, we are asked to laugh at a figure of the poet losing himself in a delusion of reference. Marston is then able to turn a lengthy history of literary convention – the elaborate discourse of anatomizing similes – into a lewd erotic fantasy of "parts." Pigmalion "views her lips," her "thigh," her "breasts," and so on:

Thus fond Pigmalion striveth to discry
Each beauteous part, not letting over-slip
One parcell of his curious workmanship.   (stanza 8)

For such a poet, even the mental activity of paying attention ("not letting over-slip") suggests the tactile fantasy of sexual touching. In an Ovidian "extasie" where figures turn into things, Marston's Pigmalion forgets himself as he forgets the minimal distinctions necessary to either verbal or visual representation.

By such means, largely inherited from Ovid, Marston builds a ludicrous scene of misplaced sexual energy out of his charge that the Petrarchan poet is a deluded Narcissus. Like Ovid's unhappy youth, Marston's Pigmalion can't see the difference between body and image, original corporeal form and its reflection or copy. As we've already noted, however, the charge of self-love would hardly surprise Petrarch. Marston's skeptical and aggressive narrator turns Petrarch's overriding (and remarkably Freudian) suggestion in the *Rime Sparse* – that a story about the self's blindness to itself inhabits any story of love – into a biting denunciation of the blindly self-serving nature of *other* people's symbolic-erotic activity. With a shift of tone and emphasis, the combined figures of Pygmalion and Narcissus turn from being at the center of Petrarch's discourse of melancholic, critical self-examination to being the means by which Marston conducts a stinging satire of others' failings. From the auto-aggression of Petrarchan melancholia, Marston derives the hetero-aggression of Juvenalian satire.

But if Marston uses Petrarch's avowed fixation on the *laura* or *figura* for which no others can be substituted to satiric advantage, however, it is not simply because such a passion can be rendered absurd – which the poem, of course, does mercilessly. (Recall, for instance, Pigmalion's enthusiastic apostrophe to "Sweet sheetes ... which nowe doe cover / The Idol of my soule ... Sweet happy sheetes, daine for to take me in" [stanza 26]. The exclamation encourages one to ask if this is Pigmalion's voice, talking about actual bedsheets, or Marston's, reminding us of the more figural "sheets" of paper on which Petrarchan poets write.) Rather, Marston's main reason for painting this satiric portrait appears to be that Petrarch's love for the written figures of his own making – compilations, as we have seen, of so many Ovidian *figurae* – spawned an entire tradition of imitators whose own claims to passion barely masked their primary (self-serving) purpose: to be recognized for the "wondrous rarenesse" of their own images, the "perfection" of their poetic "workmanship." Petrarch's obsession, like Pigmalion's, was not without issue. No further than two stanzas into Marston's poem, we understand we are in the middle of a canny reading of Petrarchan discourse as a literary movement. Conducted through the fetishistic excesses of Ovid's Pygmalion, Marston pokes fun at the conventional discourse of the *blason*:

> Her Amber-coloured, her shining haire,
> Makes him protest, the Sunne hath spread her head
> With golden beames, to make her farre more faire.
> But when her cheeks his amorous thoughts have fed,
>   Then he exclaimes, such redde and so pure white,
>   Did never blesse the eye of mortal sight. ...
>
> Her breasts, like polisht Ivory appeare,
> Whose modest mount, doe blesse admiring eye,
> And makes him wish for such a Pillowbeare. ...
>
> His eyes, her eyes, kindly encountered,
> His breast, her breast, oft joyned close unto,
> His armes embracements oft she suffered,
> Hands, armes, eyes, tongue, lips, and all parts did woe.
>   His thigh, with hers, his knee playd with her knee,
>   A happy consort when all parts agree.   (Stanzas 6, 8, and 17)

In Marston's hands, Pygmalion becomes a metapoetic figure at least as suitable as Apollo to the satiric purpose of exploding the symbolic and libidinal economy of the Petrarchan tradition from within its own terms. Marston's deliberately derivative anatomy of body parts turns into a literalist's fantasy of possible sexual positions. At once trite and lascivious, this *blason* accuses an entire literary tradition of being exhausted, its conventions no better than clichés.

But Marston's critique of the tradition goes further still. In the apostrophe to Ovid we looked at earlier, Pigmalion delivers a puerile, boasting address to his literary forbear. His trope, integral to the tradition against which it is deployed, draws attention away from the statue's erotic attractions to Pigmalion's (now eroticized) rivalry with a male poetic precursor: "when the faire portion of her thigh / Began appeare: O Ovid would he cry ..." The point of imagining such an address, of course, is that the Petrarchan poet's attempt to "move" his beloved, silent image into language and desire is merely an excuse for conducting a more interesting conversation about literary form with his male predecessors (and, presumably, contemporaries): "Did ere Corinna show such Ivorie?" Marston's scene reminds us that Petrarch's own apostrophe to Pygmalion ended a pair of sonnets that began by addressing another male artist – Simone Martini – and by describing an intense male "competition in the art of looking" that began with the Greek sculptor, Polyclitus. Deeply skeptical of this legacy, Marston makes sure that at a culminating moment in the sculptor's erotic delirium, Pigmalion addresses himself not to his statue (with words of prayer) but to another, more important, addressee: his predecessor and creator. Encouraged by the "turning away" that constitutes *apo*strophe, Marston's Pygmalion no sooner glimpses the body of his beloved – "the faire proportion of her thigh" – than he turns away from it. Thus the Petrarchan poet emerges, in Marston's critique, as a lover whose interest lies elsewhere: on the one hand, with the beauty of his own images and figures; and on the other, with the male colleagues whose poetic labor and interest give those images and figures value. Marston's point is canny and familiar. The spectacle of Pigmalion's erotic enthusiasm deflected from image's "thigh" to Ovid's poetic skill suggests precisely what modern feminists have been pointing out about Petrarchan discourse for some time: that it constitutes an elaborate homosocial tradition in which the *figura* of a beloved *donna* becomes the conduit for a more important discourse between male poets about the beauty of their own language.

As strange a transformation wrought by mee

My brief summary of the main points of Marston's satire, along with the above excerpts, should be sufficient to indicate how important it is for the sake of the poem's humor that readers feel that there are considerable differences between Marston's poetic activities and those of the belated Pigmalion he attacks. Marston's absurdist vision of Pigmalion's frenzy clearly does much to foster such distance. But at the same time, he complicates any simple division by creating a shadow portrait of himself as a Petrarchan love poet – one who therefore also fashions himself in Pigmalion's image:

> For having wrought in purest Ivorie
> So faire an Image of a Womans feature,
> That never yet proudest mortalitie
> Could show so rare and beautious a creature.
>   (Unlesse my Mistres all-excelling face,
>   Which gives to beautie, beauties onely grace).   (Stanza 2)

No later than the second stanza of the poem we find that the narrator is also an epideictic poet and that he, too, has a mistress to move. But the tone of *Pigmalions Image* couldn't be farther from Petrarch's melancholic confession that he envies his rival "if," as he puts it, Pygmalion had "a thousand times" what "I yearn to have just once." Marston's narrator may lay claim, in good Petrarchan fashion, to resembling Pigmalion. But by contrast to Petrarch, his way of imitating the deluded sculptor means that the narrator turns into a gaping buffoon whose unlovely sexual energy becomes an efficient vehicle for carrying the poem's dirty joke:

> Had I my Love in such a wished state
> As was afforded to Pigmalion,
>   Though flinty hard, of her you soone should see
>   As strange a transformation wrought by mee.   (Stanza 32)

If we follow this narrator's path through *Pigmalions Image*, we feel sometimes that he shadows Petrarch/ Pigmalion and at other times that he resembles his satiric author. By turns image of Pigmalion – the deluded lover of idols – and instrument of Marston – the self-described "barking satirist" – this metamorphic narrator gets a laugh either at Pigmalion's expense or his own. Such vacillation efficiently creates our sense that there are parties outside the poem who know better than anyone in it: Marston and his audience.

With regard to the literary history we've traced thus far, we've seen that Petrarch's melancholic autobiography collapsed the distinction that Ovid first proposed between his narrator and Pygmalion, turning that irony, instead, against himself. By comparison, Marston's satire proposes at least two levels of distinction: narrator from Pigmalion; and Marston, in turn, from both Pigmalion and his narrator. Crucial as these distinctions are to the point of the satire, however, they are not always as clear as Marston might like. Throughout *Pigmalions Image*, a complex play of proximity and distance defines these negotiations between author, narrator, and character. On one hand, Marston's derisive tone and mocking imitations work to maintain a critical distance between the poem's author and the contemporary poets he holds up to ridicule. But on the other hand, Marston's narrative *persona* copies the Petrarchan lover because the joke works only by repeating and exaggerating Petrarch's substitution of one *figura* for another – his words for the body of his beloved. Reenacting verbal fetishism to reduce it to the absurd, Marston's narrator is able to ridicule Petrarchanism. But he also runs the risk of indulging in the failings he mocks.

Notice, for instance, that it is not an an easy task to avoid the problem posed by his third stanza: "Hee was amazed at the wondrous rarenesse / Of his owne workmanships perfection." That Marston's own poem, *as a poem* – and thus a "shade" and not "substance," a "conceit" and "image" too – might recapitulate the problems Petrarch was analyzing remains an ever present possibility. It should alert us to the fact that the ostensible difference between Pigmalion and his narrator – a difference necessary to Marston's critique – is not always easy to sustain. As Bruce Smith observes of Juvenalian satire in the hands of practitioners such as Donne and Marston, this mode is peculiarly prone to succumb to the very excesses it deplores: a "spiral of power and pleasure … locks the satirist and satirized in a furious embrace."[7] An uneasy fluctuation between difference and sameness – the difference necessary for the joke on Petrarch and the corollary danger of the author's repeating the libidinal and symbolic economy he attacks – pervades *Pigmalions Image*.

Such a movement of similarity and difference can hardly surprise in a poem whose title recalls Narcissus. But of course, the charge of narcissism is dangerously two-sided. Impertinent questions arise. Isn't Marston's claim to superior knowledge at least as self-absorbed as Petrarch's melancholic admission that his understanding of himself is only ever partial, plagued by blindness and lapses of memory? Is Marston any less enamored of his "conceit" than Petrarch was of his? Or than any of his followers were of theirs? Can Marston claim in all honesty that he derives *no* pleasure out of the "wanton" *figurae* he's inventing? And with respect to his suggestion that "Pigmalion" is just as interested in getting a response from Ovid as he is in getting one from his statue, can Marston defend himself against the same charge – that the audience that really interests him isn't his "mistress" but rather his colleagues at the Inns of Court?

The "furious embrace of satirist and satirized" may help to explain the escalating tone of aggression in *Pigmalions Image*. By the end of the poem, Marston widens his satirical scope to include his audience as well as Pigmalion – an aggressive strategy of sudden attack that is designed to distance Marston from the poem's action, to suggest that certain errors belong only to others and "not to me." In a concluding apostrophe to which we will return from a different angle at the end of this chapter, the narrator maintains that any lewdness in *Pigmalions Image* comes from the audience, not its author:

> Who knowes not what ensues? O pardon me
> Yee gaping eares that swallow up my lines.
> Expect no more. Peace idle Poesie,
> Be not obsceane though wanton in thy rimes.
>   And chaster thoughts, pardon if I doe trip,
>   Or if some loose lines from my pen doe slip. (Stanza 38)

Rebuking the very audience he has summoned to listen to his erotic "conceit" for *its* lewd expectations, Marston draws his series of sexual jokes to a close by claiming that any obscenity in the poem lies not in the author's pen but in the reader's ear. Because of the contradictions built into the very form of *Pigmalions Image* – by which I mean that it quickly undermines the very distinctions between satirist and satirized it also requires – Marston ends up attacking every one of the poem's imaginary audiences by the time he is finished. Assaults such as the one on the reader's "gaping ear" allow Marston to stake out boundaries that one might otherwise say are no longer clear. As is often the case in this poem, however, Marston attacks with a double-edged sword. The stanza indicts the poem's audience for obscenity in order to distance its author from precisely that charge. But at the same time, the peculiar figure of the reader's "gaping" ear reminds us that a homosocial scene of listening shapes Marston's poem just as much as it determines the poetry of the would-be Pigmalions he holds up for ridicule.

Marston's abusive apostrophe to his audience's "gaping ears" does more than deflect blame, however. It is also part of the poem's concluding definition of its own performance – its sense of its position with regard to the moral failings it describes: "Peace idle Poesie, / Be not obsceane ..." It also amounts to a general declaration about aesthetics – about what is and is not admissible subject matter for poetry. When he delivers himself of this, his final definition of what cannot be included within poetry's orbit, however, Marston obliquely tells us that he is easily inclined to repeat the errors he sets out to censure. You will recall that in his opening summation of Ovid's story, Marston is characteristically blunt about Pigmalion's motives for shaping his work of art:

> Pigmalion, whose hie love-hating minde
> Disdain'd to yeeld servile affection,
> Or amorous sute to any woman-kinde,
> Knowing their wants, and mens perfection.
>> Yet Love at length forc'd him to know his fate,
>> And love the shade, whose substance he did hate.   (Stanza 1)

The artist loves the "shadow" yet hates "the substance" of womankind; his "love-hating minde" knows the difference between women's "wants" and men's "perfection." The inspiration for Marston's poem – a satiric attack on contemporary poetic practice – tells us that the author's opinion about "mens perfection" may differ considerably from that of his deluded character. But in the context of the volley of sexual innuendoes that follow, as well as the context of the audience at the Inns of Court to which these jokes were addressed, this opening sally raises questions that are more difficult to put aside. How much distance is there between Marston's performance and Pigmalion's "love-hating" view of women's "wants"? If Pigmalion loves "the shade" of a woman and "hates the substance" of one, how far does this generative misogyny inform his narrator's own discourse?

And indeed, Marston's closing definition of what is "fit" matter for poetry tells us that this narrator's sense of aesthetic propriety relies heavily on Pigmalion's "idolatrous" distinction – between a woman's body and its representation, "substance" and "shadow." In the concluding stanzas of the poem that end with the apostrophe to "gaping ears," Marston turns Pigmalion's artistic way of avoiding any dealings with female "substance" into a definition of the difference between verse that observes proper social decorum and verse that does not. In other words, when Marston claims to adjudicate the difference between what is merely "wanton" and what "obsceane," he argues that it is permissible to describe the details of a fetishist's "sport" in bed with a statue. The one thing in this unseemly story that isn't "fit reporting," he tells us, is intercourse with actual female "substance."

> And now me thinks some wanton itching eare
> With lustfull thoughts, and ill attention,
> List's to my Muse, expecting for to heare
> The amorous discription of that action
>> Which Venus seekes, and ever doth require,
>> When fitnes graunts a place to please desire.
>
> Let him conceit but what himselfe would doe
> When that he had obtayned such a favour,
> Of her to whom his thoughts were bound unto,
> If she, in recompence of his loves labour,

Would daine to let one payre of sheets containe
The willing bodies of those loving twaine.

Could he, o could he, when that each to eyther
Did yeeld kind kissing, and more kind embracing,
Could he when that they felt, and clipt together
And might enjoy the life of dallying,
    Could he abstaine midst such a wanton sporting
    From doing that, which is not fit reporting?   (Stanzas 33–35)

According to this narrator, a poem about ogling, groping, and touching an inanimate object is merely "wanton sport." Once the statue has metamorphosed from a poetic figure into a corporeal one, however, such sport is no longer "fit reporting." The next two stanzas reiterate the distinction: just when Pigmalion finds "that life had tooke his seate, / Within the breast of his kind beauteous love" (stanza 37) the narrator intervenes and declines to describe the newly made woman any further. He then rebukes the reader's gaping ear in order to distinguish merely "wanton" rhymes from "obscene" ones (stanza 38). Marston's narrative performance means that the hated "substance" behind the image stays on the margins, hidden by its idol or substitute. Because when the image has turned into a living woman, it would be pornographic to "heare / The amorous discription of that action / Which Venus seekes." If Pigmalion loathes female substance, his narrator is equally averse to having any truck with it.

The apostrophe blaming the reader's "gaping ears" for anything lewd in the poem brings *Pigmalions Image* to a close by placing the anticipated event – and the substance – forever beyond the narrative frame. By the end of Marston's satire, the sculptor's misogyny blossoms into a definition of poetic decorum based on an equation between female flesh and pornography. Source of desire and anxiety at once, the idea of the female body frames Marston's poem by literally being placed outside it. "Hated" by Pigmalion and unmentioned by his narrator, the idea of a woman's body becomes what Lacan calls the *interdit*. That is, what is actually said between persons ("inter") is already defined, made possible, by the prohibitive social codes organizing what cannot be said (the "obscene"). In Judith Butler's recent elaboration of Lacan's idea, the *interdit* of pornography concerns the culturally contingent, *apparently* foundational, exclusions that constitute the symbolic order. Thus for her, the ever-changing definition of pornography, as socially regulated speech, is central to a culture's production of speaking subjectivity. "Censorship is a productive form of power: it is not merely privative, but formative as well." Thus censorship of the kind Marston ironically but effectively invokes to shift blame from author to audience "seeks to produce subjects according to explicit and implicit norms." "The question," therefore, "is not what it is I will be able to say, but what will constitute the domain of the sayable within which I begin to speak at all."[8] The poem's closing idea – that the female body cannot be represented – is foundational for Marston and his audience. It determines the limits within which men (or what the poem defines as men) can speak and beyond which nothing can be said. Integral to the "implicit norms" that define the domain of the sayable, female flesh stands outside the "shadow" of *Pigmalions Image*. Yet that excluded substance, precisely *as* the excluded, hovers at the margins, telling us quite a lot about the gynephobic social criteria that allow Marston, as the poem's self-proclaimed speaking subject, to "begin to speak at all."

This closing question of what counted as "obsceane" among Marston and his peers at the Inns of Court is a new twist to a problem with which we're already familiar. We've examined representations of the female voice in relation to the "unspeakable" event of rape (Philomela's *nefas*) and to the Petrarchan predicament of writing a series of poems whose very existence violates Diana's prohibition against speech. In Marston's satire on Pygmalion, however, this deeply Ovidian problem of the conditions of representation – of what can or cannot be spoken – assumes new contours. Philomela's *nefas*, sign of her impasse as well as her narrator's, points to a criminal sexual act – rape – that is unspeakable because of its violence. This iterated *nefas* implicitly raises the question of how women may become speaking subjects at all in a symbolic order in which they are so objectified as to confront rape as the defining act of their existence as social subjects.[9] But Marston's definition of the unspeakable as "obscene" – a telling representation of the conditions of objectification that determine what can and cannot be said among male poetic colleagues – is not at all interested in Ovid's question about what it costs to be defined as "the other." Instead, Marston's concluding statement about poetic decorum expends considerable energy placing women outside the symbolic order – "the domain of the sayable" – altogether. In so doing, Marston's apostrophe moves Ovid's idea of the "unspeakable" away from an investigation of sexual trauma – experiences that exceed (and implicitly question) culturally determined conditions of intelligibility – toward a masculinist fantasy of regulated poetic speech that, by contrast, endorses and upholds those conditions. Both Ovid's and Petrarch's brush with the unspeakable, moreover, lead each poet to question the integrity of the voice. But Marston's final strategy of exclusion draws on and endorses culturally hegemonic, rigid definitions of sexual difference in order to protect the authorial speaking subject from having to entertain any of the negative figures of vocal self-dispossession that haunt Ovidian subjects. Separated from the framing narrative of Orpheus' death in Ovid's narrative, the story of *Pigmalions Image* entertains no voices like those of Ovid's Bacchae; no discordant female *clamor* sounds a note of internal distance from the misogyny on which the poem relies. Rather, the narrator tells us that if there is any error or fault in the poem's representation, we should blame either the female body or the reader's ear, but not him.

Women's wants and men's perfections

Once we have understood the satiric argument that drives *Pigmalions Image,* the major contradictions that attend its satiric vision, and the way that its gynephobic exclusion of the female body is deeply bound up with its definition of what it means to speak at all, we are ready to inquire a little more deeply into the relationship between the poem's libidinal and rhetorical economies. In my discussion of sexuality in the *Metamorphoses* and the *Rime Sparse*, I outlined an unconscious, but nonetheless powerful, tendency either to question or to refuse the discourse of sexual difference that the poems also deploy. The practice of cross-voicing in the *Metamorphoses* and the polymorphic exuberance of the poem's ever-changing desires pull against Ovid's metarhetorical and heteronormative story of rape. And in the *Rime Sparse*, the refusal of difference implicit in fetishism comes into view, however briefly, when the poet feels himself, and his voice, unaccountably "transformed into her" – when the cycle's elliptical implication of "him in her" means that the poet's voice is defined not merely by Apollo, Actaeon, and Pygmalion, but also by Diana, Byblis, Echo, and Medusa. Despite Marston's concluding stanzas – or perhaps motivating those stanzas – such Ovidian refusals of difference do occur in *Pigmalions Image*; we'll be looking closely at these moments in this section and the next. In the next section, in fact, we'll examine a number of other passages in *Pigmalions Image* where the satirist once again brushes up against the very desires and practices he satirizes, fantasies that make Marston just as much of a verbal fetishist as Petrarch.

But first it's important to look at what happens in the plot when the poem uses the conventional language of Petrachanism to establish the difference between Pigmalion and his statue. As we've noted, Marston opens the story by being very clear about the difference between male and female bodies and experiences: Pigmalion's artistry arises from his knowledge of the difference between women's "wants" and men's "perfection." But by the time the narrator begins the first of several evasive accounts about what, exactly, is going on between sculptor and statue in Pigmalion's bed, the conventional of the *blason* cuts against

Pigmalion's notion of sexual difference and hierarchy. Instead, this anatomy suggests a parity of part for part:

> His eyes, her eyes, kindly encountered,
> His breast, her breast, oft joyned close unto ...
> Hands, armes, eyes, tongue, lips, and all parts did woe.
>> His thigh, with hers, his knee played with her knee,
>> A happy consort when all parts agree.   (Stanza 17)

After this image of a mirroring, dismembered, yet "happy consort," the narrator eventually compares the lovers to "Leda's twins" (stanza 27). If Pigmalion's "image" is his reflection as well as his statue, whose bodily shape is the origin, and whose the copy, in this twinned pair?

The narrator, moreover, twice invents extended similes that illuminate Pigmalion's feelings of lust by comparing him to a woman. First he draws an analogy between the sculptor's lascivious gaze at "Love's Pavillion" to that of the "Citty-dame / In sacred church" who, "when her pure thoughts shold pray" nonetheless "peire[s] through her fingers, so to hide her shame" (stanza 10). And then, at the culminating moment when the statue melts "like Waxe," the narrator compares Pigmalion's erotic joy to a mother's relief at finding her son raised from the dead:

> Doe but conceive a Mothers passing gladnes,
> (After that death her onely sonne hath seazed
> And overwhelm'd her soule with endlesse sadnes)
> When that she sees him gin for to be raised
>> From out his deadly swoune to life againe:
>> Such joy Pigmalion feeles in every vaine   (Stanza 30)

In the middle of Pigmalion's ostensibly masculine "extasie," Marston's incongruous simile switches genders for both sculptor and statue: he is a mother, she a dead son come to life. Where the *blason* of parts dissolves both bodies into anatomized parity – a jumble that hints at positions and pleasures outside the reductive dictates of gender – the figures of the "Citty-dame" and the joyful mother remind us, despite the first stanza's economic invocation of sexual hierarchy and difference, of the fluid, elliptical reversal of male and female that characterizes either Ovid's metamorphosing bodies or Petrarch's labile fantasy of suddenly finding himself "transformed into her."

For his part, the narrator immediately moves on from the "happy" anatomy of body parts to wake us up, alongside Pigmalion, from any such utopian delusion:

> A happy consort when all parts agree.

> But when he saw poore soule, he was deceaved
> ... And saw how fondly all his thoughts had erred,

> Then did he like to poore Ixion seeme,
> That clipt a cloud in steede of heavens Queene.   (Stanza 18)

Marston intervenes in this "fond" fantasy to remind us that something is still missing – an absence at the heart of Pigmalion's unsatisfied desire that elsewhere in the poem finds precise location: first in the female body (woman's "wants") and then in the statue's voice ("remorseles ... dum and mute" stanza 14). In other words, as soon as this *blason* starts to interrogate the discourse of sexual difference in a subversively Ovidian manner, the narrator strategically reminds us that the statue is still inanimate – in Ovid's terms, lacking life and voice at once. And Marston associates any fluidity between male and female bodies, moreover, with Pigmalion and his image alone. *Pigmalion's* desire may resemble that of a "Citty-dame" or a mother, but no such figures emerge for the narrator. As if in reaction to the refusal of difference implicit in the discourse of verbal fetishism (the double epistemology of "I know but still" that simultaneously asserts and denies the culturally given "fact" of castration), the narrator tries to contain such intimations of gender confusion and reversal by attributing them to Pigmalion and his statue only. When it comes to drawing the narrator's portrait or, by implication, his own, Marston dedicates himself, with considerable vigor, to *policing* the difference between genders. The poem therefore veers back and forth between dissolving boundaries between gendered bodies and remarking them, a vacillation that ends only with the narrator's final exclusion of the female body altogether from the poem's symbolic economy.

True to the tradition from which he draws inspiration, the chief tool Marston uses for managing this uneasy libidinal economy is the idea of the female voice. For example, where Pigmalion prays that his idol, however much an "image of himself," may turn into a subject of desire – that "she may equalize affection / And have a mutuall love" (stanza 24) – Marston's narrator wishes just the opposite for his mistress. In a joking aside that draws on the masculinist cliché that women talk too much, Marston pins his narrator's erotic hopes on reversing the story of animation: "O that my Mistres were an Image too, / That I might blameles her perfections view" (stanza 11). This wish for a woman's petrification – that his mistress shut her mouth so that he may takes his pleasure – defines the rhetorical level of Marston's performance throughout. In the *Rime Sparse*, Laura's voice is at once object of Pygmalion's desire and Actaeon's fear, by turns the sound of an angel, of a prohibiting Diana, or of a breeze coming from Medusa. Though not often heard in the cycle, her voice nonetheless commands a startling sort of power. By contrast to the petrifying effects of Medusa's "aura" and Diana's prohibition, in *Pigmalions Image* Marston's narrator never quotes his "mistress," never wonders what her voice might sound like. No apostrophes are addressed to her, as if she cannot be imagined to hear, much less to respond.

Pigmalion's statue, similarly, never breaks free of the stone to which she is confined. The moment of her animation – and potential trans-formation into a speaking subject – is the one moment the poem ostentatiously does not represent; the narrator keeps pointing to it, on the margins of the poem, as a kind of vanishing point that defines erotic expectation (stanzas 27–28, 32, and 38). Integral to the poem's tempor-ality of forepleasure – its coy allusion to and evasion of the act of intercourse – the mute, "senceless" statue never comes alive. Her silence, which "seems to grant his suit" (stanza 16), therefore allows Marston to build toward the release of erotic tension twice over the course of the narrative (stanzas 34 and 38). Instead of imagining what the animated woman might say, want, or do, the narrator twice steers away from imagining her side of the metamorphosis. Instead, he imagines only the reader's side of the anticipated event and remonstrates this reader – now explicitly gendered male – for expecting it: "Let him conceit but what himselfe would doe / When that he had obtayned such a favour" (stanza 34). We hear nothing of his mistress's ear, nothing of the statue's. Nevertheless, the figure of a listening ear – "wanton" and "itching" and male – grows increasingly important to the precise extent that it is *detached* from the statue. After expanding the fantasy of what "he would doe" for a few stanzas, Marston again moves away from describing sexual relations with female flesh by invoking the reader's listening ear one more time ("O pardon me / Yee gaping eares that swallow up my lines" [38]). The only parties within the poem's imaginary erotic circuit that Marston imagines to have the capacity for thought, desire, or language are Pigmalion, the narrator, and his male readers.

When Marston does describe the ivory statue's relation to language, we find that more than merely silent. She is in every sense a stone.

> Looke how the peevish Papists crouch, and kneele
> To some dum Idoll with their offering,
> As if a senceles carved stone could feele
> The ardor of his bootles chattering,
> So fond he was, and earnest in his sute,
> To his remorseles Image, dum, and mute.   (Stanza 14)

Her muteness is not merely profound. It is "remorseless." The silence of Pigmalion's "image" is so absolute, in fact, that this "dum" and "senceles stone" threatens to mirror Pigmalion-Narcissus back to himself as if he were as mute and mindless as she – the subject of mere "bootless chattering." Were this Petrarch's narrator, the threat of such a mirroring, mute *imago* would pertain to the speaker as well as the figures in his poem.[10] We would be reminded, once again, of Medusa or Echo as surrogate figures for the poet's exile from his own tongue. But Marston ventures no such self-critique. Instead, he acts like Perseus, deflecting the statue's potentially mirroring silence by turning its image against his character. In other words, Marston indulges in the distancing language of stigmatization – "Looke how the peevish Papists crouch . . . . so fond he was" – in order firmly to separate himself from Pigmalion. Although the narrator finds it convenient to imitate Pigmalion on some occasions in the poem, here he asserts difference. Pigmalion, not he, is subject to "bootles chattering." Pigmalion, not he, is a "peevish Papist" slavishly devoted to a "dum Idol." Marston's simile neatly manages two things at once: first, it evades the slightest hint that a woman might become a speaking or listening subject; and second, it also manages to avoid the potential alienation from one's own tongue that haunted Petrarch's apostrophe in sonnet 78. At the crucial Ovidian moment of trying to use one's voice to move a stone, Marston distances himself from Pigmalion to suggest that his own satiric voice replaces Pigmalion's babbling nonsense. In Pigmalion's "bootles chattering," Marston evokes and quickly evades the Ovidian tradition's trademark critique of speaking subjectivity as a state of linguistic crisis, of constitutive alienation from within the voice itself.

There is one apostrophe in *Pigmalions Image*, however, that proves the exception to the poem's rule that women are mute, senseless objects beyond the touch of language or thought. But to those interested in the story's question of the other – that is, what the stony woman might actually want – the wording of this address takes away more than it gives:

> Marke my Pigmalion, whose affections ardor
> May be a mirror to posteritie.
> Yet viewing, touching, kissing, (common favour,)
> Could never satiat his loves ardencie:
>   And therefore Ladies, thinke that they nere love you,
>   Who do not unto more then kissing move you.   (Stanza 20)

Never speaking directly to his mistress, the narrator turns here to talk to "Ladies" as a group. It is the poem's only address to a woman. But notice the considerable ambiguity in Marston's last two lines: "thinke that they nere love you, / Who do not unto more then kissing move you." While a generous reading of Marston's sexual politics might suggest that he is referring to what a woman wants or feels – how far her passion is "moved" by her poet-lover's ardent address – the general idea and syntax of the stanza steers away from any such an interpretation. What the narrator is talking about, as throughout the poem, is the rhetorical effectiveness of male discourse: the poetic attempt, "Ladies," "to move you." Evoking just long enough to put aside the idea of a woman's feelings, "move" jokingly refers to a man's request for sex. Speaking on behalf of his fellow love poets, Marston-as-rake wittily recommends that "Ladies" interpret a request for coitus (rather than the "common favour" of "kissing" and "touching") as the only proof of love. He is telling Ladies what to "think" of male rhetoric (the attempt to move) rather than wondering what they might actually feel about it (how they are moved).

Finally, this address to "Ladies" tells us that if Marston copies his protagonist, he tries to do so insofar as Pigmalion speaks beyond the statue to address a male audience (i.e. "O Ovid!"). In other words, where Pigmalion seems to be trying to "move" his statue but turns out to be just as interested in talking to "Ovid," Marston's singular address to "Ladies" is also framed by the poem's larger address to a male audience (which we discover in the poem's final deflection: "Let him conceit but what he himselfe would do"). Addressing himself beyond "Ladies" to these "itching," "gaping" ears – presumably Marston's peers at the Inns of Court – Marston's erotico-rhetorical maneuvers recall Pigmalion's evasive apostrophe to Ovid. Thus framed, Marston's apostrophe to "Ladies" enacts the same triangular circuit of exchange that Freud famously describes as the dynamic of a dirty joke (and from which Sedgwick's analysis of homosociality derives).[11] A woman's resistance – in Ovidian-Petrarchan terms, her stoniness – is first the condition and then the conduit for male erotic discourse. As such, it means that this apostrophe to "Ladies" presumes their silence as it reaches beyond them to animate the "gaping," "itching" ears of the male readers who constitute the poem's final audience and who will, Marston presumes, laugh at his considerable effrontery.

We've seen that in the *Rime Sparse* Laura's voice could grow suddenly powerful – as Medusa, Echo, Diana – and that the sound of Petrarch's various Ovidian "female" voices unsettle the very logic of difference that defines the relationship between Laur*a* and laur*o*. In *Pigmalions Image*, therefore, Marston carefully avoids the question of the female voice altogether. He never tries to speak as a woman. He never addresses his mistress directly (as an entity capable of hearing or responding) but merely speaks *about* her to himself or to that other listening audience. And his single address to "Ladies" very effectively reduces them to the status of being mute conduits for a lewd joke enjoyed among male peers. In light of the poem's consistent rhetorical effort to return women to conventional, stony silence, we should look a little more closely at the apostrophe that explicitly states this desire:

> He wondred that she blusht not when his eye
> Saluted those same parts of secrecie:
> Conceiting not it was imagerie
> That kindly yeelded that large libertie.
> > O that my Mistres were an Image too,
> > That I might blameles her perfections view.   (Stanza 11)

Consonant with Marston's endeavor to insist with renewed vigor on the unbridgeable gulf between male voice and female silence – a difference that sometimes comes undone in the *Metamorphoses* and the *Rime Sparse* – Marston's apostrophe is not addressed to his stony mistress but to himself. Although spelled like the "O" of an appeal to an imagined other party, Marston's exclamation here is rather closer to what we now conventionally spell "oh" – the "oh" of spontaneous expression.[12] In contrast to Petrarch's Laura, his mistress cannot occupy the imaginary place of a listening ear that might, one day, make her capable of responding – of turning from stone to flesh and from silence to speech. If we understand this wish in the context of Marston's attempt to circumscribe the refusal of difference that defines the libidinal contours of Petrarch's brand of verbal fetishism, we will not be surprised that in *The Scourge of Villainy*, Marston remarked of his performance in *Pigmalions Image* that, contrary to appearances, he had "no female soul to move."

My wondrous metamorphosis

We've seen the narrator expend considerable labor to keep his distance from Petrarchan fetishism even within his satirizing repetition of it. Marston's effort to ward off the elliptical implication of male and female voices in the Ovidian tradition is relatively efficient in the poem's rhetorical economy. But its libidinal economy is another matter. We may conclude our analysis of Marston's Ovidian figures with three erotic scenes in which his effort to maintain satirico-sexual distinction encounters some difficulty. The first of these three scenes narrates Pigmalion's voyeurism. It tells us how deeply the poem's masculinist rhetoric of animation, its signifying circuit of male voice to male ear, revolves around the idea of castration, the visual perception of female bodily difference. Thus Pigmalion's gaze on "Loves pavillion" generates desire and fear at once:

> Untill his eye discended so farre downe
> That it discried Loves pavillion:
> Where Cupid doth enjoy his onely crowne,
> And Venus hath her chiefest mantion:
> > There would he winke, & winking looke againe,
> > Both eies & thoughts would gladly there remaine.   (Stanza 9)

For Pigmalion, looking on "Loves pavillion" is like looking into the dazzling light of the sun: "There would he winke, & winking looke again." He sees incompletely through blinking eyes. He sees and doesn't see her nakedness, the empirical "fact" of female bodily difference (woman's "wants") around which the poem's dirty jokes turn. The vacillation between seeing and not seeing, absence and all-too-literal presence, makes this ivory statue deeply contradictory: this "image" is a reminder that some bodies are "wanting" and at the same time is a phallic figure asserting just the opposite.

In this passage, moreover, the narrator is once again copying Pigmalion. He looks and doesn't look, teases his audience by refusing to describe the one thing he tells them they want to see. I see and I don't see: such contradictions transform the ivory statue into a fetish in the psychoanalytic sense of the term – a substitute figure that reveals and occludes the idea of castration for both Pigmalion and the narrator despite Marston's attempt to distance himself from Petrarchan idolatry. The naked image replaces woman's "wants" in stanza 1; and in this stanza, the image renders such "wants" literal – as the can't-be-seen of bodily absence – and at the same time covers them over. Replicating Pigmalion's visual hesitation at the level of imagery and narrative, Marston points to the visual signs of female sexual difference only at the margins, beyond the poem. His broad euphemisms (Cupid's "onely crowne"; Venus' "chiefest mantion") become a kind of narrative "winking." Thus the stanza alludes to female sexual difference, "so far downe," without referring to it, evoking the pleasurable titillation and castrating anxiety of what can't be seen no matter how much the viewer strives to do so. The "naked" statue, in other words, is Marston's leering version of Petrarch's more delicate image of a fetish: Laura's "veil," fluttering in the breeze yet still covering the body he so dearly longs to see (sonnet 52).[13]

The second libidinal "scene" that challenges the poem's assertion of absolute difference at the rhetorical level – male voice opposed to senseless female muteness – is really an aside. But it is also one of Marston's most self-referential and explicitly sexual jokes. At the unspeakable yet culminating moment of the statue's animation – the moment when the statue softens like melting "wax" and thus evokes a fantasy of a receptive female "part" – Marston's narrator once again feels it appropriate to mirror Pigmalion's activities.

> And now each part, with her faire parts doe meet,
> Now doth he hope for to enjoy loves crowne:
>> Now doe they dally, kisse, embrace together,
>> Like Leda's Twins at sight of fairest weather.

Yet all's conceit. But shadow of that blisse
Which now my Muse strives sweetly to display
In this my wondrous metamorphosis.
Daine to beleeve me, now I sadly say:
   The stonie substance of his Image feature
   Was straight transform'd into a living creature.   (Stanzas 27 and 28)

When Pigmalion's "conceit" fails to achieve "loves crowne," the narrator's poem, his "shadow," takes over. Marston now rivals his character with his own "wondrous metamorphosis," claiming that his poem achieves a form of "that blisse" that escapes Pigmalion's unsuccessful "part." Having learned his punning lesson from Ovid's continual movement between linguistic and corporeal "forms" and "figures," and bringing to a close his titillating, evasive series of allusions to intercourse, Marston replaces Pigmalion's "part" with his poem ("shadow of that blisse"). Such a substitution – Marston's poetic shadow for Pigmalion's bodily part – produces an exceedingly complex, deeply sexualized rhetoric of the author's body. In true Ovidian fashion, the phrase, "this my wondrous metamorphosis" seems to refer to two things at once: the words of "this," his poem (describing the statue's "wondrous" transformation); and "this," the narrator's penis (swelling in a "wondrous metamorphosis" as the result of the poem's ever more explicit descriptions of sex). The movement away from "the metamorphosis of Pigmalions image" toward "this" the narrator's "wondrous metamorphosis" is exceedingly elusive, a movement away from reference (to heterosexual intercourse) toward linguistic self-reference. Marston's wondrous metamorphosis thus proposes a fetishizing, phallic, and masturbatory verbal fantasy that repeats the excision of "hated" female "substance" in favor of "his Image feature" even at the very moment that a female body seems most to be invoked.

The idea of the poem as phallic verbal idol would, of course, sustain Marston's all-important distance from the hated "substance" of the female body. But the fantasy in this stanza is not quite so univocal as that. Where Pigmalion puts the "image" of a woman in place of the substance of one, his narrator, in this stanza's similar idolatrous gesture, tries to replace Pigmalion's disappointed bodily "part" with his ostensibly phallic poetic "shadow." The narrator wants to keep the phallus for himself: Pigmalion's experience is "but conceit" but I have produced a "wondrous metamorphosis." How wondrously phallic remains an open question. Notice that while the narrator's poem-as-body seems, on first reading, to mirror Pigmalion's erection at the long-anticipated moment of intercourse – since the joke requires this suggestion – what exactly the narrator is mirroring at this juncture remains an open question. That is,

Pigmalion is also mirrored by his "image" (here as throughout): his parts meet "her faire parts" so that the two become like twins, Leda's twins to be exact. The threat of castration hovers over Pigmalion as twin to a female image "himselfe portraied." But if the narrator is copying Pigmalion, a man mirrored by a woman, whose "part," exactly, is he shadowing? As in the scene of Pigmalion's winking, these lines betray the double epistemology of fetishism. But what interests me in the narrator's rivalry with Pigmalion, however, is the distinctive way that he invokes Ovid's sculptor as a figure to absorb his anxieties about muteness (he is the chattering papist, not me) and about the frightening "fact" of women's "wants" (by which I mean both what they might "lack" and what they might "desire"). Such displacements onto Pigmalion allow the narrator to maintain a difference between his own full voice and body and the female image's muteness and lack – a difference that the discourse of verbal fetishism constantly puts into question.

And finally, even the closing stanzas of *Pigmalions Image* contain a sudden, unexpected erosion of difference. Such erosion occurs, in fact, in the poem's seemingly gendered, final apostrophes to the male reader's "wanton," "itching," and "gaping" ear. As I suggested earlier, Marston invokes the idea of an unbridgeable sexual difference – the female body as *interdit* – in order to regulate what can and cannot be said among male literary colleagues. Copying Pigmalion's apostrophe to Ovid, Marston addresses himself to a male interlocutor – the young, cultivated ear of his literary colleagues at the Inns of Court – in order to lay the charge of obscenity at his colleagues' door and, at the same time, to define the female body as that which lies beyond representation. With so much work to do, his final apostrophes to the ears of male readers are no less aggressive than Pigmalion's rivalrous boast to Ovid. Despite Marston's appeal to transparency, however –

> Who knowes not what ensues? O pardon me
> Yee gaping eares that swallow up my lines.
> Expect no more ...

– what actually is going on in these lines remains, to my mind, somewhat opaque. The narrator wants us to move our attention from Pigmalion's sexual acts to his own rhetorical acts. This slide from sexual to rhetorical relations enacts a displacement from the homosocial competition of Petrarchanism to a strangely evasive, labile erotic fantasy. Once again, the poem alludes to the moment of intercourse only to evade it: "when he found that life had tooke his seate / Within the breast of his kind beauteous love .... Who knowes not what ensues?" (stanzas 37–38). This evasion works by putting the narrator and his pen in place of

Pigmalion and his penis and at the same time putting the reader's ear in the place of the receptive statue: "O pardon me, / Yee gaping eares that swallow up my lines ... And chaster thoughts, pardon if I doe trip / Or if some loose lines from my pen doe slip." As the "conceits" of Petrarchan figuration harden into literal, and rather lewd, idolatry, Marston's writing substitutes for Pigmalion's act, turning the flow of a writer's ink into a verbal fetishist's ejaculation. Thus the writer's "loose lines" slip from writer's pen to the waiting receptacle of the male reader's "gaping" ear. It is difficult to locate precisely *which* part of the body's erotogenic zones determine the sexual charge of Marston's figure. And it is just as difficult to determine whether this fantasy is hetero- or homo-erotic. I'd suggest that it is, rather, both. Lying behind the idea of the reader's avid, listening ear lies the newly metamorphosed "Image of a Womans feature" – repressed, perhaps, and declared "obsceane," but not entirely forgotten.

As in the scene of Pigmalion's lascivious gaze or Marston's aside about "this my wondrous metamorphosis," the elusive figure of the ivory maiden's part turned reader's "gaping ear" corresponds to fetishism's double epistemology, its paradoxical assertion and denial of the culturally sanctioned definition of what marks the difference between human bodies and organizes their pleasures. The poem's unconscious undercurrent challenges the culturally sanctioned narratives of sexual difference, hierarchy, and "natural" desire that Marston also relies upon to tell his crudely misogynist jokes and to produce his closing definition of the "obsceane." What we discover, then, is that it is chiefly in the *rhetorical* register of *Pigmalions Image* – particularly in its apostrophes – that Marston tries, not altogether successfully, to manage the poem's unruly erotic energy. Since the Ovidian practice of ventriloquizing female voices reinforces the refusal of difference in the fetishizing, double epistemology of the *Rime Sparse*, Marston pointedly declines this practice. The rhetorical economy of Marston's poem, in other words, responds to the challenge of its libidinal economy by aggressively reducing the resistant female voices of the Ovidian tradition to silence. *Pigmalions Image* reduplicates its concluding exclusion of the female body from representation at the level of the voice, working hard to refuse even the idea of a female speaking subject from the poem.

In contrast to the *Rime Sparse*, where Diana's prohibition, "make no word of this," places male and female voices in a mutually defining, elliptical relation, Marston's definition of the prohibited-as-pornographic works to return the destabilizing, Ovidian female voices of Petrarch's cycle to the "relentlesse stone" from which they came (stanza 21). Happy to imitate Ovidian rhetoric in a number of ways, the one practice

Marston does not borrow from Ovid is that of ventriloquism. Unlike his Latin predecessor, Marston never tries to speak "as a woman." Nor does he follow Petrarch's elliptical definition of two voices, the poet's predicated on – and hollowed out by – a series of Ovidian female voices (Echo, Diana, Medusa). Rather, Marston works vigorously to lay claim to his own full, authorial voice while at the same time foreclosing the questions raised by female voices in the *Metamorphoses* and the *Rime Sparse*. In his epyllion, women are imagined to be, from virtually every angle of the discourse, just like the stony statue: "remorseless, dum, and mute." At the level of the poem's social and rhetorical transactions with gender, we encounter a fiercely masculinist, gynephobic, and homosocial performance that requires the very female "substance" it designates as obscene. But at the level of the poem's labile erotic fantasies, we discover an equally fierce struggle over the meaning of sexual difference – a struggle in which precisely those distinctions between male and female experience necessary to the gendered exchanges of homosociality are constantly subject to interrogation, erosion, and revision. Over the course of *Pigmalions Image*, therefore, Marston's figures for sexual difference multiply and their tone becomes ever more insistent. But none, I submit, are stable. Understood in light of the unconscious refusal of difference implicit in verbal fetishism, or the larger struggle over the body's significance and value in the Ovidian tradition, these figures – at once erotic and aggressive – point to the culturally laden contest that Marston's poem may enact but cannot resolve.

5 "Poor instruments" and unspeakable events in *The Rape of Lucrece*

Stony ladies

In moving from *The Metamorphosis of Pigmalions Image* to its near contemporary, *The Rape of Lucrece*, we are turning our attention to another Elizabethan epyllion in which Ovid's embodied voices are integral to a critique of the unspoken assumptions behind Petrarchan convention. But there are profound differences between the way Marston and Shakespeare juxtapose Ovidian and Petrarchan rhetoric. A sense of these will allow us a better grasp of the local, contemporary inflections that shape the sexual politics of *The Rape of Lucrece*. And it is, of course, precisely the sexual politics of *Lucrece* that have been the subject of much debate: critics have argued, in various ways, that the deeply entangled issues of rape, subjectivity, and rhetoric in Shakespeare's epyllion pose particularly vexing problems for readers, problems that call upon both critical and ethical judgment.[1] The map one draws of *Lucrece*'s literary affiliations and context will therefore be a matter of no small importance, particularly since the issues that most trouble the poem's recent readers – rhetoric, rape, subjectivity, and the female voice – are, as we have seen, central to the Ovidian legacy that informs it. But before we can analyze how Shakespeare engages with this longer legacy in the voice of his Lucrece, or what difference his revisions make to our reading of the poem's sexual politics, it will be helpful first to narrow the focus briefly by comparing the symbolic and libidinal economy of *The Rape of Lucrece* to that of Marston's epyllion.

When Marston uses Ovid's figure of Pygmalion to mock the symbolic and erotic economy of Petrarchan poetry, his satire on the homosocial undercurrent of this tradition thrives on repeated fantasies that one may use one's art to silence female voices. Rather than stage the fantasy of animating his mistress or of hearing her reply to his anxious apostrophe, Marston's narrator desires only the erotic advantage of returning her to stone. In fact, repeated gestures of silencing become the engine of the poem's satire as the narrator, trying to define his own narrative against pornography, enacts the "love-hating minde" he ascribes to the shared Ovidian-Petrarchan figure of Pygmalion. That is, by representing the ivory maiden's animated flesh as the one thing he cannot write about without becoming pornographic, the narrator makes the excluded "substance" Pygmalion "hates" crucial to the poem's sense of its own performance. As the idea of the statue's muteness grows more obdurate, moreover, Marston's numerous apostrophes work hard to secure the fictions of masculinity and authorial voice by excluding female bodies and voices from the poem's symbolic economy. By the conclusion of *Pigmalions Image*, Marston is claiming that the difference between what counts as "wanton" and what "obsceane," between what can and what cannot be spoken, lies outside his poem – in the "substance" of female flesh and the lascivious hollows of the male ear.

Like Marston, the narrator of *The Rape of Lucrece* takes aim at the all-male conversation that underpins the ostensibly hetero-erotic fictions of Petrarchanism.[2] But by contrast to his contemporary imitator of Ovidian erotic verse, Shakespeare does not avail himself of the distinction between image and body implicit in Petrarchan verbal fetishism. Where Marston relies on this distinction to push Ovid's idea of the "unspeakable" into a revealing definition of the "obsceane" – a culturally hegemonic definition of what can and cannot be spoken – Shakespeare takes another, more Ovidian, approach to the relationship between language and the body. Fascinated, in his turn, by the idea of an event so traumatic as to be unspeakable, Shakespeare returns to an Ovidian problem: how to write verses in which a woman tries to represent a crime against her person that lies beyond the power of words to tell. Like Ovid's narrator, grappling with Philomela's *nefas*, Shakespeare's narrator speaks in the voice of a victim who is faced with what she calls, among other things, "so much grief and not a tongue" (1462). In a gesture characteristic of Ovidian rhetoric in general and Ovid's version of Philomela's severed "tongue" in particular, Shakespeare's narrator insists that the usually functional differences between language and body, representation and event, verge on collapse.

The distinction between shade and substance that defines virtually every level of discourse in Marston's poem therefore has very little pertinence in *Lucrece*. We've seen that Ovid signals this collapse with a pun on the corporeal and linguistic meanings of Philomela's "tongue" (*lingua*) and with the image of the bruised "purple notes" on her tapestry. Where Philomela's tongue and woven *notae* suggest a kind of body language in the *Metamorphoses*, in Shakespeare's poem Lucrece explicitly uses her body as a text, turning suicide into a kind of writing when she becomes author of her own "plot of death."[3] At first, she describes her body as a brutally literal legacy or possession: she "bequeaths" her "stained blood" to Tarquin, her body "to the knife" (1181 and 1184). But soon Shakespeare's second Philomela imagines her body itself as a kind of last testament or "will," a textual "legacy" or "example" for her husband's perusal: "How Tarquin may be us'd, read it in me" (1195). Of this characteristically Ovidian body language, Lucrece says that it is but "the brief abridgment of my will" before she passes her intention along, however abbreviated, to her husband to realize: "Thou, Collatine, shalt oversee this will" (1205). In this last word, Lucrece's corporeal legacy turns on a pun that points, like Philomela's *lingua*, toward an imagined intersection between authorship, language, and the body. Here as in the sonnets, this pun on "will" unfolds in a number of directions: the proper name of the poem's author, "will" can also signify "conscious intention" or "volition"; it can mean a written deed of testament whose efficacy depends on its author's death; at other times, "passion," "carnal desire," or "appetite"; and finally, it can also designate either the male or the female sexual organs.[4] Where Marston uses Ovid's metarhetorical story of Pygmalion's statue to separate language from female flesh, Shakespeare transforms the programmatic trope of Philomela's *lingua* into Lucrece's corporeal "will." He thereby points, like Ovid before him, to an enigmatic, violent place where writing and the sexualized body collide.

I do not mean to argue that there are no similarities between Shakespeare's narrator and Marston's. Like his contemporary, Shakespeare is interested in using various fictions about the voice – in speech and in silence – as the means to bring Ovid's rhetoric together with Petrarch's. And as we shall see in further detail, Shakespeare is as taken with the trope of apostrophe as is Marston, particularly as the rhetorical means to invoke an Ovidian presence or "voice" in his text. In addition, the idea of the silenced female voice may be as resonant as the fiction of a speaking one in both epyllia. At a certain moment in *Lucrece*, as in *Pigmalions Image*, the gesture of silencing a woman becomes crucial to the poem's understanding of its own economy of representation. The female voice that is suppressed or "controll'd" (678) in *Lucrece*, however, is even more deeply troubling than the leering version proposed by Marston. Where the narrator of that poem proposes an opportunistic reversal of Pygmalion's fantasy – "O that my Mistres were an Image too, / That I might blameles her perfections view" (stanza 11) – Shakespeare imagines a far more disturbing scene. Lucrece becomes both the Petrarchan object of praise and another Philomela, gagged by her own bed sheets: "Till with her own white fleece her voice controll'd / Entombs her outcry in her lips' sweet fold" (678–79).

Here Shakespeare, like Marston, implicates his own activity as narrator in the story he tells – in this case, the sexual assault represented as the consequence of Petrarchan epideictic metaphors. As recent critics observe, Shakespeare's narrator traces in detail a number of disquieting connections between writing and rape.[5] From Marston's narrator, a self-styled second Pygmalion, we've moved to a narrator who also does little to discourage the analogy between his own work and that of his male protagonist. The puns on Tereus' force – "*pens* her piteous clamors in her head" (681) – and his rapacious "will" underline the connection.[6] Where words like "unspeakable" and "tongue" (*nefas* and *lingua*) in Ovid's story of Philomela "insist on the convergence between speaking the crime and doing the deed,"[7] Shakespeare's "will" and "pen" follow suit, insisting on the convergence between writing the poem and carrying out the acts of violence narrated in it.

But the comparison between the narrator and Tereus is not absolute. In *Lucrece*, I will argue, there are at least two "wills." As we shall see later in close detail, many of the narrator's most self-reflexive, Ovidian moments suggest another analogy familiar to readers of the *Metamorphoses* – that between his narrator's "voice" and Lucrece's. For now, it will suffice to observe that alongside the affinities between Tereus' brutal silencing and the narrator's writing "pen," Shakespeare's *Lucrece* also sketches another, very different set of fantasies about the sound and effects of the female voice – fantasies that differ, as well, from those we found in *The Metamorphosis of Pigmalions Image*. Unlike Marston's "mistress," silenced and petrified on the margins of his narrative, or Pygmalion's statue, "remorseless, dum, and mute," the lips of Shakespeare's Lucrece are stopped only momentarily. She cries out at length both before and after the crime. As heir to Philomela, Lucrece proclaims, "My tongue shall utter all" (1076); and finally she calls, again like Philomela, for "Revenge on him that made me stop my breath" (1180).[8] Extravagantly devoted to the sound of Lucrece's voice – a devotion that has not escaped the censure of modern critics – the narrator revives Ovid's story of Lucretia from the *Fasti* by giving that silent heroine a number of voices, most of them from the *Metamorphoses*: Orpheus, Philomela, and Hecuba. We will return later to consider what these other voices, as well as Lucretia's few words about her inability to speak, imply for Shakespeare's titular character.[9] But I want to note here about this intertextual relation simply that it is as if Shakespeare, upon reading Lucretia's story in the *Fasti*, found its reticent heroine simply not "Ovidian" enough. In other words, it is as if he took up the challenge of writing a serious imitation in the mode of a grammar school exercise, rewriting Lucretia's voice "in the phrase and vein of the poet" – that is, making Ovid's virtually silent victim more truly Ovidian by imagining her as if she were speaking from either the *Metamorphoses* or the *Heroides*.[10]

Despite considerable similarities, then, Shakespeare's Ovidian critique of Petrarchanism differs profoundly from Marston's: it does not displace only to reenact what it satirizes. Where Marston's belated "Pygmalion" turns aside from his statue to speak directly to "Ovid," deftly excising the fantasy of the stony lady's response yet again for the sake of conversation with his male inventor and precursor, Shakespeare's narrator establishes a very different relationship with another one of Ovid's characters – the *Fasti*'s Lucretia.

In other words, if we read Shakespeare's poem in light of Marston's aestheticizing yet also pornographic treatment of woman as a reified, mute object to be used only as a means to enter the more interesting game of conversation with male colleagues, we see that Shakespeare, unlike his contemporary at the Inns of Court, is preoccupied with two different issues: the potentially violent consequences of this rhetorical exchange; and the precise texture of a woman's reaction to such violence. Like Marston's narrator, Shakespeare uses Ovidian figures to expose the unspoken motives behind the received rhetoric of Petrarchanism. But his critique verges less in the direction of satire, more in the direction of an ethical inquiry into this tradition's potentially violent consequences. In *Lucrece*, as we will see again in *The Winter's Tale*, Shakespeare engages with the homosocial conversation of Petrarchanism by using Ovid's female voices to pose a difficult question: what might happen if the chaste, resistant, stony lady were at last to speak back? To put the force of Shakespeare's critique another way, his Lucrece speaks as subject – "Revenge on him that made me stop my breath" – about the same symbolic-erotic exchanges of which Marston's "mistress" is never more than object.

As I have suggested throughout this book, rhetorical performance and self-reflection – particularly as embodied in tropes for lost voices – provide an extremely important route to understanding the complex fantasies about subjectivity, sexuality, and violence that are the hallmark of Ovidian poetry. We saw in the preceding chapter that in Marston's version of Pygmalion, tropes of address are central to what I have called Ovid's phonographic imaginary. Shakespeare, too, evokes this imaginary primarily through the trope of apostrophe. But he pushes his apostrophes in directions that are crucially different from those Marston takes in *Pigmalions Image*. The goal of the rest of the chapter is to analyze what these gestures of address and Lucrece's various Ovidian voices tell us about the consequences of the relationship between the narrator and Ovid's Lucretia. I will argue that the complex, often contradictory

motives behind this relationship are refracted through Lucrece's imagined duets with two other silenced Ovidian women: Philomela and Hecuba.
Running against the grain of the poem's other, prominent analogy
between the narrator and Tereus, these overlapping figures produce
somewhat surprising consequences for Shakespeare's representation of
sexuality and authorship. By exploring these apostrophes and their
consequences, we may better understand what the presence of Ovidian
rhetoric suggests about the paradoxical conditions of subjectivity,
agency, and gender in this difficult poem.

Lucrece's tongue

Two extremely influential essays – by Joel Fineman and Nancy Vickers –
turned renewed attention to the serious claims of rhetoric in *The Rape of
Lucrece*. Their work is central to my thinking about the poem; but each
reaches a conclusion from which I will, in the end, depart. As both
Vickers and Fineman demonstrate in different ways, Shakespeare's
rhetoric in *Lucrece* exaggerates the homosocial dynamic of the Petrarchan rhetorical tradition.[11] To elaborate Shakespeare's pointed emphasis on words and their effects, particularly words of praise, in the
poem, Vickers refers us to the sonnets: when Petrarchan epideixis meets
the greedy hand of the marketplace, the narrator warns, "praise not that
purpose not to sell."[12] For his part, Fineman calls attention to the way
that the narrator censures Collatine's ill-timed words of praise at the
opening of the poem and underscores the violation of his and Collatine's
act of naming Lucrece by putting "the name of 'chaste'" in quotation
marks. And so, by contrast to Marston's narrator, happy to engage in
the verbal fetishism he is satirizing, Shakespeare's is exceedingly wary of
its possible ill effects:

> Why is Collatine the publisher
> Of that rich jewel he should keep unknown
> From thievish ears, because it is his own?   (33–35)

From the fetishistic passion to possess, to hold onto "just one figure,"
that we analyzed in Petrarch's melancholy devotion to his idol ("idolo
mio"), Shakespeare deduces the (homo)social consequence: theft. But as
his concise phrase suggests, he recognizes that such Petrarchan fetishism
is a matter of property – "thievishness" – *and* of rhetoric, or "ears."
    The narrator's focus on the dangers of language comes into still
greater prominence if we read the opening of *Lucrece* against one of its
source texts, the *Fasti*. There, Ovid's narrator tells us pointedly that
Tarquin was inflamed by "deeds" or "things," not words of praise; only

when he sees Lucretia and hears *her* speak (not her husband) does Ovid's
Tarquin conceive his design.

> quisque suam laudat: studiis certamina crescunt,
>   et feruet multo linguaque corque mero.
> surgit, cui dederat clarum Collatia nomen:
>   "non opus est uerbis, credite rebus!" ait.[13]

Each praises his wife: in their eagerness the dispute ran high, and every tongue
and heart grew hot with deep draughts of wine. Then the man who took his
famous name from Collatia rose up: "No need of words! Trust deeds!" (or "Trust
things!")

Tarquin subsequently overhears Lucretia declare her desire that her
husband return and sees her weaving by the firelight; the narrator tells us
that he is, therefore, "ravished by blind love" ("caeco raptus amore"
762). From themes of vision, prominent in both this Ovidian source and
in Petrarchan poetry in general, Shakespeare's narrator turns, with
fiercely single-minded attention, to the problem of speech. To Tarquin's
"non opus est uerbis," Shakespeare's narrator seems to echo, in the wake
of much Petrarchan poetry, an observation about language also typical
of the narrator of the *Metamorphoses*: "non, opus est uerbis."

We can begin to understand the literary-historical texture of Lucrece's
voice in this poem by remembering my argument that in the Ovidian
tradition, rape is the call that interpellates the female subject. The call of
rape requires Ovid's female characters to recognize themselves as
"female" in a peculiarly violent form of socially determined subjection.
Student of Ovid that he is, Shakespeare renders this subjection by
stressing the voice: it is only after Tarquin threatens Lucrece with rape
that the poem begins to quote Lucrece's words directly. Not only does
rape propel Lucrece from silence into the poem's discursive orbit – as
speaker, writer, and reader – but her entry into the poem's discourse
follows the perverse logic of a violent pedagogical curriculum. Lucrece is
a woman who, when chaste, could not decipher sexual double meanings.
But the ravished Lucrece is retrospectively aware of the dangerous
errancies of language that once eluded her. Before the rape, the narrator
comments,

> But she, that never cop'd with stranger eyes,
> Could pick no meaning from their parling looks
> Nor read the subtle shining secrecies
> Writ in the glassy margents of such books.   (99–102)

After the rape, however, Lucrece is suddenly able to read the double
meaning or "guile" lurking in the painted face of the treacherous Sinon
because she has learned the lesson of hermeneutic suspicion from

"Tarquin's shape" (1534–40). Lucrece's traumatic entry into the lin-guistic duplicities of Shakespearean sexuality, her peculiarly violent reading lesson, parallels the trajectory of Freud's subject for whom, as Jean Laplanche elaborates, sexuality is by definition traumatic. This is so because subjects are always unprepared for the world of alien, adult meanings which they come, only belatedly, to understand and remember as significant. In Freud's theory of becoming subject of and to sexuality, knowledge and event do not coincide.[14]

But if Lucrece's retrospective understanding of hidden sexual meanings proposes a traumatic, retrospective interpellation in sexuality as a duplicitous language she learns too late, this does not necessarily mean that the rigid categories of difference proposed by the story of rape utterly saturate the question of gender identity in the poem. Collatine's word, "chaste," Tarquin's crime, rape, and Brutus' decision to "publish" the crime by displaying Lucrece's dead body through the streets of Rome (1849–55) all appear to define what it means to become a woman: it appears to mean becoming an object of symbolic as well as sexual exchanges ordered and carried out by men. But alongside this homo-social plot of violent objectification, we must also keep in mind Shake-speare's inaugural act in writing this poem: to speak as if in the voice of Ovid's Lucretia. Such ventriloquism, I suggest, troubles the certainty of Lucrece's objectified "female" identity (and distinguishes this poem's concerns from those of Shakespeare's other, quite different return to Philomela, *Titus Andronicus*). In other words, because Shakespeare criticizes the implications of Petrarchan rhetoric not by speaking in the voice of Ovid's Pygmalion, but instead by speaking in the voice of his Lucretia, this act of cross-voicing troubles conventional alignments of voice, gender, and agency that are proposed both by a cursory reading of Petrarchan discourse and also by the poem's story of rape. Indeed, the difference violently imposed by rape accounts for only half of *Lucrece*'s reflections on the relationship between subjectivity and representation. The other half emerges in the many Ovidian subtexts that inform Lucrece's complaint, subtexts from both the *Metamorphoses* and the *Fasti* that shape the poem's larger meditations on what it means to have a voice or to be an author.

Notice, as well, that the imaginary "conversation" that takes place in and around *Lucrece* summons other voices and other ears than those called upon by Marston (or, to the extent that Marston is accurate if exaggerated in his critique, by Petrarch). When Lucrece speaks of her own unspeakable violation, she does, of course, primarily address herself to Collatine and, through him, to his male political partners. In so doing, she brings the poem to a close with a collective "publication" – that of her bleeding body – in which both message and address are well suited to the cultural norms of the homosocial tradition. A new social order may be founded on the strength of such a message. But before that moment of closure, Lucrece also briefly addresses herself to women. Where Philomela sends a message to another woman, her sister, Lucrece follows suit: in her apostrophes, the ears of Ovid's Philomela and Hecuba, as well as those of Collatine, Tarquin, Brutus, and beyond, enter the imaginary horizon of this poem's circuit of address.

By giving Lucretia a voice, moreover, Shakespeare can attend to a subtlety of self-representation in the *Rime Sparse* that does not interest Marston. That is, the narrator of *The Rape of Lucrece* has an ear for the voices of the several Ovidian women echoing *within* the Petrarchan subject. The dynamic set in motion by ventriloquism suggests that Shakespeare's narrator, in short, is preoccupied with the always shifting elliptical pull between "male" and "female" bodies and voices – a differential struggle that, as we have seen, characterizes both subjectivity and gender in Petrarch's poetic cycle. This struggle bequeathed to Petrarch's heirs a discourse of difference that was at once influential and precarious. Marston's satire of Petrarchan convention calls upon a rigid, and eventually violent, reification of gender difference – a reification necessary to the objectifying work of pornographic fantasy. But as we've seen, the absolute certainty of difference eludes even Marston: the incoherence or failure at the heart of his joke goads the narrator of *Pigmalions Image* into ever more aggressive attempts to contain the poem's unruly erotic energy by insisting on stony female silence. Shakespeare's critique, by contrast, pushes the elliptical implication of genders nascent in the *Rime Sparse* further than Petrarch had done by calling extensively upon a female voice – that of Ovid's Lucretia – to entertain the hypothesis of *two* kinds of experience.

Shakespeare's narrator elaborates not only the metarhetorical genesis of Tarquin's desire to rape, as others have shown, but imagines at length what Lucrece, the culturally coded object of such symbolic and sexual violence, might have to say about that violence. More important still, he lavishes attention on what Lucrece's "uncertain" saying tells us about the effects of representation on the speaking subject as such, whether male or female. That the terrible event of rape remains beyond language's capture does not mean that Lucrece's attempt to represent herself or her understanding of the crime is entirely without effect. Out of her anxious meditations on an event that eludes the grasp of words, the ventriloquized voice of Ovid's Lucretia opens up unexpected possibilities for the representation of subjectivity and of sexual difference, possibilities rather different than those imagined by Marston through his Pygmalion. In chapter 3 I suggested that the (Ovidian) sound of Laura's prohibiting voice is the disruptive condition for the Petrarchan speaking subject "in exile." In this chapter, similarly, I will suggest that the (Ovidian) sound of Lucrece's voice is a precise index of the impasse lying at the heart of Shakespeare's speaking and writing "will."

The fault is thine

My topic here – Lucrece's voice and the difference it makes – touches on an important debate in modern criticism of *The Rape of Lucrece*. Numerous critics have judged this poem and found it wanting. Once based on aesthetic objections and most recently on political ones, critical disapprobation shadows *Lucrece*.[15] I take the approach I have because I believe that much modern dissatisfaction with the poem stems from not having fully accounted for its complex engagement with Ovidian rhetoric – particularly the *Fasti* but also many other voices from the *Metamorphoses*. Katharine Maus ably documents the dominant reason that critics in the 1960s judged *Lucrece* an aesthetic failure: Shakespeare's self-consciously rhetorical performance was found to be excessive, affected, evasive, and simply not in good taste.[16] Where Douglas Bush censures Shakespeare's "endless rhetorical digressions" in *Lucrece*, much as he condemns Ovid's ingenuity as "soulless," F. T. Prince locates rhetorical excess, and hence aesthetic failure, in Lucrece herself. Prince implicitly aligns the narrator with Tarquin when he comments that Lucrece is "*forced* to express herself in a way which dissipates the real pathos of her situation." She therefore "loses our sympathy exactly in proportion to the extent she *gives tongue*" (emphasis mine).[17] Shakespeare's Ovidian fascination with the use, abuse, and effects of rhetorical speech appears to Prince to contradict the sincere expression of "real pathos." His disapproval associates Shakespeare's verbal "force" with Tarquin's act and derives from several unspoken assumptions: sincere speech is the best index of character; a plain style is not rhetorical but naturally allied to feeling; and self-conscious rhetorical invention is a sign of tedious excess, particularly when it comes to the sound of a woman talking too much. His telling objection to Lucrece's voluble "tongue" brings together (albeit unintentionally) two of the chief issues of this study: the mysterious yet central role given to the female voice in the Ovidian tradition, whether the woman's voice in question is "giving tongue" or prevented from doing so; and the crucial importance of rhetoric to any critical understanding of the cultural and sexual violence this tradition incessantly represents. As I have argued throughout this book, if we are to grasp anything new about the complex issues raised by the representation of self, sexuality, and voice in Ovidian poetry, we must begin, as Maus aptly puts it, to "take tropes seriously."

In the last ten years, negative judgments of *The Rape of Lucrece* have shifted from aesthetic to political grounds. Like the reception of *Titus Andronicus* – the Shakespearean play most saturated by Ovidian narrative and very probably written in the same year as this poem – renewed critical interest in *Lucrece* indicates a renewed interest in the serious claims of rhetoric. Where Albert Tricomi's "Aesthetics of Mutilation" examined the painful coincidence of "language and action" in *Titus Andronicus*, recent work on *Lucrece* approaches the problem of violence in the poem by analyzing the productive or constitutive effects of Shakespeare's rhetoric rather than merely deploring it.[18] And yet, while rhetoric has, for some, become an object of critical study rather than *a priori* grounds for suspicion, Lucrece herself still carries the burden of a sense that Shakespeare's poem is somehow wanting. Fineman, for instance, concludes his study of rhetoric in *Lucrece* by suggesting that the female subject is missing from it: on his reading, Shakespeare's poem "attributes subjectivity only to the 'will' of man."[19] Similarly, after a subtle and influential analysis of the way the Petrarchan *blason* objectifies Lucrece, Nancy Vickers renders her sense that there is something missing in the poem by echoing Mary Jacobus's famous question, "is there a woman in this text?" Coppélia Kahn concurs, beginning her recent essay on *Lucrece* by quoting Jacobus's question once again. Observing that Vickers looked at "only that part of the poem in which Lucrece is simply an object of description" and a "voiceless creation," Kahn then recalls a portion of the *Fasti* to look again at the passages in which Lucrece does speak. But Kahn is interested more in the anthropological content of Roman ritual than the problems raised by Ovidian rhetorical practice; she therefore concludes that even though Lucrece may speak in Shakespeare's poem, she has no "self." For Kahn, *Lucrece* charts "a struggle between speech and the suppression of speech, a struggle in which Lucrece figures not so much as Tarquin's antagonist but rather as a telltale sign of his subjectivity rather than her own."[20]

If we look closely at the distinctively Ovidian aspects of the poem's figures for authorship, however, we discover some rather surprising things about its representation of subjectivity and gender. We can begin to take stock of such surprises by noticing that while Lucrece is certainly the written text or object of scandal in the poem, she also becomes its subject. Anticipating her dead body's final transformation into a published text paraded through the streets of Rome, Tarquin threatens to kill Lucrece, leave her in bed with a slave, and thereby turn her into the "author" of her family's future shame if she refuses his demand for sex:

> Thy issue blurr'd with nameless bastardy,
> And thou, the author of their obloquy,
> Shalt have thy trespass cited up in rhymes,
> And sung by children in succeeding times (522–25)

The specter of being turned into the object of future scandal offers Lucrece a perverse, sexually specific, interpellation. Tarquin's reference to future rhyme forces Lucrece to recognize herself in the language of others – what it means to be called by "the name of chaste," for example – and hence to understand herself as defined by a peculiarly violent form of socially determined subjection. Tarquin's threat forces more than temporary acquiescence, however. It propels Lucrece into discourse: it is here that she first speaks in the poem, and she pleads, the narrator tells us, with the eloquence of Orpheus (547 ff). From this point forward, Lucrece works to counter one kind of text (Tarquin's lie) with another, better text – one that promotes her version of her future name and that brings scandal to Tarquin's family rather than her own. The prospect of being branded with a shameful name, in other words, works efficiently to produce Lucrece as subject *of* as well as *to* language – to become author of her own story to the precise extent that she imagines herself being made the object of scandal.

Rape and the idea of scandal certainly collude to objectify Lucrece – to turn her into a victim and a text subject to the physical, political, and linguistic agency of others. Despite such objectifying collusion, I believe it is still possible to speak of Lucrece as a subject in this poem. Caught in a violent, sexualized social process of naming and authorship, Lucrece faces a situation reminiscent of the one Judith Butler describes more generally as the interpellating function of hate speech: "If to be addressed is to be interpellated, then the offensive call runs the risk of inaugurating a subject in speech who comes to use language to counter the offensive call ... The injurious address may appear to fix or paralyze the one it hails, but it may also produce an unexpected and enabling response."[21] In Butler's account of hate speech, linguistic vulnerability is also the condition of agency – the speaking subject's social survival is at once wounding and enabling. In Shakespeare's account of Lucretia's rape, violation is both physical *and* linguistic; her predicament that of being both object and *subject* of words that have the capacity to wound. And if Tarquin's reference to scandalous future rhymes implicates the poem's narrator in the future linguistic violation of which Tarquin speaks, the rhymes we actually do read tell a story quite different from the one Tarquin threatens to publish – a difference that derives from Lucrece's attempt to counter his offensive call.

Whether on aesthetic or political grounds, then, what critics find wanting in the poem is very often also found wanting in Lucrece. If only from the point of view of the history of literary convention, this seems to me a curious state of affairs. In order to give voices to the inner life of female characters, English poets in the 1590s would immediately turn to Ovid's poetry (either the *Metamorphoses* or the *Heroides*). As Drayton imitated the *Heroides* to speak in the voices of several women in *England's Heroical Epistles*, so Shakespeare turned to the *Fasti* and the *Metamorphoses* to find several voices for his Lucrece. But to attempt is not necessarily to achieve. Informing recent negative judgments of the sexual politics of *The Rape of Lucrece* is the further sentiment that, as Jonathan Goldberg puts it in another context, "it is impossible for a male author to inhabit a woman's mind or body."[22] Because *Lucrece* narrates a rape, the poem's story cannot help but reinforce this intuition. Psychoanalytically speaking, however, such crossing is by no means impossible. It is, rather, to be expected and its consequences for narratives of identity analyzed. From such a perspective, it remains an ongoing question whether a "male" author will necessarily, or always, inhabit a man's mind or body (or vice versa). From the perspective of the Ovidian tradition, moreover, we should expect that such transgendered cross-voicing will be the *norm* rather than the exception. By investigating what Shakespeare's return to Ovidian narrative tells us about the trope of the female voice, I will be pursuing what is, to my mind, a necessary corollary to any notion of "the female self" – that is, the differential signifying process that is the disruptive precondition for any perception of self or gender as such.

Lucrece's indebtedness to Ovidian figures for the voice, moreover, allows us to look at the early modern subject in a way that brings together rhetoric's formal and tropological concerns with the imaginary effects of historical and material practice. I use "rhetoric" here to designate two, interrelated, matters: first, the particular figures that give a characteristic, and influential, shape to Ovidian subjects in the *Metamorphoses* – figures that make them, as we've seen, the subjects of linguistic and erotic crisis. And second, I mean the institutional and discursive practices of England's rhetorical culture – specifically, the Latin curriculum of the humanist grammar school – that gave Ovid's texts such a crucial place in Elizabethan poetry and drama. The humanist curriculum taught in the schools ensured that for at least one generation of writers, the paradoxical conditions of subjectivity and desire in Ovid's poem became part of the discursive apparatus that helped set determining boundaries within which they represented, to themselves and to each other, what counts as the difference between male and female bodies and experiences.[23]

As Walter Ong observed some thirty years ago, the Latin curriculum of the early modern grammar school constituted a kind of "male puberty rite." And in an important discussion of the new forms of discipline practiced in the humanist grammar school, Richard Halpern draws on Lacan's concept of the imaginary to argue that rhetorical education in England did not merely reflect the social process of reproducing class and gender relations. Rather, it *intervened* in that process by installing young boys in "an imaginary relationship" with the schoolteacher. Supplementing overt forms of punishment, the teacher offered himself as an "orthopedic mirror" for emulation. In this pedagogical mirror Halpern locates the interpellation of early modem subjects – a place where the imaginary meets material practice. He cites the strictures of Vives as exemplary: "Listen to [the schoolmaster] intently – to his words, his forms of speech ... and make yourself as far as possible like him." "Make yourself as far as possible like" your teacher in words and forms of speech. Vives speaks an institutionalized demand for identification based on *verbal* as well as visual modes of imitation.[24]

If students were to become Latin-speaking subjects by means of an ongoing rhetorical practice of identification – to make themselves, "as far as possible" *like* the teacher by imitating his "words and forms of speech" – the means for attaining such likeness, however, were somewhat oblique. To emulate a master of rhetoric, a student drilled in the art of imitating other voices. The demand for imitation and identification, that is, did not stop with the teacher. In order to please the master, to be seen to be like him, pupils were to emulate a series of *others'* forms of speech. John Brinsley, the schoolmaster who translated the first book of the *Metamorphoses* "for the good of the schools," especially recommends imitating Ovid's "singular wit and eloquence": "neuer heathen Poet wrote more sweetly in such an easie and flowing veine." As I mentioned in chapter 1, teachers like Brinsley assigned their students English prose excerpts of classical poets, asking them not merely to translate back into Latin but to do so in the *style* of the author in question. Brinsley writes that this exercise of turning "the prose of the Poets into the Poets owne verse, with delight, certainty and speed, without any bodging," is "the first entrance into versifying." He advocates that pupils "continually practice" such exercises until they "grow in this facilitie for getting the phrase and vein of the Poet. "

Fellow graduates from this curriculum, like Francis Meres, eventually hailed Shakespeare as the English Ovid. In Vives's terms, Shakespeare learned to imitate Ovid's forms of speech so well that his schoolmates judged him to have made himself, "as far as possible," like Ovid. The success of the school's rhetorical intervention in the reproduction of properly masculine subjects, then, asks to be understood in light of its effects. If we attend carefully to scenes where characters of the English

Ovid try to imitate "the phrase and vein" of their Latin forbear, we get an even better sense of how precarious the business of reproducing properly gendered subjects might have been – even in the exclusively "male" world of the school. Halpern persuasively argues that when humanist pedagogy centered on classical texts – and here we should remember that Ovid was central to this curriculum – it did so by promoting a theory and practice of imitation that aimed to inculcate self-discipline in students by encouraging *identification* with a dominant model (rather than, as he puts it, an exclusively "juridical" model of regulation by punishing unruly behavior). In such a context, young students asked to reproduce Ovid's rhetorical style in order to please this master may well have learned their figures for "moving" eloquence precisely by identifying with the various suffering female voices in Ovid's poetry that they were so assiduously encouraged to imitate.

It therefore seems to me no accident that the literary figure who reminds Hamlet of his own forgotten "passion" is Hecuba – or more precisely, the sight of another man *imitating* the passion of Hecuba. "Weeping for Hecuba," identifying with *her* pain and thereby moving his audience to praise *his* skill, the actor becomes the negative example against which Hamlet lays claim to what he would call his own feelings. And imitating Hecuba, of course, is precisely what teaches Lucrece something about her own suffering: turning to the figure of Hecuba on the tapestry of Troy, Lucrece "spends her eyes" on Hecuba's "shadow," and "shapes her sorrow to the beldame's woes" (1457–58). In yet another in a long line of Ovidian apostrophes, she addresses the Trojan mother: "'Poor instrument,' quoth she, 'without a sound, / I'll tune thy woes with my lamenting tongue'" (1464–65). Understood in light of the practices of imitation inculcated by the humanist rhetorical training, the labile movement of address, imitation, and identification in Lucrece's apostrophe to Hecuba suggests that Lucrece, far from being mere object in a poem solely concerned with masculine symbolic agency, may be a prototype of Hamlet's metadramatic interiority. Beyond the teaching methods of the school, the problems central to Hecuba's speech in *Metamorphoses* 13 may tell us why she commands such rhetorical and psychological energy in Shakespeare's imagination. Ovid's Hecuba is caught, like so many other Ovidian women, in the predicament of trying to express a grief beyond words: "She was dumb with grief, her very grief overwhelmed both her voice and her rising tears" ("obmutuit illa dolore, / et pariter uocem lacrimasque introrsus obortas / deuorat ipse dolor" 13.538–40). Rendered "mute" with pain at the death of her daughter, moreover, Hecuba's first impulse when she tries to speak is to identify with the victim. She begins her lament for her daughter with the cry, "I see your

wound, my wound" ("uideoque tuum, mea uulnera, uulnus" 13.495).
Such a passage, in such a curriculum, speaks powerfully to the work that
identification can perform in defining the voice of eloquence.

In this regard, notice that after her encounter with her own unspeakable event, Lucrece reenacts the behavior usually reserved for early
modern schoolboys. To discover words adequate to address a situation
beyond speech, Lucrece undertakes a crash course in rhetorical imitation.
Searching among various figures for the right classical model to imitate,
she looks for an ancient exemplar of rhetorical eloquence who will enable
her to represent, and thus understand, her woe. Like any grammar school
student of classical texts, she attempts a series of exercises in declamation
– rhetorical set pieces against Night, Opportunity, Time – and looks to
various classical *exempla* as models for her plight. Forcibly inducted into
a "male" world of duplicitous sexual meaning, Lucrece emerges into the
poem's discursive orbit by following the dictates of Elizabethan pedagogical theory and practice. Formerly unable to "pick" the double meanings out of the "margents" of Tarquin's eyes-as-books, the violated
Lucrece becomes an avid reader of classical forbears. To persuade
Tarquin, she borrows the eloquence of Ovid's Orpheus. Later, to find
adequate disposition for words that are "too many" or "too few" for her
woe, Lucrece turns to the stories of Hecuba and Philomela to place
herself in imitative relation to the sorrow she finds there. Consonant with
the distinction Halpern makes between medieval *imitatio christi* and
humanist practices of imitation, Lucrece does not strive to imitate
perfectly, to narrow the distance between original and copy.[25] Instead,
she works to understand her own story by pursuing a path of eclectic,
wide-ranging imitation – seeking to become the "author" of her own
"will" by trying on the voices of others. Lucrece does not sing the *same*
song as Philomela, but rather imagines herself singing a "duet" with her.
She sings a "burden" to Philomela's "descant," tuning her own vocal
"instrument" by means of Philomela's pain. Leaning on Philomela's
thorn as the "fret" that makes her sing, she does not replicate Ovid's
Philomela but uses her as a model for how to suffer with affecting
eloquence. Thus the lyrical idea of the nightingale's voice, rather than the
actual words of the Ovidian character, allows her to invoke the moving
example of Philomela without being bound by an ideal of exact imitation.

She is not her own

I believe that if we look carefully at Lucrece's precarious and violated
entry into public discourse – particularly at the impact that Ovid's
phonographic imaginary has on her vexed appearance as a figure for

authorship – we learn much about the paradoxical conditions of subjectivity in Shakespeare. In making such a case, I am bringing a somewhat different view of the subject to bear upon *The Rape of Lucrece* than others have done. For what one understands by "the subject" – and the way one reads the literary history that gives this subject its distinctive color and texture – makes all the difference to one's critical judgment of this epyllion. In chapter 3, I juxtaposed the literary history of Petrarch's return to Ovid with contemporary psychoanalytic theory, arguing that to understand the place of Ovidian rhetoric in Petrarch's *Rime Sparse* means confronting the way that representing the self, for Petrarch, entails a constitutive blindness to one's own history. We saw that this blindness, in fact, is not a question of knowledge about the self (or lack of such knowledge). Rather, it is enacted in the very movement of speaking or writing within which, paradoxically, the poet most hopes to capture a "true image" of himself. In canzone 23, Petrarch takes Ovid's Actaeon, imprisoned by his changing mouth but also by the poem's iterative present tense, to be the appropriate figure for this predicament. My argument about the relationship between subjectivity and language in *The Rape of Lucrece* similarly derives from the joint vantages provided by literary history and contemporary psychoanalytic theory. Because we can better assess the claims of the latter by paying close attention to the former, however, I advance the psychoanalytic claim only after drawing a more precise map of the literary history that helps determine the shape of subjectivity in *Lucrece*.

When thinking through the poem's fictions about Lucrece's speaking voice, we must again think of Ovidian and Petrarchan rhetoric together. First, Ovid. I've suggested that one of Shakespeare's motives for writing *The Rape of Lucrece* is the desire to give Ovid's silent Lucretia a speaking voice. We can, perhaps, hear such a motive in at least three places in the poem. First, a telling Ovidian figure emerges when Lucrece tries to fend off Tarquin's threat. Though objectified and ravished as the result of her husband's ill-timed discourse and "the name of 'chaste,'" Lucrece, for a brief moment, acquires a voice as persuasive as Orpheus'. Lucrece wakes to discover Tarquin in her room and the narrator characterizes her impromptu eloquence in the following terms:

> But when a black-fac'd cloud the world doth threat,
> In his dim mist th'aspiring mountains hiding,
> From earth's dark womb some gentle gust doth get,
> Which blow these pitchy vapors from their biding,
> Hind'ring their present fall by this dividing;
> So his unhallowed haste her words delays,
> And moody Pluto winks while Orpheus plays.   (547–53)

Ovid tells us how Orpheus' voice affected several residents of the under-world: "Tantalus did not catch the fleeing water, and Ixion's wheel stopped in wonder .... and you, Sisyphus, sat down on your rock ("nec Tantalus undam / captauit refugam, stupuitque Ixionis orbis/ ... inque tuo sedisti, Sisyphe, saxo").[26] Shakespeare therefore immediately attri-butes to his momentarily Orphic Lucrece the power to "delay" even "moody Pluto" himself. And he transforms Ovid's story of Orpheus' journey to the underworld by making Lucrece a singer with the power to marshal the very atmosphere of that world. Drawing on Ovid's pneu-matic version of poetic voice in the *Metamorphoses* – the narrator's emphasis on the movement of air inside and outside the speaking body – Shakespeare's Lucrece turns the very atmosphere of the underworld into a new, and powerful, maternal song. She pleads in a voice that sounds like a "gentle gust" from "earth's dark womb" and is able to "blow" Tarquin's "pitchy vapors from their biding." Her poetic breath, a deeply Ovidian trope to which I will return at the end of this chapter, momentarily triumphs over his. Victim as she is of the male tongue, Lucrece nonetheless assumes here one of the most powerful Renaissance figures for the persuasive powers of poetry.

Second, we should note that in place of Ovid's mutilated and tongue-less Philomela – who was to become the prototype for the objectified, ravished Lavinia in *Titus* – Shakespeare invokes Philomela the night-ingale, a bird whose conventional status as a trope for the lyric voice inspires Lucrece to sing a duet.[27] It is not Philomela's missing tongue or her skilled, silent fingers, but the imagined compensations of her song that the narrator stresses. In fact, Ovid's Philomela shades rather quickly, by way of the lyric trope of the nightingale, into Ovid's Orpheus:

> Some dark deep desert seated from the way
> That knows not parching heat nor freezing cold,
> Will we find out; and there we will unfold
>   To creatures stern, sad tunes to change their kinds.
>   Since men prove beasts, let beasts bear gentle minds.   (1144–48)

Imagined through the story of Orpheus, the ravished Philomela and Lucrece together gain the recompense of song, "stern sad tunes" capable of changing "kinds."

And third, we hear a whisper of the narrator's inaugural motive – to lend a tongue – when he alludes to Philomela yet again when describing the "well painted piece" of Troy and its legendary traumas (1444). Because the "sad shadow" of mute Hecuba appears on what most believe to be a *tapestry* in a poem that continually takes the sack of a city as a metaphor for rape, the very presentation of Hecuba's "distress" (1445) resonates with that of the ravished Philomela, the woman who could turn muteness into language by visual means. Where in the first apostrophe Lucrece attributes Orphic vocal powers to Philomela and, by implication, to herself, in this scene she moves further still toward assuming these powers. Lucrece tries to give a moving voice to an inanimate picture.

> On this sad shadow Lucrece spends her eyes,
> And shapes her sorrow to the beldame's woes,
> Who nothing wants to answer her but cries
> And bitter words to ban her cruel foes:
> The painter was no god to lend her those,
>   And therefore Lucrece swears he did her wrong,
>   To give her so much grief and not a tongue.
>
> "Poor instrument," quoth she, "without a sound,
> I'll tune thy woes with my lamenting tongue."   (1457–65)

The trope of apostrophe here claims for itself a specifically rhetorical version of Orpheus' more ambitious designs on the world. By addressing Hecuba, Lucrece hopes to bring her to life, to give her a "lamenting tongue" with which to tell her story. All these Orphic moments, but especially her apostrophe to Hecuba, reveal something about the narrator's desire: the desire for a truly performative utterance so central to the Ovidian tradition. That is, the narrator, like Lucrece, is in search of words with the power to animate the inanimate (in this case, Ovid's Lucretia).

But the voice Shakespeare tries to give to his Lucrece has more than an Ovidian timbre (the revision of the *Fasti*'s Lucretia by way of Philomela, Orpheus, Hecuba). It is also Petrarchan. By this, of course, I do not mean the voice of longing and desire. Rather, I mean Lucrece's vocal predicament resembles Petrarch's autobiographical voice of self-dispossession in writing – a voice in "exile," devoted to questioning the limits of its own power to represent the self and in so doing, a voice that displaces the very self it seeks to represent. Before asking how this characteristically Petrarchan predicament pertains to *Lucrece*, note the conventionally specific way each poet establishes the fiction of a voice. Like Petrarch in the two sonnets on the painting of Laura by Simone Martini, Lucrece explores the power and limits of her own tongue by contrast to the silence of painting. The painted Laura's inability to "respond" to the poet's invocation allows him his apostrophe – a trope that moves the sonnet from the idea of her muteness to the fiction of his speech. In *The Rape of Lucrece*, too, the soundless picture of Hecuba provides Lucrece with the benefits that accrue from gestures of address. In both Petrarch's and Shakespeare's scenes of address, the fiction of a poem's speaking voice derives its persuasive force from the conventional antagonisms of the *paragone*.[28]

Yet within this traditional, compelling fiction about her speaking voice, Lucrece shares with Petrarch a keen sense of her want of verbal skill. In Petrarch's *canzone delle metamorphosi*, the self is exiled from itself at the moment of speaking or writing. In the Ovidian canzone 23, the poet complains that his words fall far short of capturing either Laura's beauty ("ben che sia tal ch'ogni parlare avanzi," "although she is such that surpasses all speech" 23.71) or his inner condition ("la penna al buon voler non po gir presso," "my pen cannot follow closely my good will" 23.91). For her part, Lucrece also finds words inadequate to the task of representing either the event of rape or her reaction to it: "In me moe woes than words are now depending," (1615). Both this event and her feelings about it escape her tongue's capacity; as Lucrece puts it, "more is felt than one hath power to tell" (1288). The narrator, too, continues to comment on Lucrece's "helpless smoke of words": "Sometime her grief is dumb and hath no words / Sometime 'tis mad and too much talk affords" (1104–05). Most important, both Petrarch and Shakespeare represent such self-alienation in language by summoning Ovidian characters (Actaeon and Philomela) to capture this plight. Ovid's narrative, that is, offered both Petrarch and Shakespeare the figural lexicon with which to characterize the contradictory condition of speaking subjectivity as that of being alienated from one's own tongue.

If we are to account fully for how Shakespeare represents Petrarchan discourse in *The Rape of Lucrece*, we must remember that Petrarch bequeathed more than the aestheticizing techniques of the *blason* to English writers. By using Ovidian metamorphosis as a figure for self-representation, he also offered them a particularly rich version of self-alienation in both writing and speech. This subject of linguistic crisis acquired its precise figural and mythographic character because of Petrarch's devotion to the many scenes in Ovid's *Metamorphoses* where the narrator defines the idea of a poetic voice by the imminent threat that a character is about to lose it. And so the Petrarchan poet, as we saw in chapter 3, takes the figure of Actaeon as his own, suggesting through him that self-dispossession is the *condition* for poetic utterance. In canzone 23, Petrarch-as-Actaeon utters his constitutive lament: "I am not my own, no" ("Non son mio, no"). Similarly, in Lucrece-as-Philomela Shakespeare imagines a self whose coming into words turns on a foundational paradox: the subject who struggles to speak and write her grief is never fully author to her own "will" because, as Tarquin tells us, "She is not her own" (241).

Like the poems of the *Rime Sparse*, moreover, *The Rape of Lucrece* draws sustained attention to the self-dispossessing force of spoken language precisely because a speaker fails in her attempt to persuade her audience to act as she wishes. Rhetorically speaking, Tereus' refusal to be persuaded is a terrible, violent transformation of the Petrarchan beloved's refusal to relent to the poet's demand. Therefore the narrator of *Lucrece* draws on the nearly exhausted convention of the lady's stony breast to characterize Tarquin's obdurate refusal to listen to her plea.[29] Begging for pity, Lucrece addresses her assailant in the following terms:

> O, if no harder than a stone thou art,
>> Melt at my tears and be compassionate.
>> Soft pity enters at an iron gate.   (593–95)

We have seen how labile and reversible are the gendered tropes of the *Rime Sparse*, a reflexive mirroring of subject and object that goes on to characterize the unstable discourse of difference in the tradition to which the cycle gave rise.[30] But the point here is not merely that Tarquin, too, can occupy the position of Petrarchan addressee and thus momentarily be as objectified by these conventions as is Lucrece. Rather, this received language of the stony heart or breast, if understood in terms of its Ovidian literary history and the influential rhetorical concerns of Ovid's narrator, reveals more about the status of the *subject* speaking these words than it does about the object who refuses to hear them. Attuned to Ovid's fascination with the scene of an impossible demand – for love, for pity, for life to return from death – both Petrarch and Shakespeare use otherwise utterly different erotic plots to stress the figural and formal problems of the failed words themselves. And by staging this failed plea, they stress that such failure has profound consequences for the inner condition of the speaker who utters his or her words of address in vain. The *Rime Sparse*, and much love poetry derived from it, elevate Ovid's many failed pleas into a virtual poetic ontology. Both the beauty of words themselves and the subjective condition of "exile" emerge as a kind of after-effect of language's failure to bring about the changes of which it speaks. Because Laura refuses his demand for love, Petrarch gains the aesthetic consolations of being a poet. Because Tarquin refuses Lucrece's demand for pity, her voice reminds the narrator of Orpheus' or Philomela's.

In the Ovidian *canzone delle metamorfosi*, Petrarch is exiled from himself – "non son mio, no" – precisely *because* he speaks: "words spoken aloud were forbid me" ("le vive voci m'erano interditte"). For the Ovidian subject called by the name of "chaste," too, her entry into spoken language is a distortion of the self that tries to articulate itself there. Before the rape, the poem never quotes Lucrece directly. After the rape, it can scarcely refrain from doing so – even though Lucrece keeps declaring those words "idle," "weak," and "unprofitable" (1016–17) and the narrator calls her speech "helpless," her tongue "untuned" (1027 and 1214). Lucrece's words neither express the truth of her own condition (compare Petrarch's "l'imago vero") nor constitute an effective instrument to alter it:

> "O peace!" quoth Lucrece "if it should be told,
> The repetition cannot make it less;
> For more it is than I can well express,
>   And that deep torture may be called a hell
>   When more is felt than one hath power to tell."   (1284–88)

Inner torment, Lucrece's "hell," is the consequence of her voice's failure to "tell" the story about the self it wants to tell.[31] It is as if, in the voice of Lucrece, Shakespeare inflects the idea of *nefas* in Ovid's version of Philomela's story – the desire to speak about an "unspeakable" crime – through the autobiographical turn of Petrarchan self-representation. In other words, Lucrece struggles, like Ovid's Philomela, to represent a crime that exceeds "the power to tell." But she amplifies the dilemma of Philomela by moving in the direction of Petrarch's autobiographical impasse: she struggles to represent *a sense of self* in relation to that unspeakable event. The best she can do, in Philomela's predicament, is "call" her inner torture "a hell," vainly pointing to her feelings by calling her words inadequate to what is "felt."

Lucrece's constitutive struggle with "moe woe than words" means that her voice emerges as subject of and to its own impossibility. Therefore the conventional phrases of both music and grammar are, in her case, disrupted: her "discord" is "restless" because it "knows no stops or rests" (1124). Her "modest eloquence" is marred because

> She puts the period often from his place,
>   And midst the sentence so her accent breaks
>   That twice she doth begin ere once she speaks.   (565–67)

Such failures of phrasing continue to disrupt Lucrece's musical and verbal discourse. The narrator, for his part, points to this failure in his analogy between Lucrece's feelings and Hecuba's on the tapestry of Troy. Not only does Lucrece try to lend her tongue to Hecuba, but Hecuba's muteness becomes a mirror for Lucrece's condition (the muteness of pictures capturing, of course, Ovid's observation that Hecuba is rendered "mute" by her pain ["obmutuit illa dolore" 13.538]). It is as if the sound, and sheer volume, of Lucrece's "untuned" and "restless" tongue derives from the poem's perception that Lucrece, like Hecuba, is wronged because she has "so much grief and not a tongue" – that at the heart of her torrent of "restless" words lies a muteness no act of ventriloquism, however sympathetic, can dislodge.

Finally, we should remember that a taboo against speaking makes the Petrarchan poet cry out for pen and ink in order to become a writer ("ond'io gridai con carta et con incostro," "whence I cried out for paper and ink" 23.99). Lucrece, too, interrupts her lament about the uselessness of spoken words ("The repetition cannot make it less") to ask her maid for writing implements: "Go, get me hither paper, ink, and pen" (1289). And it is at the moment of this writing that the poem unfolds its own signature version of what it means to be alienated in one's own tongue. For a subject who is "not her own" to write what she wants means to be torn asunder by the self-division of one, heavily laden word. In *Lucrece*, as Fineman so extensively demonstrates, we are asked to read the effects of the signature, "Will."[32] But the ramifications of that word extend beyond Tarquin's "will" to Lucrece's, moving from metaphorical pen to literal pen: Lucrece is the one character in the poem who actually tries to *write* her will. When writing, Lucrece appears to be imprisoned by the pun on her author's name. She tries to put pen to paper but finds that "what wit sets down is blotted straight with will" (1299). We might take this line to suggest a kind of battle between author, "Will," and character, "Lucrece." Such a battle makes her a competitor for, if not winner of, the name of authorship. But I would also read the pun on Shakespeare's name here as a kind of displacement or lateral movement that defines Lucrece as a subject of verbal crisis: the struggle *between* Lucrece's writing and Will's comes to define a difference *within* Lucrece, an interiority defined by the difference between "what wit sets down" and what "will" erases. In light of this struggle, one wonders: once the narrator has lent his tongue to Ovid's Lucretia, can we be certain whose "will" is speaking or writing? Like the Petrarchan poet-as-Actaeon, the move from speech to writing therefore provides only temporary relief. The movement of the pen produces from him the cry, "non son mio, no" and from her, the self-canceling movement of Will's erasure.

Lucrece speaks about the failure of her words to capture the trauma of an event that exceeds representation and, as well, the failure of words to alter the event of which they would speak. The narrator's piling up of metaphors to represent her woe, moreover, only underlines the way that these figures, like Lucrece's laments, are merely "a wind of words" (1330). One way to read the change of emphasis from Petrarch's use of Ovidian rhetoric to Shakespeare's in *The Rape of Lucrece* is to suggest that where Petrarch's exile in language revolves around Diana's taboo on his speech ("make no word of this"), Lucrece's self-dispossession in language revolves around Philomela's different, though not unrelated, problem: the unspeakable event. The crime of which Lucrece would speak exceeds both tongue and pen, although these "helpless" media remain her only means to redress that event. Both poems betray their Ovidian lineage because they articulate a theory of the subject at the limits of representation. But where the presence of Ovid's story of Actaeon and Diana in the *Rime Sparse* means that prohibition defines the limit to representation, the presence of his Philomela in *The Rape of Lucrece* defines this limit through the word *nefas*, a traumatic or wounding event that exceeds the anxious quest of a "restless" tongue.

Concerning the figure of the mute Actaeon in the *Rime Sparse*, we've understood that in Ovid's figure of Actaeon, Petrarch sees a way to dramatize the poetic subject's sudden, unexpected imprisonment by the language he had assumed to be secondary, or merely instrumental, to thought or emotion. To readers of the *Metamorphoses*, such imprisonment is familiar enough. Lucrece, in turn, feels harried by words that refuse to remain merely instrumental. In fact, the mobile array of tropes and figures Lucrece hopes to deploy become, when she "prepares to write," opposed to both wit and will: "Much like a press of people at a door / Throng her inventions, which shall go before" (1301–02). Struggling against language's sudden appearance in the guise of an unruly mob (a scene reminiscent again of Actaeon and Orpheus, who lose control of language before the onslaught of other angry crowds), Lucrece finds that to be an author means producing a document in which "the tenor of her woe" is no more than "certain sorrow writ uncertainly" (1311). After this "uncertain" writing, moreover, the narrator comments that although her words were summoned to communicate her sorrow, they work instead to diminish and thus betray it:

> 'Tis but a part of sorrow that we hear.
> Deep sounds make lesser noise than shallow fords,
> And sorrow ebbs, being blown with wind of words.   (1330–32)

"Blown with wind of words," the nature of Lucrece's oceanic "sorrow" or "woe" is altered as much as expressed by being given a voice. As in the *Metamorphoses*, the voice of the wind is fickle indeed. Remember in this context, too, that in the *canzone delle metamorfosi*, it is precisely when Petrarch tries to express a "true image" of himself ("l'imago vero") that he fears he will appear to "lie" (23.157) thereby violating the very emotion he tries to capture.

When Petrarch adopts the figure of the voiceless Actaeon in this canzone as a sign of his exile in, or displacement by, his own language, I suggested that he represents the condition of the poetic subjectivity in a way best captured by Žižek's rendering of Lacan's theory of the speaking subject: "the subject of the signifier is a retroactive effect of the failure of its own representation . . . the failure of representation is its positive condition."[33] In *The Rape of Lucrece*, I want to suggest, Lucrece's voice similarly points out that the failure of a merely instrumental (or merely representational) use of language is the positive condition for her appearance as subject. The "subjectivity-effect" called by the name of Lucrece, in short, emerges as the after-effect of a *failure* or splitting of authorial "will" in her case. And in this she most resembles the melancholy, divided subject of the *Rime Sparse*. As we have seen throughout this book, the failure of the voice – the ungovernable action of words that do too much or the failure of words that do too little – characterizes Ovid's reflections on the conditions of what it means to become a speaking subject. This literary history has profound consequences for the subject called Lucrece just as it had for Petrarch's equally influential self-portrait. In tuning the voice of his Lucrece to "the failure of representation," Shakespeare, like Petrarch, carries on the Ovidian tradition – a tradition whose many voices unsettle the very fantasy of phonocentrism they initially seem to endorse. Shakespeare's Lucrece emerges from this tradition as a speaking subject who, precisely *as* a subject, never will have a voice of her own.

Poor instruments

Shakespeare's poem, then, invokes several Ovidian figures for Lucrece's voice to tell us that a functional or instrumental view of language is, at best, extremely limited. But Lucrece herself is a character that others, both in the poem and outside it, often treat or speak about as merely an instrument – either in a symbolic-erotic rivalry between men (Collatine and Tarquin) or in an authorial game between one "will" and another (Shakespeare and Tarquin). As I hope to show, the poem makes this idea of an instrument – as well as related notions of personal agency – particularly elusive, especially when considered in light of the Ovidian literary history from which Shakespeare develops his figures for an "instrument without a tongue." To do justice to this issue in all its complexity, however, I must briefly recall Fineman's delineation of "subjectivity-effects" in *The Rape of Lucrece*. His reading entails several crucial observations about the relationship between rhetoric and masculine desire in *Lucrece* that will enable me to elaborate some unexpected complications that arise when Shakespeare uses Ovidian tropes to give Lucrece a voice.

On Fineman's account, Shakespeare's "will" is realized when the logic of the letter shapes the plot of rape (i.e., Collatine's letter is delivered by Tarquin's "post") and which the poem seems to indict in its first lines by indicting language – its own and Collatine's – as the origin of the crime.

Thus it is Collatine's "publication" of the *"name* of 'chaste,' " rather than the virtue of chastity, that "unhaply" sets the "edge" on Tarquin's "keen appetite."[34] He studies the way that Tarquin, but finally Collatine too, carry out the complex, but very literal logic of Shakespeare's writing "will." As we have seen, he concludes from this logic that in *The Rape of Lucrece*, Shakespeare "attributes subjectivity only to the 'will' of man." And indeed, when Shakespeare grafts the logic of Petrarchan praise and of publication onto the desire to rape, the poem encourages us to align masculinity with authorial activity, to see its relentless divide between male agents and their female victims as sad commentary on the movement, and possible social effects, of writing, publication, and literary history.

We must also remember the exact figural language in which the poem represents the problem of a writing "will." As Fineman aptly observes, the "will" in this poem is rather different from the will we might take it to be (i.e., an originating intention or desire). For the desire or "will" to rape becomes the product of another "will," a kind of after-effect or legacy of the letter – a legacy of circulation, deferral and suspension already suggested by the fact that this one word conveys so many differing meanings, meanings that draw on not entirely compatible semantic registers. Read as a kind of transpersonal cultural legacy that motivates characters to take action in a plot not entirely their own, such a "will" renders both author and his male characters instruments giving violent form to the larger misogynist underpinning of literary history, particularly the rhetorical and social relations subtending Petrarchan epideictic poetry. Author and male characters thus seem to straddle a fence between agency (with respect to Lucrece) and mere instrumentality (with respect to the larger movement of figural language and of literary history).[35] On this account of Shakespeare's writing "will," Lucrece, by contrast, seems *only* mere instrument. In particular, as Fineman argues, she is deprived of any verbal recourse by the perverse movement of the word, "let." Like the bars on the face of a clock, the intervening "lets" of her chamber increase the very force they resist (thus augmenting Tarquin's will) while at the same time they echo the other sense of "admit" or "allow" lurking in the pun. The differential movement of one word seems to define Tarquin's escalating desire to rape – "my uncontrolled tide / Turns not, but *swells the higher* by this let" – while it simultaneously "pens" Lucrece, turning her very attempts to dissuade him into fuel for his fire. This restless signifying movement produces a peculiarly lethal form of male desire: as Fineman puts it, to Tarquin, goaded but "the higher" by "lets," "Lucrece is asking for her rape because her 'no,' *as 'no,'* means 'yes.' "[36]

Lucrece becomes the victim of the letter, therefore, because Shakespeare's story translates its insight about language's differential movement – that one's will is emptied out, displaced, and paradoxically produced, by the movement of signifiers – into a sexual story about *male* desire that takes Lucrece as the means to its fulfillment. In that story, Lucrece becomes mere instrument playing her poor part in the poem's larger rhetorical drama about displacements of masculine authorial agency. Indeed, she is quite literally hemmed in by the duplicities of a language she can neither read nor control when she speaks: Lucrece seems, therefore, engulfed not just by the rape, but by the force of someone else's authorship.[37] On Fineman's reading, Tarquin and his author seem to collaborate in carrying out the "will" or effects of the letter that traps Lucrece: while Tarquin "pens her outcry in her lips sweet fold," Shakespeare turns her own words of persuasion against her. Though she would plead for delay, Lucrece unwittingly employs *double entendres* that only encourage the very rape she would prevent. For instance, Lucrece uses a turn of phrase that is at best unfortunate when trying to dampen Tarquin's lust: she calls herself a "troubled ocean" that tries to "soften" Tarquin's "stone" "with continual motion" (589–95). At such a discordant moment we understand that the conventions of Petrarchan discourse hold, for her, peculiar perils.

But the role of the instrument, like the role of the supplement, is a complex one. We've seen that Lucrece carries on the Petrarchan tradition not merely as epideictic object, but as the *subject* of self-dispossession in language. More important still, however, Fineman's compelling account of the rhetoric of masculine desire in this poem omits the extensive Ovidian material that also defines the poem's thinking about the effects of rhetoric on speaking subjectivity, particularly when it comes to Lucrece trying to write or speak her "will." When Vickers argues for the objectifying effect of the Petrarchan *blason* in *Lucrece*, and for the troubling absence of a "woman" in this text, similarly, she limits her discussion to Petrarchan discourse alone. Neither essay explores the complex debt that both the *Rime Sparse* and *The Rape of Lucrece* owe to the troubled, lost voices of Ovid's *Metamorphoses*.

Shakespeare may well represent Lucrece as a "poor instrument" subject to the violent effects of one kind of will – the violent legacy, and agency, of male letters. But we have also seen that his various allusions to Ovid's *Metamorphoses* – Orpheus, Philomela, Hecuba – comment on the narrator's status in his own poem by turning Lucrece, as much as Tarquin or Collatine, into a figure for the complex problems with linguistic agency that attend the writing of Shakespeare's "will." By remembering the crucial role that Ovidian as well as Petrarchan figures play in this poem, we've seen that he is at the same time implicitly exploring, through Lucrece's position with respect to sexuality and to language, another story about what it means to be an "author" – about what kind of agency the authorial subject has in what might seem to be its own language. In the passage we've already examined, in which Lucrece's first rhetorical "gust" works briefly to delay an enemy as "moody" as Pluto, her vocal power is at once tremendous and fleeting, as Ovid's Orpheus, too, would discover. The rest of the poem's figures therefore concentrate on the limits of Lucrece's Orphic voice – her inability to bring an unspeakable event into words or to change it. On the tongue of the ravished Lucrece, becoming author to one's will means further violating the very self one is trying to express. "Blown by a wind of words," such a self appears only to disappear, a vanishing rather like that of Collatine's joy: "an expir'd date, cancell'd ere well begun" (26).

This vanishing, moreover, has as much to tell us about the poem's narrator as it does about Lucrece. And here a further general resemblance emerges between the narrator of the *Metamorphoses* and the narrator of *The Rape of Lucrece*. When Lucrece offers her body-as-text to her kinsmen, that legacy enacts yet further "abridgement" of her will because it requires another's agency (Collatine's) if it is ever to be carried out. The abridgement is quite literal. To become author to her will, Lucrece requires the activity of other tongues: Collatine must speak Tarquin's name because his wife cannot. As the narrator tells us, Lucrece's "poor tired tongue" cannot say that name since it has "moe woe than words" (1615–17). She can do no more than stutter "he, he." No longer able to summon a powerful wind from earth's womb, the briefly Orphic Lucrece now commands only "untimely breathings" and "sick and short assays" that block the very name she seeks (1720). Such a scene dramatizes more than Lucrece's plight: together with Lucrece's apostrophes to Hecuba and Philomela, it dramatizes the kind of perplexities about becoming an author that also face the poem's narrator. That is: in order to achieve his will, Shakespeare must first, like Lucrece, "lend a tongue" to a literary character written by another hand (in this case, of course, Ovid's). And he must then submit his "will" to be realized only through the agency of others' collective readings (thus the poem's closing emphasis on the people's reaction to the "publication" paraded through the streets of Rome [1849–65]).

This insight into the always belated and always deferring conditions of authorship is profoundly Ovidian. It is, after all, in the final lines of the *Metamorphoses* that Ovid – himself a great borrower of other poets' figures – predicts his "better part" will live if his poem is "read aloud on the tongues" of other people. Echo's reduplicating tongue, as we have seen, is one of the *Metamorphoses'* most memorable figures for the hope, and also the contradictions, attending any attempt to realize a new voice out of someone else's words and beyond the life of the body.[38] And so, too, is Philomela's severed tongue, murmuring on the dark earth in search of the feet of its mistress, a figure for the Ovidian narrator's own anxious meditation on the distance between an author and what merely appears to be her own language. For Philomela's severed tongue is an orphaned *lingua*, a noun meaning both the literal organ of speech and language itself. Once parted from her body, this *lingua* can only mourn in the tracks of its former owner. Indeed, the severed tongue is no longer, with certainty, an index of the human, for its convulsions are briefly compared to the writhing of a snake. In a deeply Ovidian exploration of the tenuous, alienating conditions of self-authorship, Shakespeare's *Lucrece* explores an author's eccentric, dislocating place in his "own" language through a woman's "uncertain" and "untimely" voice and writing. In the poem's *sotto voce* song of another, less certain will than the will to rape, Lucrece as subject is defined in Ovidian terms as the effect of vocal crisis. To be realized, her will requires not only her tongue, but the tongues of others.

Now that we've traced the general phonographic lineaments that define a few of Shakespeare's important tropes for subjectivity and authorship in *The Rape of Lucrece*, we may ask a more pointed question. Exactly how does Ovid define the predicament of his Lucretia? As narrated in the *Fasti*, Lucretia's story reveals an author preoccupied with the connections between language, subjectivity, and chastity. Ovid tellingly defines Lucretia's maidenly *pudor* as an inability even to speak about the crime. The narrator uses a brief rhetorical question, indirect discourse, and Lucretia's bodily gestures to represent the purity of her mind and also to suggest that Lucretia's chastity is something further violated by the mere act of speaking:

Three times she tried to speak, three times she failed; and daring a fourth time, she did not lift up her eyes. "Must I owe this, too, to Tarquin? Shall I speak," she said, "shall I myself, unhappy, speak of my own shame?" ["eloquar," inquit, "eloquar?"] What she can, she narrates ["narrat"]; the end remained unspoken; she wept and her matronly cheeks grew red.[39]

In this one question, "shall I speak?," the *Fasti* shapes Lucretia's character around the contradiction between language and chastity. From Ovid's brief but telling portrait of Lucretia's *pudor* as the further violation of speaking about what she cannot bear to repeat, Shakespeare develops a lengthy series of rhetorical exercises for his Lucrece. That is, Lucrece's extensive commentary on the contradictions of self-authorship are generated out of her maidenly predecessor's rhetoric of the impossi-bility of rhetorical speech: " 'eloquar,' inquit, 'eloquar?' " Lucretia's evanescent reflection on language's impossibility in her case means that Ovid will conclude the narrative of her rape by alluding to the story of Philomela (2.855–56). But for Shakespeare, this Ovidian impasse becomes the positive condition for the tongue of his second Philomela, the woman who struggles to say what it means to be called by "the name of 'chaste.' " As a singing Philomel – the imaginary beauty of whose song seems to be the *result*, in literary history, of the memory that Tereus once tried to root out her *lingua* – Lucrece becomes a speaking subject whose words can only distort the inner state of woe they are summoned to describe. Where the Roman Lucretia finds speaking a violation compar-able to the crime of which it speaks ("shall I owe this, too, to Tarquin?"), Lucrece's attempt to speak her sorrow defines her inner "hell." When Shakespeare tries to shape his very vocal Lucrece out of Ovid's far more reticent heroine, he exaggerates Ovid's sense that, as "chaste," Lucrece is violated by every word she utters: she feels herself "blown" rather than aided by the extremely fickle Ovidian "wind of words" she tries to harness. The moving power of Lucrece's voice, like that of Philomela, the singing nightingale, derives from the idea of its impossibility.

But at the same time, by giving this self-consciously silent Lucretia a voice, the narrator is becoming to that legendary character what Lucrece hopes to be to the painted figure of Hecuba: her ventriloquist. When the narrator tells us that "the painter was no god" and therefore could not "lend" Hecuba either "cries" or "bitter words to ban her cruel foes" (1460–61), Lucrece offers her own voice in place of the sounds missing from the mute painting: "Poor instrument ... I'll tune thy woes with my lamenting tongue" (1457–65). In this apostrophe, Lucrece is doing more than embodying the narrator's general desire for a poetic voice with the power of Orpheus'. She also becomes a surrogate for the narrator since she is *repeating* his inaugural act. Like the narrator of *The Rape of Lucrece*, revisiting the story of the silent Lucretia from Ovid's *Fasti*, Lucrece is struggling to lend a voice to a legendary woman suffering in silence. Lucrece's address to Hecuba, in other words, restages the narrator's implied address throughout the poem to Ovid's Lucretia. Lucrece's two apostrophes to Philomela and to Hecuba, therefore, do more than amplify her inner state as a kind of imitative legacy of female suffering. They also revisit the poem's inaugural gesture. This gesture – throwing a voice – poses a problem of authorial agency. It proposes a complex exchange between author and the mute character (or "instru-ment") to whom he lends his "tongue." Lucrece's apostrophes to Philomela and to Hecuba remind us that Lucrece, as ventriloquist, is more than mere instrument: she is also *instrumental* in the logic of literary history as it passes from Ovid to Shakespeare. Without this "poor" instrument, there would be no song.

Lucrece's apostrophes to Philomela and to the pitiable, silent picture of Hecuba are declarations of empathy with a fellow sufferer (e.g. "Make thy sad grove in my dishevell'd hair" 1129). Each apostrophe develops a fairly strict logic of equivalence between speaker and addressee. Each implies, therefore, that part of the problem for clearly identifying the author-ventriloquist's voice as "male" is that this act of supplying a mute woman with a voice involves some form of *identification* with the victim. As Ovid's Hecuba puts it, "your wound, my wound"(13.495). More than ventriloquized scenes that attribute the power of animation to the voice, Lucrece's two apostrophes reveal the process by which a speaker identifies with the pain of the one to whom she or he speaks. Dramatizing the narrator's own larger, ongoing attempt to give a voice to Lucretia, both of Lucrece's apostrophes also claim likeness and kinship, thereby attenuating any absolute distinction we might think we can make between a poetic singer and his or her instrument.

Acts of ventriloquism work in two related, but unsettling ways, in the poem. First, consider its rhetorical effects. Lucrece speaks of lending a tongue as an act of similarity and kinship. The very resemblance between speaker and addressee may therefore produce something unrecognized, something alien, in the subject who lends his, or her, tongue to a mute partner. Where the silent instrument of Hecuba, as I suggested earlier, is a mirror for a muteness at the heart of Lucrece that no attempt to lend a tongue can dislodge, so, too, does her silent picture provide a mirror for the narrator. That is, ventriloquism may import something of the other's muteness within the "speaking" self rather than simply allow the self to lend its voice: the symmetry implied in Lucrece's gesture and the narrator's works both ways. Remember, in this regard, that just as Lucrece turns to invoke Philomela – "Come, Philomele" (1128) – she commands all other birds to be "mute and dumb" before the sound of her voice (1123). It is as if the anxious undersong to any act of apostrophe is the threat of muteness. We can think of this inversion in another way: something of the silent other's muteness ("without a sound") may be carried within the very subject who throws his or her voice because one judges the performance of ventriloquism successful *precisely when* it prompts one to ask, "whose 'voice' am I hearing?" The poem most lays claim to rhetorical excellence when the maneuvers that create the convincing fiction of Lucrece's speaking voice empty out the voice of the ventriloquizing who lends her his tongue. We might say of this narrator what everyone says of Lucrece: "he is not his own."

And second, the self-decentering movement in these apostrophes creates further unsettling effects for the poem's rhetoric of masculine "will" or desire. We've seen that the poem's various apostrophes – the fictions of voice as repeated and amplified through her apostrophes to Hecuba and Philomela – reveal Lucrece's desire to identify with the mute victim. Lucrece comes to the Trojan tapestry to find a face that resembles hers: "a face where all distress is stell'd" (1444). She wants to throw her voice to Hecuba *because* she is working to identify with the suffering of the "poor instrument without a tongue." And she wants to summon Philomela to sing with her *because* she feels likeness and kinship with the woes of the "poor bird." As Lucrece's couplet implies, the two share a common element: "burden-wise I'll hum on Tarquin still / While thou on Tereus descant better skill" (1133). The way she depicts her goal with respect to Philomela is that she wants "to imitate thee well" (1137). Such a mimetic goal informs her relation to Hecuba as well, whose woes help "shape" Lucrece's own. If Lucrece's ventriloquism repeats the narrator's inaugural gesture in lending a tongue to Ovid's silent Lucretia, then it also reveals something of the reasons for that gesture: Lucrece's apostrophes to Hecuba and Philomela tell us that the narrator, in some way, *identifies* with Lucretia's suffering. As Lucrece says to Philomela, he wants, for some reason, "to imitate [her] well."

To say "identifies with" may imply feelings of sympathy, as Lucrece's tone when addressing both Philomela and Hecuba might suggest. But it implies more than that. As various psychoanalytic theorists point out, identification is, for Freud, the fundamental mechanism by which the ego acquires its character at an unconscious level. In Freud's view of this process, such "character" is as much fractured as consolidated by it. In his extensive analysis of identification in Freud's work, Mikkel Borch-Jacobsen puts the problem succinctly. Although the "ego is everywhere" in the identifications that make up a dream, a poem, or a relationship, this exfoliating ego is nonetheless a strange one: "we must recognize" that the process of identification means that the ego "is nowhere properly itself." In fantasy, the subject "never avoids yielding to an identification and always confuses itself in some way with another ... the subject's place in fantasy is always the place of another."[40] Such an analysis tells us that the "ego" of the narrator in *Lucrece* is both omnipresent in the poem's various identifications – it fills up all figures of authorship in the poem – and yet at the same time is "nowhere properly itself" because, like the alienated and alienating Ovidian tongue, it always makes its appearance in "the place of another." The poem's movement of sympathetic address, then, tells us that the complex imaginary practice of imitation and identification mobilized by the teaching methods of the grammar school worked, as Diana Fuss might put it, both to produce identity *and* to "keep it at a distance." Interpellation by identification, in other words, works only by a kind of perpetual misfiring. "Nowhere properly itself": I suggest that this is the nowhere, this the displacement, that characterizes both Lucrece and her narrator. The process revealed in Lucrece's apostrophes to mute Ovidian women prevents the narrator's identity "from ever approximating the status of an ontological given, even as it makes possible the illusion" of a voice – an illusion of identity as "immediate, secure, and totalizable."[41]

In addition, as many of Freud's essays suggest (for instance, "A Child is Being Beaten"), acts of identification – multiple, overlapping, and contradictory – are by no means given to following culturally sanctioned narratives of gender difference or desire. Thus while many critics have suspected, or implied, that the poem's rhetoric develops an identification between the narrator and Tarquin (and thus speaks to a culturally admissible, if disturbing, heterosexual aim), Lucrece's various apostrophes, by reframing and restaging the narrator's own relation to Ovid's silent Lucretia, point toward an identification between the narrator and Lucrece. Understood this way, the fiction of the female voice – of lending a tongue to a mute victim – runs against the grain of the story of difference violently imposed by rape. For as Borch-Jacobsen points out, identification is a mimetic strategy; as the poem puts it, identification is an attempt to "imitate" someone "well." In *The Interpretation of Dreams*, Freud speculates that "identification is not simple imitation but assimilation [Aneignung = "appropriation"] on the basis of a similar etiological pretension; it expresses a resemblance [gleichwie = "just as"] and is derived from a common element that remains in the unconscious."[42] The "just as" or "resemblance" of assimilation typifies Lucrece's address to Philomela and to Hecuba, captured in lines such as this: "She lends them words, and she their looks doth borrow" (1498). If the desire to be "like" another that emerges when Lucrece speaks to mute Hecuba restages and amplifies the unspoken dynamics behind the narrator's connection to Ovid's mute Lucretia, further complications ensue for understanding the nature and direction of the narrator's desire. Borch-Jacobsen comments that the mimesis of identification is "included within the scope of the wish" that is "illuminated by the secret goal it is intended to serve." And the "goal" of identification, for Freud, "is sexual." In other words, if the mimesis that is identification "is grounded in sexuality" and "expresses a wish,"[43] then the doubled, contradictory question for the poem's narrator becomes: what does Tarquin have, and what does Lucrece have, that the narrator wants?

The answer to the narrator's various and contradictory desires, however, is not entirely a question of objects (or simply of having) but points back to the condition of becoming a subject. As Borch-Jacobsen elaborates, wish fulfillment in Freud does "not so much consist in *having* the object as in *being* the one who possesses it."[44] As usual in Freud's work, the subject is defined as the product of a relationship. While an identification with Tarquin's "will" puts the narrator in the place of being the one who can have Lucrece – the culturally sanctioned direction of his desire – his identification with Lucrece, at the same time, puts him in the far less admissible place of being the one who can have Tarquin. To put this point slightly differently, the narrating subject is fractured and displaced by contradictory identifications and desires: both hetero- and homoerotic desires traverse the phantasmatic slippage of this narrator's programmatic tropes for the voice.

That there might be a homoerotic undercurrent in a poem that opens with a scene of mimetic desire cannot surprise. The reason that I draw attention to it is that by contrast to the model of homosociality and mimetic desire proposed by Fineman and Vickers – a model in which Lucrece becomes mere object of exchanges carried out by men – a psychoanalytic and historical account of the poem's rhetorical practice maintains that these unconscious filiations require – indeed, they guarantee – Lucrece *a place as a subject* in the poem. More than *mere* instrument, Lucrece's voice is instrumental to her narrator. The hypothesis of Lucrece's will – what she has and doesn't have, what she wants and doesn't want – is crucial to the narrator's rhetorical and unconscious mimetic strategies.

When Borch-Jacobsen summarizes the work of identification – "to achieve its own pleasure, the ego has to take a detour, one that causes its own pleasure to pass through that of another" – we might understand his metaphor of the "detour" as a psychoanalytic version of Shakespeare's language of instruments. Now, one might reasonably object that the idea of "pleasure" is disturbingly inappropriate when it comes to the figure of the ravished Lucrece. But I suggest that the story of rape might be the distortion or dissimulation that allows a prohibited pleasure a way of emerging. That is, the narrator can be the one who wants Tarquin only by taking a detour through one who so resolutely does *not* want him. As Freud writes, "the wish is fulfilled only by disguising itself. Wish fulfillment coincides with distortion from the outset."[45]

From a literary historical rather than strictly psychoanalytic point of view, moreover, there may be yet another strategy at work in this question of what Lucrece has and what Lucrece wants. If the narrator's ego is displaced via a mimetic detour through the "poor instrument" that is Lucrece, that is because she has something *else* that the narrator wants:

fame. Fragile though her authorship may be, Lucrece nonetheless manages to produce – or better yet, to become – a text and a name that is wildly famous. It is a text, moreover, powerful enough to change the nature of government in the Roman state. Here, in the fantasy of Lucrece's published body as in the numerous allusions to Orpheus, we see the beginning of a desire that returns with tremendous force in *The Winter's Tale*: Shakespeare's desire for a truly performative rhetoric, a language powerful enough to change the world rather than merely represent it. Fame, scandal's more pleasing double, mobilizes a rhetoric of identification in this poem that is at odds with the rigid scheme of difference set in place by the story of rape.

The narrator's identification with Lucrece extracts a desired "common element": if I give Lucrece a voice, I can be "just like" her insofar as she is author to a famous publication and an undying name. But in order to achieve her fame and be author of this powerful text, Lucrece must kill herself. The narrator's identification with a protagonist who *dies* to be published reveals an ego that is at once "nowhere properly itself" and also, as Borch-Jacobsen observes of all such fantasies, profoundly "altruicidal." At this point in our reading of *Lucrece*, we've moved far from claims of sympathy that inform the poem's attempts to lend a tongue to a suffering, mute woman. The affect of sympathy that characterizes Lucrece's apostrophes – Hecuba's "my wound, your wound" – deflects attention from another, less altruistic undercurrent. In the narrator's desire to be Lucrece, to have her fame, moreover, we may detect one more shadow of the grammar school, with its distinctive way of mobilizing the imaginary in material practice. For it was in the school that young boys learned that ventriloquizing other voices meant that they would be seen to be worthy of love. Worthy of love in the eyes of the schoolmaster and, through him, the eyes of their newly emerging "masculine" society (a word that by this point in our analysis requires all the skeptical distance that quotation marks can confer).

Restaging the genesis of the poem itself, Lucrece's apostrophes to Ovid's mute women tell us that this narrator's very feelings of sympathy for the victim are, at least unconsciously, annihilating. On the one hand, we have seen that he imagines the conventionally silenced Petrarchan object as a speaking, and hence self-dispossessed, Petrarchan subject; that he unfolds the cruel predicament of her voice and her sense of interiority around Philomela's trauma of an unspeakable event; and that he refracts the generally unacknowledged paradoxes of his own position as author by way of Lucrece's vocal crisis. By comparison to his contemporary, Marston, Shakespeare's imaginary engagement with conventional Ovidian material is generous. I am using "imaginary" in the strong, Lacanian sense here as Laplanche defines it: a "dual relationship based on ... the image of a counterpart," of "another who is me" and that "can exist only by virtue of the fact that the ego is originally another."[46] On the other hand, the very act of lending the silent Lucretia (and Philomela and Hecuba) a tongue speaks to the narrator's other, less conscious and certainly less altruistic goals.

Despite the seeming finality of Borch-Jacobsen's neologism for the "altruicidal" subject, we would do well to remember the theory of the "speaking subject in process" – that is, that the imitative, identifying subject's contradictions are never resolved. The narrator's contradictory identifications with both Tarquin and Lucrece suggest that a continuing, paradoxical process of displacement defines *and* empties out Shakespeare's writing "will." We might conceptualize the two poles of this problem in the poem's language of instruments: as "other," Lucrece may be the narrator's "poor instrument," but she is also instrumental to him. It is therefore insufficient for her to remain merely the object of his anxious address. Without a distinctive sense of Lucrece's difference – a subject with her own strategies, desires and goals – no identification and therefore no writing "will" could occur.

Where breath most breathes

The overlapping ideas of ventriloquism and instruments now lead us back by a different route to Ovid's *Metamorphoses*. But it, too, will have much to tell us about the paradoxical conditions of subjectivity and authorship in *Lucrece*. The various Ovidian resonances associated with the idea of ventriloquism tell a story about the relationship between self and other which, as I hope to show, further substantiate the psychoanalytic argument that Lucrece's position as a subject is necessary to the narrating ego – that something of Lucrece must resist the aggressive, annihilating force of the narrator's identification if that identification is to be set in motion in the first place. The implied questions that guide my analysis of the Ovidian contours to Lucrece's voice will be: what kind of necessary difference does Lucrece bring, as other, to the poem and its narrator? And which of the poem's figures allow that difference to emerge?

To approach the first question by provisionally answering the second, notice that throughout *Lucrece*, the narrator imagines the act of lending or borrowing a tongue in intricate musical terms. Lucrece wants, for instance, to "sing" a duet with Philomela and "tune" their heartstrings together; she speaks of Hecuba as we have seen, as an "instrument." Both these apostrophes point to one final, prominent element of Ovidian rhetoric in Shakespeare's poem: the language of music. It is an element that, as we have seen in chapter 2, has much to tell us about the paradoxical conditions of subjectivity and authorship in the tradition Ovid inaugurated. Remember, for example, the metarhetorical figures of Daphne as *flamen* or the Asiatic cacophony of the Bacchae.[47] I've been suggesting that the narrator uses Lucrece's apostrophes to comment on "his" own rhetoric as much as Lucrece's suffering (in the case of Ovidian cross-voicing, pronouns become particularly confining). Where we saw that in the *Rime Sparse* the poet's dream of animating one's mute interlocutor was refracted most explicitly through the story of Pygmalion, in *Lucrece* the musical figures of the nightingale, the singing Orpheus, and the instrumental Hecuba carry the burden of this Ovidian imaginary (again in the strong sense). Lucrece's elaborate musical figures – the "strain," "descant," "instrument," "fret," and, most of all, the singer's "voice" and "breath" – carry a profound intertextual resonance, pointing to the phonographic pressure of Ovidian rhetoric.

Let me begin with the idea of Lucrece's breath – by turns persuasive "gust" and wasted "wind of words." We've seen that Shakespeare's narrator is keenly aware of his own rhetorical maneuver in "lending" Lucrece a tongue: he circumscribes apostrophe's fantasy of animation by turning it into a ventriloquist's ruse. In Lucrece's apostrophe to Hecuba, the language of borrowed tongues points to the poem's nature as a *fantasy* about the power of a voice to animate the inanimate and also suggests that its fictional "voices" emanate from no one certain speaker. The distance implicit in the idea of ventriloquism suggests that Shakespeare was a very canny reader of the irony that constantly unsettles the most convincing fictions of "voice" in Ovid's epic. He is a canny reader, that is, of the way Ovid's poem proposes only to satirize a "metempsychotic" rhetoric about language's power to vivify, personify, or animate.[48] As we've seen, Ovid's continuing fascination with the vocal apparatus – the tongue, the lips, the mouth (the *os*) and its breath – and the poem's continuing fantasies about the voice's power to animate – derive from the long oral tradition of epic poetry as a "song" and from the etymological resonance between mind (*animus*), soul (*anima*), and the movement of air internal or external to the body (ἄνεμος). According to these connections, the "unheard" voice of Orpheus, exhaling his "anima" to the winds, and the severed "tongue" of Philomela, betray a deeply ingrained anxiety about the voice that haunts Ovid's own self-representation as a poet singing the "song" that is the *Metamorphoses*. Both these lost voices inflect Shakespeare's portrait of Lucrece's, telling us what the poem tells us elsewhere in many ways: that their failure is the paradoxical condition for Lucrece's self-authorship; and that her predicament with respect to language reflects her author's.

Making its way to Petrarch's punning on "l'aura" or the "wind" of inspiration, Ovid's rhetoric of animation surfaces again at several crucial moments in *Lucrece*. To understand how important a figure Lucrece's "breath" or "wind of words" might be to the "hony-tongued" poet in whom "the sweete wittie soule of Ovid" was thought to live, we should briefly remember Shakespeare's sonnet 81.

> Or I shall liue your Epitaph to make,
> Or you suruiue when I in earth am rotten,
> From hence your memory death cannot take,
> Although in me each part will be forgotten.
> Your name from hence immortall life shall haue,
> Thou I (once gone) to all the world must dye,
> The earth can yeeld me but a common graue,
> When you intombed in mens eyes shall lye,
> Your monument shall be my gentle verse,
> Which eyes not yet created shall ore-read,
> And toungs to be, your beeing shall rehearse,
> When all the breathers of this world are dead,
>   You still shall liue (such vertue hath my Pen)
>   Where breath most breaths, euen in the mouths of men.[49]

This sonnet elaborates the cycle's most profoundly phonographic, animating wish: "So long as men can breathe or eies can see / So long liues this, and this giues life to thee" (18.13–14). To adumbrate this Ovidian wish, it unfolds as a complex echo of Ovid's concluding lines to the *Metamorphoses*. Shakespeare's sonnet will become an "epitaph" in place of the "opus" that is Ovid's "indelible" monument (15.876); the "name" (5) that will survive beyond the body's death replays the *nomen* to which Ovid's narrator aspires (15.876). And "life" will be perpetuated by means of the poem itself, when "toungs to be your beeing shall rehearse" (11), a prediction that slightly transforms Ovid's final claim that he will live beyond death when his verses are "read on the lips of the people." The single and crucial alteration, of course, is that Shakespeare shifts the conceit of the narrator's perpetual life through the vocalized written word to the poem's addressee, the young man.[50]

Sonnet 81, in short, restages the Ovidian narrator's self-portrait, associating the idea of poetic song that underpins the *Metamorphoses* with the idea of the breath that speaking mouths lend to a poet's written words ("Where breath most breaths, euen in the mouths of men"). Shakespeare's extended return to these metapoetic Ovidian associations in the sonnets alerts us that such images as Lucrece's "wind of words" (1330), her ability to summon a "gentle gust" that blows away "pitchy vapors" (549–50), and her "untimely breathings" (1720) stem from a figural network that not only derived from Ovid, but that remained foundational to Shakespeare's own self-representation as poet ("such vertue hath my pen"). It is the central place of Ovid's phonographic imaginary in Shakespearean figures for authorship and subjectivity, moreover, that accounts for the precise wording of Lucrece's cry for retribution. At a crucial moment in inventing her own "plot of death," Lucrece doesn't point to her violated body but cries, rather, for "Revenge on him *that made me stop my breath*" (1180). In the Ovidian universe of *The Rape of Lucrece*, Lucrece's very breath – and not only her voice and her song – gives her the status of a poet. Her cry for "revenge" might be addressed to a coterie of Petrarchan writers as much as to Tarquin, devoted as they were to talking about silent ladies made of stone.

Recall another brief but telling line about Lucrece's "breath." Just before her plea for pity, when the narrator first represents Lucrece as Orpheus ("And moody Pluto winks while Orpheus plays"), we learn how beautiful she is while Tarquin hovers over her bed. Helpless before Tarquin's rapacious gaze, the sleeping Lucrece resembles death: "like a virtuous monument, she lies / To be admired of lewd unhallowed eyes" (391–2). At first, the narrator follows Tarquin's gaze, drawing on stock Petrarchan figures to anatomize her beautiful parts: "Her lily hand her rosy cheek lies under ... Without the bed her other fair hand was ... Her eyes like marigolds had sheath'd their light ... " and so on (386–397). But then the narrator prepares for his allusion to Orpheus by depicting "life's triumph" over these monumental fragments in the following, Ovidian, terms: "Her hair, like golden threads, *played with her breath*" (400). By contrast to the "altruicidal" dynamic we explored in the last section, this figure, if understood in the context of its literary history, suggests the narrator's desire to animate Lucrece – not from death, but from the reifying conceits of received poetic convention. It is as if he wants to give this verbal "monument" life and breath from "the map of death" that is the inherited, objectifying language of the Petrarchan *blason*.

This tantalizing line – "Her hair, like golden threads, played with her breath" – does more than merely shift registers from the rhetoric of the Petrarchan *blason* to that of Ovidian animation. Evoking the idea that Lucrece is herself a kind of musical instrument, it touches on our earlier discussion of the poem's complex thinking about poetic agency. This trope for Lucrece as an instrument unto herself revisits a crucial motif from the *Metamorphoses*: the relationship between a poet's breath or voice and that poet's instrument. In order to move the inanimate world with his voice, for instance, Orpheus must first "move the sounding strings" of his lyre ("fila sonantia mouit," 10.89) and fails in his attempt only when drowned out by other, discordant instruments. More important still for the thematics of rape, when the narrator of Book 1 depicts the singing power of both Apollo and Pan as a triumph of wind and breath, that triumph relies on a woman's metamorphosis into the poet's instrument (especially wind instruments).[51] When Lucrece's golden hair "plays" with her breath, Shakespeare is representing the sleeping Lucrece, under the threat of rape, as if she, too, were a kind of instrument. In this line, the narrator condenses a number of the *Metamorphoses*' chief stories about masculine poetic inspiration and poetry's success as the triumph of breathing. But he is also modifying Ovid's sexual distribution of labor in the production of poetry's music in Book 1. Rather than merely playing the part of instrument for the poet-rapist's breath or voice – a Daphne or a Syrinx – Lucrece herself is the one to achieve a poetic voice upon waking. *Lucrece* is the one whose vocal power is compared to Orpheus'. And, as we have seen, she is the one to turn words into a poetic "gust" with the power to dispel a threatening "black-fac'd cloud" (547–51). Even in sleep, her hair plays with her breath as if she were a kind of eolian harp, or perhaps Orphic lyre, unto herself. Her passivity in sleep may suggest an instrument waiting for a musician's hand. Indeed, this passivity may lead readers of Ovid to expect that Tarquin's hand or breath will be the one to play her. But instead, Lucrece is awakened by rape into poetic (that is to say, Orphic) eloquence. It is *her* hair that plays with her breath in sleep and *her* words that effect some "delay" by transforming Orpheus' song in the underworld to powerful air issuing from "earth's dark womb."

It is thus the female instrument, and not the "penning" rapist, whose breath draws the narrator's attention. For a moment, Lucrece achieves a kind of autopoetic self-sufficiency when brought to life from a conventional "map of death." As I've suggested with respect to Petrarchan self-representation, her predicament – either the impossibility of persuading Tarquin or, later, of representing her own wretchedness – turns out to be the "positive condition" for Lucrece as a poetic subject. Petrarch's self-dispossession in language is not the only one that matters in the literary history central to *Lucrece*: so, too, is Orpheus' double failure to reanimate Eurydice or have his moving voice be heard above Bacchic cacophony crucial to the poem's representation of authorial subjectivity. Shakespeare's various figures for Lucrece's voice – Orpheus, Philomela, Hecuba – tell us that like Petrarch before him, he is exploring Ovid's conflation of erotic and rhetorical problems by representing the desiring self only in, or more accurately through, the failure of its own language –

the failure, rather than the triumph, of a "voice." In the "brief abridgement" of Lucrece's "will," her "untimely breathings," and the tunes played upon various "poor" instruments, we see what I take to be the most Ovidian aspect of Shakespeare's representation of a writing will: for both poets, figures for such authorship – male and female – produce the speaking subject as, or in, linguistic crisis.

We may now move from the language of breath to the language of instruments. Understood within the particular contours of the literary history at issue here, the complex imagery of musical instruments in Lucrece's lament – images of "tuning" woes and "untuned" tongues, "stops," "rests," and "frets" – troubles any sense of the self's singular agency in its own speech. That is, this musical imagery unsettles the poem's persuasive fictions of a "voice" by inviting reflection on the equivocal status of an instrument and its player. To the theatrically minded Shakespeare, when Lucrece strives to "imitate" Philomela in order to give "frets" to the "instrument" on which to "tune" her woes (1135–41), she is both playing an instrument (singing a song and achieving a kind of voice) *and acting the part of* an instrument: she is, in both a musical and a dramatic sense, "playing." But in Lucrece's case, the Ovidian battle between a male singer and the female body he desires becomes a battle *within* one body, the female body. Indeed, Lucrece understands the female body (her own and others') to be the appropriate instrument for her song: together she and Philomela will "tune" their "heart-strings to true languishment" (1141). Where once her breath "played" with the strings of her hair, now her music will be tuned on the strings of her heart. In these figures, Lucrece vacillates between being the player who tunes her woes and the instrument on which that song is played. In them, we can trace the origin for the sound of her woe to neither singer nor instrument. We must, instead, attribute it to both.

Shakespeare's tendency to explore challenges to singular agency – particularly the agency of passion – by combining figures for the theater with those for music would, of course, continue to operate in these puns on "frets" and "instruments." Thus Hamlet rebukes, "Call me what instrument you will, though you can fret me, you cannot play me" (3.2.388).[52] And Macbeth describes the player as "poore" because he "struts and frets his hour upon the stage" (5.5.25). Along the continuum between these two figures, Lucrece vacillates between being like Hamlet – in becoming an Orpheus who alone can "play" the song of her inner distress – and the "poore player," made "poore" – impoverished and pitiable – because she finds the very means for articulating her feelings only further "frets" or aggravates them. Thus calling on Philomela, she says she will imitate the bird by placing a knife at her breast:

> To imitate thee well, against my heart
> Will fix a sharp knife to affright mine eye,
> Who if it wink shall thereon fall and die.
>   These means, as frets upon an instrument,
>   Shall tune our heartstrings to true languishment.   (1137–41)

"These means" are both an occasion for pain (fixing the sword) and for poetry (the act of imitating the bird). Her self-wounding verses, in yet a further turn, become the "frets" that allow Lucrece to play her music. And like the knife, "these means" fret or worry the very player who requires them. Lucrece's eloquence therefore becomes "too much talk," and her discourse, like the rape, a violation of the very "will" who speaks it.

We've now arrived at a very important, if largely ignored, figure that reveals much that is distinctive to Shakespeare's thinking about the rhetorical conditions of subjectivity and authorship in *Lucrece*: the "fret." Philomela's "fret," of course, stands in opposition to the other extremely persuasive figure analyzed by Fineman: Tarquin's "let." Tarquin, in fact, is the first one to utter this rhyming pair. And when he does so, he compares Lucrece's pleading voice to a wind that fans the flame of his will, an association that should, by now, alert us to the Ovidian contours that define Lucrece as the subject of linguistic crisis. Tarquin interrupts her plea:

> "Have done," quoth he, "my uncontolled tide
> Turns not, but swells the higher by this let.
> Small lights are soon blown out; huge fires abide,
> And with the wind in greater fury fret.   (645–48)

The "huge fire" that surges because of Lucrece's "wind" or voice here means Tarquin's lust. But soon the windy work of fretting begins to fan the flames of Lucrece's eventually suicidal woe. As Fineman demonstrates, the "let" introduces a seemingly ineluctable and violent version of masculine desire into *Lucrece*. But Lucrece takes up Tarquin's rhyme, speaking of her joint suffering with Philomela as the "frets upon an instrument" – frets that enable the movement of song just as Tarquin's "lets" on the face of a clock mark the movement of time. Both the "fret" and the "let" seem to prop human passion – the desire to rape or for self-annihilation – on a particular site of a mechanical instrument. Lucrece's frets become significant, and therefore enable the swelling of passion or of a melody, because they are positioned in relation to other bars whose "differential articulation" makes the song, and its attendant emotion, possible.[53]

Lucrece's complaint acquires its very moving, affective character by still further associations that cluster around the idea of the differential mechanical parts on an instrument that enable a player to play a song.

She calls her lament a "restless discord" because it "loves no stops nor rests" (1124). Playing upon the "rest" or "interval of silence occurring in one or more parts of a movement" to portray a sense of her own restlessness, Lucrece achieves the sound of "discord" because she claims to play her lament without heeding the intervals of silence whose difference from each other and from sound makes a song possible.[54] And she also leans the "discord" of her emotion's tune not only on an instrument's "fret" but also on its "stop." The stop signified the closed finger hole of a wind instrument or the part of a string where pressure is made in order to produce a required note which was "sometimes mechanically marked as by the frets on a guitar or lute."[55] Tarquin's lust once "swelled the higher for these lets" and now, for her part, Lucrece sings a song "by means of" "frets," a song that "loves no stops or rests." She therefore becomes the violated singer of "restless discord." I suggest that it is in this swelling of emotion – either Lucrece's or Tarquin's respective passions – from a sheerly differential, mechanical relation on the surface of an instrument that the poem makes Lucrece and Tarquin equally complex figures for the production of subjectivity as a linguistic effect.[56]

Lucrece continues to imagine her duet with Ovid's Philomela, and thus the precise timbre of her own emotion's tune, in the differential language of music. Her figures for this duet, moreover, further undermine the fiction of a singular voice. At the same time, they also associate Ovidian self-dislocation from one's own tongue with the predicament of inhabiting a female body. Where Philomela's musical "strain" compels her to "strain a tear," Lucrece's pun on her own part in their duet vacillates between music, pain, and the female body at once:

> Come, Philomele, that sing'st of ravishment,
> Make thy sad grove in my dishevell'd hair;
> As the dank earth weeps at thy languishment,
> So I at each sad strain will strain a tear,
> And with deep groans the diapason bear;
> For burthen-wise I'll hum on Tarquin still,
> While thou on Tereus descants better skill.   (1128–34)

As in the apostrophe to Hecuba, we can attribute the sound of Lucrece's woe here to no single agent. She sings a duet together with Philomela, keeping a "diapason" accompaniment of lower pitch. Her undersong or "burden" is an affliction (a "blame, sin or sorrow"), a responsibility (a "load" or perhaps the "burden of proof" for rape that Lucrece's body alone provides), and it designates a peculiarly female condition: the "burden" connoted elsewhere in Shakespeare by the child borne in the womb.[57] No longer vying with the singular voice claimed by such singers as Ovid's Orpheus or Apollo, Lucrece figures her peculiar position in language and sexuality as that of an accompaniment and "burden." The idea of the pregnant, maternal body troubles quotidian notions of singular vocal agency in these lines just as much as it troubles more general discussions of agency today.[58]

Lucrece's Orphic duet with Philomela may be played only on the instrument of the female body, a self-annihilating version of the symbolic-libidinal economy proposed in Ovid's narratives of rape. The rhetorical complications that we've outlined for this song, in addition to its complex literary heritage, make it a "strain" that "strains," a tune that "frets" the very instrument that makes it possible, a burden that afflicts even as it represents. In true Ovidian fashion, however, such figures as the fret, the diapason, and the "burden" mean that Lucrece's voice defies precise location – despite its seemingly intuitive engendering and despite the fact that such tropes as the "burden" are working hard to embody this voice as female. The product of imitation and identification with another song of suffering, Lucrece's apostrophe to Philomela produces two voices rather than one. The apostrophe both restages the narrator's generative relation to the silent Lucretia and at the same time defies any precise determination of vocal agency. The "burden" of Lucrece's song, I submit, is to prompt readers to wonder: whose voice, and whose emotion, do I hear in her song? It is a question that, once posed, eventually draws the supposedly "male" author into the orbit of its restless uncertainty.

The burden of these collective voices and their collective suffering might return us to the problem of identification with a slightly different emphasis from Borch-Jacobsen's. Jean Laplanche distinguishes between modes of identification in terms of a matter of degree, a process of displacement that requires two distinct poles – a definition reminiscent of the difference necessary to metaphor. In the "centripetal" mode, the subject "identifies the other with himself," drawing the other towards his center; in the "centrifugal," the subject identifies away from his center or axis, identifies, "his own self," that is, *"with the other."*[59] This last mode most reminds us that two distinct poles are necessary to this process. And it is in Lucrece's voice, her diapason accompaniment with Philomela, I suggest, that one can hear this latter, centrifugal mode of identification in *The Rape of Lucrece*. Lucrece can be a force that pulls the narrator away from his central axis only if she acquires enough gravitational weight of her own to enter into this imaginary, elliptical relation of mutual influence and displacement. And because this poem, as it keeps reminding us, is based on an inaugural act of ventriloquism, its own rhetorical success *requires* that Lucrece's voice acquire precisely such weight. Both libidinally and rhetorically, the narrator requires the idea of Lucrece's difference as a subject. What one hears in her moving duet with Philomela, in sum, is something one can never actually hear in any voice: the permanent, elliptical dislocation of ego and other that is the eccentric condition for any self, or voice, at all.

In the subtle modulations of the poem's several musical moments, Shakespeare extends and complicates his thinking about the agency and difference of this literary "instrument" to whom he has given a tongue. The poem's Ovidian allusions and rhetorical self-reflection leave it very unclear where to locate Lucrece, as player or instrument. That uncertainty only mirrors the narrator's predicament as he tries to take a place in literary history. Lucrece's voice takes us beyond what we can actually hear in any one "voice," provoking questions about whose "Will," exactly, is singing or playing Lucrece's restless tune. The problematic language of instrumentality is, I submit, but a further elaboration of the poem's inaugural gesture, that of "lending" or borrowing a "tongue." If the narrator imagines the affective tones of female suffering from the unspeakable event of rape as the crisis of a severed tongue, Lucrece's relation to Hecuba (the attempt to lend a tongue) and to Philomela (the attempt to borrow another's tongue) restage Shakespeare's relation to Ovid's silent Lucretia (as well as to the many other voices he borrows from Ovid's narrative to make her "speak"). Shakespeare's highly self-conscious act of playing ventriloquist to Ovid's character from the *Fasti* raises a complex problem of authorial agency and explores that problem both musically and theatrically through the imitations of Lucrece, the figure whose voice is both necessary (instrumental) and mere apparatus or instrument. This "mere" instrument remains the only means of realizing the author's intention. Like the supplement, it can never quite be done in. Further still: as the musical imagery for this problem with the fiction of an authorial "voice" implies, these are instruments that have been, and will continue to be, played by other hands or "tuned" by other tongues. The fame the narrator desires to acquire by imitating Lucrece begins with an other and will continue to depend on a series of future others – as if he, too, were captured by the insight, "and toungs to be, your beeing shall rehearse."

The poem's several figures for Lucrece's voice, self-consciously drawn from the *Metamorphoses*, and its representation of her productively crisis-ridden attempt to be the author of her own "will," ask us to think again about what relationship it establishes between sexual difference and its own rhetoric of rape. The Ovidian language of music – a breath, a voice, a duet, and an instrument – represents Lucrece as somehow "not her own" because she is violated – fretted and burdened – by the very words she speaks. A virtual crisis of vocal agency, unfolded in a haunting oscillation between player and instrument, ostensibly defines the relationship between language and "female" subjectivity in the poem. But this crisis, in fact, turns out to be the condition of the poem's own authorship. A strange displacement of "authorial" voice occurs when Shakespeare represents, through her two apostrophes to Philomela and Hecuba, his own attempt to lend a "lamenting tongue" to the "poor instrument without a sound" that is the Lucretia of Ovid's *Fasti*. For a moment, in the duet with Philomela, the poem moves beyond the claims of a singular voice or ego. It ushers onto another, imaginary stage where collective, dislocating, voices emerge "to keep" authorial and gendered identity "at a distance."

By resituating Shakespeare's ventriloquism and language of instruments within the phonographic Ovidian tradition from which it derives, I hope to suggest that the poem does not "attribute subjectivity only to the will of man." There are, in my view, *two* wills in this poem. I do not believe we can speak of either a "male" or a "female" voice in *The Rape of Lucrece* without considerably distorting the elliptical work of the poem's imaginary. The poem's apostrophes tell us that the very act of giving a voice to silent female suffering blurs the genders and desires conventionally associated with this story of rape. These several acts of lending a tongue, moreover, tell us that the narrator's identifications are multiple, contradictory, overlapping; and that we considerably reduce the complexity and texture of speaking subjectivity in this poem if we strain too hard to reconcile these various voices into a single figure for authorship. While the poem's story of rape may produce in us a sense of certainty that we know what we mean by the words "man" and "woman" – or what we mean when we say a "male" or "female" desire, a "male" or "female" voice – its figural language of imitation and ventriloquism continue to disturb that seemingly self-evident knowledge.

6 "You speak a language that I understand not": the rhetoric of animation in *The Winter's Tale*

Between Leontes' opening imperative, "Tongue-tied our queen? Speak you" (1.2.28) and the final act, where Hermione as living statue returns to her husband yet says nothing directly to him, *The Winter's Tale* traces a complex, fascinated, and uneasy relation to female speech.[1] A play much noted for interrogating the "myriad forms of human narration"[2] – old tales, reports, ballads, oracles – *The Winter's Tale* begins its investigation of language when Hermione tellingly jests to Polixenes:

> Verily,
> You shall not go; a lady's "verily" is
> As potent as a lord's. (1.2.49–51)

Leontes' swift turn to suspicion hinges on the power of his wife's speech. Unable to persuade Polixenes to stay, he first expresses annoyance when Hermione is able to do so. Polixenes has just assured his boyhood friend, "There is no tongue that moves, none, none i' th' world, / So soon as yours could win me" (1.2.20–21). Nonetheless, it is Hermione's tongue, not her husband's, that "wins" Polixenes. "You, sir, / Charge him too coldly," she chides Leontes before persuading their friend to stay (1.2.29–30). Leontes therefore moves quickly from "well said, Hermione" to churlish acknowledgment of her rhetorical power. He understands her persuasive speech not as obedience to his desire – since he is the one who commanded, "speak you" – but as a force that eclipses his own:

> LEONTES: Is he won yet?
> HERMIONE: He'll stay, my lord.
> LEONTES: At my request he would not. (1.2.86–87)

From her success, jealous deductions quickly follow. Indeed, the first hint that something is amiss in their marriage is this seemingly minor quibble over who speaks to better purpose and who is the better rhetorician. When Leontes broaches Polixenes' decision to stay with Camillo, he confirms his suspicions from his own failure to persuade:

> CAMILLO: You had much ado to make his anchor hold,
> When you cast out, it still came home.

LEONTES: Didst note it?
CAMILLO: He would not stay at your petitions, made
His business more material.
LEONTES: Didst perceive it?   (1.2.212–216)

Outdone in rhetorical power by his wife, Leontes makes two interpretive
moves to reassert control over her language. First, he reminds Hermione
of her answer to his proposal of marriage – in fact, he quotes her words
of assent, "I am yours forever" (1.2.105) – and calls those words a
"better" speech than the one that persuaded his friend to stay. And
second, he reads as evidence of infidelity the conversation he has himself
induced between Hermione and his friend: "Too hot, too hot!" (1.2.108).
Making himself arbiter of Hermione's language, Leontes quotes the
words he prefers while giving a fixed, suspicious meaning to the ones he
does not. The scene's pronounced interest in acts of persuasion, one
failed and the other successful, produces an odd effect: plunging into
Leontes' jealousy, it makes his unreasonable emotion appear to be the
consequence of this rivalry between male and female speech. As the
drama quickly unfolds, we watch the king turn a rhetorical anxiety – why
do her words achieve the desired effect where mine do not? – into a
sexual one, minimizing his wife's superior rhetorical skill by interpreting
it narrowly as the consequence of her erotic power. In Act 5, however,
Hermione returns as a theatrical version of Pygmalion's silent statue to
the husband who was once so jealous of her tongue. Almost, but not
quite, "tongue-tied," she chooses her words carefully. Saying nothing to
Leontes, Hermione addresses herself to her lost daughter only. I will
return to those words to Perdita at the end of this chapter. After her
theatrical metamorphosis, Hermione does not speak to the man who
doubted her to the brink of annihilation. Her voice once triggered a
terrible response; now she evades the problem by saying nothing to
Leontes.[3]

I am tempted to say Hermione has learned her lesson. But as I hope
to show, *The Winter's Tale* defies an intuitive understanding of the
difference between speech and silence – or, for that matter, the
difference between agency and impotence, male and female, often allied
with it. The elaborate Pygmalion fantasy offered in the last scene as a
way to resolve the problems inaugurated by Hermione's "potent"
tongue in the first tells us that before we can begin to hear the full
resonance of her concluding silence, we must understand the relationship
between the trope of the female voice in the Ovidian-Petrarchan tradition
that Shakespeare inherits and transforms in this play and the quite
specific rhetorical concerns through which *The Winter's Tale* reads that
tradition, turning it into theatrical metacommentary. Any reading of the

play's uneasy fascination with the female voice, that is, must take account of the complex literary legacy of Pygmalion's obsession with his mute *simulacrum*. As this silent figure passes from Ovid to Petrarch to Shakespeare, it criticizes even as it perpetuates a mysterious tie between love of art and hatred for women. Narratives of rape and of repulsion from womankind frame the figure of the animated statue, tarnishing the luster of a story that otherwise seems to be about love for beautiful form, visual as well as verbal. The literary legacy of Pygmalion's statue asks readers, therefore, to think again about the consequences of the many kinds, and discourses, of love.

Renaissance revisions of the *Metamorphoses* routinely adopt such stories as that of Ovid's Pygmalion as a way to comment on the very medium of their appearance; Shakespeare is no exception. Ovid's own generic experimentation, rhetorical and poetic self-reflexivity, and habit of linking oral/aural dilemmas to visual ones encouraged a highly self-conscious practice of borrowing in Renaissance imitators.[4] Erotic stories from the *Metamorphoses* became highly charged reflections on the power (and dangers) of the story's very medium – be that medium painting, poetry, music, or drama. Such self-conscious visitations prepare us for Shakespeare's much noted – and celebrated – effort to turn Ovid's story of Pygmalion into one about the transforming powers of theatrical representation, about a theater that succeeds where even Orpheus failed: "I'll fill your grave up" (5.3.101). Because the idea of the living statue plays a crucial role in Shakespeare's claims for the theater and in our own critical reception of those claims, it becomes vital to account for the epistemological and ethical consequences of the rhetoric of animation. For Shakespeare's final invocation of the living statue's "magic" draws on a story that self-consciously proposes a close yet opaque alliance between aesthetics and misogyny. I will suggest that in silence as in speech, the trope of the female voice in *The Winter's Tale* allows us to interrogate the terms and the limits of that alliance.

Consonant with my usage throughout this book, when I speak of a "female voice" in *The Winter's Tale*, I mean to designate a pervasive and seductive figure – a discursive effect, not prediscursive fact. Through the sound of the very "female" voice that inaugurates Leontes' jealousy, I will argue, the play distances itself from the king's essentializing effort to dismiss Hermione's rhetorical power by understanding it as erotic power only. Of course, the arbitrary force of Leontes' jealous interpretation of his wife's tongue raises troubling questions about the violence latent in such culturally persuasive ideas as those of "male" speech and "female" silence. Because *The Winter's Tale* was written for a transvestite theater, moreover, I do not presume there to be a given – or more importantly, intelligible – phenomenon anterior to the language that gives it shape (for instance, "woman" or "the female subject"). In moving from *The Rape of Lucrece* to *The Winter's Tale*, we've moved from the plot of rape to the plot of sexual jealousy, both of which are extremely efficient fictions for producing a convincing *effect* of gendered identity. Our shift of genres from the last chapter means that this analysis of Ovidian rhetoric must similarly move from a focus on narrative cross-voicing to the material practice of cross-dressing. In the last chapter, we saw that *The Rape of Lucrece* tends to emphasize its inaugural, transgendered figures of cross-voicing in such tropes as the "diapason," or the need to "lend" or "borrow" a tongue. But *The Winter's Tale* does not, in contrast to many other Shakespearean plays, work hard to draw critical attention to its inaugural act of cross-dressing or to the historical, material practice of transvestism that was the condition for its performance of a "female voice." I will demonstrate, nonetheless, that at a crucial moment in the play – in the trial scene, precisely when we are supposed to be most moved by a wronged Hermione's protesting "female voice" – Shakespeare's rhetoric nonetheless profoundly disturbs its own fiction or femininity effect. Most telling for our purposes, it is his fascination with the Ovidian problem of rhetoric's shaping force and performative function that carries on the work that apostrophe performs in *The Rape of Lucrece* – that of loosening the natural, inevitable, or transparent connection between gender, voice, and body that the plot proposes. This chapter suggests that if we attend to the play's Ovidian rhetoric of animation, its dream about a truly performative utterance, we see first that Hermione's (transvestite) body, like Daphne's, evades the capture of the play's figurative language of gender; and second, that the voices of Hermione and Leontes affect and implicate each other – that once again in this tradition, male and female voices are locked in a mutually defining, differential embrace. An analysis of the "female voice" in *The Winter's Tale* is important, in other words, because it must change our understanding of that term.

"Shall I be heard?"

To apprehend the burden Shakespeare assumes when Hermione is told to "bequeath to death" her "numbness" and speak, we must briefly remember the symbolic and libidinal economy that informs this story in the two chief texts that gave it such tenacity as a fiction about voice, masculinity, and desire: Ovid's *Metamorphoses* and Petrarch's *Rime Sparse*. As Leonard Barkan writes, Hermione's metamorphosis enacts "a kind of marriage between Pygmalion and Petrarchanism."[5] It therefore transfers the central concerns of chapters 3 and 4 to the Shakespearean stage. As I explored in chapter 3, Petrarch brings Ovid's story of Pygmalion into the cycle as a particularly compelling analogue for his own predicament in a pair of sonnets praising a painting of Laura by Simone Martini.[6] The rhetorical issues central to Petrarch's version of Ovid's Pygmalion and to Shakespeare's are two: the trope of apostrophe and the language of praise or epideixis. As we have seen, Petrarch creates the fiction of his own voice through a series of apostrophes and by opposing the picture's silence – "if only she could reply to my words!" (78.11) – to his own poetic "speech." The sonnet's concluding tercet further draws attention away from the silent painting back to his own verbal art when a second apostrophe accentuates the fiction of a voice and the language of epideixis at once: "Pygmalion, how much you must praise yourself ("quanto lodar ti dei") for your image, if you received a thousand times what I yearn to have just once!"[7] I argued that in these concluding lines of address, Petrarch rewrites Ovid's story according to one of the *Rime Sparse*'s controlling signifiers: *lodare*. He thereby refashions Ovid's Pygmalion in his own image, reading him as an artist devoted to *praising* himself for the excellence of his *simulacrum*. Derived from the Latin *laudare*, the verb for praising is one from which, among other things, Petrarch derives the name, "Laura" – a name that, according to the *Secretum*, he loves just as much as the lady herself.[8]

In *The Winter's Tale*, Shakespeare reads Petrarch's poetry and the tradition it inaugurated in precise rhetorical terms – as a question of the power of address and of epideixis. Long before staging his own kinds of address to the shared Ovidian-Petrarchan figure of Pygmalion's statue ("Chide me, dear stone" or "descend; be stone no more; approach" 5.3.24 and 99–100), Shakespeare fits the representation of Hermione (and Leontes' relation to her) into a meditation on epideictic speech. Where *The Rape of Lucrece* explores the violent consequences of Petrarchan epideixis – because "Collatine unwisely did not let / To praise" Lucrece to other men, rape is the consequence[9] – *The Winter's Tale* gives us a Hermione who, in jest, offers herself as the beloved object of praise:

> What? have I twice said well? When was't before?
> I prithee tell me; cram's with praise, and make's
> As fat as tame things. One good deed dying tongueless
> Slaughters a thousand waiting upon that.
> Our praises are our wages.   (1.2.90–94)

Understood in light of Shakespeare's critique of praise in *The Rape of Lucrece*, Hermione's pose as epideictic object for her husband while in the presence of another man should alert us that their rhetorical competition may already have entered the troubled world of Petrarchan verbal exchanges gone awry. Indeed, Hermione's very participation in a rhetorical competition with one man to vie for another man's ear alerts us that culturally dominant alignments of gender and rhetoric do not pertain. Her "potent" rhetoric disrupts received expectations for either forensic or epideictic speech. And so in this play, terrible consequences attend *Hermione*'s speaking, not Leontes', the character who her playful remarks about praise might lead us to believe will follow Collatine as ill-fated epideictic rhetorician. Instead of hearing more from Leontes, however, we hear from Hermione; and what she speaks about is her own power of speech. Her balanced syntax hints to the jealous ear that, just as they are matched in her discourse, the two men may be equivalent objects for her exchange: "I have spoke to the purpose twice: / The one for ever earn'd a royal husband; / Th' other for some while a friend" (2.2.106–08). As if following her lead into the language of payment and exchange (e.g., "our praises are our wages"), Leontes begins to "angle" for proof by changing Hermione's equation of the two men into a suspicious marketplace where she is *their* commodity: "Hermione, / How thou lov'st us, show in our brother's welcome; / Let what is dear in Sicily be cheap" (1.2.173–5). While the rest of the play may seem to return to expected discursive convention by making Hermione (and her fidelity) the enigmatic object of others' discourse – in praise and in slander – that predicament, we should remember, is inaugurated in Act 1 by the unexpected power of her persuasive tongue.

The play's most striking debt to the Ovidian-Petrarchan tradition, of course, emerges in the final scene, a scene that reads the *Rime Sparse*'s rendition of Pygmalion together with Ovid's and in so doing further complicates its own interrogation of the relationship between rhetoric and sexuality. For both Ovid and Petrarch use what Kenneth Gross aptly calls "the dream of the moving statue" as an erotic, synaesthetic investigation of the status of the human voice and the consequences of rhetorical speech. In both, as in Shakespeare's play, this investigation occurs by way of a meditation on the success or failure of an *address*. In all three texts, this address draws our attention to the way that all parties present are implicated in and defined by the verbal event.

Consonant with the phonographic imaginary of the *Metamorphoses*, Pygmalion's wishes come true because he addresses words of prayer to Venus. The story of animation, the event of the statue's motion, offers an erotic version of a rhetorician's dream. The scene's action and considerable dramatic effect (waiting for a statue to move) derives, as we've seen Marston was quick to notice, from a pun on the desired end of rhetorical speech. Drawing on the contemporary word for rhetorical power – to "move" (*mouere*) – the narrator tells us that in his statue, Pygmalion believes he has an audience that "*wants* to be moved" (10.251).[10] And because the narrator of the story is the grieving Orpheus, yet another powerful fantasy about the voice's power informs the ivory maiden's animation. Shakespeare, too, connects these stories. After the "statue" moves, Paulina warns Leontes: "Do not shun her / Until you see her die again, for then / You kill her double" (5.3.105–7). Paulina's imperative deftly combines the story of Pygmalion's statue with that of Orpheus' Eurydice by suggesting two things: like the statue, Hermione has come to life; and because of this animation, she may, like Eurydice, die twice. Indeed, Golding's translation of Ovid's text may have suggested Paulina's wording. For Ovid's version of Eurydice's "twin" death – "stupuit gemina nece coniugis Orpheus" – Golding renders, "This double dying of his wyfe set Orphye in a stound."[11]

The interwoven stories of Orpheus and Pygmalion seem, at first glance, to propose a familiar hierarchy between male verbal agency on the one hand and female silence and death on the other. Where the sculptor's prayer succeeds, the statue says nothing and has no name; where Orpheus' song momentarily takes over the narrative of the poem – thus predicating Book 10 of the *Metamorphoses* itself on Eurydice's absence – Eurydice utters a barely audible *uale* before "falling back again to the place whence she had come" (10.63). As Petrarch realized, the first (male verbal agency) seems to depend upon the second (female silence and death). But as we saw in chapter 2, trouble soon disturbs this too sanguine version of male vocal power. Once able to move the inanimate world by "moving his voice in song" ("uocem carmine mouit," 10.147), Orpheus dies because Bacchic (female) noise drowns out his voice: the "huge uproar" of discordant flutes, horns, drums "and the howlings of the Bacchanals" overwhelms the sound of Orpheus's lyre ("ingens / clamor ... et Bacchei ululatus" 11.15–17). Formerly listening stones turn to weapons, stones now "reddened with the blood of the bard whose voice was unheard" ("saxa / non exauditi rubuerunt sanguine uatis" 11.18–19). And where Pygmalion succeeds in animating his beloved, his narrator fails. Winning Eurydice only to do the one thing he knows will send her back again, Orpheus then sings a song in which we hear the story of yet another beloved woman given life through art. Orpheus's *failure* underwrites the story he tells, making the fantasy of the statue's animation part of the wishful *fort-da* game of his impossible desire. These interwoven narratives therefore tell us that power is fleetingly, intermittently, and only fantasmatically granted the male voice. And they tell us, moreover, that his voice may not be the only sound that matters.

Still, we must acknowledge that Eurydice's death and the unnamed statue's silence in the Orpheus–Pygmalion sequence conform to a larger fantasy, first proposed in Book 1 of the *Metamorphoses*, in which male vocal triumph requires female absence or resistance. Two stories of attempted rape – Apollo's pursuit of Daphne and Pan's of Syrinx – tell the origins of epideictic and pastoral poetry by proposing a rigid sexual division of labor in the production of song. Close on Daphne's heels, the god of poetry fails to persuade and so becomes himself – sings an epideictic poem rather than "imperfect words" – *because* she eludes his grasp.[12] And hard on the heels of that silencing follows Pan's pursuit of Syrinx, an attempted rape that repeats and intensifies the first. Where Apollo's breathing down Daphne's neck becomes the breath of poetry, Pan's breath turns into music as he sighs through the newly immobilized body of Syrinx: "the soft air stirring in the reeds gave forth a low sound like a complaint" (1.708). In the context of these violent pursuits, remember that yet other forms of misogyny underwrite the Orpheus–Pygmalion sequence. Grieving for Eurydice, Orpheus "shunned all love of womankind," becoming the "author" in Thrace of "giving his love to tender boys."[13] Pygmalion's "disgust" for female sexual behavior repeats his narrator's aversion: having seen the prostitution of the Propoetides, he creates a statue more beautiful than "any woman born" ("qua femina nasci / nulla potest," 10.248–9) to eradicate the "faults that nature had so liberally given the female mind" ("offensus uitiis, quae plurima menti / femineae natura dedit," 10.244–5). For rejecting women, Orpheus will soon die at the hands of Bacchantes. Ovid thus qualifies Pygmalion's seeming aesthetic triumph twice, suggesting that it is rooted in misogyny; aversion to women is its inaugural gesture.[14] The Bacchic cry upon seeing Orpheus – "here is the man who scorns us!" ("hic est nostri contemptor!" 11.7) – claims that revenge from women (or from stones) is the best this erotic-symbolic economy can expect.[15]

As we've seen, such misogyny was not lost on later writers: Marston summarizes his reading of Pygmalion's "love-hating mind" concisely in the opening stanza of *The Metamorphosis of Pigmalion's Image* as knowledge of women's "wants, and mens perfection." Shakespeare's only other direct reference to the story suggests that he is more than familiar with this "love-hating" tradition. In *Measure for Measure*, "Pygmalion's image" means "prostitute," exactly recalling the reason for Pygmalion's creative act. In Lucio's version of the story, the fantasy of animation *is* the moment of sexual penetration (i.e., "to make a woman" as deflowering a virgin): "What, is there none of Pygmalion's images newly made woman to be had now, for putting the hand in the pocket and extracting [it] clutch'd?" (3.2.44–47).[16] Both Shakespeare and his audience were well aware of the sexual and misogynist aspects of the story that are omitted in order to achieve closure to *The Winter's Tale*. If we ignore the negative aspects of the Pygmalion tradition, we foreclose the possibility of thinking about the work and effects of repression in the play's last scene – or, for that matter, about the problem that Ovid's narrative so memorably posed: what, precisely, *is* the relationship between misogyny and art?[17]

In the first three acts, Leontes' skepticism places the "truth" of Hermione's body (her innocence or her guilt) beyond the reach of words – beyond the reach, even, of oracular speech. Similarly, the final scene turns to a story in which evasion of the female body is representation's foundational premise: the statue is *not* mimetic; its beauty supersedes that of any living woman ("qua femina nasci / nulla potest"). From this troubling gap between language and the world, transferred from Ovid's statue to Hermione, Shakespeare aspires to a mode of representation that can move beyond the impasse. If, as most critics agree, the spectacle of Hermione's pregnancy troubles the play's language from the start (most obviously in Polixenes' opening reference to "nine months"), this spectacle works together with her potent tongue to spark her husband's suspicions. The final scene of animation therefore works to reclaim another, "better" mode of generation than the one that so disturbs Leontes' understanding of the world. In so doing, Shakespeare tries to replace the animating power of the maternal body with the language and visual spectacle of the theater.[18]

The play's implied claim for theatrical power, then, derives from a literary history of aversion to female flesh. But this is not the only story the play tells about its own fiction. I want to suggest not only that Hermione's concluding silence criticizes the symbolic-erotic economy inaugurated in Book 1 of the *Metamorphoses* and developed further in the Orpheus–Pygmalion sequence, but that this economy itself tells us something important about why Hermione's speech is so unexpectedly powerful. To understand the question the play shares with *The Rape of Lucrece* – what would happen if the stony lady actually did speak back? – we need do more than remember that Pygmalion's statue has no name and says nothing. Or that Eurydice, lost again, says only "farewell" before finally disappearing in death. Although the first book of the *Metamorphoses* initially proposes a sexual division of labor in the production of poetry, and the Orpheus segment adds death to rape as one of the possible positions for women in the process of inventing poetic song, we have already heard the murmur of a different story than the one that emerges when we focus on the activities of Apollo, Pan, or Orpheus. As I suggested in chapter 2 of Pan's music, Ovid leaves it unclear exactly *whose* voice one hears in these pipes: "Instead of [Syrinx] he held nothing but marsh reeds … and while he sighed in disappointment, the air stirring in the reeds gave forth a low sound, like a complaint" ("sonum tenuem similemque querenti" 1.708). Ovid lets us wonder, whose sound is this? The complaining sound seems as much hers about rape as his for disappointed desire. Similarly, we saw that the female voice troubles the Apollo–Daphne story, too. It therefore disturbs one of the *Metamorphoses'* most prominent narratives about the origins of poetry. Where Apollo's "imperfect" rhetoric fails to persuade her to stay, Daphne's prayer to lose the "figure" that provokes such violence convinces her father to change her shape. Her words acquire a persuasive force that Apollo's do not; they inaugurate the change of form to which the poem is dedicated. If Book 1 leads one to expect that the poem will focus on male vocal power, that expectation is soon thwarted. In a series of influential stories, Ovid ventriloquizes numerous women, obliquely yet consistently hinting that these female characters are violated by the very mode of representation available to them. Echo's mimicking "voice," Syrinx's complaining reed, Philomela's severed tongue, Medusa's fearsome face, mark female experience in the *Metamorphoses* as a struggle against the restrictive conditions within which they must represent themselves.[19]

Remembering this aspect of Ovid's poem – where female voices indicate that they are betrayed by the very words they speak – we may better understand Hermione's protest in the courtroom scene that she stands somehow outside the restrictive terms of Leontes' accusation: "Sir, / You speak a language that I understand not" (3.2.79–80). To the woman about to be restored to life as a version of Pygmalion's statue, her husband's "language," like his jealousy, violates her sense of herself. Hermione's ensuing remark about the deadly effects of fantasy – "My life stands in the level of your dreams, / Which I'll lay down" (81–82) – then provokes Leontes' most concise statement of his Pygmalionlike revision of womankind: "Your actions are my dreams" (82). As both Apollo's desire and figurative language ensnare Daphne yet give her voice an unintended efficacy, so the collusion between language and male fantasy frames Hermione yet does not deprive her voice of all power. *The Winter's Tale* may mark her words as insufficient to tell the truth or command belief, yet it also gives her voice the power to unhinge her husband's sense of the world itself: "Is this nothing? / Why then the world and all that's in't is nothing" (1.2.292–93).

And the corollary aspect of Ovid's poem – where female voices suggest that male voices are not so powerful as the stories of rape or of animation might lead one to believe – illuminates why Leontes, once he has lost the rhetorical competition with his wife, spends much of the play trying (and failing) to control his own language and the language of others. For Leontes, the fact that tongues other than his own can speak becomes an increasing source of irritation. When his lords voice their initial opposition to his accusation of adultery, Leontes snaps: "Hold your peaces" (2.1.139). He then dismisses their comments as an infringement of his power:

> Why, what need we
> Commune with you of this, but rather follow
> Our forceful instigation? Our prerogative
> Calls not your counsels . . .
> We need no more of your advice. The matter,
> The loss, the gain, the ord'ring on't, is all
> Properly ours.   (2.1.162–170)

Leontes always speaks as if his voice alone should be heard. When accusing Hermione, he leans on the implicit power of his own voice: "*I have said* / She's an adult'ress, *I have said* with whom" (2.1.87–88, my emphasis). The mere existence of a king's saying, he believes, should be enough to establish facts. Where Orpheus tried, and failed, to use his voice to master death, Leontes tries and fails to use the power of his tongue to master truth.[20] In both cases, women's bodies become the signifiers of that desire. Leontes, moreover, pairs his sense of his own linguistic prerogative with a declaration designed to preempt all other voices whatsoever: "He who shall speak for her is afar off guilty / *But that he speaks*" (2.1.104–5, my emphasis). The mere existence of anyone else's discourse becomes, to Leontes, but further sign of "guilt." This is so, I submit, because Leontes, like an Orpheus singing alone in the woods, can bear to hear only the sound of his own tongue.

Though the king aspires to "order" all linguistic exchanges in Sicily, Hermione's voice continually teaches him that any such ordering, belongs, "properly," to no one. Just as she obeys his command, "speak you," in Act 1 only to challenge Leontes' sense of authority over acts of persuasion, so in Act 2 Hermione speaks to obey his command yet does so with words that prompt Leontes to protest that his voice has again been eclipsed. Although Leontes has just ordered, "Away with her, to prison" and that order is obeyed, nonetheless by the end of Hermione's speech Leontes protests that somehow he has gone "unheard." Hermione addresses herself to the court in words that obey the king's command and yet seem to him to undermine it:

> HERMIONE: . . . Beseech you all, my lords,
> With thoughts so qualified as your charities
> Shall best instruct you, measure me; and so

The King's will be perform'd!
LEONTES: *Shall I be heard?*
HERMIONE: Who is't that goes with me? ...   (2.1.112–16, emphasis mine)

Although she cedes the power of action to Leontes' word, Hermione's token of obedience makes that word ring hollow. The mere act of "going" – an act that follows the letter of the king's order – begins, in her mouth, surreptitiously to sound like a declaration of alliance: "Who is't that goes with me?" To counter her question, Leontes can do no more than repeat himself as he tries to reassert power over one word: "Go, do our bidding; hence!" (125).

Indeed, the play as a whole instructs Leontes that the linguistic marketplace he hopes to master cannot be negotiated by the careful parsing out of what he calls "the loss, the gain." He finds that it cannot be ordered by the logic of equivalence at all: language, in this play, continually exceeds Leontes' demand. Certain that the oracle's voice will prove him right, Leontes finds himself proclaimed a "jealous tyrant" (3.2.133). Calling the oracle a lie, Leontes nonetheless finds that Apollo will win. The action that follows on the heels of "this is mere falsehood" suggests that Mamillius' death *results* from Leontes having doubted oracular speech. Or so Leontes understands it: "Apollo's angry, and the heavens themselves / Do strike at my injustice" (3.2.146–7). And so, because he acts as if his voice alone should be heard, Leontes finds himself, like Ovid's Orpheus, brought low by the clamorous noise of a crowd. In Shakespeare's interrogation of the fear of losing one's rhetorical power, however, Leontes' distrust of other voices turns into an imaginary scene in which he is encircled by "whisp'ring" gossip rather than Bacchic cries:

LEONTES: [Aside] They're here with me already, whisp'ring, rounding:
"Sicilia is a so-forth." 'Tis far gone,
When I shall gust it last.   (1.2.217–19)

Consonant with the work of internal distance that we traced in the trope of the female voice in the *Metamorphoses*, however, it is the tongues of Hermione and Paulina together that best instruct Leontes in what I take to be the lesson of Orpheus: that power resides only fleetingly in one's voice, even if it be the voice of a poet or a king. In the scene of arrest, Hermione notifies her husband, as she did indirectly in the first act, that he cannot bring all language – even his own – under his control. Though Leontes may claim that "the matter" and "the ord'ring" of his accusation of adultery is "all / Properly ours," she instructs him otherwise. Once published, Hermione reminds him, a text will go its own way. It can be controlled by no mere speaking:

> How will this grieve you,
> When you shall come to clearer knowledge, that
> You thus have publish'd me! Gentle my lord,
> You scarce can right me thoroughly, then, to say
> You did mistake.   (2.1.96–100)

Having lost his attempt to master the truth by mastering other voices, Shakespeare's second Orpheus soon finds himself heavily beset by the tongue of Paulina. In her, Leontes contends with a voice that exceeds all ordering:

> LEONTES: [What] noise there, ho?
> PAULINA: No noise, my lord, but needful conference
> About some gossips for your Highness.
> LEONTES: How?
> Away with that audacious lady! Antigonus,
> I charg'd thee that she should not come about me:
> I knew she would.   (2.3.39–44)

Like an Ovidian bad penny, Paulina returns to avenge her mistress: "I knew she would." "A callat / Of boundless tongue" who, Leontes claims, "late hath beat her husband" (2.3.92–93), Paulina plagues Leontes with her "noise." A domestic version of the Bacchic horde, Paulina has a tongue that no man controls. Thus the harassed Leontes rebukes her husband, "What? canst not rule her?" (46). Paulina, the somewhat softened spirit of a revenging Ovidian woman, goes about her work with a tongue that will, after sixteen years, cure Leontes rather than kill him.

By the time he wrote *The Winter's Tale*, certain crucial stories from the *Metamorphoses* had become foundational to Shakespeare's delineations of character. This play suggests that Ovidian mythography can inform even the subtlest fantasy. Where the story of Pygmalion circumscribes that of Leontes' desire in Act 5, in Acts 1 and 2 Orpheus, the narrator of Pygmalion's desire, also plays his part in defining the mythographic shape of Leontes' delusions, his all too authoritarian anxiety about losing linguistic control of his world.

"Not Guilty"

We have seen that when Shakespeare adopts the imagined scene of speaking to a stony lady as a way to repair the devastation caused by Leontes' jealousy, he turns the conflict between male and female verbal power into a meditation on Ovidian and Petrarchan rhetoric in general and on the role of the female voice in that literary legacy in particular. Before looking more closely at the telling role female voices play in *The Winter's Tale*, however, we must recall some of the vicissitudes of the voice in the *Rime Sparse*, particularly for the Ovidian characters Petrarch borrows as so many figures for his own predicament. Like many of his contemporaries, Shakespeare frequently juxtaposes Ovidian rhetoric with Petrarchan in order to derive a flexible lexicon of figures for sexual experience, whether erotic or violent. Recall, for instance, that Marcus greets the mutilated Lavinia, Shakespeare's second Philomela, with the conventional language of a *blason* in praise of her beauty and talent (*Titus Andronicus*, 2.4.22–47). And as we saw in the last chapter, the narrator of *The Rape of Lucrece* sets his critique of Petrarchan epideixis in a larger Ovidian context, rewriting the story of Lucretia from the *Fasti* in terms of several other Ovidian characters: most notably Philomela, Orpheus, and Hecuba.

In sonnet 78, Petrarch's apostrophe to Ovid's Pygmalion epitomizes the rhetorical and erotic concerns of the *Rime Sparse*, bequeathing yet further strategies, tropes, and effects on one of the most influential modes of Renaissance self-representation. Because Petrarch, as a second Pygmalion, cannot make the picture speak, the speaker's desire for words replaces Ovid's scene of desire for a new and improved woman. Words, not sex, become the focus of the poet's longing: "if only she could reply to my words!" ("se risponder savesse a' detti miei!" [78.11]). From Petrarch's repression of Ovid's blunt sexual scene, "verbal fetishism" is born. And so, too, is an imaginary conversation born – not between Petrarch and Laura, but between Petrarch and Pygmalion ("Pygmalion, how much praise you must give yourself for your statue ..." 78.12–13). Laura's stony silence, of course, is the necessary condition for this all-male conversation about aesthetic merit. And her silence also deeply influenced English Petrarchanism as well: Barkan recalls Daniel's figure of the "marble brest" and "stony heart." And we've already considered Marston's distinctly lascivious use of the metaphor ("O that my Mistres were an Image too, / That I might blameles her perfections view.")

Despite Marston's telling barb about the erotic advantages of female silence to the would-be Petrarchan poet, however, and despite Petrarch's rhetorical turn in sonnet 78 to "speak" to another male artist about her silence, the distinctions of power proposed by such figures as Pygmalion's silent statue are not absolute in the *Rime Sparse*. As we have seen, the seemingly silenced female voice does, on occasion, ruffle the surface of Petrarchan self-reflection. The poet who takes Apollo's story as his own also represents himself as "Echo," exiled by the very language in which he represents his fate. Like Echo, or Daphne, the poet is betrayed by his own speech; in canzone 23, his echoing song (lines 13, 64–66, 138–40) angers Laura as Diana, who imprisons the poet in rock, stone, and flint.

Echo's may not seem the kind of verbal power an aspiring Apollo would want to claim, since it disrupts any sure sense of intention or origin. Yet it remains a kind of power nonetheless. Like Echo, Petrarch is never able to make his pain "resound" sweetly or softly enough so as to persuade ("né mai in sì dolci o in sì soavi tempre / *risonar* seppi gli amorosi guai / che 'l cor s'umiliasse aspro et feroce" ["nor was I ever able to make my amorous woes *resound* in so sweet or soft a temper that her harsh and ferocious heart was humbled"] 23.64–66). But such failure finds its Apollonian solace in the aesthetic pleasures of Petrarchan autobiography: "every valley *echoes* to the sound of heavy sighs which prove how painful my life is" ("et quasi in ogni valle / *rimbombi* il suon de' miei gravi sospiri, / ch'acquistan fede a la penosa vita," [23.12–14]). As is the case with both Ovid's and Shakespeare's reflections on male and female voices, Petrarch's trope of echo implicates the fate of one voice in that of another; the "male voice" prominently leans on various female voices from Ovid's text in order to define itself. As I suggested in chapter 3, Petrarch uses both female and male Ovidian characters to indicate that he is alienated from his own tongue; Actaeon's story, as well as those of Echo and Daphne, appears in canzone 23 for this purpose. Ovid no sooner proposes the story of male poetic control over language in Book 1 than he dissolves it; this dissolution subtends Petrarch's poetic self-portrait. Ovid, and Petrarch after him, suggest that alienation from one's own tongue is the condition of having a voice whatsoever, male or female. But in both poets the trope of a female voice appears strategically, as the place in the text where one can hear the greatest strain on the voice, on such cherished illusions about artistic vocal power as those initially proposed by Apollo, Pan, Pygmalion, or Orpheus. It is the diacritical function of Ovid's female voices, their ironic juxtaposition to such ostensibly "male" fantasies, that is most important for understanding Shakespeare's representation of the tongues of Hermione and Paulina.

In addition, though Laura rarely speaks in the *Rime Sparse*, her few words wield significant authority. As Diana, she utters the taboo against speaking that subtends the cycle: "make no word of this" ("Di ciò non far parola" [23.74]). Her prohibition enables Petrarch to portray himself as one driven by compulsion to write about what is forbidden. Laura's sentence against his speech becomes, paradoxically, the positive condition for Petrarch's appearance as the speaking subject in "exile." Like the undertone in the complaining sound that issues from Syrinx's reed, Laura's spoken taboo is that without which we would not "hear" his voice. Indeed, in the *Rime Sparse* as a whole, Laura's voice, when heard, carries the force of prohibition or revelation. "Sweet" and "angelic," it attracts her lover like "the sound of the sirens" (207.82). I understand the seeming polarity between male speech and female silence in Petrarch's rendition of the Pygmalion story, therefore, in light of the larger fantasies about the poet's own symbolic and erotic condition that gives the female voice, though infrequently heard, an unsettling power.[21]

This voice articulates the specific rhetorical concerns that preoccupy Shakespeare as he transforms this Ovidian-Petrarchan legacy into a figure for the theater. Act 1, scene 2, the scene of rhetorical competition, opens with a brief meditation on the power and limits of a particular speech act: Polixenes complains of the imbalance between "thank you" and the time it takes to say it. Lest he remain in debt for staying long enough to utter words of thanks equal to his friend's hospitality, Polixenes leans on other, better words than "thank you" to assist him in evading time: "like a cipher ... *I multiply* / With one 'We thank you' many thousands moe / That go before it" (1.2.6–9). From the very opening of the play, words are somehow not equal to the world; they can but measure the very time they strive to overcome.

> Time as long again
> Would be fill'd up, my brother, with our thanks,
> And yet we should, for perpetuity,
> Go hence in debt.   (1.2.3–6)

The phrase "I multiply" is invoked to assist its speaker in clearing his debt to his friend and to time. Leontes' reply, however, only reopens the debt that this phrase was meant to close: "Stay your thanks a while, / And pay them when you part" (1.2.9–10). Polixenes' verbal maneuvers usher in a rhetorically self-conscious play in which Shakespeare continues to test language's power as a mode of action rather than mere vehicle of representation, to search for a kind of voice that can effect the changes of which it speaks. Moreover, the verbal power that Polixenes desires in this scene and that Paulina finally stages in the last raise the same question – the question of language's ability to erase indebtedness to time. As the concluding scene's greater success might suggest, Shakespeare asks this question most pointedly through the sound of the female voice – Leontes' less than "tongue-tied" queen and the "boundless tongue" of her faithful Paulina (2.3.92). He does so in such a way, I submit, that the (barely) suppressed undercurrent of illicit sexuality in Polixenes' opening reference to nine months and "standing in rich place" comes to define the very notion of time.

Let us examine exactly how this happens. Beginning with Polixenes' desire for words that can discharge a debt – for some kind of verbal action – the play's rhetorical concern is precisely delimited by its often repeated doublet, "to say" and "to swear." Preoccupied with the inability of any statement to prove Hermione's innocence and the concomitant failure of all speech to persuade Leontes of the truth, the first three acts of *The Winter's Tale* continually present us with this pair, "to say" and "to swear." The doublet appears early: in the first scene of rhetorical and sexual competition, Hermione says to Leontes of Polixenes, "But let him say so then, and let him go; / But let him swear so, and he shall not stay, / We'll thwack him hence with distaffs" (1.2.35–37). Similarly, when Leontes charges Hermione directly, "'tis Polixenes / Has made thee swell thus," she responds: "But I'ld say he had not; / And I'll be sworn you would believe my saying / Howe'er you lean to th' nayward" (2.1.62–64). This iterated pair of verbs draws a distinction similar to the one made by J.L. Austin in his theory of the difference between constative and performative utterances, between "saying" – words that "'describe' some state of affairs ... either truly or falsely" – and "swearing" – words in which saying something is "to do it."[22] In *The Winter's Tale*, oath-taking and swearing faith take on the peculiar (Ovidian) urgency of futility, since neither utterances aspiring to state the truth nor words convention-ally designated as actions exercise any force.

Indeed, we might say that this pair, saying and swearing, precisely distinguish the two halves of the play. For in Act 3, Paulina is the first woman whose spoken words command belief: "I say she's dead; I'll swear't. If word nor oath / Prevail not, go and see" (3.2.203–4). Before Paulina's oath – "I say she's dead; I'll swear't" – no proof or belief attended woman's word. For women, according to Leontes, "will say anything" (1.2.131). After Paulina's oath, Leontes views female speaking differently: "Go on, go on," he says to her, "Thou canst not speak too much" (3.2.214). But just as Leontes invokes the evidence of sight without ever having visual proof – Hermione's adultery "lack'd sight only" (2.1.177) – Paulina's imperative makes the "fact" of Hermione's death, like the "fact" of her innocence, a kind of metatheatrical crime: for the one thing the audience *cannot* do is "go and see." The truth of Hermione's body – its innocence and its death – is always held from view; all that remains is the evidence of "word" and "oath." Where neither "word nor oath" allow Hermione to testify to the truth of her innocence, Paulina's oath marks the moment where a woman's words do finally work – but only to testify to a lie. Only a lie – Hermione is dead – establishes the trust in Leontes necessary for her to live as innocent. Only this lie to the audience, moreover, allows Shakespeare the surprise ending of the living statue that claims such powers for the theater. Between Hermione's vain yet truthful swearing of innocence and Paulina's successful yet false swearing of death, *The Winter's Tale* uses the female voice to point beyond truth or falsehood, beyond a conception of language as transparent

description. Instead, it asks us to consider the *effects* of language –
particularly female language but also theatrical language – in relation to
the fugitive truth of the female body and the "old tale" it tells.[23]

In the courtroom scene, saying and swearing come together at the
moment of their failing. The oracle, for instance, is truth telling's last
chance. That telling is supposed to be secured by another performative,
for the officers, swearing "upon the sword of justice" that they have been
"at Delphos, and from thence have brought this seal'd-up oracle," open
it and read: "Hermione is chaste, Polixenes blameless ... Leontes a
jealous tyrant" and so on (3.2.132–34). Leontes merely declares, "There
is no truth at all i' th' oracle" (140). But in this scene, it is Hermione's
voice in particular that puts performative language on trial by stressing
its failure and, at the same time, connecting that failure to the central
problem of the play. For her commentary on her own speaking, like
Paulina's false oath that Hermione is dead, connects the passing of
language into action with the play's two chief preoccupations: the
"truth" of the female body and the effects of theatrical representation.
Brought forward to testify, Hermione declares her innocence by commenting on her own lack of vocal power. She quotes the one performative for which she longs but which, in this context, will not work:

> Since what I am to say must be but that
> Which contradicts my accusation, and
> The testimony on my part no other
> But what comes from myself, it shall scarce boot me
> To say, "Not guilty."   (3.2.22–26)

Quoting the performative that in her mouth and in this place must
misfire, Hermione's meditation on the inefficacy of saying "Not guilty"
does two things. First, it constructs Leontes as tyrant for bringing her
forth in a courtroom where no words can acquit her. Commenting on her
own inability to speak, Hermione claims that viewed by a higher, divine
witness, her predicament "shall make / False accusation blush, and
tyranny / Tremble at patience" (3.2.30–32). The necessary misfiring of
Hermione's "Not guilty" becomes the verbal event that marks Leontes,
against his hopes, as "tyrannous" (line 5). Second, Hermione's meditation on the necessary failure of "Not guilty" recalls an earlier "Not
guilty." This one is first spoken offstage, but it defines the entire time of
the play as the fallen time of sexuality. In Act 1, Polixenes remembers a
prelapsarian idyll of male bonding very specifically. Of his young friendship with Leontes, Polixenes remarks,

> We were as twinn'd lambs that did frisk i' th' sun,
> And bleat the one at th' other. What we chang'd

> Was innocence for innocence; we knew not
> The doctrine of ill-doing, nor dream'd
> That any did.   (1.2.67–71)

Had this Edenic state continued, he claims, "we should have answer'd heaven / Boldly, 'Not guilty'; the imposition clear'd" (1.2.73–74). In the decidedly less than innocent time of the play, "Not guilty," though boldly declared, will *not* "clear" "the imposition." For the immediate action of a prelapsarian performative is nullified by the mere sight of the female body:

> HERMIONE: By this we gather
> You have tripp'd since.
> POLIXENES: O my most sacred lady,
> Temptations have since then been born to's: for
> In those unfledg'd days was my wife a girl;
> Your precious self had then not cross'd the eyes
> Of my young playfellow.   (1.2.75–80).

Like Leontes' suspicious interpretation of her pregnancy, of course, Polixenes' comments on Leontes' fall from "innocence" to "cross'd" eyes mark Hermione's body as a sign of transgression. But the echoing of "Not guilty" across the play turns the female *voice*, too, into the mark of another transgression. For the possibility of saying a "Not guilty" that performs the action of absolving belonged only to a world without women. When young men answered to heaven there was no human convention to be violated and so deprive these words of efficacious action. With a language so natural as that of lambs bleating, heaven automatically witnesses and ratifies all performatives; the one who enters a plea simultaneously delivers his own verdict. Between the two, very different circumstances for saying "not guilty," Shakespeare defines the play's fallen time as a time of broken linguistic conventions – conventions broken, moreover, around the question of sexual "guilt." Turning what Shoshana Felman calls "the scandal of the speaking body" into the scandal of the speaking *maternal* body, Shakespeare sets *The Winter's Tale* in a time when the performative "Not guilty," in a woman's mouth, cannot act.[24]

The failure of Hermione's "Not guilty" is implicit in Austin's definition of the performative. As Felman demonstrates of Austin's work, the performative is "defined ... through the dimension of failure."[25] That failure is, however, not simple; it produces further effects. If the conventional rules governing a performative utterance are not in effect – if, as Austin writes, when we say "I do" in a marriage ceremony, "we are not in a position to do the act because we are, say, married already" – that does not mean that "I do" will be "void or without effect." Instead, "lots of things will have been done": for instance, "we shall most interestingly have committed the act of bigamy."[26] What other effects, then, follow from the "position" in which Hermione speaks about the inevitable failure of her "Not guilty"? As we have already seen, her infelicitous position turns Leontes' courtroom into a mockery, the ruse of a tyrant who has already determined the verdict. Within the fictions of the play and of Leontes' justice, the inevitable failure of Hermione's plea defines, by rhetorical means, the extent of the king's tyranny.

But more radically still, the self-reflexivity that defines all performatives reminds us, suddenly, that we are not only in the mock courtroom of a tyrant. We are also in the mock courtroom of a play. Of such a fictive situation, Austin observes that "a performative utterance will ... be *in a peculiar way* hollow or void if said by an actor on the stage."[27] I do not cite Austin's observation here in order to endorse his distinction between a "non-serious" "theatrical" use of language and a "serious" "ordinary" use of language. Jacques Derrida, Barbara Johnson, and Shoshana Felman have amply discussed how such a distinction is untenable. And if they dared say anything at all after their own unhappy experiences of language's unanticipated effects, Cephalus, Cydippe, and Daphne might similarly remind us how deep a chasm can suddenly open up between a speaker's utterance and his or her intentions – a chasm that tells us how incomplete our account of the Ovidian subject's relationship to linguistic action will be if it is based solely on Austin's distinction. But Derrida, Johnson, and Felman argue that this distinction, while flawed, is extremely revealing. When Austin writes that something "peculiar" is at work on stage or in a poem, his choice of words reminds us that his work is "often more fruitful in the acknowledgment of its impasses than in its positions."[28] I recall Austin's unsuccessful distinction, rather, because of the considerable theoretical work on the status of the speaking subject it has enabled. For Derrida, Austin's attempt to exclude "non-ordinary" poetic or theatrical language from his theory of performative action turns on a foundational belief in consciousness or intention: "the conscious presence of the intention of the speaking subject in the totality of his speech act."[29] In chapter 2, we examined numerous Ovidian stories – among them, Cephalus, surprised by the deadly effects of his spontaneous lyric to the wind; Cydippe, bound against her will by the marriage vow she pronounces but did not mean to take; and Daphne, transformed due to the duplicity of one word – that make it difficult to grant intention pride of place when it comes to accounting for the volatile field of verbal action that permeates Ovid's rhetorically self-conscious poetry. Derrida argues, moreover, that Austin's exclusion allows him to avoid acknowledging the problem raised most insistently by Ovid's Echo: that is, a "general citationality" or "general iterability" is the "risk" or "failure" internal to all performative intentions – their "positive condition of possibility." It is not that the "category of intention will disappear," only that intention, as Narcissus might readily acknowledge, will no longer "govern the entire scene and system of utterance." In a turn of phrase revealing for our study of Ovidian rhetoric and its influence, Derrida writes: "the intention *animating* the utterance will never be through and through present to itself and its content." He therefore argues that an "absence of intention" is "essential" to performative utterances; and he calls such absence the performative's "structural unconscious."[30]

In *The Literary Speech Act* Felman elaborates the full psychoanalytic resonance of such a phrase, discussing the consequences of the performative's "structural unconscious" for her understanding of the condition of speaking subjectivity. Reading Austin together with Lacan, she rephrases Lacan's "deliberately superficial" notion of the unconscious in terms of a poststructuralist theory of the failure implicit in performatives. "It is precisely from the *breach in knowledge* ... that the act takes its performative *power*: it is the very *knowledge that cannot know itself*, that [in the speaking subject] *acts*."[31] But in order to specify what such a definition of the "structural unconscious" of performative utterances means for *The Winter's Tale*, we must remember one further comment about what Austin finds so "peculiar" in a performative uttered on stage. As Barbara Johnson succinctly puts it, when Austin tries to distinguish between ordinary language and theatrical language for the purposes of his theory, he is "objecting not to the use of the verb but to the status of its subject." For in a poem or on the stage, "the speaking subject is only a persona, an actor, not a person." A theatrical performative is "peculiar" insofar as it reveals how all performatives put personae in place of persons. It reminds us that the necessity of speaking *in persona* – intrinsic to the conventionality of all performatives – opens up a difference *within* the speaker. Johnson evokes *Hamlet* to illustrate her point: "the nonserious-ness of a performative utterance 'said by an actor on the stage' results, then, not from his fictional status but from his duality, from the spectator's consciousness that although the character in the play is swearing to avenge his dead father's ghost, the actor's own performative commitments lie elsewhere."[32]

In the case of the trial scene in *The Winter's Tale*, Shakespeare presents us with an escalating succession of performatives. The series opens with the somber tones of an indictment that, because it is uttered in a play, divides its speaker from himself: "Hermione, queen to worthy Leontes ... thou art here accused and arraigned of high treason, in committing adultery," and so on (3.2.12–14); the messengers follow suit, swearing that they have fetched the oracle and left it unopened ("All this we swear," line 130). And it culminates in an oracular message that should provide the last word by enacting the verdict it announces. In the case of Hermione, who explains why she will plead "Not guilty," the play's rhetorical move here is pointedly and internally citational: she repeats Polixenes phrase, thereby reminding us that he, in turn, was quoting a conventional utterance, despite the fantasy of his youthful friendship with Leontes as a utopian moment prior to language (lambs bleating rather than boys talking). Hermione's quotation, then, makes us uncertain of the status of the subject who is giving her voice to these deeply conventional words by elaborately refusing to say them. The conceit of her impossible "Not guilty" tells us that "Hermione" is at once a (persuasive) character terribly wronged by her doubting husband *and* an actor "whose own performative commitments lie elsewhere." When Hermione evanescently evokes the action her words cannot achieve if uttered, she reminds us that this is so, in part, because we are listening to an actor speak in a play. Hermione's words do pass into action but not entirely the act she intended and certainly not one that the character, "Hermione," could know. What she knows (that these words will fail) and what she does (reveal herself to be an actor playing a falsely accused Hermione) do not coincide.

Hermione also protests that she has been "proclaim'd a strumpet," and "hurried / *Here to this place, i' th' open air*" to proclaim innocence in vain (ll. 104–05, my emphasis). It is "here" in "this place" – the place of the theater – that Hermione puts her impossible "Not guilty" in quotation marks. Her deictics refer us, within the fiction, to Leontes' mock courtroom. Due to the self-reflexive nature of performative utterances, however, they also refer us to the story's frame – to the "here" and now of "this" stage on which Hermione speaks.[33] The disjunction or misfiring that happens in "this place" of the theater is what Felman might call the unconscious action of *The Winter's Tale*, a "knowledge that cannot know itself" and therefore disarticulates the speaking subject, Hermione, from within the sound of her own voice. Further still, Felman's psycho-analytic view of the import of performative misfiring suggests that we must examine the relation between the play's unsettling rhetorical performance and its story of sexuality. I have argued that Hermione's "Not guilty," echoing Polixenes' "Not guilty," colors the entire question of performative misfiring with Leontes' (Pygmalion-like) obsession with female sexual guilt; only in the prelapsarian world inhabited by male twins do plea and verdict coincide. But if we read Hermione's rhetoric in light of the material conditions of the theater for which her lines were written – the here and now of the English transvestite stage – we are confronted with a division within the speaking subject that is "peculiar" indeed. We are reminded not merely that Hermione is an actor, but that the voice speaking these lines was that of a boy-actor playing a falsely accused wife and mother. Leontes' suspicions may reduce Hermione's tongue to her body; similarly, the story attached to the two versions of "Not guilty" may work to engender "Hermione" by claiming a necessary link between the female body and the sexual guilt of "man"kind. But the material practice of the early modern English stage, to which the rhetoric of Hermione's speech also refers, would tell a far different story about Hermione's body [34] – a story in which the alleged difference (and implicit hierarchy) between two sexes is in fact a difference within one. The hollowness or duality of "her" "female" voice, then, mirrors a division internal to the play's representation of gender. That is, the metatheatrical echo implicit in the performative and Hermione's deictics reminds us, as I suggested at the opening of this chapter, that Shakespeare's representa- tion of a "female" voice – what it can and cannot say and what effects it achieves – is a dramatic trope. It is, quite literally, a "travesty" of womanhood, a femininity-effect rather than a revelation of anything essential to what the play continues to call the "female" tongue.

We might understand the tropological status of what counts as a female body and voice in *The Winter's Tale* in one further way. As we have seen, what Felman calls an unconscious "breach in knowledge" is marked by the inevitable misfiring of "Not guilty" in Hermione's case. The precise content of the phrase itself will not let us forget that, for Shakespeare, a specific sexual story informs what might otherwise seem a strictly rhetorical failure. Indeed, Felman's discussion of the affinities between Austin and Lacan suggests something further still about Her- mione's mysterious body. Through its constant meditation on the failures of its own language to reveal the truth or to act as intended, the play turns the secret of "female" sexuality – the question raised by Hermione's pregnancy – into what Lacan calls the missed encounter. One might say of the play's relation to Hermione's elusive body what Lacan says of the speaking subject's mediated, eccentric relation to "the Real": "Misfiring *is* the object."[35] On such an understanding of the discursive limits to knowledge, we might describe what Stanley Cavell aptly calls Leontes' "skeptical annihilation of the world" in other terms – as the vanishing of the maternal body before the joint pressure of language and culturally inflected fantasy. That is, Shakespeare is exploring the (Cartesian) problem of radical doubt by designating a specific body – a "mother's" body – as the privileged object that resists the play's knowledge and its verbal action.[36] A psychoanalytic perspective, moreover, reminds us that it is not a philosopher's idea about a deceptive, malignant deity, but a husband's idea about a deceptive, pregnant wife, that sets the process of "skeptical annihilation" in motion. Foundational to the way *The Winter's Tale* rhetorically defines the limits to knowledge, the "female" body as staged in this play remains, like Daphne, forever fugitive.

"Be stone no more"

The literary figure to whom Shakespeare turns to explore such a vexed relation to the world is Ovid's Pygmalion. For both skepticism *and* projection join hands to fashion Leontes' misery (e.g., "Your actions are my dreams"). On David Ward's persuasive argument for retaining the punctuation of the First Folio and for remembering the contemporary meaning of "co-active" as "coercive" or "compulsory" (and not merely "acting in concert"), Leontes' speech about "affection" is stressing "the *coercive* nature of affection," its "action upon the 'nothing' it generates in the imagination" (as Ward parses it, "Affection ... Thou ... Communicat'st with dreams ... / With what's unreal: thou co-active art, / And fellow'st nothing").[37] In addition, it is through Ovid's Orpheus–Pygmalion sequence – particularly as given the influential contours of Petrarchan linguistic self-consciousness – that Shakespeare can explore the subject's missed relation to the world of objects not as a process of doubting alone, but as a meditation on the simultaneously productive and aberrant effects of rhetoric – on language conceived not merely as a representation *of* the world, but as a mode of action *in* the world. As I suggested above concerning Hermione's vain yet truthful swearing of innocence and Paulina's successful yet false swearing of death, such action, precisely by distinguishing the two halves of the play, turns the relation between the subject and the world of which it speaks into a recurrent misfiring. On the one hand, neither saying nor swearing reestablishes the faith in Leontes required for Hermione to live as herself, outside Leontes' "dreams" or beyond the "language" of male fantasy she "understands not." And on the other, when Paulina's words do have effect, they do their work through a lie. That such misfirings as these or Hermione's impossible "Not guilty" are inaugurated by the mere sight of her pregnant body or the sound of her voice I understand as a symptom of a deeply entrenched – though not necessary or inevitable – collusion between the representational and libidinal economies of patriarchal culture.

When the truth of Hermione is the object of representation, representation fails, drawing attention to the opacity of language rather than the clarity of truth.[38] And when Hermione speaks, something happens that she does not intend: though she intends to persuade Polixenes to stay, her words trigger Leontes jealousy; though she intends to speak of her innocence, her speech about the failure of "Not guilty" in her case also reveals her to be an actor and "this" place to be the space of the theater. Though her words of defense may be profoundly moving, may create the convincing effect of Hermione as wronged wife and mother, their misfiring paradoxically underscores the transvestite performance required to produce such a gendered fiction. That a failed performative still has power to act despite having dislocated language's action from intention becomes vividly clear when the scene ends. For this self-reflexively theatrical trial produces further unintended effects. We hear that Mamillius, "with mere conceit and fear / Of the Queen's speed" (3.2.144–45) has died. And the report of his death becomes, in turn, words with the power to kill: "This news is mortal to the Queen" (line148). Hermione's unintended act – the "Not guilty" that produces the effect of theatricality – and the lethal effects that attend the play's reflection on its own fictive enactment darken Shakespeare's attempt to evoke consciously and artistically controlled theatrical effects through Paulina's staging of Pygmalion's statue. That story works through yet another woman's voice to rein in the action of a now-benign theater in which language appears to perform the act its speaker intends: "Music! awake her! . . . descend; be stone no more" (5.3.98).

Paulina's imperative to the statue, we should note, is not literally a performative utterance. Rather, her command represents an *idea* about language as performance. Shakespeare inherits this idea from Ovid's Orpheus and calls it "magic": the dream of a voice so persuasive that it can effect the changes of which it speaks.[39] It is the dream of a language that, when it acts, "fills up" the grave, makes good our debt to time. Paulina's spectacle of Hermione-as-statue offers more than a meditation on the desire to see in the theater: it becomes a visual analogue for the play's evident desire for a truly performative utterance. The long-awaited verbal event – signaled by such performatives as "Not guilty," the incessant taking of oaths, and the search for oracular truth – finds its culminating visual icon in the event of Hermione's "animation." Drawing on verbal and visual fictions, Shakespeare nonetheless accentuates the power of the voice in Paulina's heavily weighted moment of invocation and, eventually, the much-desired event of Hermione's speech. Although Leontes declares himself content to be a "looker-on" (line 85), thus including the audience in the theatrical circuit of his desire, and though Paulina apologizes for the "sight of my poor image" (line 57), what everyone waits for is to hear Hermione's voice. As the doubters in Paulina's audience demand, "If she pertain to life let her speak too" (line 113) and "make it manifest where she has liv'd / Or how stol'n from the dead" (lines 114–15). The scene, however, both claims and disavows the Orphic power for which it longs. Availing itself of a language at once oral and visual, this theater seems to "steal" Hermione, like Eurydice, "from the dead." At the same time, we hear a warning, through Paulina, that the Orphic story of life, were it "told ... should be hooted at / Like an old tale" (lines 116–17).

The acts that words do in the courtroom scene exceed intention and, by so doing, turn the theater into the space of these unpredictable effects. The final scene attempts to control verbal action through Paulina's careful stage management, her magically effective voice. Yet such an attempt may all too easily recall Leontes' disastrous desire to master the world by controlling all language. It therefore does not go unqualified. On the one hand, when Paulina proclaims "descend; be stone no more," a woman's successful voice in *The Winter's Tale* appears to replace Pygmalion's successful prayer to Venus in the *Metamorphoses*. On the other hand, just as Hermione once reminded her husband that even his own language exceeds his control, so now her voice is the one to remind us that the play's seeming animation is only a fiction. Despite the ruse of death, she has "preserv'd" herself somewhere else (line 127). Hermione, moreover, says nothing to the man who now longs to hear her speak. She seems poised to speak to him – "Still methinks / There is an air comes from her. What fine chisel / Could ever yet cut breath?" (lines 77–79) – but does not. Leontes' question should remind us that throughout the *Metamorphoses*, "breath" is the etymological root for Ovid's rhetoric of animation: Apollo's "breath," the "wind" streaming through Daphne's hair, and the Orphic *uox* telling the story of Pygmalion's art all derive from the narrator's trope of ἄνεμος and his fascination with the vicissitudes of speech, the all-too-uneasy relationship between voice and mind.[40] In this image of the chisel that can "cut breath," Leontes signals his, and the play's, desire for a rhetoric of animation, for a theatrical version of the "l'aura" or "breeze" that blows through the figures of the *Rime Sparse* or the "breath" that Ovid asks the gods to bestow on his song (1.1–3).

What Hermione does and does not say in this scene tells us something about the cost of that desire. Given the gendered relations of power passed down through literary history as the "air" that seems to "come from her," very much indeed hangs on Hermione's voice. I take the fact of Hermione's silence toward Leontes – and the fact that after she moves, Leontes never asks her a direct question – to be Shakespeare's way of acknowledging the problems raised by her voice in the first three acts. Nothing she says to Leontes diminishes the force of his projections; the language she "understand[s] not" limits the field of her possible responses; and any answer she makes must still be read by him, a reading she cannot control. This awareness of the limits that Leontes' fantasy places on the stony lady's possible reply stems, in part, from Shakespeare's understanding that, in Ovid as in Petrarch, the stories of Pygmalion and Narcissus are deeply intertwined.[41] Leontes has, of course, always viewed others through the mediating screen of his own form. Observing his son in Act 1, he begins testing his theory about his wife's guilt according to whether or not Mamillius is his mirror: "Looking on the lines / Of my boy's face, methoughts I did recoil / Twenty-three years, and saw myself unbreech'd" (1.2.153–55). Even Leontes' admission of culpability in the final scene, prompted when he gazes on the "statue," surreptitiously imports Narcissus' story into Pygmalion's. Repentant though he may be, Leontes still reads Hermione as a version of himself: "does not the stone rebuke me / For being more stone than it?" (5.3.37–38). To Leontes, even her stoniness is not "hers." If anything of the world is to return to Leontes that does not stand at the level of his dreams, it cannot do so within the reflexively binary terms proposed by Petrarchan rhetoric. Rather, Paulina's intervention tells us that if Hermione is to be restored to Leontes and not fade away again before the force of fantasy and doubt, it is on the condition that she *not* respond to his words only, that she not conform utterly to his language and his desire. Therefore a third party (Paulina) must manage this meeting from outside the restrictive frame of Pygmalion's desirous yet annihilating address.

And finally, what Hermione *does* say – precisely not to Leontes but to her lost daughter – offers a telling index of how constraining have been the terms of that address. What Pygmalion loathes, what his phantasmatic love for his *simulacrum* pushes aside, Ovid tells us, is not simply female sexuality but "the female *mind*" ("menti / femineae," 10. 244–45). And so, one final allusion to the *Metamorphoses* tells us something about that mind. Hermione's allusion prompts a question that seems not to occur to Petrarch: what does *she* want? The shift from Petrarchan autobiography to Shakespearean ventriloquism marks a subtly but, crucially, different return to Ovidian narrative. In *The Winter's Tale*, Shakespeare stages Petrarchan tropes in order to perform an ethical critique of them, particularly the rhetoric of address and its role in Petrarch's story of love and the self. When Shakespeare returns to listen once more to Ovid's female voices, he shifts the emphasis away from the otherness within the self (Petrarch's "exile" of blindness, obsession, and forgetting) to pose, instead, a question: the question of the other's desire. And for a moment, that "other" – the Petrarchan stony lady – has something else in mind than "responding" to the speaker whose apostrophe restricts them both ("se risponder savesse a' detti miei!" [78.11]). What "moved" Hermione, her last words tell us, were thoughts of

Perdita. Turning to a daughter who has already coded herself as Proserpina at the moment of dropping her flowers, Hermione models herself on Ceres as a mother unable to forget her lost, though still living, daughter:

> Tell me, mine own,
> Where hast thou been preserv'd? where liv'd? how found
> Thy father's court? for thou shalt hear that I,
> Knowing by Paulina that the oracle
> Gave hope thou wast in being, have preserv'd
> Myself to see the issue. (5.3.123–28)

Hermione's questions to Perdita – "Where hast thou been preserv'd? where liv'd?" – obliquely recall Ovid's story of violent rape and maternal grief by making her the reason for living the hope of being reunited with her daughter.[42]

Where the suspicion of female sexual "guilt" defines the relation between time and language's action in the first half of the play, in this final scene both are redefined by another story – that of rape and maternal grief. Hermione's allusion to Book 5 of the *Metamorphoses*, of course, echoes the title, place, and time of *The Winter's Tale*. For Ceres' grief over Proserpina's rape brought winter into the world. Golding's translation of that grief brings the story of Ceres closer still to that of the animated statue in Act 5. When the nymph Arethusa tells Ceres why her daughter vanished, Golding renders Ovid's lines as follows: "Hir mother stoode as starke as a stone ... And long she was like one that in another worlde had beene" (5. 632).[43] It is left to Shakespeare's Hermione to return from that "other world" of stone in order to be reunited with her Proserpina. Alongside Pygmalion's prayer and Orpheus' suppliant song, then, we must also remember Ceres' curse. In Ovid's text, we find yet another story, often less well remembered, about a voice that can bring about the changes of which it speaks. Orpheus' mother, the muse Calliope, tells us that when Ceres saw Proserpina's girdle floating on the surface of the pool, she "reproached all the lands loudly, calling them ungrateful ... but *Sicily above all other lands*, where she had found the traces of her loss ... She ordered the plowed fields to fail in their trust and spoiled the seed" (5.474–80). Setting his "old tale" of Leontes' winter in Sicily, Shakespeare invokes but finally turns attention away from the fantasy of the animated statue.[44] He thereby suggests that Pygmalion's self-reflexive fantasy so narrowly constricts female speech that there is, quite literally, *nothing* Hermione can say. Yet by recalling Proserpina's rape and Ceres' powerful reproach, he grants her voice a different authority. Her last words to Perdita fleetingly testify to the violence against the female body that subtends such "old" and "sad" "tales" as that of an animated statue or the first appearance of winter.

Carrying on the critical work that Ovid's narrator grants to such figures as the howling Bacchae, the moan from Syrinx's reed, or the curse of Ceres, the trope of the female voice in *The Winter's Tale* acquires an oblique but nonetheless telling power. Like the many female characters in the *Metamorphoses* whose protests mark the poem's internal distance from the very ideology of gender on which its representations of voice and body also rely, Hermione and Paulina allow us to hear that received stories such as that of Pygmalion's triumph, however "poetic" their claims may seem to be, nonetheless entail tremendous violence against the female body. Troubling Ovidian-Petrarchan tropes for "male" vocal power when they thwart Leontes' desire to control all speech, the tongues of Hermione and Paulina recall Ovid's rhetorically self-conscious narratives of rape, misogyny, and female vengeance that form the background for Orpheus' descent into the underworld. Not necessarily conscious, that violence nevertheless insists, emerging in what might otherwise seem to be the unlikely circumstance of metapoetic or metatheatrical reflection. When heard in the context of transvestite performance, moreover, the voices of Hermione and Paulina also stage the kind of critique that Ovid's transgendered *prosopopoeiae* inaugurated: that is, the play's "female" voices also allow us to hear something about the violence directed against those bodies whose meaning and value are said to be saturated by the contents of that one culturally laden word. When Shakespeare returns to Ovidian narrative in *The Winter's Tale*, he reminds us that if we isolate Pygmalion's story from Orpheus', or Persephone's from Ceres', we fail to notice the fierce, unresolved struggle over the body's significance that is woven into the very fabric of Ovid's rhetorical self-consciousness (and by that route, into Ovid's phonographic definition of subjectivity as the after-effect of the voice's failure). Investigating the causes and effects of verbal action through these seemingly disparate figures, Shakespeare invites reflection on the intricate connections between rhetoric and sexuality proposed by Ovid's interwoven stories. Because of this investigation, however, the "structural unconscious" of the play's performative misfiring – particularly as inflected by the material practice of the transvestite theater – restages the discordant tones of internal distance that Shakespeare inherited from the *Metamorphoses'* most influential stories about voice, gender, and the body. Like the Ovidian poem to which it is deeply indebted, Shakespeare's *Winter's Tale* allows the cost of its foundational tropes for poetic authority to emerge. Part of a cautionary story about the uncanny returns of cultural inheritance, the voices of Hermione and Paulina allow us to catch something of the sound of that cost.

Notes

1 "Illa vero frigida et puerilis est in scholis adfectatio, ut ipse transitus efficiat aliquam utique sententiam et huius velut praestigiae plausum petat, ut Ovidius lascivire in Metamorphosesin solet, quem tamen excusare necessitas potest res diversissimas in speciem unius corporis colligentem" (Indeed, there is a pedantic and childish affectation in vogue in the schools of marking the transition with some epigram and seeking to win applause for this trick. Ovid is given to such lack of discipline in the *Metamorphoses*, but there is some excuse for it because he is compelled to assemble the most diverse things into the appearance of a unified body [Quintilian, *Institutio oratoria*, 4.1.77. I have modified the translation of H. E. Butler, Cambridge, MA: Harvard University Press, 1964]).

2 For further comment on the way Lactantius' treatment of the *Metamorphoses* influences its reception, see Joseph Loewenstein, *Responsive Readings: Versions of Echo in Pastoral, Epic, and the Jonsonian Masque* (New Haven, CT: Yale University Press, 1984), pp. 35–36.

3 "radix micat ultima linguae, / ipsa iacet terraeque tremens inmurmurat atrae" *Metamorphoses*, 6. 557–58. All citations are to Ovid, *Metamorphoses*, trans. F. J. Miller (Cambridge, MA: Harvard University Press, 1968) unless otherwise specified. I have consulted Miller's translation but have made silent emendations throughout.

4 For such an account, see Leonard Barkan, *The Gods Made Flesh: Metamorphosis and the Pursuit of Paganism* (New Haven, CT: Yale University Press, 1986), to which this book is indebted. There have also been a number of books written on the relationship between single European authors and Ovid. See Jonathan Bate, *Shakespeare and Ovid* (Oxford: Oxford University Press, 1993); Richard DuRocher, *Milton and Ovid* (Ithaca, NY: Cornell University Press, 1985); John Fyler, *Chaucer and Ovid* (New Haven, CT and London: Yale University Press, 1979); and Rachel Jacoff and Jeffery Schnapp (eds.), *The Poetry of Allusion: Virgil and Ovid in Dante's Commedia* (Stanford, CA: Stanford University Press, 1991).

5 Ovid's evident interest in the female voice and the female reaction to rape has drawn the attention of numerous feminists, although judgments about the political valence of Ovidian narrative are extremely mixed. The following essays range over a wide array of literary topics; each takes up at least one of Ovid's stories as crucial for assessing the sexual politics of certain modes of

representation: Kathryn Gravdal, *Ravishing Maidens: Writing Rape in Medieval French Literature and Law* (Philadelphia: University of Pennsylvania Press, 1991); Karen Greenberg, "Reading Reading: Echo's Abduction of Language" in *Women and Language in Literature and Society*, ed. Sally McConnell-Ginet, Ruth Borker, and Nelly Furman (New York: Praeger, 1980); Mary Jacobus, "Freud's Mnemonic: Women, Screen Memories, and Feminist Nostalgia," *Michigan Quarterly Review* 26 (Winter 1987): 117–139; Ann Rosalind Jones, "New Songs for the Swallow: Ovid's Philomela in Tullia d'Aragona and Gaspara Stampa," in *Refiguring Woman: Perspectives on Gender and the Italian Renaissance*, eds. Juliana Schiesari and Marilyn Migiel (Ithaca, NY: Cornell University Press, 1991) and "Dematerializations: Textile and Textual Properties in Ovid, Sandys, and Spenser" in *Subject and Object in Renaissance Culture*, ed. Margreta de Grazia, Maureen Quilligan and Peter Stallybrass (Cambridge: Cambridge University Press, 1996), pp. 189–212; Patricia Klindienst Joplin, "The Voice of the Shuttle is Ours," *Stanford Literature Review* 1, 1 (Spring 1984): 25–53; Amy Lawrence, *Echo and Narcissus: Women's Voices in Classical Hollywood Cinema* (Berkeley: University of California Press, 1991); Elissa Marder, "Disarticulated Voices: Feminism and Philomela," *Hypatia: A Journal of Feminist Philosophy*, 7, 2 (Spring 1992): 148–66; Nancy K. Miller, "Arachnologies: The Woman, the Text, and the Critic," in *The Poetics of Gender*, ed. Nancy K. Miller (New York: Columbia University Press, 1986); Tanya Modleski, "Feminism and the Power of Interpretation: Some Critical Readings," in *Feminist Studies/Critical Studies*, ed. Teresa De Lauretis (Bloomington: Indiana University Press, 1986); Claire Nouvet, "An Impossible Response: the Disaster of Narcissus," *Yale French Studies* 79 (1991): 95–109; Amy Richlin, "Reading Ovid's Rapes," in *Pornography and Representation in Greece and Rome*, ed. Amy Richlin (Oxford: Oxford University Press, 1992), pp. 158–179; Naomi Segal, "Echo and Narcissus," in *Between Feminism and Psychoanalysis*, ed. Teresa Brennan (London: Routledge, 1989); Gayatri Spivak, "Echo," *New Literary History* 24 (1993): 17–43.

6   See Barkan, *The Gods Made Flesh*; Nouvet, "An Impossible Response"; Marder, "Disarticulated Voices;" and Spivak, "Echo." In an early, sustained defense of rhetoric in the European tradition as one that poses a serious epistemological and ontological critique, Richard Lanham selects Ovid as an appropriate place to begin "redeeming" rhetoric in the west (*The Motives of Eloquence: Literary Rhetoric in the Renaissance* [New Haven, CT: Yale University Press, 1976]). In the last ten years, renewed critical interest in the serious claims of rhetoric means that the approach to Ovid has begun to change. In particular, see Stephen Hinds, *The Metamorphoses of Persephone: Ovid and the Self-conscious Muse* (Cambridge: Cambridge University Press, 1987).

7   Loewenstein, *Responsive Readings*, p. 35. In contemporary feminist work, Ovid's Echo, Philomela, Arachne, and Ceres (to name a few) have all served their part in projects searching for an alternate, critical, view of literary history and the literary inscription of the social subject. But feminists often turn to the *Metamorphoses* by isolating one story from the rest of the narrative. Such selective treatment, in part the result of the way Ovid's poem

was handed down, occludes a more expansive view of the relationship between rhetoric, poetic form, sexuality, and violence in the *Metamorphoses* as a whole (and hence, the many European poems indebted to it). That so many figures appealing to a feminist sensibility, whether critical or affirmative, are drawn from one poem suggests that it is important to ask why this should be the case.

8 "Disarticulated Voices," p. 158.

9 See *Oxford Latin Dictionary* (Oxford: Oxford University Press, 1992), hereafter cited as *OLD*. For the last sense, *OLD* cites Q. Curtius Rufus (first century AD), "confuderat oris notas pallor."

10 Of Philomela's *notae*, Marder writes: "Although alienated from her body, this form of writing through weaving represents and writes the mutilated body" ("Disarticulated Voices," p. 161)

11 William Keach, review of John Fyler's *Chaucer and Ovid*, in *Helios* 12 (1985): 78.

12 For the influences of Roman rhetoric on Ovid's style, particularly the techniques of declamation, see S. F. Bonner, *Roman Declamation* (Liverpool: University Press of Liverpool, 1949): Ovid was "a poet among declaimers and a declaimer among poets" (p. 156). But to assess Bonner's judgment that "declamatory rhetoric gave to Ovid virtue as well as vice; without it he might never have attained to the cleverness and sparkle which we admire in him at his best" (p. 155), see Alison Goddard Elliot's discussion of the reasons for this dominant critical tradition ("Ovid and the Critics: Seneca, Quintilian, and 'Seriousness,'" *Helios* 12 (1985): 9–20). As she points out, received suspicion of Ovid's exuberant *ingenium* was born, in part, from the blindness of historical circumstance: "One may suspect ... that the Roman rhetoricians were not predisposed to like Ovid, who was, after all, a talented speaker (on Seneca's admission) who abandoned oratory for poetry, who therefore appeared to have 'sold out'" (p. 16). Following Quintilian's assessment that Ovid was "nimium amator ingenii sui" (excessively fond of his own talent), the usual assessment of the *Metamorphoses* condemns it for lack of moral seriousness. In the sixteenth century Giraldi Cintio judges that Ovid is "more ingenious than profound, more licentious than attentive to law, more copious than diligent"; a Victorian critic registers annoyance when "artifice and labored ornament corrupts the sincerity of situation and characters and even slips into ineptitude and perversity"; and as recently as 1965, Clarence Mendell dismisses Ovid for a "frivolous gaiety undisturbed by any concern for morals or politics" (discussed by Elliott in "Ovid and the Critics," pp. 12–14). Douglas Bush, too, takes Ovid's rhetorical facility as evidence of insincerity: therefore "the soulless Ovid does not now hold high rank" ("Foreword" to *Ovid's Metamorphosis Englished, Mythologized and Represented in Figures by George Sandys*, ed. Karl K. Hulley and Stanley T. Vandersall [Lincoln: University of Nebraska Press, 1970], p. xiii). Responding to such charges in 1968, J. M. Frecaut had first to contend with a general consensus that rhetoric is merely ornament to thought: Ovid is not "too ingenious and artificial"; rather, the virtuoso transitions in the *Metamorphoses* have deep "artistic and psychological" significance ("Les transitions dans les Metamorphoses d'Ovide," *REL* 46 (1968): 247–63).

13 Perhaps most famously, T. S. Eliot declared *Titus* to be "one of the stupidest and most uninspired plays ever written" (*Selected Essays: 1917–1932* [New York: Harcourt, Brace, 1932]). Coleridge wrote that the play's violence, "to our ears shocking and disgusting," was "intended to excite vulgar audiences" (*Coleridge's Shakespearean Criticism*, ed. T. M. Rayson [Cambridge, MA: Harvard University Press, 1930], vol. II, p. 31). Eugene Waith's 1957 article on *Titus* is the *locus classicus* for serious reconsideration of the relation between violence and rhetoric in the play; in this regard, he pays close attention to Shakespeare's debt to Ovid, although not all commentators interested in this conjunction follow suit ("The Metamorphosis of Violence in *Titus Andronicus*," *Shakespeare Survey*, 10 [1957]: 39–49). Waith's work informs Albert H. Tricomi's essay, "The Aesthetics of Mutilation in *Titus Andronicus*" (*Shakespeare Survey*, 27 [1974]: 11–19), which locates the "relationship between language and event" as the play's central concern. For related work, see Clark Hulse, "Wresting the Alphabet: Oratory and Action in *Titus Andronicus*," *Criticism* 21 (1979): 106–18; Gillian Murray Kendall, "'Lend Me Thy Hand': Metaphor and Mayhem in *Titus Andronicus*," *Shakespeare Quarterly* 40 (1989): 299–316; Karen Cunningham, "'Scars Can Witness': Trials by Ordeal and Lavinia's Body in *Titus Andronicus*," for a reading of Lavinia's body as sign. For an account of the relationship between dismemberment in *Titus* and early modern conceptions of agency, see Katherine Rowe, "Dismembering and Forgetting in *Titus Andronicus*," *Shakespeare Quarterly* 45 (1994): 279–303.

14 From Pierre Ronsard, *Les Amours*, poem XX, ed. Henri Weber and Catherine Weber (Paris: Editions Garnier Frères 1963). Translation mine. Following Barkan's suggestive reading of the pun on "blandissant," I have leaned to one side – "whitening" rather than the synonyms the editors provide as a gloss ("caressant, seducteur" i.e. affectionate, tender, or seductive). As Barkan suggests, the pun stresses both the color (the bull is white in Ovid's story) and the process of metamorphosis that Ronsard captures with his participles, "a metamorphic poetics of constant motion" (*Gods Made Flesh*, p. 220).

15 For a discussion of the relationship between metamorphosis and sexuality in this poem, see Barkan, *The Gods Made Flesh*, p. 221. For the poem's complex engagement with its Ovidian and Petrarchan predecessors, see Thomas Greene, *The Light in Troy: Imitation and Discovery in Renaissance Poetry* (New Haven, CT: Yale University Press, 1982), pp. 197– 219.

16 See Gravdal's discussion of the evolution of the sense of *ravissant* in *Ravishing Maidens*, pp. 4–5: from the twelfth-century sense of "the action of carrying off a woman," a new term, *ravissement* in the fourteenth, becomes "the action of carrying a soul off to heaven." It refers to "the state of being 'carried away' emotionally, a state of exaltation. From this psychological troping comes a sexual trope: the state of sexual pleasure or rapture. *Ravir* is to bring someone to a state of sexual joy" (p. 5). She also discusses the subtle shifts in the subject of rape in literary history from Ovid to Chrétien de Troyes, observing that where Ovid's narrator concentrates on the victim's reaction, Chrétien, by contrast, "shifts focus away from the literal representation of the female experience of violence, toward the moral, erotic, and

symbolic meaning rape holds for male characters" (p. 158). The specific transfer of sensibility enacted in Ronsard's revision of Europa is not grief or horror but the capacity to appreciate aesthetic form – a capacity that includes the poem's speaker, object, and reader.

17 For a series of important reflections on the problem of aesthetics in contemporary criticism and theory, see *Aesthetics and Ideology*, ed. George Levine (New Brunswick, NJ: Rutgers University Press, 1994).

18 It took a long time before critics confronted the issue of rape directly in Ovid's poem. Leo Curran was the first to break the silence. For him, Ovid mounts a serious critique: the narrator represents rape as "both an outrage committed upon a woman and a grotesque caricature of masculinity" ("Rape and Rape Victims in *The Metamorphoses*," *Arethusa* 2 [1978]: p. 218). More recent critics who agree with this position are Gravdal, *Ravishing Maidens*, and Julie Hemker, "Rape and the Founding of Rome," *Helios* 12 (1985): 41–47. One of the strongest critics of Curran's argument is Amy Richlin: she sees far greater collusion between the narrator and his various male agents – a collusion suggested by her title, "Reading Ovid's Rapes." Richlin's method is more empirically and thematically oriented than my own. In order to build on this feminist effort to reread classical texts by investigating the relation between fantasy, violence, and representation, I argue that rape is not only thematically central to the *Metamorphoses*, not only a question of narrative tone or one's position in relation to the narrated event, but is also woven into the poem's rhetorical (and frequently metarhetorical) structure. Ovid's distinctive treatment of rape puts the very notion of "position," as well as what one means by author, reader, and above all, "experience," "agency," "representation," and "fantasy," in question.

19 On the conceptual impasse arrived at in the debate over the canon (of which Richlin's "Reading Ovid's Rapes" is a part) when critics think of textual "representation" as an image or reflection of this or that social group, as well as the consequences of the recent slippage between "the subject" and "identity" in the American academy, see John Guillory, *Cultural Capital: The Problem of Literary Canon Formation* (Chicago: University of Chicago Press, 1993), pp. 3–84.

20 Marder, "Disarticulated Voices," pp. 157 and 162.

21 In the pair of letters that constitutes *Heroides* 20 and 21, we learn that Cydippe unwittingly betrothed herself to Acontius in the temple of Diana when her suitor threw an apple in front of her on which he had written the oath, "I swear by the sanctuary of Diana that I will wed Acontius." Like most readers in the ancient world, Cydippe read the words aloud and thereby bound herself to Acontius by pronouncing words that were not her own. The considerable distance between language and experience in Lucretia's story is a matter to which I return in chapter 5.

22 Felman, *The Literary Speech Act: Don Juan with J. L. Austin, or Seduction in Two Languages* (Ithaca, NY: Cornell University Press, 1980). Reading Lacan together with Austin, Felman defines a "material knowledge of language" that is not a question of the difference between language and matter – the traditional definition of reference – nor of a kind of knowledge about which one makes constative statements. Rather, "language makes

itself part of what it refers to (without, however, being all that it refers to). Referential knowledge of language is not knowledge about reality (about a separate and distinct entity), but knowledge that *has to do with reality*, that acts within reality, since it is itself – at least in part – what this reality is made of" (p. 77). It is in Felman's sense that I use the terms "the performative," or "a material effectivity of rhetoric," when describing Ovid's rhetorical self-consciousness. This book traces the ways in which Ovid's characters discover what it means to be subjects of and to language, drawing attention to moments when they find themselves deeply and unpredictably affected by the ways in which their language is part of reality – as much "modification of reality" as description of it. To take an example I explore further in chapter 2, Cephalus' apostrophe to the breeze (*aura*) profoundly changes the world he thinks he merely sets out to praise.

23   See Jacques Derrida, *Of Grammatology*, translated by Gayatri Chakravorty Spivak (Baltimore, MD: The Johns Hopkins University Press, 1976).

24   *The Riverside Shakespeare* (Boston, MA: Houghton, Mifflin Co., 1974), line 646. All subsequent citations from this edition. I rely here on Joel Fineman's reading of rhetoric in "*Lucrece*, Shakespeare's Will: The Temporality of Rape," in *The Subjectivity Effect in Western Literary Tradition* (Cambridge, MA: MIT Press, 1991), pp. 165–221 which I explore further in chapter 5.

25   I use the verb "persuade" in the strong sense, since both Ovid and his interpreters understand the story of Apollo's plea to be a story about rhetoric as much as about love. Raphael Regius, for instance, writes approvingly of Apollo's speech: "hac oratione Apollo conatur daphnem persuadere ne se fugiat ... elegans repetitio amatoriae orationi maxime conueniens" ("By means of this speech, Apollo tries to convince Daphne not to flee ... skillful repetition is especially appropriate for the language of love") (Venice, 1527).

26   "Medusa's Head," in *The Standard Edition of the Complete Works of Sigmund Freud*, trans. James Strachey (London: Hogarth Press, 1974), vol. XVIII, pp. 273–74.

27   These are the first four meanings for "os, oris" in the *OLD*. In *Metamorphoses* 5, for instance, we hear of one of the daughters of Pierus who challenge the muses to a singing contest in which the fountain of Medusa is the prize. When the first sister begins, the narrator refers to her mouth: "ad citharam uocalia mouerat ora" (5.332). Other references to the poet's mouth or lips are common among Ovid's contemporaries: see Vergil, *Georgics* 3.294; Horace, *Odes*, 3.25.8; Tacitus, *Annals*, 14.16.

28   Charles Segal, "The Gorgon and the Nightingale: The Voice of Female Lament and Pindar's Twelfth *Pythian Ode*," in Leslie C. Dunn and Nancy A. Jones, eds., *Embodied Voices: Representing Female Vocality in Western Culture* (Cambridge: Cambridge University Press, 1994), pp. 18–19. In Pindar's Twelfth *Pythian Ode*, the subject of Segal's essay, Athena turns the lament of Medusa's sisters for her death into flute music. To contextualize Pindar's use of the female voice, Segal reminds us of Hesiod's Gorgons: they "have heavily emphasized oral features, licking tongues and gnashing teeth" (*Shield of Heracles*). In artwork, the Gorgon's grotesque face, as Thalia Phillies-Howe suggests, "conveys to the spectator the idea of a terrifying

roar," ("The Origin and Function of the Gorgon-Head," *American Journal of Archeology* 58 [1958]: 211–12) while the extended tongue may suggest verbal incoherence, a sub-verbal vocality closer to the bestial than the human" ("The Gorgon and the Nightingale," pp. 18–19).

29 For a recent argument for the importance of the female voice to the Petrarchan tradition, see Heather Dubrow, *Echoes of Desire* (Ithaca, NY: Cornell University Press, 1996).

30 *The Tears of Narcissus: Melancholia and Masculinity in Early Modern Writing* (Stanford, CA: Stanford University Press, 1995).

31 For commentary on the alignment of chastity with silence and loose morals with a loose tongue in the early modern period, see, *inter alia*, Ann Rosalind Jones, "New Songs for the Swallow"; Karen Newman, *Fashioning Femininity and English Renaissance Drama* (Chicago: University of Chicago Press, 1991); and Patricia Parker, *Literary Fat Ladies: Rhetoric, Gender, Property* (London: Methuen, 1987).

32 The most extensive account is by T. W. Baldwin, *William Shakespere's Small Latin and Lesse Greek*, 2 vols. (Urbana, IL: University of Illinois Press, 1944). For a description of the way texts like Ovid's were taught in the schools, see Jonathan Bate, *Shakespeare and Ovid*, pp. 19–32. Richard Halpern offers a compelling account of the role of humanist pedagogy in the reproduction of ideology in *The Poetics of Primitive Accumulation: English Renaissance Culture and the Genealogy of Capital* (Ithaca, NY: Cornell University Press, 1991).

33 *Ovids Metamorphosis translated grammatically, and also according to the propriety of our English tongue, so farre as Grammar and the verse will bear* (London: Humfrey Lownes, for Thomas Man, dwelling at the signe of the Talbot in Pater-noster rowe 1618), pp. 75–86. The text is Brinsley's translation of *Metamorphoses* Book 1. His explanatory gloss translated Raphael Regius, the most influential of Ovidian commentators. As Apollo looks on Daphne's mouth, Regius had written, "Os autem paruum maxime uirginem commendat" (Venice, 1527). Brinsley generally borrows only sparingly from Regius' copious notes, but in this instance he seems to have approved of Regius' gloss. Another English edition of the poem also borrows from Regius for a similar comment on proper female conduct (London, 1582). The text is systematically divided and annotated with marginalia explaining what is happening in the story; the editor offers no allegorizing glosses and few moral exempla, except for a brief but revealing gloss on the story of Pygmalion and his statue. Ovid's satiric comment that the sculptor is deluded enough to believe the statue "wants to be moved" ("uelle moueri" 10. 251) is one I return to frequently in the following chapters because Ovid's pun on "moving" one's listener makes this story an erotic rendition of a rhetorical desire. To expand the idea of the inanimate statue, this text cites only one of Regius' many comments: "out of modesty, well educated virgins will scarcely dare move under the gaze of men" ("uirgines bene educatae prae pudore in conspectu uirorum uix se audent mouere").

34 Gravdal, *Ravishing Maidens*, p. 158, note 9.

35 Harvey, *Ventriloquized Voices: Feminist Theory and English Renaissance Texts* (London and New York: Routledge, 1992).

36   Harvey's introduction to *Ventriloquized Voices* concisely summarizes the problems inherent in such concepts as voice and persona in current critical practice, arguing for the need to pay closer attention to "transvestite ventriloquism," not in the theater alone, but in lyric and narrative poetry as well.

37   Just after I completed the chapter on Petrarch, "Embodied Voices," I was pleased to find that others had been thinking along similar lines: see Leslie Dunn and Nancy Jones, ed., *Embodied Voices: Representing Female Vocality in Western Culture* (Cambridge: Cambridge University Press, 1994). Readers interested in this problem should refer to this collection.

38   Bate, *Shakespeare and Ovid*, p. 28. For accounts of this transition, see Jean Seznec, *The Survival of the Pagan Gods: The Mythological Tradition and Its Place in Renaissance Humanism and Art* (New York: Pantheon Books, 1953); Douglas Bush, *English Literature in the Earlier Seventeenth Century* (Oxford: Oxford University Press, 1952).

39   On the crucial role that Petrarch's autobiographical rendition of Ovidian metamorphosis played in the Renaissance imagination, see Barkan, *The Gods Made Flesh*, pp. 206–41. As he observes, "The performance of metamorphosis in the arena of the psyche is the first of the great Renaissance innovations, and the source for this connection between passion and transformation can be traced directly to the *Rime* of Petrarch … More widely read and copied than any other of Petrarch's self-explorations," the *Rime* "codify the psyche in terms that are closely linked with paganism and metamorphosis" (p. 206).

40   Canzone 23. 98–100, from the edition by Robert Durling, *Petrarch's Lyric Poems: The Rime Sparse and Other Lyrics* (Cambridge, MA: Harvard University Press, 1976). All translations are Durling's, though I have made silent emendations where necessary.

41   Halpern, *The Poetics of Primitive Accumulation*, p. 29; Ong, "Latin Language Study as a Renaissance Puberty Rite," *Studies in Philology* 56 (1959): 103–24.

42   *Ludus Literarius: or, The Grammar Schoole* (London, 1612), p. 193, as cited in Bate, *Shakespeare and Ovid*, p. 22.

43   Bate, *Shakespeare and Ovid*, p. 20. From *Drama of the English Renaissance I: The Tudor Period* (New York: Macmillan Publishing, 1976).

44   Robert Cawdry, *A Treasurie or Store-house of Similies* (1600), p. 538, as cited in T. W. Baldwin, *William Shakspere's Small Latine and Lesse Greeke*, vol. I, p. 117.

45   Halpern, *Poetics of Primitive Accumulation*, p. 47.

46   *On Education: A Translation of the "De trandendis disciplinis" of Juan Luis Vives*, trans and ed. Foster Watson (Cambridge: Cambridge University Press, 1913). Quoted in Halpern, *Poetics of Primitive Accumulation*, p. 47.

47   Meres, *Palladis Tamia*, in *Elizabethan Critical Essays*, ed. G. Gregory Smith, 2 vols. (Oxford: Oxford University Press, 1904), vol. II, pp. 317–18; Nashe, *Works*, ed. R. B. McKerrow, 5 vols. (1904–10; reprint Oxford: Oxford University Press, 1958), vol. I, p. 193. For further comment on the similarity between the ways in which Shakespeare and Ovid were commended for rhetorical facility, see Bate, *Shakespeare and Ovid*, pp. 20–22.

48 Ahl, *Metaformations* (Ithaca, NY: Cornell University Press, 1985), pp. 104–05. For the many forms of wordplay in Ovid's handling of the story, see pp. 105–109.

49 See Curran, "Rape and Rape Victims in the *Metamorphoses*," Hemker, "Rape and the Founding of Rome," and Richlin, "Reading Ovid's Rapes."

50 On interpellation, see Althusser's "Ideology and Ideological State Apparatuses," in *Lenin and Philosophy*, trans. Ben Brewster (New York: Monthly Review Press, 1971), pp. 133, 152–156. Since the metamorphosis that results from Caenis' request – she becomes a powerful warrior – gives Ovid a new character with which to carry on his satire against Vergil's account of Troy in the *Aeneid*, one might say that this successful transsexual hero/ine continues to remind us of Ovid's considerable distance from received narratives that define gender in more conventional terms.

51 For discussions of the changing definitions of *raptus*, see Kathryn Gravdal, *Ravishing Maidens*; James Brundage, *Law, Sex, and Christian Society in Medieval Europe* (Chicago: Chicago University Press, 1987); and Barbara J. Baines, "Effacing Rape in Early Modern Representation," *ELH* 65 (1998): 69–98.

52 Althusser, *Lenin and Philosophy*, p. 222.

53 To take one resonant instance: as Patricia Joplin pointed out some years ago, Ovid's version of Philomela's story pointedly makes Tereus' desire to rape seem but a mere extension of patriarchal privilege. Tereus is first inflamed when he sees Philomela's father kiss her; the narrator tells us that he wishes he were in her father's place. The narrative stresses the proximity between the father and Tereus and does so in the context of the exchange of women that constitutes the father's power ("The Voice of the Shuttle is Ours"). Tereus' wish tells us that the violence of rape is, in fact, merely an extreme form of business as usual – a notable instance of "internal distance." For commentary on how the fantasy of paternal rape is implicit in a patriarchal symbolic order, see Mary Jacobus, "Freud's Mnemonic."

54 "Arachnologies," p. 287. Wanting to "read Arachne's story as a parable of women's writing" – what John Guillory might call a conception of representation as reflection or image of subordinate groups – Miller personifies Ovid's character, Arachne, as "a woman" only by castigating her narrator. She assumes, as well, that the battle is always between genders and persons rather than *within* sexuality or the speaking subject. Her sense of Ovid's culpability with respect to Arachne – that demoted from an artist to "a woman," Arachne is "returned to the domain of the natural" – similarly glosses over a larger problem that pervades the *Metamorphoses*: every body, including the narrator's, is returned to the domain of the natural. Focusing on Arachne alone from Ovid's epic permits Miller to elide a complex question: why does Ovid so frequently stage his own predicaments as a writer through violated female voices and bodies?

55 Charles Segal, "Ovid: Metamorphosis, Hero, Poet," *Helios* 12 (1985): 49–63, see p. 57. Segal charts the various ways that in the *Metamorphoses*, Ovid consistently undoes epic assumptions: he is fascinated with the dissolution rather than consolidation of identity; he concentrates on metamorphosis rather than the monuments of fame; and he avoids narrative focus in favor

of rhetorical self-reflection. I disagree only with Segal's final suggestion that the final lines bestow heroic *kleos* on "the poet himself, the poet as hero" because of the poem's claim for the power of artist-figures. Rather, as Eleanor Winsor Leach points out ("Ecphrasis and the Theme of Artistic Failure in Ovid's *Metamorphoses*," *Ramus* 3 [1974]: 102–42) with obvious relevance here to the fate of Arachne, it is the *failure* of art that the poem documents. That art and rhetoric are central to the poem's critique of epic assumptions is indeed true. But as post-structuralist theory would suggest, the poem's focus on its own language does not necessarily make its user a "hero." For a critique of the desire to make the subject merely "user" of language as a code rather than subject of and to it, see Rosalind Coward and John Ellis, *Language and Materialism: Developments in Semiology and the Theory of the Subject* (Boston, MA: Routledge and Kegan Paul, 1977).

56   Placing Horace's use of "doctus" (1.1.29), in light of the emphasis on *sophos* in Greek poetry and *doctrina* in Roman, R. G. M. Nisbet and Margaret Hubbard suggest that "'learned' is too heavy, and 'cultured' too pretentious ... The adjective is particularly common in verse, and is applied impartially to the poet, the poet's lady, and the muses themselves," *A Commentary on Horace Odes Book I* (Oxford: Clarendon Press, 1970), p. 13.

57   Anderson, *Ovid's Metamorphoses, Books 6–10* (Norman, Oklahoma, 1972), p. 167, note to lines 127–28. For "the wearing of ivy by poets," Nisbet and Hubbard draw attention to Pliny, *Historia naturalis* 16.147, Juvenal 7.29, and Propertius 4.1.61, as well as Horace's 1.1.29.

58   Miller notes this signature effect in "Arachnologies," but consonant with her will to personify Arachne as an image of and for women, she attributes the signature to Arachne only. We should note two things: Arachne's weaving is much closer to Ovid's mode of narration than Athena's; and Ovid is a poet very fond of signing his own name. The *Ars Amatoria*, for instance, ends with such a signing ("Naso magister erat"). Arachne signs her weaving much as Ovid signs his poetry, and does so with an indeterminable mark hovering between literal and figural that is characteristic of Ovid's poetic technique throughout the *Metamorphoses*. The problem remains, then: whose signature is this?

59   Many readers have argued for a close connection between Ovid and Arachne, although until recently they have not done so within the frame of a feminist critique of gender. W. S. Anderson argues that the sympathies of Ovid's narrator are clearly with the human weaver, drawing attention to the considerable affinity between Ovidian poetry and Arachne's composition. For him, Ovid is "suggesting the value of Arachne's kind of composition: freer, more mannered, more dramatic and distorted, less specifically didactic" (*Ovid's Metamorphoses* p. 160, note to lines 70–102). François Rigolot points to the resemblance between the narrator and his character in "Les 'subtils ouvrages' de Louise Labé, ou: quand Pallas devient Arachné," *Etudes Littéraires* 20 (Autumn, 1987): 43–60, as does Frederick Ahl in *Metaformations*, p. 227. Most recently, Ann Rosalind Jones follows the telling reversals of this story as it passed from Ovid's hands to Velasquez, Sandys, and Spenser, reading Arachne's story once again to understand the politics of engendering in various texts; she argues that all three Renaissance

artists, to varying degrees and by different means, suppress the affinities between poet and Arachne that are so prominent in the *Metamorphoses*. See "Dematerializations," pp. 189–212.

60 Both Gravdal, *Ravishing Maidens*, and Hemker, "Rape and the Founding of Rome," point out how frequently Ovid stresses the victim's reactions to the situation.

61 Loewenstein, *Responsive Readings*, p. 67.

62 Rubin,"The Traffic in Women," *Towards an Anthropology of Women*, ed. Rayna R. Reiter (New York: Monthly Review Press, 1975), pp. 156–210; Sedgwick, *Between Men: English Literature and Male Homosexual Sexual Desire* (New York: Columbia University Press, 1985).

63 Nancy Vickers, "Diana Described," in *Writing and Sexual Difference*, ed. Elizabeth Abel (Chicago: University of Chicago Press, 1982), p. 109.

64 Bergstrom "Enunciation and Sexual Difference, Part 1," *Camera Obscura* 3/4 (1979), p. 58 and Jacqueline Rose, "Introduction II" in *Feminine Sexuality: Jacques Lacan and the Ecole Freudienne*, ed. Juliet Mitchell and Jacqueline Rose (New York: Pantheon Books, 1982), pp. 27–57.

65 I borrow Richard Halpern's apt rendering of the idea of determination. See *The Poetics of Primitive Accumulation*, p. 11.

2 MEDUSA'S MOUTH: BODY AND VOICE IN THE *METAMORPHOSES*

1 In a chapter titled "Travestis et modèles de la rhétorique," Simone Viarre systematically sets out the various ways in which Ovid's poem plays with this fusion between poetry and rhetoric (*Ovide: Essai de lecture poétique* [Paris: Société d'édition les belles lettres, 1957], pp. 55–69). Viarre traces the presence of three important parts of ancient rhetoric in the poem – *inuentio*, *dispositio*, and *elocutio* – and concludes with particularly evocative comments on the connection between metamorphosis and metaphor (an important element of *elocutio*). For Barthes's observation that the conversion of rhetoric into "une techné poétique" is characteristic of the Augustan age see "L'ancienne rhétorique," *Communications* 16 (1970): 172–223. See also F. J. E. Raby, *A History of Secular Latin Poetry in the Middle Ages* (Oxford: Clarendon Press, 1957), vol. I, p. 28. On the role of rhetorical training in Roman education and speculation about its effect on poetry, see S.F. Bonner, *Roman Declamation in the Late Republic and Early Empire* (Liverpool: University Press of Liverpool, 1949). As Bonner observes, "It is clear to any student of the Roman educational system that preparation for public speaking was the chief preoccupation of teachers, parents, and pupils alike, and that education was accordingly mainly linguistic and literary in its earlier stages, and predominantly oratorical and legal in its more advanced forms. Successful declamation was the crowning achievement to which the long study of grammar, essay-writing, paraphrase, character-delineation, commonplaces, panegyric and invective, and the other exercises which filled the Roman school curriculum, was designed to lead" (p. vi). In a more recent exploration of Ovid's linguistic self-consciousness, Stephen Hinds reads Ovid's two versions of Persephone's rape (*Metamorphoses* 5 and *Fasti* 4) in light of his consistent practice of "poetic self-reference" (*The Metamor-*

phosis of Persephone: Ovid and the Self-Conscious Muse [Cambridge: Cambridge University Press, 1987]). This inquiry into the connections between Ovidian self-reference – which I construe broadly as rhetorical, poetic, and linguistic – and his representations of desire and sexual difference is indebted to the studies of Viarre and Hinds.

2   For considerable detail on the programmatic aspects of two rapes – those of Persephone and of Medusa – see Hinds, *The Metamorphosis of Persephone*.

3   For evocative comments on the importance of ventriloquism for a feminist reading of Renaissance poetry, see Elizabeth Harvey, *Ventriloquized Voices: Feminist Theory and English Renaissance Texts* (London and New York: Routledge, 1992).

4   *Institutio Oratoria*, 3.8.49–52.

5   Althusser, *Lenin and Philosophy*, trans. Ben Brewster (New York: Monthly Review Press, 1971), p. 222.

6   I use the term "programmatic" in accordance with the practice of classical scholars to signify a moment in which a narrative reflexively points to itself.

7   Arguments about Pythagoras' status in the poem abound. For an overview of critical opinions, see Leonard Barkan, *The Gods Made Flesh: Metamorphosis and the Pursuit of Paganism* (New Haven, CT: Yale University Press, 1986), pp. 86–88.

8   On the importance of the lapse from culture to nature in the poem, see Alison Goddard Elliott, "Ovid and the Critics: Seneca, Quintilian, and 'Seriousness,'" *Helios* 12 (1985): 17, and Charles Segal, "Metamorphosis, Hero, Poet," *Helios* 12 (1985): 49–63, see p. 57.

9   Elliott considers the failure to communicate to be integral to the way the poem draws boundaries between self and other ("Ovid and the Critics," p. 17).

10 Perhaps the most resonant story for a Lacanian analysis of these lost voices would be that of Midas. Because Midas does not know what he wants or means when he makes his fateful request for gold, it is only after his words return to him in inverted or literal form that he finds out that he hates his own desire (11.100–34).

11 See Jacques Derrida, *Of Grammatology*, trans. Gayatri Chakravorty Spivak (Baltimore, MD: The Johns Hopkins University Press, 1976).

12 John Brenkman, "Narcissus in the Text," *Georgia Review* 30 (Summer, 1976): 309; Clare Nouvet, "An Impossible Response: the Disaster of Narcissus," *Yale French Studies* 79 (1991): 95–109; Gayatri Spivak, "Echo," *New Literary History* 24 (1993): 17–43.

13 Nouvet, "An Impossible Response," pp. 106–07. Her claim about an "inaudible echo" inhabiting one's words as soon as one speaks derives in part from the difference between Narcissus' *coeamus* ("let us come together") and Echo's ("let us copulate"), where the same signifier does indeed signify two different meanings. Nouvet's reading is an extremely important one for contemporary accounts of Ovid's poem, but because this is the case it is perhaps necessary to correct a grammatical error at the heart of her critique. Nouvet argues her case most strongly about the echo within from the repetition of *ueni* in the line, "uoce ueni magna clamat: uocat illa uocantem." She claims that "the statement 'Come!' might mean 'come' as well as 'I am

coming.'" Such a claim is grammatically inaccurate: Narcissus' "ueni" could never mean "I am coming." The imperative of *uenio*, *ueni* is indeed *ueni* ("come!"), but the first person present ("I am coming") is *uenio*. Although the first person perfect form of the verb, *ueni*, ("I *have* come") might be what she means here as the second "inaudible echo" implicit in the first imperative form (*ueni*), that suggestion too would ignore the quantitative vowels of Latin. The long e in the perfect stem of the verb distinguishes the imperative from the first person perfect (*ueni*, "come," from *uēni*, "I have come"). The meter of this line offers no recourse either, for the short e of the imperative is required ("uŏcĕ uĕnī māgnā clāmāt: uŏcăt īllă uŏcāntēm"). If, as she observes, Narcissus "looks around" when he hears his *ueni* repeated "and sees no one coming" ("respicit et rursus nullo ueniente"), it is because he thinks he is being commanded, "come," by the echo. Even if one were to argue that Narcissus hears a "slant" echo of *uĕni* as *uēni* (since Echo's actual word does not appear in the text), it would seem to me, then, that what the line is doing is alerting readers to that trick (like a slant rhyme). One could say, along with Brenkman, that such a trick reveals Saussure's insight about the structure of difference out of which meaning is produced (I distinguish *ueni* with a short e because it is not *ueni* with a long one). Echo's "alteration" of *coeamus*, of course, does support her general argument, so I offer this comment only in the spirit of remaining as faithful to the text as possible. Narcissus' response – to turn around when he hears this word – does put him in a strange position, as Nouvet rightly demonstrates: he is a speaker who doesn't recognize his own words. I would add that it is a particularly Ovidian touch that the contingency of meaning emerges from the division of one word into sexual and nonsexual registers.

14   Brenkman, "Narcissus in the Text," p. 309.
15   Frederick Ahl, *Metaformations* (Ithaca, NY: Cornell University Press, 1985), pp. 146–7, traces a complex network of transformations for this and other words throughout the poem, arguing that the narrator also plays on the similarities between *os*, *oris* and *os*, *ossis*. He finds such wordplay, for instance, in the story of Deucalion and Pyrrha's interpretation of the oracle to throw the bones of their mother over their shoulders (p. 117) and in other Roman poets (p. 56). Ahl also draws attention to the interplay between *ego* and *echo* in the story of Echo and Narcissus (pp. 237–38).
16   See *Of Grammatology*.
17   For the clearest presentation of the epic aspects of Ovid's poem, see Otis T. Brooks, *Ovid as an Epic Poet* (Cambridge: Cambridge University Press, 1970).
18   Bakhtin, *The Dialogic Imagination*, ed. Michael Holquist (Austin: University of Texas Press, 1981), p. 3. For discussions of the poem's epic characteristics, see Otis T. Brooks, *Ovid as Epic Poet*; Otto Steen Due, *Changing Forms* (Copenhagen: Gyldendal, 1974); E. J. Kenney, "Ovid," in *The Cambridge History of Classical Literature*, ed. P. E. Easterling and E. J. Kenney, 2 vols. (Cambridge: Cambridge University Press, 1983) 2: 124–26; Segal, "Ovid: Metamorphosis, Hero, Poet."
19   Franz Bömer (in *Metamorphosen* [Heidelberg: Universitätsverlag, 1986], I, p. 4) compares Ovid's invocation, for instance, to Vergil's in *Aeneid*, 9.525, "uos, o Calliope, precor, adspirate canenti." What interests me here is not a

taxonomy of genre – whether the poem is or is not an epic – since the *Metamorphoses* is evidently a hybrid work experimenting encyclopedically with many genres (concerning which, see A.S. Hollis, *Metamorphoses Book VIII* [Oxford: Oxford University Press, 1970], pp. xiii–xiv). Rather, what concerns me is what the epic trope opening the *Metamorphoses* implies for the narrator's self-representation.

20 Simon Goldhill, *The Poet's Voice: Essays on Poetics and Greek Literature* (Cambridge: Cambridge University Press, 1991), p. 292.

21 I suspect that it is precisely Ovid's consciousness of his own late position in literary history that made many of his tropes so appealing to writers like Petrarch and Shakespeare who were similarly struggling with a sense of their own belatedness – with the situation Shakespeare calls his attempt to renovate a "forebemoaned moan" and Petrarch the predicament of finding only an "echoing" voice.

22 See pp. 6–7.

23 See Viarre, *L'Image et la pensée dans les Métamorphoses d'Ovide* (Paris: Presses Universitaires de France, 1964), pp. 211–47.

24 We know from Seneca's *Controuersiae* (2.2.8–14) that Ovid frequented such declamatory exercises and was himself schooled in the art. On the retreat of oratory to "the safer arena of the schools," S. F. Bonner remarks that "under the Republic, oratory had been essential for success in public life, and the whole subject was alive and keenly debated; but under the principate it had lost much of its political value. It was not so much that the courts had lost a great deal of their power; there were still civil and criminal cases to attract the advocate. It was rather the lack of assured success in public life, which the good orator in Republican days could naturally expect. Under the principate, so much depended upon Imperial and Court patronage; and it became necessary to choose one's words rather too carefully when speaking in public for the practice to be a popular one" (*Roman Declamation in the Late Republic and Early Empire*, p. 43). On contemporary reactions to Ovid's relationship to this history, see *Helios*, 12 (1985).

25 Bonner, *Roman Declamation*, p. 21.

26 Ἄνεμος derives "from 'ane-,' blow, breathe, cf. Sanskrit, 'anti-ti,' 'breathes,'" *Greek–English Lexicon*, ed. Henry Liddell and Robert Scott (Oxford: Clarendon, 1968). They cite Hippocrates, *Gunaikeia* 2. 179 for the sense of wind in the body.

27 *Tusculanae Disputationes* 1,9.19 "ipse animus ab anima dictus est." As Cicero's derivation of one word from the other suggests, *anima* is sometimes, but not always, distinguished from *animus*. *Anima* denotes the air as an element (Lucretius 1.715) – i.e. the air which one inhales, and the air one exhales when dying; the animal or vital principle of life (in Lucretius, distinct from the *animus* or reasoning principle); the soul or spirit; and yet *anima* is sometimes used in place of *animus* for consciousness (Lucretius 3,598).

28 Arguing for important connections between Ovidian metamorphosis and Pythagoreanism, Viarre draws attention to the frequency with which *anima* (as well as its less favored companion term, *spiritus*) appears in the poem (*L'Image et la pensée*, pp. 232–34).

29 For similar references see also 5.62; 6. 247; 7.581 and 861; 11.43; 15.528.

30   Translation by E. J. Kenney, *The Cambridge History of Classical Literature*, p. 145.
31   See Bömer, *Metamorphosen*, vol. VII, pp. 490–91.
32   *OLD* (Oxford: Oxford University Press, 1992), *deleo*, definition 1.
33   *Tristia ex ponto*, 2.119–20. All quotations from the Loeb edition, edited and translated by A. L. Wheeler (Cambridge, MA: Harvard University Press, 1988).
34   *Ars Amatoria*, 3. 811–12. All quotations from the Loeb edition, edited and translated by E. H. Warmington (Cambridge, MA: Harvard University Press, 1969).
35   Jean Laplanche and J.-B. Pontalis, *The Language of Psychoanalysis*, trans. Donald Nicholson-Smith (New York: Norton, 1973), p. 210.
36   Bakhtin, *The Dialogic Imagination*, p. 3. John Bender and David E. Wellbery, commenting on the history of rhetoric in relation to practices of reading and writing, contrast classical rhetoric, which "took its point of departure from the direct and oral encounters of classical civic life" and thus "inevitably referred back to a face-to-face situation" to the Enlightenment, a "culture of print," in which "rhetoric drowned in a sea of ink" ("Rhetoricality," in *The Ends of Rhetoric: History, Theory, Practice*, eds. John Bender and David E. Wellbery [Stanford, CA: Stanford University Press, 1990] 3–42 esp. 19–20). On the difference between speaking and writing to classical treatises on rhetoric, see Barilli, *Rhetoric*, trans. Giuliana Menozzi (Minneapolis: University of Minnesota Press, 1989), pp. 24–37.
37   Bernard Knox, "Silent Reading in Antiquity," *Greek, Roman and Byzantine Studies* 9 (1968): 421–435.
38   Sonnet 81. From Stephen Booth, *Shakespeare's Sonnets* (New Haven, CT: Yale University Press, 1977).
39   *Heroides* 21.1–2. All quotations from the Loeb edition, edited and translated by Grant Showerman (Cambridge, MA: Harvard University Press, 1969).
40   Numerous conversations with Patricia Rosenmeyer were invaluable for giving me insight into these letters and their possible place in Ovidian poetics.
41   See Bömer, *Metamorphosen*, vol. VII, p. 488.
42   On the presence of Vergil and Horace in these lines, as well as an overview of the general topoi, see Bömer, *ibid.*, pp. 488–91; for the echoes of various fragments of previous Roman poetry, see Heinrich Dahlmann, *Zu Fragmenten römischer Dichter* (Heidelberg: C. Winter, 1982), p. 19.
43   It is perhaps worth noting that Renaissance authors were given to reading such conventional claims personally. The frontispiece of George Sandys's translation offers an elaborate engraving of a monument surmounted with Ovid's portrait; the verses below identify the picture as "Ovids Counterfeit," a picture equivalent to the one Ovid "with his owne pensil drew." The final line then invites us to "view" "The Poet in his deathless Poems."
44   Kenney, *The Cambridge History of Classical Literature*, p. 140.
45   J. Derrida, *Limited Inc.*, trans. Jeffrey Mehlman (Evanston, IL: Northwestern University Press, 1988), p. 49. Of particular relevance to my concern here with Echo's repetition and Ovid's signature – as "Naso," "magister," or "indelebile nomen" – are his comments on pp. 48–49: "The 'shopping list for myself' would be neither producible nor utilizable, it would not be what

it is nor could it even exist, were it not possible for it to function, from the very beginning, in the absence of sender and of receiver: that is, of determinate, actually present senders and receivers ... At the very moment 'I' make a shopping list, I know ... that it will only be a list if it implies my absence, if it already detaches itself from me in order to function beyond my 'present' act and if it is utilizable at another time, in the absence of my-being-present-now ... The sender and receiver, even if they were the self-same subject, each relate to a mark they experience as made to do without them, from the instant of its production or of its reception on; and they experience this not as the mark's negative limit but rather as the positive condition of its possibility".

46   Nouvet, "An Impossible Response," pp. 106–07.
47   Barkan, *The Gods Made Flesh*, p. 87. For a similar account of the poem's ending, see Segal, "Ovid: Metamorphosis, Hero, Poet," p. 57.
48   That such a reading considerably distorts the *Aeneid* does not mean that it is not to Ovid's advantage to suggest it. For an important account of the skeptical undercurrent to Vergil's depiction of the Augustan empire, see William Johnson, *Darkness Visible: a Study of Vergil's Aeneid* (Berkeley: University of California Press, 1976).
49   In *Amores* 1.1 the narrator explains that he was trying to compose an epic (that is, he was trying to rival Vergil by beginning with the word "Arma"), but Cupid came along and stole away one metrical foot, thus making him write in elegiac verses. Laughing, Cupid shoots an arrow at the aspiring narrator of epic verse and says with high irony, "take that, *uates*." (" 'quodque canas, uates, accipe' dixit 'opus' " [" Singer,' he said, 'here take what will be the matter for your song' "]).
50   For a different reading of the role of epic fame or *kleos* in Ovid's concluding lines, see Segal, "Ovid: Metamorphosis, Hero, Poet." My account diverges from his because I take a different view of what it means to be subject to language. One does not obviate a post-structuralist or psychoanalytic critique of subjection by repositioning the subject as user of the code. For a critique of such attempts, see Rosalind Coward and John Ellis, *Language and Materialism: Developments in Semiology and the Theory of the Subject* (London and Boston: Routledge, 1977).
51   Murnaghan, "Body and Voice in Greek Tragedy," *Yale Journal of Criticism* 1,2 (1988): 25.
52   Vernant, "Dim Body, Dazzling Body," in *Fragments for a History of the Human Body*, ed. Michel Feher (New York: Zone, 1989), p. 33.
53   Bömer, *Metamorphosen*, p. 488, compares Ovid's closing figure to Horace *Odes* 3.30 as one of many Roman variations on the Greek topos of the epitaph. This monumental imagery – particularly funeral monuments – becomes particularly important for Shakespeare.
54   Jesper Svenbro, *Phrasiklea: anthropologie de la lecture en grèce ancienne* (Paris: Editions la Découverte, 1988) studies the epistemology and erotics of reading as an oral practice in ancient Greece. Patricia Rosenmeyer kindly brought this book to my attention
55   *Tusculanae Disputationes* 1.117; 1.34.
56   Segal, "Ovid: Metamorphosis, Hero, Poet," p. 57.

57 This is, of course, the question that de Saussure asked, and failed to answer, of Ovid's poem when he thought he detected a complex series of anagrams. That de Saussure abandoned his attempt gave rise to Michael Riffaterre's answer – to stabilize the aleatory force of language through appeal to intentionality and code – and Paul de Man's important comments on that "solution" to the problem in "Hypogram and Inscription: Michael Riffaterre's Poetics of Reading," *Diacritics* 11,4 (Winter, 1981): 17–35.

58 Interested readers should see Viarre, "L'Image et la pensée," for an extended analysis of mind–body dualism in the *Metamorphoses*.

59 Viarre, *ibid.*, p. 241.

60 Ahl observes that *forma* in Ovid's poem signifies both physically and linguistically, venturing that Ovid "probably accompanies his descriptions of change in physical shape with changes in the shape of the words with which he describes those changes" (*Metaformations*, p. 51).

61 On physical beauty, see *Aeneid*, 8.393; as style of composition, see Quintilian 12.10.2; as rhetorical form of speech, see Cicero, *Brutus*, 69 and *Orator*, 220.

62 See Ahl's discussion of the grammatical and sexual *formae* in Varronian etymologizing and its pertinence to Ovid's poem (*Metaformations*, pp. 24–31). He draws attention to the double sense of *forma* in Varro's text as well, since the grammarian describes linguistic "forms" as if they were living, physical forms: for instance, "fertile" words give birth to new "forms" where "sterile" words do not. On *forma* as a sign of difference between words, see *De Lingua Latina*, 9.109: "utrum in secunda forma uerbum temporale habeat in extrema syllaba as an is, ad discernendas dissimilitudines interest" (see also 9.101). In 8.9 he uses *forma* to designate a grammatical paradigm. See also Quintilian. 10.1.10.

63 The *OLD* lists the following sense for *membrum*: 1. a part or organ of the body, limb; 2. the limbs regarded as composing the whole body; 3. one of the main divisions or component parts of a thing; 4. a member of a body of people; 5. a small section of a speech or literary work; and a rhetorical term for the member of a period or clause (translation of Greek *kolon*).

64 "The Garden," lines 29–32.

65 For the corporeal sense, the *OLD* cites "sic mea uibrari pallentia membra uideres" (Ovid, *Heroides*, 11.77); for the vocal, "haec uox ... sonat adhuc et uibrat in auribus meis" (Seneca, *Dialogi* 1.3.3).

66 This may be why the statue takes on the graphic form of wax – because such a material form resists the iron stylus.

67 See W. S. Anderson's account of Ovid's less than sublime rendition of the story in Charles Segal, ed., *Orpheus: The Myth of the Poet* (Baltimore, MD: Johns Hopkins University Press, 1989), pp. 111–32.

68 Nisbet and Hubbard, *A Commentary on Horace Odes Book 1* (Oxford: Oxford University Press, 1970), p. 236. They trace a similar moment in Horace *Odes* 1.18.13 as well as in Varro, Lucretius, and Catullus. Whether or not *tibia*'s only other meaning – "shinbone" or *os* (with a short o) – helped determine Ovid's choice here for an instrument capable of conquering Orpheus's *os*, I leave for individual readers to decide.

69 In light of the role of the Bacchae in the story of the voice, remember that the name "Gorgon" derives from an Indo-European root meaning "shriek"

or "shout" and that in ancient Greek art, the Gorgon's face "conveys to the spectator the idea of a terrifying roar" (Thalia Phillies-Howe, "The Origin and Function of the Gorgon-Head," *American Journal of Archaeology* 58 [1958]: 211). For further comment, see chapter 1, note 28.

70   See Hinds, *The Metamorphoses of Persephone*, for a detailed account.

71   See Valerie Traub's argument that erotic difference is not reducible to sexual difference in "Desire and the Difference it Makes," in *The Matter of Difference: Materialist Feminist Criticism of Shakespeare*, ed. Valerie Wayne (Ithaca, NY: Cornell University Press, 1991), pp. 221–36.

72   Curran, "Rape and Rape Victims in the *Metamorphoses*," *Arethusa* 2 (1978).

73   For example, 7. 53–4; 8.72–3; 9.745 ff; 9.500–01; 10.329–30.

74   Here one might discriminate between Ovid's representation of love and Petrarch's. Where Ovid is fascinated by the overwhelming *force* of *amor*, Petrarch switches allegiance to the object. Only one object, *Laura*, will do; all the other Ovidian stories on which he builds his self-portrait are subsumed as metaphors for this single object-relation. Freud, of course, distinguishes between ancient and modern attitudes to love along precisely these lines in *Three Essays on the Theory of Sexuality*, published in *The Standard Edition of the Complete Works of Sigmund Freud*, trans. James Strachey (London: Hogarth Press, 1974), vol. VII, pp. 123–243. Whether or not one agrees with his generalization about the history of erotic life from antiquity to the modern era, Freud's remark usefully distinguishes between *eros* in the *Metamorphoses* and the *Rime Sparse*.

75   Laplanche, *Life and Death in Psychoanalysis*, p. 21.

76   Jean Laplanche and Jean-Bertrand Pontalis, "Fantasy and the Origins of Sexuality," in *Formations of Fantasy*, ed. Victor Burgin, James Donald, and Cora Kaplan (London: Methuen, 1986), pp. 5–34. For Laplanche, the necessity of inventing such histories speaks to the way in which sexuality is inherently traumatic for speaking beings who come to experience the adult world of sexual meanings belatedly, as the retrospective intrusion of an "alien internal entity" (see *Life and Death*).

77   See Bruce W. Holsinger, "Sodomy and Resurrection: The Homoerotic Subject of *The Divine Comedy*," in *Premodern Sexualities*, ed. Carla Freccero and Louise Fradenberg (New York and London: Routledge, 1996), pp. 243–74 for a compelling discussion of this aspect of Ovid's narrative and what it means for Dante's return to this moment in Ovid's text.

78   I borrow Samuel Weber's useful phrase. See *Return to Freud: Jacques Lacan's Dislocation of Psychoanalysis* (Cambridge: Cambridge University Press, 1991). For an account of the elliptical or differential production of sexual identity in Renaissance poetry, see my *The Tears of Narcissus: Melancholia and Masculinity in Early Modern Writing* (Stanford, CA: Stanford University Press, 1995).

3 EMBODIED VOICES: AUTOBIOGRAPHY AND FETISHISM IN THE
RIME SPARSE

1   Most recently, see Lawrence Kritzman, *The Rhetoric of Sexuality and the Literature of the French Renaissance* (Cambridge: Cambridge University

Press, 1991); and Ann Rosalind Jones, "New Songs for the Swallow: Ovid's Philomela in Tullia d'Aragona and Gaspara Stampa," in *Refiguring Woman: Perspectives on Gender and the Italian Renaissance*, ed. Marilyn Migiel and Juliana Schiesari (Ithaca, NY: Cornell University Press, 1991). For discussions of Ovid and Petrarch, see Leonard Barkan, *The Gods Made Flesh: Metamorphosis and the Pursuit of Paganism* (New Haven, CT: Yale University Press, 1986); Robert Durling, *Petrarch's Lyric Poems: The Rime Sparse and Other Lyrics* (Cambridge, MA: Harvard University Press, 1976); and Sara Sturm-Maddox, *Petrarch's Laurels* (University Park, PA: University of Pennsylvania Press, 1992).

2   Unless otherwise noted, quotations and translations of Petrarch are from Robert M. Durling, *Petrarch's Lyric Poems* (Cambridge, MA: Harvard University Press, 1976) and quotations of Ovid are from W. S. Anderson, *Ovidius Metamorphoses* (Leipzig: Teubner, 1977). Translations of the *Metamorphoses* are mine.

3   For a similar reading, see Lavinia Lorch, "Human Time and the Magic of the Carmen," *Philosophy and Rhetoric* 15, 4 (Fall 1982): 262–71.

4   See Frederick Ahl's detailed account of anagrams in *Metaformations* (Ithaca, NY: Cornell University Press, 1985), esp. p. 138. J. N. Adams, *Latin Sexual Vocabulary* (London: Duckworth, 1982), p. 120 cites *ramus roborascit*, "his branch is hardening."

5   Ovid also plays with the letters of *laurus*: struck by a golden arrow ("*aura*tum est," 470), the god seeks to touch her hair, blown about by the breeze ("dabat *aura* capillos," 529), gets the *laurus*, and sings a song in praise of Rome. For Petrarch's revisions, see #5, 23, 30, 194 and 196–98.

6   See E. W. Leach, "Ekphrasis and the Theme of Artistic Failure in Ovid's *Metamorphoses*," *Ramus* 3 (1974): 102–42; and Donald Lateiner, "Mythic and Non-Mythic Artists in the *Metamorphoses*," *Ramus* 3 (1974): 1–31.

7   For example: "Né pur il mio secreto e 'l mio riposo / fuggo, ma più me stesso" ("Nor do I flee my secret place nor my rest, but I flee more from myself" [234.9–10]).

8   See Thomas Roche, *Petrarch and the English Sonnet Sequences* (New York: AMS Press, 1989). For analysis of the splitting of the subject as a defense, see David Rodowick, *The Difficulty of Difference: Psychoanalysis, Sexual Difference and Film Theory* (New York and London: Routledge, 1991).

9   I refer to Augustinus' position in Petrarch's *Secretum*, which is to be distinguished from Saint Augustine's own project. Were one to read Saint Augustine's text carefully (particularly in terms of the address to God that frames it), his autobiographical subject would look rather less stable than Petrarch would have it. On the difference between Augustinus and Saint Augustine, see Charles E. Trinkaus, *In our Image and Likeness: Humanity and Divinity in Italian Humanist Thought* (Chicago: University of Chicago Press, 1970).

10 *Secretum*, in *Prose*, ed. G. Martellotti, P. G. Ricci, E. Carrara, and E. Bianchi (Milan: Sansoni, 1955), pp. 156–58. All citations are to this edition. Critics often note that Petrarch disrupts the Augustinian autobiographical narrative of conversion he invokes. See Robert Durling, *The Figure of the Poet in Renaissance Epic* (Cambridge, MA: Harvard University

Press, 1965), p. 84; Giuseppe Mazzotta, "The *Canzoniere* and the Language of the Self," *Studies in Philology* 3 (1978): 271–96; Marguerite Waller, *Petrarch's Poetics and Literary History* (Amherst, MA: University of Massachusetts Press, 1980), pp. 21, 56, and 91. Although Augustine is not mentioned, a good recent discussion of what the split self implies for the subject of autobiography is Vincent Crapanzo's "'Self'-Centering Narratives," *Yale Journal of Criticism* 5, 3 (1992): 61– 80.

11   Both the *Secretum* and the "Ascent of Mont Ventoux" attest to the enormous effect that Augustine's reflections on time had on Petrarch's representation of himself. See Victoria Kahn, "The Figure of the Reader in Petrarch's Secretum," (*PMLA* 100 [1985]: 154–66) for an acute account of Petrarch's relation to Augustinian definitions of reading, memory, and self. "In the *Secretum*," she argues, the text that might seem a place to "preserve memory" in fact becomes a "means of self-forgetfulness." Important for this analysis of Petrarch's verbal fetishism and Pygmalion's place in that fantasy, she adds that the *Secretum* itself becomes an "object of desire" (160).

12   Mazzotta, "The Language of the Self," 291. See also his discussion of Petrarch's "disjunctive consciousness" in sonnets 77 and 78 in *The Worlds of Petrarch* (Durham, NC and London: Duke University Press, 1993), pp. 28–29.

13   As Lacan puts it, the signifier, like the purloined letter, "will be and not be where it is, wherever it goes" ("Seminar on 'The Purloined Letter,'" *Yale French Studies* 48 [1975]: 54).

14   Freccero, "The Fig Tree and the Laurel: Petrarch's Poetics" in *Literary Theory / Renaissance Texts*, ed. Patricia Parker and David Quint (Baltimore, MD: Johns Hopkins University Press, 1986), p. 22.

15   See Barkan, *The Gods Made Flesh*, for analysis of the way Ovid's stories inform the conventional antagonisms of the *paragone*.

16   Such a reading of Pygmalion and Narcissus was not uncommon. Petrarch is clearly leaning on Jean de Meun's representation of the lover in the *Roman de la Rose*, a text in which the two Ovidian figures appear together. Jean's Pygmalion calls himself happier than Narcissus who loved a mere shadow; in these lines, Pygmalion interestingly refers to the form that Narcissus cannot touch as a *woman*'s shadow ("Mais cil ne poait aveir *cele* / Qu'il voait en la fontenele" l.20887–8). For an overview, see Louise Vinge, *The Narcissus Theme in Western Literature up to the Early Nineteenth Century* (Lund, Sweden: Gleerups Press, 1967) 86– 87.

17   Translation by William H. Draper, *Petrarch's Secret* (London: Chatto, 1911), p. 134. All subsequent citations are to this translation unless otherwise noted. Mazzotta similarly observes, "Like Narcissus, who gazes at his reflected image – discovers that he, too, is a shadow – Petrarch looks at Simone's painting of Laura and 'sees' in it his own mute reflection" (*The Worlds of Petrarch*, p. 31).

18   See H. Frankel, *Ovid: A Poet Between Two Worlds* (Berkeley and Los Angeles: University of California Press, 1945), p. 96; and G. Karl Galinsky, *Ovid's Metamorphoses: An Introduction to the Basic Aspects* (Oxford: Basil Blackwell, 1975), p. 30.

19   For Freud's analysis of the game little Hans played in reaction to his

mother's absence, see *Beyond the Pleasure Principle*, in *The Standard Edition* (London: Hogarth Press, 1974), vol. XVIII, p. 1416.

20 See Kritzman, *The Rhetoric of Sexuality*, p. 6. The most extensive, and influential, treatment of dismemberment in the *Rime Sparse* remains Nancy Vickers's "Diana Described: Scattered Woman and Scattered Rhyme" in *Writing and Sexual Difference*, ed. Elizabeth Abel (Chicago: University of Chicago Press, 1982), pp. 95–110. For an account of the *blason* in terms of property relations, see Patricia Parker, *Literary Fat Ladies: Rhetoric, Gender, Property* (London and New York: Methuen, 1987), pp. 126–54.

21 11.24–27. Vickers compares Actaeon, Orpheus, and Pentheus in "Diana Described," pp. 99–100. Ovid's preoccupation with *mutatas formas corpora* has the uncanny habit of returning: Quintilian, for instance, excuses Ovid's rhetorical excess because of the necessity of "collecting exceedingly diverse" material into "the semblance of a unified body" (*Institutio oratoria*, 4.1.77).

22 Jane Gallop comments, "The *corps morcelé* is a Lacanian term for a violently nontotalized body image, an image ... accompanied by anxiety" (*Reading Lacan* [Ithaca: Cornell University Press, 1985], p. 79).

23 "Diana Described" pp. 103–05.

24 *Rime Sparse*, 11.12. See Freud's "Fetishism" and "The Splitting of the Ego in the Defensive Process" in *Sexuality and the Psychology of Love*, translated by Robert Strachey (New York: Macmillan, 1963). References are to this translation, modifications noted where made. Freud writes that "the devotees of fetishes regard them as abnormalities, it is true, but only rarely as symptoms of illness; usually they are quite content with them or even extol the advantages they offer for erotic gratification" ("Fetishism," p. 214).

25 The first quotation is from Freud, "The Splitting of the Ego in the Defensive Process," p. 218; the second is Constance Penley, *The Future of an Illusion: Film, Feminism, and Psychoanalysis* (Minneapolis: University of Minnesota Press, 1989), p. 27.

26 "The Splitting of the Ego," pp. 222–3 and 221. "The boy did not simply contradict his perception, hallucinating a penis there where none was to be seen, but undertook a displacement of value [*Wertverschiebung*], transferring the significance of the Penis [*die Penisbedeutung*] to another part of the body" (222, translation modified). For original, see "Die Ichspaltung im Abwehrvorgang," *Studienausgabe*, 12 vols. (Frankfurt: Fischer Taschenbuch, 1982), III, 393. German texts are cited from this edition. On the "role of the father" see "Fetischismus," pp. 387–88.

27 "Diana Described," pp. 103 and 104–05. To those familiar with Petrarch and Petrarchan criticism, Kaja Silverman's "Lost Objects and Mistaken Subjects: Film Theory's Structuring Lack," *Wide Angle* 7, 1 and 2 (1985): 14–29, sketches a movement in 1980s film theory concerning fetishism similar to the one from Freccero to Vickers. But because Freccero turns away from Freud and Vickers does not make use of Lacan, the relationship between a semiotic and a psychoanalytic theory of the "speaking subject" has not been developed as extensively in the criticism of Petrarch as it has in the critique of film. From the semiotics of film as a language constructed around lack or absence (of the referent, the site of production, or of the subject of enunciation) to a rethinking of that lack in filmic signification as

one that takes place *for* the subject, one can hear an echo of the theory in Freccero's "The Fig Tree and the Laurel." Thus Petrarch constructs an effect of poetic "presence" in relation to the fetishized veil, a symbol of the lack constituting his own autobiographical discourse (Laura becomes the single, privileged, missing "referent"). In describing the veil as a "fetish," Freccero makes a move comparable to that of Stephen Heath, who argues that the cinematic subject is installed in relation to the fetish ("Lessons from Brecht," *Screen* 15, no. 4 [1980]: 107–08). He then explicitly turns away from any engagement with the comparable linguistic analysis of subjectivity developed in psychoanalytic and film theory. This engagement is left to Vickers, whose largely Freudian account of fetishism argues that castration is central to Petrarch's "scattered rhymes." In contrast to film theory's exploration of fetishism in language, however, Vickers focuses primarily on the erotic problem and on the body; she does not explore the relationship between the sexual and the linguistic order beyond the symbolic process of defense. I understand the problem of verbal fetishism in these poems as a problem that joins one to the other. Therefore I suggest we recall that according to Lacan's work on "castration" as a linguistic as well as a sexual problem, this fetish would mark a cultural, not a natural, story: the imposition of the organizing prohibition of the Oedipal story on the displacements necessary to linguistic functioning.

28   In *Sexuality and the Psychology of Love*, Strachey translates, "the fetish itself has become the vehicle both of denying and of asseverating the fact of castration" (218). "The fact of castration" is the translator's wording; Freud writes only "castration" (*Studienausgabe* III. 387). In both "Fetishism" and "The Splitting of the Ego," castration is socially constructed – the traumatic recognition of a *taboo*, not an unmediated encounter with the female body. As Freud suggests, the threat "by itself" might not "produce a great impression" (*für sich allein muß nicht viel Eindruck machen*); the sight alone of the female genitals "might" convince him of the possibility (*von einer solchen Möglichkeit überzeugen können*) – but he might "draw no conclusion from this alone" (III. 392). What Freud studies is the social and psychic *construction* of *die Realität der Kastrationsgefahr*. This construction is produced for the subject when taboo and memory coincide: meaning is transferred to a sight that first meant nothing. The joint work of taboo and retrospection produces the verdict of "reality" or fact, and fetishism reveals that this "fact" is something that *may or may not* be believed. Either a little boy disregards what he "sees," or a previously "harmless" scene is revived in memory and recognized, the second time, as a threat because a look and a prohibition "happen" to coincide: "the little boy believes that he now understands" (*Der Knabe glaubt jetzt zu verstehen*). See Jean Laplanche's study of temporality and the production of "meaning" for the traumatized sexual subject in *Life and Death in Psychoanalysis*, trans. Jeffrey Mehlman (Baltimore, MD: Johns Hopkins University Press, 1976), pp. 35–47 and esp. 40.

29   Mazzotta "The *Canzoniere* and the Language of the Self," p. 283. Mazzotta adds that the strictly differential nature of this subject/object, male/female relationship also produces an internal split: "the shift insinuates a doubleness at the moment in which the self is constituted: *Petrarch is at the same time*

both Actaeon and Diana but he is also neither, a double, like the two foci of an ellipsis always implicating each other and always apart" (pp. 283–84, emphasis mine). Vickers similarly remarks on this implication in "Diana Described," p. 104.

30 See Rodowick, *The Difficulty of Difference*, p. 68, and Janet Bergstrom's "Enunciation and Sexual Difference," (*Camera Obscura*, nos. 3–4 [Summer 1979]: 33–70) for insightful work on the bisexual mobility and contradictory multiplicity of subject positions in psychoanalytic work on fantasy.

31 See Slavoj Žižek, who stresses the insistence of synchronic structures and the contingency of any new intervention in those structures: analysis "produces the truth; that is, the signifying frame which gives the symptoms their symbolic place and meaning. As soon as we enter the symbolic order, the past is always present in the form of historical tradition and *the meaning of these traces is not given; it changes continually with the transformations of the signifier's network.* Every historical rupture, every advent of a new master-signifier, changes retroactively the meaning of all tradition, restructures the narration of the past, makes it readable in another, new way" (*The Sublime Object of Ideology* [London: Verso, 1989], p. 56, emphasis mine).

32 A number of scholars suggest Pygmalion's name (*pygmaios*) evokes a "phallic dwarf": see Franz Bömer, *P. Ovidius Naso, Metamorphosen*, vol. V (Heidelberg, 1969), p. 93; and Ahl, *Metaformations*, pp. 256–57. As we'll see in the next chapter, John Marston was particularly alert to such resonances.

33 See, for example, J. Hillis Miller, *Versions of Pygmalion* (Cambridge, MA: Harvard University Press, 1990).

34 One continually reads, "one day x happened to be somewhere and saw y ..." Not only does desire not conduct itself along heterosexual lines or according to the demand for exogamy, it doesn't always stick to the human (e.g. Pygmalion loves a statue, Narcissus an *imago*).

35 Mazzotta, "The *Canzoniere* and the Language of the Self," p. 284.

36 "Fetishism," p. 217; translation modified. *Studienausgabe* III, 385–6.

37 *The Sublime Object of Ideology*, pp. 45 and 37. Žižek asks how an external "symbolic machine" becomes "the place where the fate of our internal, most 'sincere' and 'intimate' beliefs is in advance staged and decided," and trauma becomes the mechanism by which the unconscious is constituted as a social "affair of obedience to the dead, uncomprehended letter." For him, trauma is the condition of the subject's "unconscious economy." His revision of Althusserian "interpellation" clearly pertains to Freud's theory that the subject recognizes what it means to be "male" (and what it means for his mother to be a "woman") because of the trauma called "castration": "How does the Ideological State Apparatus ... 'internalize' itself; how does it produce the effect of ideological belief ... [or] recognition of one's ideological position? .... This external 'machine' of State Apparatuses exercises its force only in so far as it is experienced, in the unconscious economy of the subject, *as a traumatic, senseless injunction* ... It is precisely this non-integrated surplus of senseless traumatism which confers on the Law its unconditional authority ... Far from hiding its full authority, this traumatic, non-integrated character of the Law is a positive condition of it" (*The Sublime Object of Ideology*, pp. 43 and 37, emphasis mine). With similar

emphasis on the subject's traumatic insertion into the Symbolic order, Laplanche argues that it is the disjunction between the intelligible and the as yet unintelligible, the "senseless," that characterizes Freud's understanding of any subject's entrance into sexuality. In Laplanche's linguistic account of "latency," the interference between the not-yet significant and the significant inducts the always unprepared subject into the system of sexual meanings, an interference that makes the necessarily "retrospective" work of rendering sexuality legible traumatic (*Life and Death in Psychoanalysis*, pp. 35–47 and esp. p. 40).

38　"Within the limits of this book," Greene writes, the lady "is never created." *Laura* is "unable to create her supposed lover as laureate ... the closed system of an autonomous universe remains permanently out of reach" (*The Light in Troy: Imitation and Discovery in Renaissance Poetry* [New Haven, CT: Yale University Press, 1982], p. 115).

39　See my "'Myself/Before Me': Gender and Prohibition in Milton's Italian Sonnets," in *Milton and the Idea of Woman*, ed. Julia Walker (Urbana, IL: University of Illinois Press, 1988), pp. 32–51.

40　Mazzotta, "Petrarch's Song 126," in *Textual Analysis: Some Readers Reading*, ed. M. A. Caws (New York: Modern Language Association of America, 1986), pp. 125, 129, and 130.

41　In *S/Z*, Barthes writes of fetishism in *Sarrasine*: "the sentence can never constitute a total; meanings can be listed, not admixed: the total, the sum are for language the promised lands, glimpsed *at the end* of enumeration ... As a genre, the *blazon* expresses the belief that a *complete* inventory can reproduce a total body ... description ... accumulates in order to totalize, multiplies fetishes in order to obtain a total, defetishized body; thereby, description *represents* no beauty at all: no one can *see* La Zambinella, infinitely projected as a totality impossible because linguistic, *written*" (trans. by Richard Miller [New York: Hill and Wang, 1974], p. 114).

42　Lacan, first quotation: "Desire and the Interpretation of Desire in *Hamlet*," as reprinted in *Literature and Psychoanalysis: The Question of Reading: Otherwise*, ed. Shoshana Felman (Baltimore, MD: Johns Hopkins University Press, 1982), p. 28. Second quotation: *Ecrits: A Selection*, trans. Alan Sheridan (New York: W. W. Norton and Co., 1977), p. 67, emphasis mine. See "L'instance de la lettre" (*Ecrits*, pp. 493–528) and "La chose freudienne" (*Ecrits*, pp. 414–15) for a summary of the "gap" or "béance congénitale" in the subject's "natural relations" as translated by "l'omniprésence pour l'être humaine de la fonction symbolique."

43　*The Seminar of Jacques Lacan: Book II, The Ego in Freud's Theory and in the Technique of Psychoanalysis 1954–55*, trans. Sylvana Tomaselli (New York: W. W. Norton and Co., 1988), pp. 238 and 239.

44　See *Ecrits: A Selection*, p. 40.

45　*Reading Lacan*, p. 20.

46　*The Sublime Object of Ideology*, p. 175. Compare here Thomas Greene's observation that "one might argue" that Petrarch "creates himself out of failed signifiers" (*The Light in Troy*, p. 116).

47　Compare the similar formulation by Nicholas Abraham and Maria Torok – that to become a subject, one must join a linguistic exchange within a community of "empty mouths" (*L'Ecorce et le noyau* [Paris: Aubier-Flammarion, 1978], p. 268).

48 Ovid's Actaeon appealed widely to male writers representing internal states. See Ioan Couliano's discussion of Actaeon's role in Giordano Bruno's *Eroici Furori* in *Eros and Magic in the Renaissance*, trans. Margaret Cook (Chicago: University of Chicago Press, 1984), pp. 72–80. But Actaeon's accidental vision proved useful in a yet larger cultural domain than the lyric. As Wendy Wall demonstrates, early book prefaces represented reading as "voyeurism," thus "mediating and suppressing" a set of cultural anxieties released by printing technology" ("Disclosures in Print: The 'Violent Enlargement' of the Renaissance Voyeuristic Text," *Studies in English Literature* 29 [1989]: 53). For her, Actaeon's presence in prefatory material figures and deflects the anxieties of the new democratizing, anti-aristocratic trade in books; making the reader a voyeur allows an "aristocratic" disavowal of the stigma of print while also constituting a marketing strategy.

49 *Life and Death in Psychoanalysis*, pp. 82–83.

50 See *The Seminar of Jacques Lacan, Book II*, pp. 166–67.

51 For commentary on the important role of the *paragone* or competition between visual and verbal art in medieval and Renaissance appropriations of Ovid, see Barkan, *The Gods Made Flesh*.

52 Here I rely on Joel Fineman's work on Petrarch and depart from it. The idealizing language of vision, which he takes as the hallmark of Petrarchanism, is clearly crucial to these sonnets (*Shakespeare's Perjur'd Eye: the Invention of Poetic Subjectivity in the Sonnets* [Berkeley: University of California Press, 1986]). But Petrarch's complex engagement with the *Metamorphoses* also offers a critique of that heavenly ideal as a fantasy. In the *Rime Sparse*, Ovidian figures like Actaeon and Medusa lie behind Pygmalion: they signal an ironic hollowing out of idealized vision, a visual estrangement of the self from its body's perceptions that echoes the poet's equally Ovidian alienation from his own tongue.

53 The combined attention of Ovid and Petrarch to the poetic subject's verbal and visual displacement, of course, means that the penchant for ekphrasis in the Ovidian tradition will have as much to do with the conditions of subjectivity as it has to do with the beauty of works of art.

54 As Hillis Miller observes, "For Pygmalion, the other is not really other. Pygmalion has himself made Galatea. She is the mirror image of his desire … For Galatea, to see at all is to see Pygmalion and be subject to him. It is as if Narcissus' reflection in the pool had come alive and returned his love" (*Versions of Pygmalion*, 4–5). In the context of the weight given the proper name in Ovid's text, however, we must remember that the poem never names the statue; following Pygmalion's colonizing narcissism closely, albeit ironically, the poem keeps the "other" not quite an other precisely by *not* giving her a name.

55 There is, in Ovid's text, always an exception. In this case it is Narcissus: he attains knowledge of the poem's ironic split, an accession to Ovidian irony that results in "iste ego sum." It is an exception which may, in part, explain the extraordinary influence of his predicament on literary history and which suggests, as well, why Petrarch is so drawn to the Narcissus.

56 *The Worlds of Petrarch*, p. 31.
57 "The Fig Tree and the Laurel," p. 32.
58 Marjorie Garber similarly suggests that the figure of the Medusa's head, in *Macbeth*, is a sign of gender indeterminacy. See *Shakespeare's Ghost Writers: Literature as Uncanny Causality* (New York: Methuen, 1987).
59 See notes 25 and 27.
60 See my analysis in chapter 2, pp. 79–83.
61 "quantum motu formosi suspicior *oris* / uerba refers aures non peruenientia nostras," 3. 461–2.
62 "uox nulla secuta est. / ingemuit: uox illa fuit, lacrimaeque *per oral non sua* fluxerunt," 3.201–03.
63 See chapter 2, pp. 79–83.
64 It might be worth remembering here the story of Pan and Syrinx, because this sonnet reverses the trajectory of that story, making the male body the vessel through which the wind passes.
65 Kristeva, *The Revolution in Poetic Language*, trans. Margaret Waller (New York: Columbia University Press, 1981), pp. 65–67.

4 "BE NOT OBSEANE THOUGH WANTON": MARSTON'S *METAMORPHOSIS OF PIGMALIONS IMAGE*

1 This is Barbara Johnson's useful summary of the assumptions behind the trope. See *The Critical Difference* (Baltimore, MD: Johns Hopkins University Press, 1980).
2 *The Metamorphosis of Pigmalions Image*, stanza 12. As printed in Elizabeth Story Donno, *Elizabethan Minor Epics* (New York: Columbia University Press, 1963). All subsequent citations are from this edition. I retain Marston's spelling of the name throughout to distinguish his character (P*i*gmalion) from Ovid's (P*y*gmalion).
3 See Philip J. Finkelpearl, *John Marston of the Middle Temple* (Cambridge, MA: Harvard University Press, 1969) for an account of the social, demographic, and educational background of the Inns of Court.
4 Compare the accounts of Finkelpearl, *John Marston of the Middle Temple* and S. F. Bonner, *Roman Declamation in the Late Republic and Early Empire* (Liverpool: University Press of Liverpool, 1949).
5 Critics often note that the chief object of Marston's satire was contemporary amatory poetry, though the terms of these discussions differ from my own. See Anthony Caputi, *John Marston, Satirist* (Ithaca, NY: Cornell University Press, 1962), pp. 1–22; Finkelpearl, *John Marston of the Middle Temple*; Clark Hulse, *Metamorphic Verse: The Elizabethan Minor Epic* (Princeton, NJ: Princeton University Press, 1981).
6 Arthur F. Marotti, *John Donne: Coterie Poet* (Madison, WI: University of Wisconsin Press, 1986). For further comment on the agonistic atmosphere at the Inns of Court, see Marotti pp. 26–31. On Marston's well-earned reputation as a particularly "combative" writer, see T. F. Wharton, "'Furor Poeticus' – Marston and his Contemporaries," in *The Critical Fall and Rise of John Marston* (Columbia, SC: Camden House, 1994).

7   Bruce R. Smith, *Homosexual Desire in Shakespeare's England* (Chicago: Chicago University Press, 1991), pp. 178–81.

8   Butler, *Excitable Speech: a Politics of the Performative* (New York and London: Routledge, 1997), p. 133.

9   For further discussion, see my comments in chapter 1 and Elissa Marder's analysis of the discourse of rage in the story of Philomela ("Disarticulating Voices: Feminism and Philomela," *Hypatia: A Journal of Feminist Philosophy*, 7, 2 [1992]: 148–66).

10 For an analysis of the way Laura's *imago* reflects the poet back to himself as "mute," see Giuseppe Mazzotta, *The Worlds of Petrarch* (Durham, NC and London: Duke University Press, 1993).

11 Eve Kosofsky Sedgwick, *Between Men: English Literature and Male Homosocial Desire* (New York: Columbia University Press, 1985).

12 I am indebted here to Barbara Johnson's canny discussion of this distinction in Shelley's "Ode to the West Wind" in *A World of Difference* (Baltimore, MD: Johns Hopkins University Press, 1987).

13 For further comment. see pp. 103–106.

5   "POOR INSTRUMENTS" AND UNSPEAKABLE EVENTS IN *THE RAPE OF LUCRECE*

1   For the details of this debate, see my discussion below in the section headed "The fault is thine."

2   See Joel Fineman, "Shakespeare's Will: the Temporality of Rape" in *The Subjectivity Effect in Western Literary Tradition* (Cambridge, MA: MIT Press, 1991), pp. 165–221 and Nancy Vickers, "The Blazon of Sweet Beauty's Best: Shakespeare's *Lucrece*," in *Shakespeare and the Question of Theory*, ed. Geoffrey Hartman and Patricia Parker (New York: Methuen, 1985), pp. 95–115.

3   Line 1212. All quotations from *The Riverside Shakespeare* (Boston: Houghton and Mifflin, 1968).

4   See the comments of Stephen Booth on sonnets 135 and 136 in *Shakespeare's Sonnets* (New Haven, CT: Yale University Press, 1977), pp. 466–67. For the last two meanings he cites "this night he fleshes his will in the spoil of her honor," *Alls Well That Ends Well*, 4.3.14; Lear's "O indistinguish'd space of woman's will" 4.4.271 and sonnet 135.5, "thy will is large and spacious."

5   See both Fineman, "Shakespeare's Will" and Vickers, "Blazon of Sweet Beauty's Best."

6   See Fineman, "Shakespeare's Will," p. 189.

7   Elissa Marder, "Disarticulated Voices: Feminism and Philomela," *Hypatia*, 7, 2 (1992): 158.

8   Ovid's Philomela protests: "ipsa pudore / proiecto tua facta loquar: si copia detur / in populos ueniam; si siluis clausa tenebor / inplebo siluas et conscia saxa mouebo; / audiet haec aether et si deus ullus in illo est" ("I myself, casting shame aside, will report your deeds: if I have the chance, I will go among other people; if I am detained in these woods, I will implore the woods and move even rocks to share knowledge; the air of heaven will hear and even god himself, if there is a god, will hear" 6. 544–7).

9   For ease of reference, I distinguish Shakespeare's character from Ovid's by retaining the difference between the Latin and the English spellings of her name.

10 The phrase is from John Brinsley's *Ludus Literarius: or, The Grammar Schoole* (London, 1612), 193, as cited in Bate, *Shakespeare and Ovid* (Oxford: Oxford University Press, 1993) p. 22.

11 Fineman, "Shakespeare's Will" and Vickers, "The Blazon of Sweet Beauty's Best." For an analysis that develops the problem of homosociality in relation to the visual representation of Lucretia's rape and suicide, see Mieke Bal, *Reading "Rembrandt": Beyond the Word-Image Opposition* (Cambridge: Cambridge University Press, 1991), pp. 60–93.

12 Vickers, "The Blazon of Sweet Beauty's Best," p. 97.

13 *Fasti*, 2. 731–34, translation by Sir James G. Frazer modified (Cambridge, MA: Harvard University Press, 1989).

14 See Laplanche's reading of retrospection in *Life and Death in Psychoanalysis*, trans. Jeffrey Mehlmann (Baltimore, MD: John Hopkins University Press, 1976).

15 As Katharine Eisaman Maus points out, such disapprobation is modern. The poem was extremely popular among its contemporaries; Gabriel Harvey compared it to Hamlet as a work designed to intrigue "the wiser sort" ("Taking Tropes Seriously: Language and Violence in Shakespeare's Rape of Lucrece," *Shakespeare Quarterly* 31 [1986]: 66).

16 "Taking Tropes Seriously," pp. 66–67.

17 F.T. Prince, introduction to *The Poems*, Arden Shakespeare Paperbacks (London: Methuen, 1969), xxvi.

18 Tricomi, "The Aesthetics of Mutilation in *Titus Andronicus*," *Shakespeare Survey*, 10 (1957): p. 12. In addition to Fineman, "Shakespeare's Will" and Vickers, "The Blazon of Sweet Beauty's Best," see Maus, "Taking Tropes Seriously." None of these essays take up the problem of Ovidian rhetorical practice, but I could not have written this chapter without them.

19 "Shakespeare's Will," p. 195. In a footnote he adds that "Lucrece is not the 'author' of her 'will.'" On his argument, which I examine in greater detail below, "neither Tarquin nor Lucrece can ever be the authors of these letters that perform them, and so it is the very crossing of letters that calls forth the figure of an author who can serve as the inscribing agent of the way letters cross." Whether this "figure of an author" is decidedly male, or the achievement of a "subjectivity-effect" attributed exclusively to "the 'will' of man" is worth exploring further, particularly by looking at what happens to the figures for Lucrece's attempt to write a "will." For Fineman, however, it is *Collatine* who is the "*only* anthropomorphic figure in the poem who possesses ... a specifically psychologistic literary power" (p. 200); neither Tarquin nor Lucrece achieve "the characteristic density ... and affective pathos we associate with Shakespeare's fully developed psychologized characters" (p. 199). Read against Petrarchan rhetoric alone, Collatine may well emerge as an important authorial figure. But read against the poem's Ovidian backdrop, Lucrece acquires, to my ear at least, as much (if not more) status as a "psychologistic" character than Collatine.

20 Coppélia Kahn, "Lucrece: the Sexual Politics of Subjectivity," in Lynn A.

Higgins and Brenda R. Silver, *Rape and Representation* (New York: Columbia University Press, 1991), p. 143; see also p. 148.

21   Butler, *Excitable Speech: a Politics of the Performative* (New York and London: Routledge, 1997), p. 2.

22   Goldberg, "Shakespearean Inscriptions: the Voicing of Power," in *Shakespeare and the Question of Theory*, ed. Patricia Parker and Geoffrey Hartman (New York and London: Methuen, 1985), p. 117.

23   For discussions of humanism in Tudor grammar schools, see Lisa Jardine and Anthony Grafton, *From Humanism to the Humanities* (London: Duckworth, 1986); Richard Halpern, *The Poetics of Primitive Accumulation* (Ithaca, NY: Cornell University Press, 1991), pp. 29–32; T. W. Baldwin, *William Shakspere's Small Latine and Lesse Greeke* (2 vols., Urbana: University of Illinois Press, 1944).

24   Ong, "Latin Language Study as a Renaissance Puberty Rite," *Studies in Philology* 56 (1959): 103–24, and Halpern, *The Poetics of Primitive Accumulation*, p. 32. See my earlier discussion in chapter 1, pp. 24–27.

25   Halpern, *The Poetics of Primitive Accumulation*, p. 44.

26   *Metamorphoses* 10.41–44. Translations mine unless otherwise noted.

27   For a different interpretation of the political implications of the way Philomela appears in this poem, see Jane O. Newman, "And Let Mild Women to Him Lose Their Mildness: Philomela, Female Violence, and Shakespeare's *The Rape of Lucrece*," *Shakespeare Quarterly* (Fall, 1994): 304–26.

28   For further comment on the central role that scenes of competition between visual and verbal arts plays in Ovidian narrative, see Leonard Barkan, *The Gods Made Flesh: Metamorphosis and the Pursuit of Paganism* (New Haven, CT: Yale University Press, 1986).

29   The trope derives originally from Dante's *Rime Petrose*, was inflected by Petrarch's rivalry with his predecessor, and so passed into countless English Petrarchan lyrics.

30   By the time the convention of Laura or the poet turning to stone reaches Shakespeare's hands, for instance, we find both male and female characters fashioned after this predicament: Venus, Lavinia, Titus, Paulina, and Leontes all try to plead their cases with flinty addressees.

31   Here I disagree with Fineman, who reads such phrases as "unprofitable sounds" and "this helpless smoke of words" as evidence of "a long and familiar history of anti-rhetorical sensibility," which means that "there is nothing in any way novel about either Lucrece's or Tarquin's stated thoughts about the issue of rhetoric" ("Shakespeare's Will," p. 190). If we understand these sentiments as I propose – in light of their Ovidian literary history and thus in light of a tradition in which the failure of the voice is a revealing index of a profoundly rhetorical sensibility – we may well discover something interesting (if not entirely "novel") about the subject of rhetoric.

32   See Fineman's extensive discussion of this pun in relation to Tarquin in"Shakespeare's Will."

33   Žižek, *The Sublime Object of Ideology* (London: Verso, 1989), p. 175.

34   See Fineman, "Shakespeare's Will," pp. 173–74.

35   Thus Fineman argues that Shakespeare emerges as "the immanent authorial

agency governing the poem's rhetorical production, even though this authorial agency is itself an *effect* of the way the poem rhetorically unfolds" ("Shakespeare's Will," p. 191). It is the decidedly tenuous status of such governance that seems to me emerges through Lucrece – particularly in her capacity as "instrument" and ventriloquist and, as well, as the after-effect of the failure of representation.

36   Fineman, "Shakespeare's Will," p. 186.

37   To this analysis I would briefly add that Lucrece's inability to hear otherwise, to listen for the sexual second meaning lurking in the margins, is precisely what defines "chastity" in this poem; it is her initial exclusion from the literary system of this "will" that recasts this Ovidian problem – Lucretia's inability even to speak about the crime in the *Fasti* – in Shakespearean terms.

38   The hope surfaces most forcefully at the end of Echo's story: it is voice – "voice" and "sound alone" – that "live in her" ("*uox* tantum atque ossa supersunt: / *uox* manet ... *sonus* est, qui uiuit in illa" [3.398–401]).

39   *Fasti* 2. 823–28. From the Loeb edition, edited by Sir James George Frazer. Translation mine.

40   Borch-Jacobsen, *The Freudian Subject*, trans. Catherine Porter (Stanford, CA: Stanford University Press, 1982), p. 21.

41   Fuss, *Identification Papers* (London and New York: Routledge, 1995), p. 2.

42   As quoted in Borch-Jacobsen, *The Freudian Subject*, p. 14. Readers interested in the larger context of this discussion should see Freud, *The Interpretation of Dreams* (*The Standard Edition*, trans. J. Strachey [London: Hogarth Press, 1974], vol. IV, p. 150).

43   Borch-Jacobsen, *The Freudian Subject*, p. 15.

44   *Ibid.*, p. 18.

45   *Ibid.*, p. 23. As Freud puts this idea, "these identifications should then make it possible for me to bring into contact with my ego certain ideas whose acceptance has been forbidden by censorship" (*The Interpretation of Dreams*, pp. 322–23).

46   Jean Laplanche and J. B. Pontalis, *The Language of Psychoanalysis* trans. Donald Nicholson-Smith (New York: Norton, 1973), p. 210.

47   See chapter 2, pp. 68–69 and pp. 76–77.

48   See my discussion of the shift from metamorphosis to metempsychosis in Pythagoras' soliloquy in chapter 2.

49   From Booth, *Shakespeare's Sonnets*.

50   For further comment on Ovidian motifs in the sonnets, see Jonathan Bate, *Shakespeare and Ovid*, pp. 32–43.

51   See chapter 2, pp. 67–70.

52   Lucrece's status as instrument is this poem's way of examining the problematic relationship between selves – or the "authenticity" of emotions – that in *Hamlet* is articulated as a confrontation between feeling and acting. In the play, as in *Lucrece*, it is the possibility of identifying with Hecuba's suffering, weeping "for" Hecuba, that produces an "inward" turn. Where the self-reflexive rhetoric of ventriloquism in *Lucrece* turns on some claim of likeness with Hecuba – and Philomela and Lucretia – and produces Lucrece as a subject in relation to that claim, Hamlet's confrontation with a scene of

acting someone else's passion produces his claim to having his "own" feelings. He declares the player's sorrow for Hecuba mere hypocrisy in order to claim his own, sincere cause for sorrow. Explicitly rejecting identification along with acting, Hamlet nonetheless makes a claim to his own sorrow in a scene that derives from the movement of identification articulated by both Lucrece and the Player as each contemplates Hecuba. I owe what I understand of the force of Hecuba's story on Shakespeare's representation of theater to Scott McMillin. I am also indebted to Adela Pinch's evocative reading of the way that, at crucial junctures in eighteenth-century literary and philosophical texts, one's feelings may turn out not to be one's own but, instead, someone else's (*Strange Fits of Passion: the Epistemology of Emotion from Austen to Hume* [Stanford, CA: Stanford University Press, 1996]).

53 This formulation is Samuel Weber's, *Return to Freud: Jacques Lacan's Dislocation of Psychoanalysis* (Cambridge: Cambridge University Press, 1991).

54 The "rest" also designates the "character or sign" by which this pause is noted on the musical score (*Oxford English Dictionary*).

55 *Oxford English Dictionary*. Compare *Much Ado*, "His jesting spirit, which is now crept into a lute string, and now govern'd by stops" (3.2.61).

56 The uncertainty about linguistic agency that is explored in the imagery of instruments is, it seems to me, one of the reasons that the poem also spends so much time considering the question of who is responsible for the rape (Tarquin's lust, Lucrece's beauty, "Time," "Opportunity," and so on). As Fineman tellingly suggests concerning the subjective and objective genitive in the title, Tarquin and Lucrece "together make the rape of Lucrece" just as "the two of them," because "chiasmatically imagined," "come together 'in her lips sweet fold' " ("Shakespeare's Will," p. 187). The crisis of agency usually provoked by narratives of rape here serves as a metaphor for the problems with authorial agency that haunt both Ovid's poem and Shakespeare's.

57 See "burden" and "bourdon" in the *OED*, definitions 1–4 and 9. For another Shakespearean meditation on a woman's singing burden, see Celia to Rosalind in *As You Like It*, 3.2.247, "I would sing my song without a burthen, thou bring'st me out of tune."

58 See Barbara Johnson's comments on the difference that the idea of pregnancy makes for the trope of apostrophe in "Apostrophe, Animation, Abortion" (*The Critical Difference* [Baltimore, MD: Johns Hopkins University Press, 1984], pp. 122–38).

59 Jean Laplanche and J.B. Pontalis, *The Language of Psychoanalysis*, p. 206. Choice of pronouns is the translator's.

6 "YOU SPEAK A LANGUAGE THAT I UNDERSTAND NOT": THE RHETORIC OF ANIMATION IN *THE WINTER'S TALE*

1 All quotations from *The Riverside Shakespeare* (Boston: Houghton, Mifflin Co., 1974).

2 William Morse, "Metacriticism and Materiality: The Case of Shakespeare's *The Winter's Tale*," *ELH* 58 (1991): 297.

3 How to read Hermione's silence has been an important question in much

criticism of the play. I am particularly indebted to Kenneth Gross, *The Dream of the Moving Statue* (Ithaca, NY: Cornell University Press, 1992), pp. 105–09 and Leonard Barkan, "'Living Sculptures': Ovid, Michelangelo, and *The Winter's Tale*," *ELH* 48 (1981): 639–67.

4   For an overview, see Leonard Barkan, *The Gods Made Flesh: Metamorphosis and the Pursuit of Paganism* (New Haven, CT: Yale University Press, 1986). As Barkan comments of "Diana and Actaeon," Titian turns Ovid's story of Actaeon's visual transgression into a painting that comments on the act of looking at a painting. Actaeon, poised "on the threshold," lifts a curtain to gaze on Diana; therefore "the bath almost becomes a picture within a picture. The result is a powerful identification between the viewer and Actaeon as both participate in the visual, the voyeuristic, and the visionary" (p. 201). One could make similar comments about the resonance between Petrarch's many allusions to Ovid's stories about the human voice and the characteristic fiction that a lyric poem is a spoken utterance – particularly in light of its favored trope, apostrophe. Such aesthetically self-reflexive allusions to Ovid's *Metamorphoses* are not a purely "Renaissance" phenomenon. On Dante's poetically self-conscious appropriations of Ovidian narrative, for example, see Rachel Jacoff and Jeffrey T. Schnapp, ed., *The Poetry of Allusion: Virgil and Ovid in Dante's "Commedia"* (Stanford, CA: Stanford University Press, 1991).

5   "'Living Sculptures,'" p. 660.

6   Sonnets 77 and 78.

7   78.12–14. I have modified the translation of Robert Durling (*Petrarch's Lyric Poems: the Rime Sparse and Other Lyrics* [Cambridge, MA: Harvard University Press, 1976]) to capture the rhetorically specific sense of the verb, *lodare*, "to praise." Barbara Johnson distinguishes between the two apostrophes in Shelley's "Ode to the West Wind" in a way that is useful for reading Petrarch's two: the first, emotive "if only" lays stress on the first person and the second, vocative "Pygmalion" on the second person. The typography of Shelley's poem marks this difference as one between "Oh" and "O," a difference Johnson allies with the one between Jakobson's emotive function, or "pure presencing of the first person" and his conative function, "or pure presencing of the second person" (*A World of Difference* [Baltimore, MD: The Johns Hopkins University Press, 1987], p. 187).

8   In the *Secretum*, Franciscus acknowledges the truth of Augustinus' rebuke that he is "captivated no less by the beauty of her *name* than of her person" ("non minus nominis quam ipsius corporis splendore captus") in *Prose*, ed. G. Martellotti, P. G. Ricci, E. Carrara, and E. Bianchi (Milan: Sansoni, 1955), p. 158. Petrarch's anagrams and puns on the "laurel" derive from Ovid's own verbal wit in the story of Apollo and Daphne, *Metamorphoses* 1. 451 ff.

9   On epideixis and gender in Petrarchanism, see Joel Fineman, "Shakespeare's Will: the Temporality of Rape," in *The Subjectivity Effect in Western Literary Tradition* (Cambridge, MA: MIT Press, 1991) and Nancy Vickers, "The Blazon of Sweet Beauty's Best: Shakespeare's *Lucrece*," in *Shakespeare and the Question of Theory*, ed. Geoffrey Hartman and Patricia Parker (New York: Methuen, 1985).

10 All quotations of the *Metamorphoses* from the text edited by Frank Justus Miller (Cambridge, MA: Harvard University Press, 1927). Translations are my own, although I have consulted Miller's.

11 *The. xv. Bookes of P. Ouidius Naso, entytuled Metamorphosis, translated oute of Latin into English meeter, by Arthur Golding Gentleman* (London: 1567), X. 69.

12 The association between the stories of Orpheus and Eurydice and Apollo and Daphne is commonplace. The most influential commentator on Ovid's poem, Raphael Regius, claims that Orpheus is Apollo's son, adding that the singer received his lyre from Apollo as a gift. A French translation of Orpheus' song (published in 1537) transposes the two, having Apollo narrate the story of Orpheus' descent and Pygmalion's creation.

13 "omnemque refugerat Orpheus / femineam Ueneram ... fuit auctor amorem / in teneros" (10.79–84). Here as elswhere in the *Metamorphoses*, we feel the tug of war between a controlling heterosexual imperative and the various polymorphous desires that undermine this story.

14 See Harry Berger's recent argument that a gynophobic and misogynist discourse informs Book 10, "Actaeon at the Hinder Gate," in *Desire in the Renaissance*, ed. Valeria Finucci and Regina Schwartz (Princeton, NJ: Princeton University Press, 1994).

15 Leontes signals an awareness of this punitive possibility. But he does so in the domestic register, containing the threat no sooner than uttered: "Chide me, dear stone, that I may say indeed / Thou art Hermione; or rather, thou art she / In thy not chiding; for she was as tender / As infancy and grace" (5.3.24–27). Hermione's being as "Hermione" is defined by an Ovidian economy of return in order to transcend it.

16 For a history of this misogynist tradition, see Barbara Rico's "From 'Speechless Dialect' to 'Prosperous Art': Shakespeare's Recasting of the Pygmalion Image," *Huntington Library Quarterly* 48 (1985): 285–95. Except for the two scenes I am discussing here – the last act of *The Winter's Tale* and Petrarch's paired sonnets (77 and 78) – the Pygmalion story is generally not a positive one in the middle ages or the Renaissance. Misogynist diatribes inform it, and the story of prostitution, too, clings to it: John Marston uses Pygmalion to adjudicate between the "wanton" and the "obscene" and George Pettie's *A Petite Palace* alludes to the story of the statue in overtly misogynist ways.

17 Jonathan Bate, in a book otherwise dedicated to tracing the minutiae of Ovid's *presence* in Shakespearean poetry, oddly dismisses the relevance to *The Winter's Tale* of the misogynist genealogy in Ovid. It seems to me no accident that the artist Shakespeare chose for his Pygmalion, Giulio Romano, was known not only as a painter but as a pornographer. The nature of Shakespeare's reference to Giulio Romano has been much debated. For a useful summary of the debate as well as an account of a contemporary English conduct book for young women that refers to the excellent work of "Iules Romain," see Georgianna Ziegler, "Parents, Daughters, and 'That Rare Italian Master': A New Source for *The Winter's Tale*," *Shakespeare Quarterly* 36 (1985): 204–12. For Romano's notorious, if not often seen, collaboration with Aretino, see David O. Frantz, *Festum*

Voluptatis: A Study of Renaissance Erotica (Columbus: Ohio State University Press, 1989), pp. 46–8, 119–23, and Frederick Hartt, *Giulio Romano* (New Haven, CT: Yale University Press, 1958). As Hartt points out, Giulio's prints, though suppressed, were also widely copied and widely destroyed; Frantz points out that when Perino del Vaga and Agostino Carracci imitated Romano, they do so in an Ovidian vein by calling them the "loves of the gods" (Frantz, p. 123). It is the rumor of Romano's work, rather than an actual copy in England, that seems to me important to Shakespeare's reference.

18 See Janet Adelman's account of dreams of male parthenogenesis and the problem of the maternal body in this play in *Suffocating Mothers: Fantasies of Maternal Origin in Shakespeare's plays, "Hamlet" to "The Tempest"* (London: Routledge, 1992).

19 For further elaboration of this issue, see chapter 2.

20 For an analysis of the role bodies – especially female bodies – play in the relationship between desire and "the drive to know" in modern narrative, see Peter Brooks, *Body Work: Objects of Desire in Modern Narrative* (Cambridge, MA: Harvard University Press, 1993). Leontes' devotion to speaking about the fantasized "truth" of Hermione's body might usefully be considered part of what Brooks calls "epistemophilia," a project in which we "tell stories about the body in the effort to know and to have it" and which results "in making the body a site of signification – the place for the inscription of stories – and itself a signifier, a prime agent in plot and meaning" (*Body Work*, pp. 5–6).

21 Recently, Heather Dubrow has argued that we must attend carefully to the complex and often contradictory role of Laura's voice if we are to understand the "relationship among speech, power, and gender" in the *Rime Sparse* and beyond. See *Echoes of Desire: English Petrarchism and its Counterdiscourses* (Ithaca, NY: Cornell University Press, 1995), esp. pp. 40–48.

22 *How To Do Things With Words*, ed. J. O. Urmson and Marina Sbisa (Cambridge, MA: Harvard University Press, 1962), pp. 1 and 6. Austin lists "I swear" as part of a class of "commissive" performatives in which conventional phrases are deployed to "commit the speaker to a certain course of action" (along with such other verbs as "promise," "give my word," "pledge myself," etc. [*How to Do Things With Words*, pp. 157–58]. Over the course of his lectures, Austin renders his "provisional" performative/constative distinction problematic; he eventually rejects any absolute dichotomy between the two, finding that constatives may well have a performative aspect (i.e. "I state that …" p. 91). Readers interested in the qualifications of Austin's initial theory should consult *How to do Things with Words*; the details are not necessary for this argument. My point here, rather, is simply to note that in *The Winter's Tale*, Shakespeare is exploring a distinction analogous to Austin's provisional one – between statements that report some state of affairs truly or falsely (in this case, the "state of affairs" in question being Hermione's fidelity) and other, conventional statements (like "I swear") in which saying and doing explicitly appear to converge. For a study of performatives in Shakespeare with an emphasis on cultural and

institutional authority, see Susanne Wofford, "'To You I Give Myself, For I Am Yours': Erotic Performance and Theatrical Performatives in As You Like It," in *Shakespeare Reread: The Texts in New Contexts*, ed. Russ McDonald (Ithaca, NY: Cornell University Press, 1994), pp. 147–69.

23 For my thinking about the relationship between performativity and sexuality I have drawn on several important discussions: Shoshana Felman, *The Literary Speech Act: Don Juan with J. L. Austin, or Seduction in Two Languages* (Ithaca, NY: Cornell University Press, 1983); Lynne Huffer, "Luce et veritas: Toward an Ethics of Performance," *Yale French Studies* (1995): 20–41; and Barbara Johnson, *The Critical Difference: Essays in the Contemporary Rhetoric of Reading* (Baltimore, MD: Johns Hopkins University Press, 1980).

24 *The Literary Speech Act*, p. 94. Analyzing performative language in relation to the story of Don Juan and of Oedipus, Felman's work is equally telling for the central dilemma of *The Winter's Tale*: the relationship between theatrical representation and the female body or, more generally in Ovidian narrative, between body and voice. Felman writes that "the problem of the human act," in psychoanalysis as well as performative analysis, "consists in the relation between language and body ... because the act is conceived ... as that which problematizes at one and the same time the separation and the opposition between the two. The act, an enigmatic and problematic production of the speaking body ... breaks down the opposition between body and spirit, between matter and language." She reminds us of Austin's comment that "in the last analysis, doing an action must come down to the making of physical movements with parts of the body; but this is about as true as ... saying something must ... come down to making movements of the tongue" (as quoted in *The Literary Speech Act*, p. 94).

25 As quoted in *The Literary Speech Act*, p. 82. Austin explores the contingent and context-bound nature of any speech act in "the doctrine of Infelicities" (*How To Do Things with Words*, pp. 14–24). Jacques Derrida's critique of Austin constitutes a sustained analysis of "the failure" that is an "essential" risk of performative utterances; see Derrida, "Signature Event Context," first published in *Glyph* 1 (1977) and translated by Samuel Weber and Jeffrey Mehlman in *Limited Inc* (Evanston, IL: Northwestern University Press, 1988), pp. 1–24. For other, related, approaches to the performative in Shakespearean drama, see Joseph Porter, *The Drama of Speech Acts: Shakespeare's Lancastrian Trilogy* (Berkeley: University of California Press, 1979) and Susanne Wofford, "'To you I give myself, for I am yours': Erotic Performance and Theatrical Performatives in As You Like It," in *Shakespeare Reread: the Texts in New Contexts*, Russ McDonald, ed. (Ithaca, N.Y.: Cornell, 1994): 147–69.

26 *How To Do Things With Words*, pp. 16–17.

27 *Ibid.*, p. 22.

28 *Limited Inc*, p. 10.

29 *Ibid.*, p. 14.

30 *Ibid.*, pp. 17 and 18.

31 *The Literary Speech Act*, p. 96; emphasis in original.

32 *The Critical Difference: Essays in the Contemporary Rhetoric of Reading*

(Baltimore, MD.: Johns Hopkins University Press, 1980), p. 60. Emphasis my own. Johnson adds, "if one considers the conventionality of all performative utterances (on which Austin often insists), can it really be said that the chairman who opens a discussion or the priest who baptizes a baby or the judge who pronounces a verdict are persons rather than personae? ... The performative utterance thus automatically fictionalizes its utterer when it makes him the mouthpiece of conventionalized authority." Or one could say that read rhetorically, the performative utterance may uncover the *theatrical* nature of such "ordinary" social transactions.

33   In light of the duality of Hermione's deictics, we might read the specification "i' th' open air" within the historical context as well. The stage in London's earliest commercial theaters projected into a yard and therefore placed actors "i' th' open air." On the physical conditions of London's public amphitheaters and private halls, see Andrew Gurr, *Playgoing in Shakespeare's London* (Cambridge: Cambridge University Press, 1987), pp. 13–18. Most critics believe *The Winter's Tale* to have been written for the closed theater of Blackfriars. But a note on the play by Simon Forman tells us that at least one contemporary remembers having seen the play performed at the Globe (on 15 May 1611).

34   For an interesting analysis of how important Ovid's poetry was for "the homoerotics of marriage," see Mario Di Gangi, *The homoerotics of early modern drama* (Cambridge: Cambridge University Press, 1997), pp. 29–63. Even in the story of sexual jealousy that orients *The Winter's Tale*'s heteronormative impulses, this sudden reminder of Hermione's transvestite body and voice, as well as the unruly libidinal currents of the Orpheus story that informs the play's dream of a voice that can bring about the changes of which it speaks, continue to trouble the story of gender difference on which the plot relies. On Orpheus as a figure for libidinal contradiction in the *Metamorphoses*, see my chapter 2, pages 83–87. For a discussion of where Orpheus' "misogyny and its homoerotic consequences" surfaces in early modern English texts, see De Gangi, especially pp. 44–50.

35   *Encore* (Paris: Seuil, 1975), p. 55. On the frequent misprision of Lacan's theory as one about "lack" rather than the productive process of misfiring, see *The Literary Speech Act*, pp. 82–84. We can rephrase this issue in the literary language that proposes it: like Daphne's *figura*, forever receding from Apollo's rapacious *figurae*, Hermione's "maternal" body exceeds the tropes that point to her.

36   *Disowning Knowledge in Six Plays of Shakespeare* (Cambridge: Cambridge University Press, 1987), pp. 193–221, especially p. 214. Cavell is, of course, most concerned with Leontes' doubts about his son and his own paternity. But in light of Janet Adelman's work on the play one is led to wonder, when poised between these two powerful essays, why it is that the idea of the *maternal* body sparks Leontes' radical doubt. I would add to Adelman's analysis only that it is Hermione's language – the effects of her voice – as well as her body that unsettles her husband's sense of himself. To Cavell's approach, similarly, I would add only that the play explores the action of Leontes' doubt through the action of language as much as of thought. For the scandal of what cannot be known – the truth about Hermione – turns, as

we have seen, into an interrogation of the power and the limits of theatrical representation as well as of two kinds of discourse: saying and swearing.

37 David Ward, "Affection, Intention, and Dreams in *The Winter's Tale*," *Modern Language Review* 82 (1987): 545–54, especially p. 552. Ward offers a precise discussion of Leontes' "affection" in relation to sixteenth-century faculty psychology, particularly in medical discourse. Looking at discussions in Hooker and Burton, Ward suggests that by "affection" Leontes is designating a "disease of the mind" linked to the faculty of the appetite rather than to the will or to reason; for Hooker, affection is both involuntary ("Wherefore it is not altogether in our power") and a desire for the impossible, for "any thing which seemeth good, be it never so impossible" (as quoted in Ward, p. 546). For Shakespeare, Ovid's combined stories of Pygmalion and Orpheus give a distinctive mythographic and erotic turn to affection's involuntary aspect (revulsion from womankind out of grief or disgust) and its connotation of a desire for the impossible (for art to conquer death).

38 See Howard Felperin, "'Tongue-Tied Our Queen?': the Deconstruction of Presence in *The Winter's Tale*," in *Shakespeare and the Question of Theory*, ed. Patricia Parker and Geoffrey Hartman (New York: Methuen, 1985). Although I clearly agree with Felperin's emphasis on the play's self-consciousness about its own failure to refer, it seems to me that, by framing the question in terms of a continued possibility that Hermione may be guilty, Felperin participates in the very logic he critiques; his reading repeats what it might otherwise analyze – the question of *why* language's misfiring should be represented in cognitive terms as the truth or falsity of the maternal body.

39 As attested with particular force in the final lines of the *Metamorphoses*, Ovid both entertained this dream and remained skeptical of it (see pp. 52–61). For my understanding of this scene, I am indebted to conversations with Thomas M. Greene on the relationship between poetry and magic. See his essays, "The Balance of Power in Marvell's 'Horatian Ode,'" *ELH* 60 (1993): 379–96 and "Poetry as Invocation," *New Literary History* 24, no. 3 (1993): 495–517.

40 See chapter 2, pp. 50–53. Notice, too, that in addition to the other meanings we have explored, *animus* can designate "a disembodied spirit, soul, or ghost." A hint of such a meaning appears when Polixenes asks Paulina to "make it manifest where she has liv'd, / Or how stol'n from the dead" (5.3.112–14). For interesting comments on the ghostly undertone in the scene, see Kenneth Gross, *The Dream of the Moving Statue*.

41 As we have seen, the link became one of the mainstays of a traditional reading of Ovid's poem. See Louise Vinge, *The Narcissus Theme in Western Literature up to the Early Nineteenth Century* (Lund: Gleerups Press, 1967). I learned to attend to the crucial role that Pygmalion and Narcissus play in the *Rime Sparse* from Giuseppe Mazzotta (*The Worlds of Petrarch* [Chapel Hill: Duke University Press, 1993]).

42 Stephen Orgel argues that rather than "mere local allusion," the Proserpina story is foundational to the play as a whole. As he observes, the story is pertinent not only to the play's preoccupation with time, but also to its dark view of male sexuality – a view that includes Florizel, the suitor who invokes

Ovid's chief predators, Jove and Apollo, as precedents for his own behavior and also calls Perdita Flora, the name that Ovid tells us in the *Fasti* was given to the nymph Chloris after being raped by Zephyrus (see the "Introduction" to Orgel's edition of *The Winter's Tale* [Oxford: Oxford University Press, 1996], pp. 43–46). As we have seen throughout this book, a text's internal distance from its own ideology of gender – particularly as defined by the story of rape – is central to both Ovid's poem and Shakespeare's revisions of it. In addition, the Proserpina story, as Orgel observes, is well suited to convey the importance of the daughter's return: "for Shakespeare's age," it is not the restoration of the marriage but "the restoration of Perdita" that is "the crucial element" ("Introduction," p. 78).

43   Ovid uses the simile of turning to stone, but says nothing of "another worlde." For another approach to what Ceres' grief means for the play, see T. G. Bishop, *Shakespeare and the Theatre of Wonder* (Cambridge: Cambridge University Press, 1996): 125–75.

44   Golding, too, preserves the detail of Sicily in his translation: "But bitterly aboue the rest she banned *Sicilie*, / In which the mention of hir losse she plainely did espie" (5.590–92). Understanding Hermione's proximity to Ceres may tell us why Shakespeare makes an otherwise puzzling change of location. Where Greene begins *Pandosto* in Bohemia and later moves to Sicily, Shakespeare opens the story of winter in Sicily only to move, in Act 4, to Bohemia's pastoral landscape. Others attending to the play's Ovidian texture have noticed and speculated about this change (see T.G. Bishop, *Shakespeare and the Theater of Wonder*; E.A.J. Honigmann, "Secondary Source of *The Winter's Tale*," *Philological Quarterly* 34.4 [1995]: 27–38; and Stephen Orgel, "Introduction" to his Oxford edition of *The Winter's Tale*).

Index

Cambridge Studies in Renaissance Literature and Culture

General editor
STEPHEN ORGEL
Jackson Eli Reynolds Professor of Humanities, Stanford University